Umiker's Management Skills for the New Health Care Supervisor

Fourth Edition

Charles R. McConnell, MBA, CM
Human Resources and Health Care Management
Consultant
Ontario, New York

JONES AND BARTLETT PUBLISHERS
Sudbury, Massachusetts
BOSTON   TORONTO   LONDON   SINGAPORE

World Headquarters
Jones and Bartlett Publishers
40 Tall Pine Drive
Sudbury, MA 01776
978-443-5000
info@jbpub.com
www.jbpub.com

Jones and Bartlett Publishers Canada
6339 Ormindale Way
Mississauga, ON L5V1J2
CANADA

Jones and Bartlett Publishers International
Barb House, Barb Mews
London W6 7PA
UK

Jones and Bartlett's books and products are available through most bookstores and online booksellers. To contact Jones and Bartlett Publishers directly, call 800-832-0034, fax 978-443-8000, or visit our Web site www.jbpub.com.

Substantial discounts on bulk quantities of Jones and Bartlett's publications are available to corporations, professional associations, and other qualified organizations. For details and specific discount information, contact the special sales department at Jones and Bartlett via the above contact information or send an email to specialsales@jbpub.com.

Library of Congress Cataloging-in-Publication Data

McConnell, Charles R.
  Umiker's management skills for the new health care supervisor
  / by Charles R. McConnell.—4th ed.
      p.   ;   cm.
  Rev. ed. of: Management skills for the new health care supervisor
  / William Umiker. 3rd ed. 1998.
  Includes bibliographical references.
  ISBN 0-7637-2878-0
  1. Health facilities—Personnel management. 2. Supervision of
  employees. I. Umiker, William O. Management skills for the new
  health care supervisor. II. Title. III. Title: Management skills for the
  new health care supervisor.
  [DNLM: 1. Health Facility Administrators. 2. Personnel Management—methods.   WX 155 M4775u 2006]
  RA971.35.U526 2006
  362.1906893—dc22

                                                                                    2005008276

Production Credits
Acquisitions Editor: Michael Brown
Editorial Assistant: Kylah Goodfellow McNeill
Production Director: Amy Rose
Production Editor: Renée Sekerak
Production Assistant: Rachel Rossi
Associate Marketing Manager: Marissa Hederson
Manufacturing Buyer: Therese Connell
Composition: Auburn Associates, Inc.
Cover Design: Kristin E. Ohlin
Printing and Binding: Malloy, Inc.
Cover Printing: Malloy, Inc.

Printed in the United States of America
09 08 07 06 05   10 9 8 7 6 5 4 3 2 1

Contents

Preface

I felt flattered to be asked to prepare a fourth edition of Dr. William Umiker's *Management Skills for the New Health Care Supervisor*. I had experience working with Dr. Umiker via long-distance on article-length publications, and I've always found his style appealing. He employs a straightforward, uncluttered way of conveying information and advice in clear and concise terms. His approach to the material has been, I firmly believe, exactly what the aspiring, new, or even experienced first-line supervisor needs to survive in what has become a position of increasing responsibility, importance, and difficulty.

I believe that the strengths of the earlier editions lie, to a considerable extent, in the clarity and simplicity of presentation, making the book an extremely usable text and reference. In addressing the fourth edition it has been my intent to preserve the tone of the earlier editions, so I have retained the level of language, the chapter divisions, and order of presentation of the third edition. A number of chapters were updated to some extent, but much of my contribution to this work consists of the addition of questions, exercises, and case studies intended to enhance the book's value for classroom work, continuing education activities, and self-study purposes.

This book was written primarily for health care workers who have had little or no management training but who may be, or have been, promoted to supervisory positions, or who aspire to such positions. Seasoned first-line as well as middle managers will also find many practical suggestions for improving their effectiveness.

Supervisors continue to wrestle with smaller budgets, fewer professional workers, greater responsibilities, and more time pressure. Morale continues to decline in many organizations, and eroding job security is adding additional stress to an already stressful environment. This fourth edition addresses these continually changing circumstances and their impact on supervisors.

To a considerable extent, this book is about solving people problems, the difficult, frustrating, and time-consuming problems that go with the territory wherever working people provide goods or services for other people. The supervisor may sometimes feel that never-ending people problems take away from one's ability to address the "real work." For the supervisor, however, that specialized worker who exists to make it possible for employees to get the work done as efficiently and effectively as possible, the people and their problems are in fact the core of the real work. It's certain that if there were far fewer people problems to address, far fewer supervisors would be needed.

Supervisors and other managers are judged not only by their personal performance but also by the performance of their subordinates. This book provides the information they need to get maximum effort and results from staff.

Not a great deal of theory will be found within these pages, and little will be said about managing an organization from a top-down perspective. The focus throughout is providing practical advice about getting things done through and with the people who do the hands-on work day in and day out. This includes not only what to do but also exactly how to do it.

The advice and guidance provided by this book can enable you to:
- Survive the transition from professional or technical employee to supervisor.
- Improve customer satisfaction.
- Plan, organize, and delegate work to achieve greater productivity.
- Improve policies, position descriptions, and work standards.
- Recruit, select, orient, and train new employees more skillfully.
- Implement organizational changes and build high-performing teams.
- Improve safety and cope with violence in the workplace.
- Enhance your leadership, coaching, counseling, and disciplinary skills.
- Cultivate your communication, meeting, and negotiating expertise.
- Provide your employees with helpful performance feedback.
- Cope with cultural diversity, conflict, and problem employees.
- Adjust to changes, the requirements of managed care, and the demands of cost-control.
- Encourage creativity, solve problems, and delegate more.
- Stimulate staff development and groom a potential successor.
- Improve your personal use of your time and reduce time lost from external influences.
- Reduce workplace stress and prevent burnout.
- Increase your personal marketability and career development.
- Develop an efficient personal network.
- Sharpen your workplace political skills.

Charles R. McConnell

PART I

Planning and Organizing

Chapter 1

Do You Really Want to Be a Supervisor?

Be careful what you wish for—you might get it.

CHAPTER OBJECTIVES

- Encourage the individual reader or student to carefully examine his or her reasons for aspiring to supervision and assess the willingness of this potential supervisor to accept the responsibilities along with the apparent advantages.
- Provide simple, functional definitions of management and supervision and establish the relative importance of the supervisory role in the organizational structure.
- Convey an understanding of the basic functions of supervision, and place the performance of these in perspective with their applicability at other levels of management.
- Outline the various skills and capabilities essential for success in supervision.
- Review some of the significant changes the individual may experience in making the transition from member of a work group to leader of a group.
- Highlight the elements of a new supervisor's relationships with subordinates, peers, and superiors.
- Enumerate potential pitfalls that can interfere with the growth and development of the supervisor.
- Offer some practical advice for achieving success in a supervisory career.

Unfortunately, not all health care organizations provide supervisory training on a timely basis to the technical or professional employees who are promoted to supervisory positions. We might go so far as to say that the majority of organizations do not provide an adequate orientation to supervision. This failure compounds the problems caused by the tendency to promote technically skilled employees who show no particular leadership skills or who have little interest in becoming supervisors.

Many workers accept promotion to supervision only because of the salary increase or because they feel obligated to do so. However, insightful employers and employees know that "doing" skills do not convert easily to "leading" skills; that is, the good worker does not necessarily make a good supervisor.

If you have never been in a position of leadership, promotion to supervisor represents a major vocational change. You must give up some tasks that you might enjoy to take on others you either dislike or feel uncomfortable doing. It is highly likely that you were promoted because of your professional knowledge, technical skills, and seniority, with little or no attention to the fact that you are inexperienced as a leader.

Of course, to be offered the supervisory job is flattering. You can use the extra pay, and your family will be proud of you. Yet accepting the position could be a decision you will regret. For one thing, your relationship with former teammates will never be the same. You are now part of "them," not "us." Your daily routine, your interpersonal relationships, and your self-concept all must change. Your primary loyalty must now lie with management.

Assuming a supervisory position separates you from your coworkers. Occasionally you will feel alone. Your decisions and your efforts to enforce policies and rules will not always be popular. Your decisions and actions may create adversaries. New peers (mostly supervisors and other managers) may be reluctant to accept you, especially if you continue to identify closely with your old group, a clear danger if you are elevated to supervision of a group of which you were formerly a member.

If you have not thought about or prepared for the necessary role change, proceed with care. Weigh the advantages and disadvantages of the change. Think through all that seems to be involved, considering questions such as the following:

- Do I truly want to become a supervisor, or am I considering doing so because I need the increased income or because I feel I really have no choice?
- Do I honestly want the opportunity to get things done the way I believe they should be done?
- Am I prepared to take the risk and let go of old patterns of behavior?
- Will I enjoy instructing people and evaluating their performance?
- How will I react to the necessity of enforcing policy and counseling and disciplining employees when needed?
- Am I willing to engage in budget preparation and, inevitably, participate in workplace politics?
- Do I stand ready and willing to adopt an attitude of continuous learning about supervision?

As you wrestle with questions such as these, seek the advice of your present supervisor, mentors, if any, and experienced employees whose judgment you trust. Also, think hard about the apparent advantages and disadvantages of the supervisory role. There may be much you find appealing about being a supervisor, and thus part of management, but you need to take care to prevent that which is appealing from obscuring your view of possible drawbacks.

DEFINITIONS AND ESSENTIALS

Management is getting things done through people. The term "manager" is used in both a generic and a titular sense. In the generic sense it refers to any member of the management team, from newest first-line supervisor to chief executive officer. As a position title it describes someone who is ordinarily at an organizational level below executive but above first-line supervisor. We generally use "manager" to describe those above the rank of supervisor and "executive" to describe members of top management. However, considerable care must be taken in using various labels and titles; that which means one thing in one organization or department may mean something entirely different in another setting. For example, "supervisor," as used in these pages, refers to the lowest level of management, but in some nursing service structures "supervisor" has been used to describe someone in charge of a wing or collection of units having authority over several head nurses who, in that capacity, are the first-line supervisors.

A distinguishing characteristic of supervisors, as the term is used in this book, is that they oversee the activities of the people who perform the hands-on work; that is, the people who report to them do not oversee the work of others. In this book the terms supervisor, first-line supervisor, and first-line manager are synonymous.

For a frequently cited legal definition, the Taft-Hartley Act of 1947 a supervisor is "any individual having the authority to hire, transfer, suspend, recall, or discipline other employees; or responsibility to direct them, or to adjust their grievances."[1]

The supervisor is often depicted as the person in the middle, beset by the opposing forces of higher management and the workers. Higher management wants work quality, productivity, and low costs. Workers want higher pay, more benefits, and greater job satisfaction. Although the primary loyalty of the supervisor is to the organization and its customers, clients, or patients, subordinates expect their supervisors to represent their needs and to be their spokespersons.

Supervisors spend most of their time meeting goals, implementing plans, and enforcing policies. At the next higher level, that which is often referred to as "middle management," managers spend most of their time setting goals, planning, and making policies. Supervisors are more likely to be able to fill in for absent workers than are managers. In small departments, supervisors may spend much of their time performing technical or professional work alongside the people who report to them.

Anyone who would aspire to a successful career in supervision, perhaps leading to middle management or higher, would do well to always remain aware of two essential characteristics of supervision. First, supervisors need subordinates more than subordinates need supervisors. A group can function without a supervisor, perhaps not overly well but still it can function. However, a supervisor alone, with no one to supervise, cannot accomplish the work. Second, supervisors do not get paid for what they know or what they do. Rather, they are paid for what their subordinates do, and they are paid for bearing the responsibility for ensuring that the work gets done and gets done correctly.

In the past, supervisors were primarily "bosses." Today's supervisors, however, must be leaders. They are the primary source of answers, instructions, assistance, and guidance for the employees who report to them. Their primary function is to help their employees get the daily work done. Many employees feel that their supervisors have forgotten this, so as a supervisor, you must accept full responsibility for the success or failure of your personnel.

ESSENTIAL MANAGEMENT FUNCTIONS OF SUPERVISORS

In addition to the professional and technical duties from which a supervisor never completely separates, a supervisor has management responsibility related to the following five essential functions.

1. Planning: for example, budgets, new methods and procedures, goals and objectives, and continuing education programs.
2. Organizing: for example, position descriptions, locations of equipment, workstations, and storage areas.
3. Directing: including selection and indoctrination of new personnel, scheduling, making assignments, training, coaching, and resolution of employee grievances.
4. Controlling: applying policies and rules, enforcing standards of performance, conducting performance appraisals, and addressing issues of quality, safety, cost, inventory control, counseling, discipline, and such.
5. Coordinating: cooperation with other sections of the department, other departments, and various staff activities and services.

According to Marvin, the typical supervisor spends about 40% of his or her time leading other people and 40% performing technical or professional work.[2] Another 15% of the time is spent training, counseling, and appraising, and about 5% is devoted to other tasks.[2]

ESSENTIAL SUPERVISORY SKILLS

First, a supervisor must be technically and professionally competent. Most supervisors help with some technical tasks, and in larger units supervisors serve as pinch hitters. In either case, supervisors need professional competency for making decisions and solving problems.

Your influence as a leader must not be limited to the authority granted to you by your employer. Your knowledge and experience give you much more power. Most health care workers promoted to supervisory roles have specific professional or technical competencies. This does not mean they must know more about everything or be technically more proficient than their subordinates but rather that their expertise must be sufficient to earn the respect of subordinates.

Basic Skills for Every Supervisor

Successful supervisors need leadership skills in the following areas:

- Communication
- Employee motivation
- Problem solving and decision making
- Delegation
- Time management
- Career development

The importance of these vital leadership skills comes through loud and clear in the experiences related by some health care supervisors. Wilder reported that laboratory supervisors found the following activities to pose the most difficulties for them.[3]

Preparing letters and memos

- Interviewing, whether for employee selection or discipline
- Setting goals for themselves and subordinates
- Offering suggestions for improving work processes
- Delegating authority
- Developing data for budgets
- Developing job descriptions
- Resolving conflicts among subordinates

Traits Exhibited by Effective Supervisors

Certain traits are exhibited by effective supervisors:

- Self-confidence. Good supervisors do not become defensive when criticized. They accept responsibility for their own actions and the actions of their subordinates.

- Respect for others. Good supervisors welcome input from all sources and are effective listeners. They praise more often than they criticize.
- Sense of humor. Competent supervisors can laugh at themselves. They seldom lose their temper.
- Ability to make decisions. Effective supervisors make decisions promptly but not before careful consideration. They do not pass the buck.
- Flexibility and resiliency. Good supervisors adjust rapidly to changing situations, conditions, and demands. They overcome setbacks without becoming bitter.
- Energy and enthusiasm. Good supervisors possess a strong work ethic. They are optimistic and cheerful, even when under stress.
- Creativity. Good supervisors are always thinking about better ways of doing things. They encourage others to be innovative.
- Customer awareness. Good supervisors know their external and internal customers and strive to exceed the expectations of these customers.
- Quality oriented. Good supervisors insist on things being done right the first time. They support all quality improvement measures.
- Empowering. Good supervisors practice participative management and are effective team builders.
- Risk taking. Good supervisors are willing to express opinions, encourage creativity, and accept responsibility.

Supervisors As Seen by Their Employees

Following is a list of statements that workers can be heard to make about the supervisors they respect.

- "He discusses problems with me and listens to what I have to say."
- "She shares credit, telling the big boss when we do a good job."
- "She lets me know how she feels about my work, whether good or bad."
- "I can trust him to go to bat for me."
- "He means it when he pays me a compliment, and I know exactly what I did that he liked."
- "He always has time to listen to me."
- "She tries to help me do a better job."

TRANSITION TO SUPERVISION

Moving into a supervisory position in the department in which you have been working has both advantages and disadvantages. On the plus side, you know the people and the territory. On the other hand, you must establish new relationships with former peers and friends and must henceforth identify with management. The transition is easiest if you have

- already been accepted as an informal leader within the department,
- previously served in leadership roles, such as committee chair, trainer, or substitute supervisor,
- had experience performing administrative tasks,
- prepared for this eventuality through formal educational programs or self-study.

Leading vs Doing

Your new role requires you to spend more time getting the work done through others and less time doing the work yourself. Many new supervisors simply cannot stop doing what they did before they were promoted. This is partly because they did their former tasks well and partly because they were not trained to be supervisors. Some supervisors become frustrated when they realize they no longer can do everything better than their subordinates; however, although a supervisor must understand the work, he or she does not need not to be able to perform every task in a superior manner. Trying to serve as both a full-time leader and a full-time worker simultaneously ends in burnout or failure.

Supervisors must maintain enough technical or professional expertise to be able to answer questions and serve as a resource. They must often pitch in and help with the daily work. Some positions, especially in smaller units or on evening, night or weekend shifts, legitimately call for hybrid leadership–worker roles.

RELATIONSHIPS WITH SUBORDINATES

As a supervisor you will naturally want to be liked by the people you supervise, but you cannot continue to be part of the old gang. Strive for the respect of the employees rather than their affection. Be firm, fair, and consistent. Make up your mind to develop your managerial skills while maintaining your professional knowledge.

If you previously earned the respect of your teammates, you are off to a good start. On the other hand, if they resent your promotion, think someone else was more deserving, or believe you were selected because of favoritism, you may experience some rough going.

Honeymoon Phase

Immediately after the promotion, you and your subordinates will most likely make a special effort to cooperate. Your former pals will have mixed feelings toward you; this is referred to as the phenomenon of ambivalence. They want to like and trust you, but they resent your control over them. Sure, they congratulate you and say they are happy to have you as their new leader. You reciprocate with equal enthusiasm. You tell them that nothing has changed and that with their help you will correct all the problems and annoyances that have long bothered the group. During this phase, those at organizational levels both above and below you will watch you carefully and will be judging your competence.

After the Honeymoon

The honeymoon phase, in which everyone cooperates, acts friendly, and conceals problems, lasts about as long as a typical marital honeymoon. It may give way abruptly to a phase of discomfort when a sensitive problem, such as the need for a reduction in personnel, arises. More often, the honeymoon ends gradually as the new supervisor turns down requests or exhibits ineffectiveness. In their desire to be liked, new supervisors often go too far with the friendship approach. This ultimately hampers their ability to provide direction, criticize work performance, or make unpleasant decisions. It is necessary to risk friendship to gain respect. Like it or not, you finally realize that you are now one of "them," and no longer one of "us."

Some subordinates take advantage of the goodwill of the supervisor; the rest take a wait-and-see attitude. The chronic complainers, cynics, passive-aggressives, and negativists cannot stay silent long. They soon begin to describe all the weaknesses of the new boss, compare this boss unfavorably with predecessors, and point out how things have been getting worse, not better.

Work should be the primary topic of conversation. This does not rule out casual conversation, but your main job is to ensure that the work is completed. You must enforce orders from your superiors, even when these orders do not seem sensible or fair to you or to your subordinates. You will feel an urge to dissociate yourself from these orders. If you yield to that temptation, however, you will lose the respect of your subordinates. Instead, discuss such an order with your manager and try to change it. At least find out and explain to your people the reasons for the directive. Above all, do not discredit management with statements such as "What do you expect from those idiots?"

If you let your authority go to your head and lower the boom on your charges, they will unite against you. It is essential to meld humility with firmness. Micromanaging is largely one-way communication: no listening and a great deal of ordering. This may occur either because a new supervisor wants to do a good job or because he or she enjoys the feeling of authority.

Because of all your new supervisory responsibilities, you should spend less time with former teammates and more with your fellow supervisors. This should extend to time spent in social activities. Others are more likely to charge you with favoritism if you have close social ties with your old buddies. You are also more likely to reveal confidential information while socializing. As a supervisor, you must remember that your words carry more weight. Comments you make about others are more often repeated and can get you into hot water.

On the other hand, do not destroy old relationships. The temptation to please management may reduce your sensitivity to your employees. You should take time to continue personal, positive contacts with each person, chiefly during brief encounters on the job or during breaks. Do not be afraid to ask questions or solicit help from them.

RELATIONSHIPS WITH OTHER SUPERVISORS: YOUR NEW PEERS

Your new peers, the other supervisors, will not accept you unless you start meeting with them and acting as though you are one of them. These contacts are important for other reasons. Sharing problems and ideas with other supervisors enhances your growth as a supervisor. In the health care industry, there has been too much emphasis on strictly professional growth. We tend to identify with fellow professionals rather than with fellow managers.

Another reason for moving closer to fellow supervisors is the increasing need for coordinating the flow of work. Sharing equipment and overlapping services requires close cooperation between and among departments and other units.

RELATIONSHIP WITH YOUR MANAGER

If you have been promoted from the ranks, you already know something about the person who is now your immediate boss. You know whether he or she prefers to communicate verbally or in writing. You have learned how to interpret the boss's body language, when to stay out of the way, and what pleases or displeases this manager. If you are new to the department, learn these things as soon as you can.

Good supervisors help their managers control their time by handling trifles themselves. They give the managers all necessary information, even when the news is bad. They admit their mistakes and do not make the same mistake twice.

ADJUSTING TO THE NEW ROUTINE

The transition phase consists of preparing for your behavioral changes. This involves enhancing your communication processes, learning how to best get the work completed effectively and efficiently, and applying the right skills at the right time: "situational leadership." Shandler advises new supervisors to find a coach or mentor.[4] He also recommends that they modify their leadership style after learning how the employees react.

Endeavor to balance a task-oriented style with people-oriented needs. Model the behavior you want to encourage in others.

PITFALLS

Supervisors should do their best to be aware of and to avoid the following potential shortcomings in supervisory behavior.

- Lack of flexibility in dealing with attitudes, biases, perceptions, emotions, and feelings. Previous experience depended on objective measurement and on circumstances one could objectively control and measure, but now the ambience is murky and decisions are more frequently based on subjective factors.
- Lack of assertiveness. Introverts often struggle with leadership roles.
- Unwillingness to pay the price of loneliness, fewer peers, and more stress.
- Striving to be liked rather than respected.
- Unwillingness to determine specifically what superiors expect.
- Failing to maintain technical and management competence and thus not remaining marketable.
- Withholding important information from peers, subordinates, or superiors.
- Becoming a bottleneck rather than a supporter and expediter.

Refer to Chapter 11 for more information about leadership.

LAUNCHING A SUCCESSFUL SUPERVISORY CAREER

To give yourself the best possible chance of succeeding as a supervisor, there are several things you should do.

- Know what is expected of you. Be thoroughly familiar with all aspects of your job description.
- Periodically hold a one-to-one meeting with each of your employees.
- Work to build relationships and establish a personal network.
- Learn to trust your intuition more than you ever had to before you became a supervisor.
- Remain available to help others. Become a great listener.
- Be sensitive to the feelings, needs, and desires of the people who report to you.
- Share knowledge and keep your people informed.
- Maintain high ethical and moral standards; be a model of integrity.
- Be willing to ask for help when needed and to ask questions.

- Join professional organizations serving your field and attend their meetings.
- Maintain an active self-education program.
- Insist on good performance, and acknowledge and reward it.
- Remain calm under stress. Avoid shouting and pouting.
- Display self-confidence at all times.
- Remain fair. Be sure your conduct is free from favoritism or discrimination.
- Defend your employees from hostile people and tormentors.
- Display the courage to make unpopular decisions and see them through.

Think About It

Entering supervision is not a matter of simply accepting a promotion and performing tasks different from what you had been doing. Entering supervision is literally the adoption of a second career.

Questions for Review and Discussion
1. Why should the first-line supervisor be proficient in both doing and leading? Explain.
2. Do you believe it is better to rise to supervision from within the group or move into the position from outside? Why?
3. What do you believe are the fundamental differences between a traditional "boss" and a true leader?
4. Why is it necessary for the first-line supervisor to be technically or professionally competent as well as a capable leader?
5. Why is delegation a critically important supervisory skill?
6. Concerning the section "Supervisors As Seen by Their Employees," write one additional statement that you would like to hear said of you as a supervisor. Explain why you wrote this particular statement.
7. Why is it of particular importance for the supervisor to identify primarily with management?
8. As a first-line supervisor, how would you attempt to relate honestly with your immediate superior if that manager's attitude strongly suggests that "bad news" is never welcome?
9. As a newly hired or recently appointed supervisor, how would you go about trying to determine what expectations you will be called upon to meet?
10. What would you do if you found yourself in strong disagreement with a mandate your immediate superior expects you to implement through your employees?

Exercise: Pros and Cons
Consider once again the title of this chapter: "Do You Really Want to Be a Supervisor?" This is a legitimate question for anyone thinking of accepting a supervisory position, and it is a question to be taken seriously because not everyone is equally suited for supervision.

Take a full sheet of paper and divide it into two columns. Label the left column "Advantages" and label the right column "Disadvantages." List both the advantages and disadvantages of the supervisory role as you perceive them affecting you personally. A suggestion: do not attempt to work one column completely and then move to the other. Rather, move back and forth, listing one or two advantages, one or two disadvantages, and so on. Develop the lists to the greatest extent you can; don't worry about entries that seem to partially overlap each other in meaning. When you have finished, write a single sentence completing the following: "I believe I (should or should not) accept a supervisory position because. . ."

If this is done in a classroom setting, consider opening up the results of this exercise for discussion by the group.

Case: Sarah's Promotion

After spending several years as a staff nurse in the same medical-surgical unit, Sarah was promoted to the position of head nurse of that unit. Immediately after the staff meeting at which her promotion was announced, Sarah was surrounded by several of her coworkers, members of her lunch time "coffee club," offering congratulations.

"Great news," said Jane, "but does this blow the carpool? I don't think your hours will be the same as ours any more."

Emily said, "There goes the coffee club. Management commitments, don't you know." Sarah felt she detected a sarcastic edge to Emily's mention of management.

Debbie said, "Well, maybe now we can get someone to listen to us. Don't forget, Sarah, you used to complain just like the rest of us."

Helen said, "Complaining has been a way of life around here. I personally don't think that our recently departed supervisor ever passed any of our concerns up the line." Her tone turned sharp as she added, "Now that Sarah's going to be in a position to do something, let's hope she doesn't forget who her friends are."

Following a brief, awkward silence, the group broke up and the nurses went their separate ways.

Questions:
1. Describe the advantages Sarah may enjoy in taking over as supervisor for this group of which she has long been a member.
2. What principal disadvantages might Sarah face?
3. Put yourself in Sarah's position and describe the approach you would take in attempting to alter her relationships with her small group of friends.

REFERENCES

1. Taft-Hartley Act of 1947 (Labor-Management Relations Act of 1947), Section 101, Subsection 2(11).
2. Marvin, P. 1990. *Executive time management.* New York: AMACOM, 4.
3. Wilder, R. 1981. How one lab gauges job satisfaction. *Medical Laboratory Observer* 13:35–9.
4. Shandler, D. 1993. *From technical specialist to supervisor.* Menlo Park, CA: Crisp, 13.

RECOMMENDED READING

J.G. Liebler et al. *Management Principles for Health Professionals*, 4th ed. (Sudbury MA: Jones and Bartlett Publishers, 2004).
C.R. McConnell, *The Effective Health Care Supervisor*, 5th ed. (Gaithersburg, MD: Aspen Publishers, 2002).
D. Shandler, *From Technical Specialist to Supervisor* (Menlo Park, CA: Crisp Publishers, 1993).

Chapter 2

Customer Service

It is not the employer who pays the wages.
Employers only handle the money. It is the
customer who pays the wages.

—Henry Ford

CHAPTER OBJECTIVES

- Develop an understanding of what the various customers served by the health care organization and its employees need from their relationship with health care provider organizations.
- Briefly describe the impact of managed care on the delivery of services to the customers of the organization.
- Identify the essential elements of customer service.
- Address techniques that can be applied in improving the personnel systems so important in providing and sustaining superior customer service.
- Identify the elements of an effective customer satisfaction system.

WHO ARE OUR CUSTOMERS AND WHAT DO THEY WANT?

Any activity in any business has both external and internal customers. Customers external to health care organizations include patients, patients' families and visitors, referring physicians, doctors' offices, blood donors, and third-party payers. Internal customers include nurses, staff physicians and other professionals, students, trainees, employees, departments, and committees.

There is a distinct difference between a person's wants and that individual's genuine needs. As the widow in the retirement home said, "I need a husband; I want Tom Selleck." Patients are ordinarily aware of their wants. By and large they want quiet, clean rooms with all the conveniences of a first-rate hotel. They want tasty food served hot and on time. They want painless procedures and no waiting on gurneys or in ready rooms. They want courteous, attentive, skillful, and professional-looking staff. Most of all, they want to leave the institution alive and feeling better than when they arrived. On the other hand, few patients are completely aware of their needs for diagnostic tests or therapeutic modalities.

Physicians are not always cognizant of what they should order for their patients until they learn about some new diagnostic or therapeutic procedure. Then they demand it. They invariably want fast and courteous service and all the latest technology.

Insightful care providers take steps to determine what their customers must have (their needs), what they want, and what they do not want. To stimulate or modify the needs and wants of their customers, health care providers make their customers aware of new services or products as they become available. What they often forget to do is find out what new services or products their external customers want or need.

INFLUENCE OF MANAGED CARE

The shift to managed care has had considerable impact on customer service. In terms of their effects on customers, managed care organizations—such as health maintenance organizations and preferred provider organizations—have placed certain restrictions on access to care. Government and insurers have forced providers to find ways of operating on less money than they might have received in the absence of managed care. Provider organizations have had to adjust to the financial limitations imposed on them. As a result the health care industry has experienced numerous mergers and affiliations and other forms of restructuring, making it necessary to tighten staffing overall at precisely the same time managed care is forcing an increase in customer service communication with an increasing number of internal and external customers.

Under managed care, for the first time in the history of American health care, significant restrictions have been placed on the use of health care services. Customers have been introduced to the use of the primary care physician as the "gatekeeper" to control access to specialists and other services. Under the gatekeeper concept visits to specialists and certain others are covered only if the patient is referred by his or her primary care physician.

As managed care continues to mature and individuals gain more experience in dealing with it, enrollees are becoming more sophisticated in their knowledge of what is promised and what is delivered. Many are increasingly critical of how they are handled, especially concerning real and perceived barriers to their access to medical specialists and expensive procedures. Customer inquiries and complaints are on average becoming more complex and articulate and thus more difficult to address.

Although all agencies claim that quality care and patient satisfaction remain important, the emphasis on cost control and limitation of services is unmistakable. Managed care has been directly or indirectly responsible for staff reductions and for the replacement of numerous highly trained personnel with employees who have been educated to a lesser level and thus are paid less.

The impact of managed care is not likely to diminish in the foreseeable future. Many people depend on managed care plans. During late 1998 and 1999, some 160 million Americans were enrolled in managed care plans, and while overall managed care participation seems not to have grown appreciably since then, neither has it diminished.[1] Present membership may represent the overwhelming majority of people suitable for managed care. In-and-out participation of some groups, such as the younger aging and Medicaid patients, is expected, but the bulk of people on whom managed care plans can best make their money are already enrolled.

THREE ESSENTIALS OF CUSTOMER SERVICE

The basic essentials of customer service in any activity in which employees deal directly with customers are systems, strategies, and employees.

Systems

Systems include policies, protocols, procedures, arrangement and accessibility of the physical facilities, staffing, operations, workflows, and performance monitoring. Policy statements and procedure manuals provide behavior guidelines, rules, and regulations. For effective and customer-friendly policies there are several things that must be done.

1. Eliminate policies that adversely affect client satisfaction (for example, unnecessarily strict visiting hours).
2. Annually review all policies affecting customer service.
3. Establish a policy committee or a quality circle to address policy matters.
4. Introduce new policies that improve client service (for example, a special parking area for blood donors, more convenient locations and times for specimen collections).
5. For each new service that is introduced, consider a policy specific to that service.

A later discussion will address policies relating to personnel selection, orientation and training, reward systems, communication, empowering people, and building teams.

Strategies

Strategy in customer service consists of developing a customer-oriented culture. A customer-oriented culture is achieved when every employee understands that good service is expected, that exceptional service is rewarded, and that unsatisfactory service is not tolerated. Such strategy involves statements of vision, values, mission, goals, objectives, and action plans.

Customer feedback is essential to strategy. We obtain feedback from a number of sources, including complaints, suggestions, incident reports, surveys, interdepartmental meetings, cross-functional work groups, task forces, and focus groups.

Employees

Employees are our best customers in that we must satisfy them before we can please other customers. Concerning employee satisfaction, the major personnel responsibilities of supervisors are to

1. determine and respond to the legitimate needs and wants of their employees,
2. field the best possible team of employees,
3. empower employees to solve problems. (Can each of your employees say: "I rarely need anyone else to help me handle customer problems or questions?"),
4. teach by example, and
5. insist on excellent customer service and constantly monitor the delivery of this service.

TECHNIQUES FOR IMPROVING PERSONNEL SYSTEMS

Position Descriptions

In the summary statement of every position description there should appear the word "customer" and an indication of how the customer is to be regarded. (For example, "The goal of this position is to meet or exceed customer expectations and needs. Our external and internal customers include...").

Modify performance standards to include items addressing quality and customer service. Here are some examples.

- Exercises discretion with patient information
- Accepts night and weekend assignments willingly
- Displays tact in personal interactions with customers and staff
- Frequently reports customer comments and suggestions

Recruiting Process

Your goal should be to hire employees who are competent, caring, and resistant to turnover. Assist in the recruiting process by providing the employment section of your human resources department with concise, up-to-date position descriptions. Be sure the attractive aspects of each job are prominent in those descriptions. Help the recruiters by recommending the most effective means for identifying potential job candidates. Answer inquiries about jobs enthusiastically, and interview candidates promptly.

Selection Process

> *Hire for attitude, train for skill.*

The ability to sell jobs to candidates is important. The stronger the candidates appear to be, the more likely it is that other organizations will be trying to hire them. You can learn a great deal about a candidate's attitude toward customer service by asking questions such as: What does superior service mean to you? What gives you the strongest feeling of satisfaction about your workday? Provide an example of how you made an extra effort to serve a client.

Orientation and Training System

Make certain that new employees know who their external and internal customers are. Orient them toward exceptional customer service. Infuse them with the latest ideas in quality improvement. Emphasize the importance of a "can do" attitude and how this can affect performance ratings. Review workflows and each provider–recipient interface. Alert new employees to questions that customers frequently ask, and let them know where the answers can be found. Describe what you regard as proper telephone and electronic etiquette. Introduce them to the department's major customers.

Performance Review and Reward Systems

Refocus performance objectives and performance appraisals to strongly address customer satisfaction. Discuss customer service when reviewing past performance and when formulating objectives for future activities. Encourage employees to set objectives such as attending seminars on communication skills or customer service, visiting internal customers, or learning to speak customers' languages.

Tie your recognition and reward strategy to customer service. Unfortunately, the health care personnel who have the most client contact are among the lowest paid, receive the least training, and have the least opportunity for promotion.

Inservice Educational Programs

Inservice topics for all employees should include customer identification, recognition of customer expectations, customer problem solving, presenting new services, and communication skills, telephone courtesy in particular. Topics for employees responsible for contact with customers should also include empathic interactions, listening skills, dealing with complaints, assertiveness, and how to cope with angry people.

Personnel Retention

Turnover of personnel presents a major impediment to customer service. Unfortunately the employees who provide the majority of hands-on service experience the highest turnover rates. (These topics are covered in greater detail in subsequent chapters.)

DESIGNING A CUSTOMER SATISFACTION SYSTEM

Principles of effective customer service for supervisor and employees include the following:

- Always treating customers as you would like to be treated
- Anticipating your customers' needs and wants
- Hiring employees who have a caring attitude, and retraining, reassigning, or getting rid of those who do not
- Including customer satisfaction in your orientation and training programs
- Making yourself a model of good customer service
- Making customer satisfaction a condition of satisfactory performance
- Monitoring the behavior of your service providers and coaching those who demonstrate any deficiencies
- Obtaining frequent feedback from internal and external customers
- Underpromising and overdelivering; whenever possible give customers more than they expect
- Working the right way the first time
- Recognizing and rewarding those who make special efforts to please customers
- Giving your employees the authority to resolve customer complaints

Address Complaints

Patients are most likely to complain about noise, food, their rooms, waiting, and lack of courtesy. Customers are displeased when

- they do not receive what is expected or promised,
- they have to wait for what they consider excessive amounts of time,
- someone who represents the organization is rude, patronizing, or indifferent,
- they feel they are getting the brush-off or the runaround, or
- someone expresses a "We can't do it" attitude or hits them with the rule book (for example, "It's our policy").

Always regard complaints as suggestions for improving service. Complaints are the least costly source of customer feedback. Invite additional comments and ask for specific suggestions for improvement. Encourage your staff to report complaints and make suggestions for eliminating them, and record these suggestions. Express your appreciation of these suggestions at performance reviews as well as at the time they are offered.

Ask for customer comments and suggestions at every staff meeting. Suggestions need not be elaborate or complicated. In one large hospital, for example, music was piped into the waiting room for visitors, most of whom were waiting for patients undergoing surgery. The results of a study of this practice indicated that self-reported stress levels of visitors were reduced.[2]

Maintain a comment log. Empower your front-line troops to solve customer problems. Most customers will be understanding if they feel that providers care about them, so give your employees the authority they need.

When faced with a complaint, acknowledge its validity and offer an apology as appropriate. Accept responsibility without blaming others. Empathize with the complainers and ask them what they would like done. If you receive no response, make an offer. Thank the person for bringing the matter to your attention. Promise to do what you agreed to do, then do it promptly.

Think About It

> *A satisfied customer is your best advertisement. The customer who believes he or she received good service may or may not tell others about the experience, but you can be certain that the customer who received poor service will tell others, perhaps many.*

Questions for Review and Discussion
1. Why is it necessary to concern ourselves with internal customers?
2. Why are employees our best customers?

3. How would you respond to customer demands that were clearly unreasonable?
4. Why do you suppose hospital patients are likely to complain most about food, cleanliness, and staff treatment rather than about the quality of care?
5. Do you believe managed care has made customer service more difficult? Why or why not?
6. How are the quality of health care and excellence in customer service related to each other?
7. How does present day customer service relate to the increasing tendency toward competition among health care providers?
8. Is employee turnover ever a significant barrier to good customer service? Why or why not?
9. What do you believe has the greatest influence on an employee's willingness to deliver excellent customer service?
10. Relative to customer service, why is it suggested that we "underpromise" and "overdeliver"?

Exercise: Identifying Customers and Their Needs

Designate a specific health care organization function or department (for example, nursing service, physical therapy, housekeeping, or food service). Make it the one you presently work in or one you have worked in at one time. If you are not experienced, select any function or department with which you are comfortable.

Create two blocks of space on a sheet of paper, upper half and lower half, and label one "Internal Customers" and the other "External Customers" (with "internal" and "external" referring to the organization, not just the department—in other words, employees of another department remain your "internal" customers). In each half-page space list as many internal and external customers as you can for your designated department. Next, for each customer designation write a one-sentence description of the services you provide to that customer. If this exercise is done in a classroom setting, compare your lists with others and attempt to reconcile any differences that arise.

Case: The Crabby Receptionist

"I don't know what I'm going to do about Louise," said section supervisor Missy Clare to her friend and fellow supervisor, Janet Stevens. "She was a good worker for the longest time, but now I'm getting complaints."

Janet asked, "What kinds of complaints?"

"That she's brusque to the point of rudeness when she answers the phone and that she snaps at other employees when they just ask simple questions. I've had at least three doctors tell me I'd better get someone more pleasant out front, and obviously someone complained to Carson—you know, *my* boss—because he asked me about the crabby receptionist in my section he was hearing about."

"Has she been experiencing any kind of problem that you know of? Something personal that's bothering her?"

"I don't know," Missy answered, "and it's a cinch she doesn't want to talk about it even if there is a problem. I've given her every opportunity to talk but she's not having any of it."

Janet said, "Well, to be completely honest with you, I've heard a few things about Louise."

"Like what?"

"Like how some of your outpatients are afraid to approach her because they don't know if they're going to be snapped at, glared at, or ignored."

Missy said, "Louise is such a long-time employee I hate to just lower the boom on her."

"Well, kiddo," said Janet, "you'd better lower something before Carson and his higher-ups get any more complaints."

Questions:

1. How would you go about trying to balance the customer service needs of the section with the apparent needs of Louise, the long-time employee?
2. Which of the section's customers are likely to cause Missy the most grief over Louise's behavior? Why?
3. Recommend an approach for Missy to consider in addressing the problem with Louise.

REFERENCES

1. Ginzberg, E., et al. 1998. Healthy debate. *Human Resource Executive* (May 5): 57–59.
2. Routhieaux, R.L., and D.A. Tansik. 1997. The benefits of music in hospital waiting rooms. *Health Care Supervisor* 16,(2): 31–9.

RECOMMENDED READING

K. Albrecht and R. Zemke, *Service America* (Homewood, IL: Dow Jones-Irwin, 1985).

J. Carlzon, *Moments of Truth* (Cambridge, MA: Ballinger, 1987).

R.Y. Chang and P.K. Kelly, *Satisfying Internal Customers First* (Irving, CA: Richard Chang Publishers, 1994).

W.H. Davidow and B. Uttal, *Total Customer Service* (New York, NY: Harper & Row, 1989).

R.L. Desatnick, *Managing to Keep the Customer* (San Francisco, CA: Jossey-Bass, 1988).

L. Goldzimer, *"I'm First." Your Customer's Message to You* (New York, NY: Rawson, 1989).

W. Umiker, *The Customer-Oriented Laboratory*, 2d ed. (Chicago, IL: ASCP Press, 1997).

Chapter 3

Planning

*Great success in any enterprise comes from a
balanced combination of three elements: the
mission, the leadership, and the people who make it
happen. By far the most important is the mission.*

—Roger Dawson[1]

CHAPTER OBJECTIVES

- Establish the benefits of planning and convey an understanding of the implications of the failure to plan.
- Provide familiarization with the types of plans employed in business activity and identify and explain the key elements of planning.
- Establish the role of planning in an organization's vision and mission.
- Establish the significance of goals and objectives in planning.
- Define action plans and examine the elements of a typical action plan.

Planning is the most fundamental of the management functions, and as such it logically precedes all other functions. Planning is the projection of actions intended to reach specific goals. In other words, a plan is a blueprint for the future; it is our expression of what we wish to accomplish or our best prediction of what might occur in the future. Planning begins with the questions of what and why, then focuses on the how, when, who, and where.

BENEFITS OF PLANNING

Planning ensures that we work effectively and efficiently or at least improves our chances of doing so. Planning reduces procrastination, ensures continuity, and provides for more intelligent use of resources.

27

Planning improves our chances of doing things right the first time, resulting in the satisfaction of having everything under control at present and knowing what to do next.

Planning is proactive. It decreases the need to manage from crisis to crisis. It is a prerequisite for practically all necessary managerial activities, including teaching or mentoring, preparing for and running committee and staff meetings, conducting performance appraisals or employment interviews, preparing budgets, and numerous other activities.

Planning is essential for coping with crises such as fires, natural disasters, strikes, bomb threats, or hostage incidents.

Some may occasionally ask, Because plans work out exactly as anticipated only once in a while, why bother? Isn't planning just effort that's wasted, consuming time that could be better spent *doing*? Perhaps those whose thinking runs along such lines feel uneasy because they can see the amount of time spent in planning but are aware that nothing concrete is happening during that time to advance the completion of the work. However, those who discount the value of planning often discover that without planning their efforts are wasted on false starts and misdirection such that excess time is consumed in setting things right.

If things often do not happen exactly as we planned for them to happen, what have we gained by planning? We have been able to apply our efforts more effectively than without a plan, and even though we might not have hit the target precisely, we nevertheless have acquired some important information. As a result we know by how much the target was missed, and we can proceed to determine whether (1) we need to readjust our direction to attain the target or (2) conditions have changed such that the target should be adjusted. In any case, the effort expended in planning is never wasted.

We have all undoubtedly heard the expression "If we fail to plan, we plan to fail." This is largely true. Without planning, even that which does get done suffers to an extent because it has consumed more time and effort than necessary, and without direction established through planning, the pursuit of any particular end result can be an expensive journey into chaos.

CLASSIFICATIONS OF PLANS

Strategic plans are plans made for achieving long-range goals and living up to the expectations expressed in statements of mission and values. Without strategic planning, few visions are realized. *Tactical* plans translate broad strategies into specific objectives and action plans.

Organizational plans begin with a table of organization. They include position descriptions, staffing, and channels of communication. *Physical* plans concern topography (for example, the site of a building, the layout of an office, or the location of diagnostic and therapeutic equipment.)

Functional plans are plans concerned with the workings of major functional units such as a nursing service, clinical laboratory, human resources department, financial or clinical services, and others. *Operational* plans address systems, work processes, procedures, quality control, safety, and other supportive activities.

Financial plans address the inflow and outflow of money, profit and loss, budgets, cost and profit centers, charges, and salaries.

Career planning, time management, and daily work planning are also vital forms of planning.

KEY ELEMENTS OF PLANNING

The essential elements of planning are vision, mission, goals, objectives, strategy, and action.

Vision

> *A vision is an image without great detail. It acts as*
> *a flag around which the troops will rally.*
>
> —Michael Hammer[2]

Vision statements and mission statements deal with purpose and alignment at an organizational level. Without these, the energy of an organization scatters rather than focuses. Leaders create a vision around which people rally, and managers marshal the resources to pursue that vision. Vision provides a premise that leaders commit to and dramatize to others. A vision statement should not read like a financial report. Rather, it must conjure up a compelling positive vision that fires people up. Martin Luther King, Jr., provided the best and simplest example of a vision statement with his "I have a dream" speech.

An organization's vision statement should be clear and exciting and should leave broad latitude for the pursuit of new opportunities. The vision of top management must be broad enough that the visions of the lower echelons of the organization fit within it.[3]

One segment of an organization's vision can be aimed at the consumer (for example, "Our vision is to have a fully staffed, high-quality, committed workforce that is efficient and effective in providing the highest quality service in our community"). Another portion can be directed at employees. For example:

> We envision an organization staffed by dedicated, enthusiastic, customer-oriented people who act as partners. Our people readily adapt to change, seek continuous technical improvements, and exhibit a caring attitude.

Our organization is preferred by most patients and admitting physicians. It is the darling of third-party payers and a local preferred employer.

The vision must be sustained through action. A vision is translated into a mission statement. Goals are enunciated, strategy is developed, and action plans are constructed.

Mission

Mission statements proclaim the purpose of an organization or department, literally stating why this entity exists. Like visions, mission statements should serve to define the organization and inspire its employees. Most mission statements are too vague, platitudinous, and quickly forgotten. Most of them cannot pass the "snicker" test. Organizations work hard to develop vision and mission statements, then let them become just framed pieces of paper decorating a wall.

An effective mission statement must be expressed clearly in one paragraph or less and in simple language. When workers participate actively in the formulation of mission statements, they understand why the organization exists and what their work is all about. They will do their best to make the virtual visions come to life.

Some mission statements include the vision, goals, and strategy. They answer the key questions of why (Why does this organization or department exist?), what (What is our goal?), and how (What strategy will we use?). What follows is a departmental mission statement appropriate for a small hospital unit. Note that it begins with a goal, adds objectives, and ends with a strategy.

We seek a service that surpasses the expectations of our clinician customers. We will improve the quality of reported results, shorten turnaround time, reduce costs, and promote a spirit of cooperation between our staff, our customers, vendors, and associates in other departments. To accomplish this we will meet weekly to analyze service needs, investigate complaints and suggestions, and explore new methods or equipment. We will make recommendations to management, monitor progress, and evaluate results.

Before accepting a mission statement, experienced originators ensure that it answers four critical questions.

1. Do you know where you want to be 5 years from now?
2. Is it clearly and definitely expressed in one paragraph or less?
3. Is it expressed in language that a 10th grader can understand?
4. Will it be believable to everyone in the organization?

Goals and Objectives

Leaders share their visions and involve their associates in setting goals and objectives. Goals have ends or conclusions, while mission statements usually do not. Employees prefer things that have conclusions. For example, they usually prefer to work on projects rather than perform routine work because projects have clear destinations. All riders know when they have arrived at the station. Retirees sometimes die shortly after retiring because mentally their goal (end of employment) has been reached and they lack a clear mission that deals with the future.

Targets become more specific when you subdivide goals into objectives. Objectives relate to milestones passed on the way toward reaching a goal. Objectives should be realistic, understandable, measurable, behavioral, achievable, and specific. An objective such as "reduce inventory costs" is not sufficiently specific. Instead use "reduce inventory costs by 10% within 12 months." Assign priorities to objectives and set target dates. Written objectives get more attention and provide a permanent record. Although there should be some degree of challenge—employees are motivated by achieving difficult but not impossible tasks—objectives must be attainable. If a plan holds little chance of success, it will frustrate rather than motivate. Here are some examples.

- Within 12 months, a repeat survey of employee morale will show an increase in the average employee satisfaction rating from the current level 3 to level 2.
- By the end of the next quarter, we will provide point-of-care testing for all patients in the north wing.

These are examples of objectives for a more comprehensive goal for customer satisfaction.

- Hire employees who are client oriented in addition to being technically or professionally competent and who will remain onboard.
- Provide an orientation-training program that stresses client satisfaction.
- Anticipate changes in customers' needs or expectations, and monitor their satisfaction using multiple feedback sources and techniques.
- Encourage all employees to participate in the planning and execution of new or improved services and in solving customer problems.
- Provide an intensive continuing education program that features client satisfaction.

Strategy

Successful organizations build on their existing strengths and eliminate their weaknesses or render them irrelevant. They constantly search for innovative ways to please their customers. The moves they make to please their customers, to position themselves relative to their markets, to adapt to the changing environment, and to address their relationships to their competition are reflections of their strategy. Keys to success in the pursuit of an organizational strategy include

- vision, mission, goals, objectives, and action plans,
- support of top management,
- effective and efficient systems, processes, and procedures,
- quality tools and techniques,
- sufficient time to carry out plans, and
- empowered, caring, competent employees.

Action Plans

Action plans typically contain five steps.

Step 1. Identify the Problem or Need

To identify and understand the problem or need, answer the following questions.

- Why is there a need for change? What is wrong with the present service or system?
- What are our strengths and weaknesses and those of our competitors?
- What are the potential gains, losses, or risks of a change?
- Who will be affected? What will it cost?
- What is likely to happen if no action is taken?

Step 2. Obtain and Analyze Data

Select a method of collecting information and build a data bank. Be thorough when you collect information. Become familiar with statistical analysis and the use of charts, electronic data interchange, electronic mail, and workflow automation. Document current deficiencies and opportunities for improvement.

Step 3. Determine the Best Action

Appropriate action plans should answer the following questions.

- What is to be done?
- Why must it be done?
- When should it be started and when should it be completed?
- Who is to do it?
- Where is the action to take place?
- How should it be done?

Step 4. Carry Out the Plan

It is essential that a plan be doable, understandable, comprehensive, cost-effective, approved, and periodically reviewed. Complex plans should always include an executive summary. The summary should state how the proposal affects the mission statement and how it will affect service quality and operational costs. Also to be added is your assessment of how you believe clients and employees will react to the changes wrought by the plan. The implementation process includes

- identifying resources (for example, people, supplies, equipment, facilities, time, and funds),
- preparing checklists of important tasks to be performed,
- assigning tasks, authority, and responsibility,
- preparing work schedules,
- providing necessary training, and,
- as necessary, formulating new policies, systems, and procedures

Sequencing and Scheduling of Tasks

Use Gantt charts, flowcharts, and flow or other logic diagrams to document tasks and analyze the times required for the work processes. On a chart, chronologically list the tasks to be done on one side opposite the appropriate calendar periods. See Chapter 35 for more information on charting.

Budget Preparation

Estimate all costs associated with each task. Build in some slack for inflation or other unanticipated costs. Prepare a cost spreadsheet with tasks listed vertically and cost factors (for example, labor, supplies) listed horizontally and totaled at the right of each line.

Establish Priorities

Priorities are a vital part of any plan. To avoid frustration, be flexible; that is, prepared to modify your priority list as circumstances change. Unexpected interruptions are the rule rather than the exception.

Step 5. Monitor Process, Report Progress, and Make Adjustments

Formal control is planned control and consists of data gathering and analysis. Informal control consists of day-by-day observations and impromptu meetings with other participants. Informal controls are more proactive than formal controls. Issue periodic status reports for large projects.

Monitoring progress usually necessitates tying up some loose ends. These may involve changes in plans, reassignment of tasks, removal of barriers, or seeking additional resources. The earlier a problem is identified, the easier it is to correct.

Think About It

Conditions change, circumstances change, the environment is forever in a state of flux, so oftentimes plans are themselves not particularly useful. However, the planning process is invaluable.

Questions for Review and Discussion

1. If we believe that planning is so important, why, knowing this, do we so often rush directly into doing without pausing to plan?
2. What do we stand to gain from applying planning principles to supposedly routine activities?
3. What are two significant reasons why a particular objective or target may not be attained as planned?
4. What are the principal characteristics of planning that apparently cause many to bypass it altogether?
5. What kinds of plans are of most concern to the working supervisor? Why?
6. What are the primary differences between mission and vision?
7. What are the three essential components of an appropriate objective?
8. Assume the organization has a 5-year plan. When would formal planning again take place: 5 years in the future? A year in the future? Some other time? Explain your answer.
9. What is the fundamental difference between goals and objectives?
10. Create an example of a sound objective to apply at the departmental level.

Exercise: Your Planning "Manual"

You are to write, preferably using full sentences but arranged in outline form, a departmental planning manual; that is, a guide for you and other supervisors to follow in preparing action plans for improving work methods, solving productivity problems, and addressing issues of quality. Be sure to provide for all of the required elements of an action plan.

Case: And Here We Go Once More

The position of business manager at Smalltown Hospital has been a hot seat, with incumbents changing frequently. When the position was vacated last May, the four senior employees in the department were interviewed. All were told that because they were at the top of grade and the compensation structure for new supervisors had not yet caught up with that of other positions, the position would involve just a miniscule increase in pay, an increment one could readily consider insultingly small. All four refused the position, and all were given the impression that they were not really considered qualified just yet but that they might be considered for supervision again at a later date.

That same month a new business manager was hired from outside, and the four senior employees were instructed to show their new boss in detail how things worked in the department. Over the following several months the business manager's boss, the finance director, told all four senior employees that they had "come along very well" and would be considered for the manager's position should it again become vacant.

In October of that same year the manager resigned. However, none of the four senior employees got the job; the process was repeated, and again a new manager was hired from the outside.

Instructions:

1. You are advised upfront to avoid allowing the most blatant errors and transgressions revealed in the case description to lead you to focus exclusively on the inappropriate management behavior. Rather, we are concerned here with operational planning. Viewing the department and its needs from the perspective of the finance director, describe how this shoot-from-the-hip manager, with appropriate forethought, could have properly planned for the department's supervisory transition.
2. Also, summarize what you believe to be the inappropriate consequences of the finance director's failure to plan.

REFERENCES

1. Dawson, R. 1992. *Secrets of Power Persuasion.* Englewood Cliffs, NJ: Prentice Hall, 277.
2. Hammer, M., and J. Champy. 1993. *Re-engineering the corporation.* New York: Harper, 155.
3. Fisher, K. 1993. *Leading self-directed work teams: A guide to developing new team leadership.* New York: McGraw-Hill, 136.
4. Dawson, R. 1992. *Secrets of Power Persuasion.* Englewood Cliffs, NJ: Prentice Hall, 278.

Chapter 4

Organizing, Coordinating, and Reengineering

Organization is the art of getting people to respond
like thoroughbreds. When you call on a
thoroughbred, he gives you all the speed, heart, and
sinew in him. When you call on a jackass, he kicks.

CHAPTER OBJECTIVES

- Provide a working definition of organizing and describe its place among the basic management functions.
- Convey the importance of values in organizational life, at both the corporate and personal levels.
- Explain the concept of authority and describe how authority is apportioned to those responsible for its application.
- Define the concepts of *unity of command* and *span of control* as they apply to the role of the first-line supervisor.
- Explain the staffing process and describe how the work to be done is apportioned among the appropriate staff.
- Define the informal organization and describe its potential impact on organizational functioning.
- Define the coordination process and identify its various components.
- Provide a working definition of reengineering and describe how it is intended to reduce costs or improve productivity, quality, or customer satisfaction.

Organizing is the process of gearing up to implement decisions that result from the planning process. It concerns delineating tasks and establishing a framework of authority and responsibility for the people who will carry out these tasks; that is, building the structure within which the work gets done. It involves analyzing the workload, distributing it among employees, and coordinating the activities so that work proceeds smoothly.

Supervisors perform organizing functions using authority assigned to their positions in the organizational hierarchy or "table of organization" as it might be described. Essential organizing tools include policies, procedures, work rules, position descriptions, and the all-important activities of assigning and delegating.

VALUES

Corporate Values

In value statements most employers express what they regard as evidence of loyalty, expected behavior, or ethical practice. Organizational cultures consist of the values that guide an organization in its daily activities; that is, the sum total of all the ways people are expected to act in pursuing the goals and objectives of the organization. As work crosses departmental boundaries (for example, the flow of patients moving from unit to unit), inevitable differences in values affect what, how, and when things are done.

When corporations or supervisors violate their own values, employees become cynical. They remember what they have been told, and they talk of past promises that have been broken. They use such descriptors as "unfair" or "double-talk."

Personal Values

What we as individuals consider ethical and unethical depends on our personal value systems, the things in which we believe. Personal values concern what is important regarding work (for example, challenges, tasks, recognition, creativity, and authority). These values encompass relationships, personal finances, living and recreational activities, hobbies, and entertainment. Other values may include ambition and desire for fame or the wish to own one's own enterprise. Attitudes continually reflect the core beliefs and values of individuals. Attitudes can change when beliefs and values change, but that does not happen very often.

AUTHORITY

Authority is delegated power or formal power passed on down the hierarchy to the point at which it will be applied. Supervisors require authority to fulfill their responsibilities. It is axiomatic that people should not be given responsibilities without sufficient authority to get the job done. Although authority is the power that makes a managerial job a reality, it can be relatively weak. To be effectively applied, authority must be supplemented by conditions or characteristics such as

- expertise (for example, licensure, certification, knowledge, skill, or experience),
- credibility, as in being trusted and respected,
- leadership skill, whether natural or acquired,
- persuasiveness or charisma, and
- influence (often as determined by whom one knows or is related to).

Ideally the extent of a supervisor's authority is expressed in the position description. Some of the more important activities over which supervisors possess variable amounts of authority fall into three categories: personnel administration, fiscal administration, and procedures.

Personnel administration includes

- selecting, orienting, and training new employees,
- assigning or delegating to subordinates,
- scheduling and approving overtime, and
- coaching, counseling, and disciplining employees.

The tasks of fiscal administration include

- selecting supplies or equipment or approving such purchases,
- selecting vendors, and establishing inventory levels.

The third category, procedures, involves

- selecting or modifying methods,
- formulating or enforcing policies and rules, and
- participating in administrative activities (for example, quality management, safety, and education).

UNITY OF COMMAND

The principle of unity of command originally meant that each employee reported to one and only one superior. However, matrix management arrangements and other complex organizational patterns have eroded that concept. Presently, unity of command simply means that for each task that must be done, the employee who performs it is directly accountable to someone. From the first-line supervisor's viewpoint unity of command ordinarily represents a normal working arrangement under which every task that must be done is assigned to someone, and each person responsible for performing a specific task is accountable to the supervisor. This means that never, at any time, should there be cause for the department's employees to wonder, Whose job is this?

SPAN OF CONTROL

In simplest terms span of control refers to the number of employees who report to a single leader. In practical terms it is a reckoning of how many employees a single supervisor can effectively manage; how many the supervisor can keep track of and still provide with the necessary supervisory attention.

Factors such as computers and autonomous work teams have led top management to expand spans of control and strip away layers of management. Organizational flattening, which often accompanies reengineering or reorganizing efforts, can also reduce management layers and force more responsibility down to lower management levels. The result is that many supervisors are likely to find themselves directing greater numbers of people, and staff reductions, which have sometimes had the effect of replacing highly qualified personnel with workers of lesser overall qualifications, have placed an additional burden on overworked supervisors. This condition is compounded by the fact that most of today's supervisors are left with fewer fellow superiors from whom to solicit advice and support.

A supervisor's effective span of control depends on numerous factors, including the skill level of the employees, employee mobility, and the variability of the department's work, so it is not possible to supply a magic number representing an ideal span of control. However, when the number of people who report to a supervisor is too low, the supervisor, having too little to do at times, often micromanages, much to the discomfort of the employees. When the number of people reporting to a supervisor is too great, there is the danger of problems and needs going unaddressed and the likelihood that some employees will not receive the supervisory attention they require.

STAFFING

The staffing process starts with human resource planning, recruitment, personnel selection, and orientation of new employees. It continues with training, career development, control, and the appraisal of performance. It may lead to promotion, transfer, demotion, or separation.

Avoid staffing with people who are clearly overqualified; these people will not remain long, so personnel costs and turnover can be excessive. Underqualified candidates may or may not represent good investments; some may make it, some may fail. The key factor is whether you can train them without excessive cost or loss of time. These individuals, when trained, are less likely to be bored with routine tasks, and their turnover rate is generally lower than that of overly qualified people.

You enhance personnel availability and morale when you can adjust work hours to suit your employees. The majority of health care workers are women, and many prefer work hours that allow them to take care of their family responsibilities. Part-time employment, flextime, and job-sharing opportunities can be powerful incentives. The use of these staffing strategies also helps provide the needed flexibility for jobs that experience peaks and troughs of activity.

ASSIGNING

Assigning and delegating have one thing in common: if they are not done, the supervisor is left to do all the work, a clearly unrealistic situation. Assigned tasks are those described in position descriptions. They are activities ordinarily performed by employees in each particular category, and the employees have limited choice in their specific assignments. A delegated task, on the other hand, involves transfer of a responsibility and authority from supervisor to employee. It is often voluntary. Delegation is addressed in more depth in Chapter 31.

A composite list of the qualifications of all your employees is like all the pieces in a set of Tinkertoys®. All the pieces (qualifications) are not used; in fact, some pieces may be missing. Your task is to match the expertise and available work hours to the requirements of your unit.

Supervisors who maintain an inventory chart of the skills of their employees find such charts helpful in assigning backup services. They also use the information when designing educational and cross-training programs.

Supervisors make the specific assignments and ensure that the assignments are carried out. To do this effectively, supervisors must know

- what must be done
- what equipment and supplies are needed
- what authority the supervisor has
- what quality and productivity requirements must be met
- what the cost constraints are
- where each task is to be performed
- where supplies and service supports are found
- where to obtain help
- who does what
- when the work must be done (deadlines, turnaround time, etc.)
- when changes must be made
- how the work is to be performed (procedure or methodology)
- how well, how quickly, and how economically the work must be done
- why the work is done (how an employee's work affects the big picture)

It is also necessary for a supervisor to make an honest effort to match each assignment with an individual's ability. The supervisor must

- ensure that the employee to be assigned has time available in which to accomplish the work. Overloading an employee, even inadvertently, is unfair to the individual and it creates the risk of failing to do justice to the task;
- provide all necessary training. It is never appropriate to hand a task to an individual and let that person learn by trial and error;
- explain each assignment without overloading the explanation with trivial details. Ask the employee to repeat the instructions or perform the work under observation to ensure he or she understands;
- provide complicated orders in writing, perhaps in procedural form;
- alert the assignee to potential pitfalls, barriers, or constraints, and let the person know how, when, and where to report problems or ask for help;
- whenever possible, make holistic assignments; that is, assign a complete task to an individual rather than breaking it up. For example, many nurses prefer being responsible for all the nursing care of an individual patient rather than providing only part of that care such as passing medications.

THE INFORMAL ORGANIZATION

Every organization has beneath its visible surface a network that constitutes another arrangement of interrelationships that is not represented in any organizational chart. This is the informal organization, at times perhaps even more powerful simply because of its lack of visibility. This informal organization even has its own communication system; we refer to it as the grapevine.

There are, of course, labor unions, which are certainly visible and have their share of power and influence. In addition to unions, there are also groups of workers that have no formal power but are able to intimidate or ostracize coworkers and, at times, even negotiate with management in an unofficial sense. Within formal work groups there are cliques that select informal leaders based on expertise, personality, persuasiveness, or physical power. Often informal leaders and union leaders possess more power than the formal leaders. When members of these informal groups are frustrated or are led to feel disloyal, they may sabotage equipment, block workflow, start malicious rumors, or even inflict physical harm.

Supervisors must be aware of informal networks. An astute supervisor can often tap into the grapevine and use it to advantage. The grapevine can carry correct information when formal means cannot be trusted or when formal means are not fast enough to squelch rumors by circulating the truth. The supervisor who is well tuned to the grapevine is often in a position to learn what is really going on at employee level. The astute supervisor also identifies the informal leaders and makes a special effort to get along with them. These informal leaders sometimes turn out to be strong candidates for promotion to supervisory positions and likely employees to handle important delegated tasks.

COORDINATION PROCESS

Coordination is the process of synchronizing activities and participants so that they function smoothly with each other. When coordination fails, conflict and confusion run rampant. Proactive coordinating involves activities intended to anticipate and prevent problems. Reactive coordinating consists of regulatory activities aimed at the maintenance of existing structural and functional arrangements and corrective activities that rectify errors after they have occurred.

The more steps and the more gatekeepers involved in a workflow process, the greater the need for coordination. Joint projects and services that require interdepartmental cooperation also demand active coordination. Breakdowns in coordination are largely a result of faulty communication, personality conflicts, turf battles, and job design problems. Other causes include training deficiencies, flawed physical arrangements, conflicts of authority, and lack of appropriate policies or procedures.

Workflow coordination is easier when each employee interaction is regarded as a customer service engagement with a provider and a service user (customer). Recipients are encouraged to provide positive or negative feedback to the providers and make suggestions for improving such interactions.

Coordinating Requires Persuasive Ability

The definition of management can be expanded to include not only getting things done through people but also getting things done *with* people. "With people" signifies the importance of influencing persons who are neither bosses nor subordinates. These relationships are lateral, or collegial, rather than hierarchical. As organizations grow more complex and more highly specialized, supervisors spend less time with superiors and subordinates and more time with their peers. Peer groups include internal and external customers, vendors, and other outside providers, as well as employees who precede or follow them in workflows.

Most managers and supervisors are involved in both intradepartmental and interdepartmental coordination. The inability to function effectively and efficiently as a coordinator in such relationships can impair careers.

Tools of Coordination

Committees

A major purpose of committees is to increase coordination, but committees are costly, time consuming, and often ineffective. The strength of committee action comes through a synthesis of divergent viewpoints.[1]

Coordinators

As interdepartmental coordination becomes more important, new coordinating and facilitating roles may be established. Coordinators play an important role in quality management, employee safety, risk management, customer service, staff training, and cost containment.

Communication Modalities

Up-to-date tables of organization, policy and procedure manuals, standard operating procedures, computers, memos, reports, and newsletters are important, as are telephones, intercoms, e-mail, voice mail, and meetings.

Clinical Paths

A clinical path is a linked series of activities and processes intended to guide the performance of a multistep clinical task with optimum efficiency. In medicine clinical paths are important in planning, coordination, communication, and evaluation of care. For example, the clinical path for a routine inpatient surgery case would perhaps begin with preadmission testing, proceed through admission, continue through all activities performed with and for the patient including the surgery itself, and eventually conclude with the patient's discharge. Having been thoroughly thought out in advance and established as a protocol, this path would represent the most efficient of a number of possible paths to the same end. Somewhat related to clinical paths, there are also algorithms that guide clinicians through the "if, then" decision-making process; that is, at each of any number of steps the clinician responds: *if* this occurs, *then* take this particular action.

Improved Interdepartmental Coordination

To achieve improved interdepartmental coordination, and with it improvements in communication and cooperation, keep in mind the following points.

- Make all service requests clear and direct. Whenever possible, make the requests directly to the person or persons who provides the service.
- Anticipate negative responses to requests and problems, and be ready to respond positively.
- When a request is initially made, secure agreement on the date or time by which the necessary action will be taken.
- Always follow up a verbal request with the same in written form; a verbal request can be forgotten or ignored, but it is less likely to fall by the wayside if documented.
- Listen to the problems of employees and do your best to empathize.
- Seek collaborative (win-win) solutions whenever possible, but be prepared to compromise when necessary.

- Treat others as partners or collaborators; let them know this is "ours" rather than "mine."
- Always place teamwork above competition.
- Be patient and reasonable, never demanding or critical.
- Avoid becoming upset and avoid upsetting the other person; anger only hinders the cooperative process.
- Eliminate all kidding and sarcasm from your repertoire. You never know when innocent kidding could be taken to heart. Also, sarcasm is never found among the legitimate tools of communication.
- Always strive to know your staff and your colleagues better and to improve your understanding of their work.
- Always express sincere appreciation for the efforts of others. Honest appreciation of work well done is one of the surest ways of ensuring that future work is well done.

REENGINEERING

Reengineering is a significant and powerful tool for managers who wish to change a system or process for the better or design a new approach or procedure. Smith defines reengineering as the redesign of processes and the systems, policies, or structures that support them.[2] It means, quite literally, to engineer again, to go back to square one, as it were, and start over as though there was nothing presently in place. The purpose of reengineering is usually to optimize workflow and improve productivity. The ultimate goal may be increased productivity, reduced costs, improved quality, greater customer satisfaction, or some combination of these.

An example of an operational process is the sequence that begins when a physician writes an order and ends when the patient receives whatever has been ordered. Although it usually involves charting, reengineering is not merely modifying flowcharts. It includes abandoning obsolete systems, forming cross-functional teams, amalgamating jobs, discarding old rules and assumptions, introducing new technologies, and creating new principles for task organization. Reengineering often proves to be far more difficult than it first appears. Many find it is extremely difficult to take their thinking back to square one to begin anew without being unduly influenced by the manner in which the process presently proceeds.

On a macro level reengineering concerns downsizing, strategic alliances, decentralization, structural changes, reorganizing, and mergers and affiliations. On a micro level it deals with quality circles, team building, and operational efficiency.

Successful reengineering requires a leadership style that features participative management, delegation, employee empowerment, and self-directed teams. It also requires a great deal of sensitive employee relations; to a great many employees in today's health care organizations the mere mention of "reengineering" is taken to mean that layoffs are on the way.

Systems or processes are more likely to be the cause of medical service problems and patient complaints than are issues of employee performance. For example, an audit of hospital inpatients found that the most common complaints were noise, quality of food, the temperature and appearance of rooms, and time spent waiting for admission, discharge, or x-rays. Most of these problems were attributed to faulty processes.[3]

How well departments work together is fully as important as the performance of individual departments. This is regularly illustrated in the treatment of patients in emergency departments. In this critical unit, collaboration of physicians and nurses with the laboratory, blood bank, respiratory therapy, radiology, and electrocardiographic services is essential.

Successful reengineering eliminates much monitoring, checking, waiting, tracking, and other unproductive work. Thus there is more time for doing real work. In one hospital a cross-functional team cut patient admission waiting time by 17%. Another team at that facility reduced the paperwork process of hiring from an average of 9.5 days to 4.5 days.[4]

Many health care processes are complex and nonlinear and cannot be simplified into strings of quick sequential tasks. The desired result often requires a high degree of collaboration between individuals and functions.

Processes often are more efficient if they consist of multiple operational channels. For example, a large emergency department may be more efficient if one section cares for major trauma cases, another handles minor injuries, and a third treats nonsurgical patients.

Selection of a Process for Reengineering

A current process may be dysfunctional in that things are just not working as they should. There may be chronic problems, frequent breakdowns, excessive losses of time or money (for example, too much waiting in the admissions office, slow turnaround time for laboratory or radiology work, difficulties obtaining physician discharge notes, excessive inventory, or a breakdown in quality).

Another factor in the selection of a process for reengineering includes the importance of the process, such as an assessment of how seriously customer service, employee morale, or profitability is affected, for example. Feasibility also enters into the equation. It is necessary to ask, Do we have the wherewithal to accomplish a significant change? Is the desired change cost effective?

Hospital processes that will receive increasing attention are those that cut across departmental lines. These systems involve multiple compartmentalized functions, many different employees, and diverse priorities. Because of their complexity and the need for cooperation, these systems are the most difficult to modify, but they promise the greatest dividends in terms of time and money saved. Such a process may be as complicated as the handling of a trauma patient from the time of admission to the time of discharge, or it may be as simple as getting a blood transfusion for an outpatient.

Preparation and Implementation

What is the problem and how is it presently being handled? Start with customer input. Learn more about what the customers want or need. Watch them go about their daily routines. For example, laboratory workers can make rounds with physicians when they order laboratory tests and when they receive the test results. Talk with customers about your billing process. Visit a physician's office and talk with the office manager or nurse about the ease of requesting services. Talk with your front-line service providers such as patient care technicians, phlebotomists, nurses, and others who meet the customers. These people can give you more useful information than you will ever get from consultants or in-service specialists.

Determine what tasks can be eliminated. Should any of the work be outsourced? How could technology help?

Visit facilities that have reputations for outstanding service and learn what you can from them. Consider innovative approaches. Identify and attack assumptions or time-honored practices such as paying suppliers only after they have delivered the goods. Consider eliminating a large inventory storage space to force the use of a just-in-time inventory system.

Identify variables that can be readily measured, and create temporary problem-solving teams to improve a specific metric. For faster action, avoid too many open-ended initiatives. When a team finds itself alone with a specific problem and a deadline, the thinking often comes with startling ease.

Establish a measurement system. Such a system includes schedules, overhead costs, employee and customer satisfaction gauges, and any conditions that would trigger a variant that would require attention.

Barriers to Reengineering

Barriers to reengineering include cost, time, and risks (to customers, employees, or vendors). There may also be problems of team function or turnover. Outsiders and in-house executives may toss in a few monkey wrenches. New challenges or management initiatives may divert attention away from the reengineering efforts.

The two most common causes of reengineering failure are the loss of interest and support on the part of top management and the resistance of the workers who must implement the initiative. Employees who are not convinced of the need for change or who perceive change as a threat may drag their feet or even refuse to participate.

Think About It

To a considerable extent the typical supervisory job is a constant exercise in coordination. If certain events do not happen in the proper temporal relationship to each other, gross inefficiencies are often the result. Coordination's opposite number is chaos.

Questions for Review and Discussion

1. Fully describe the relationship between planning and organizing.
2. As a supervisor, why is it important for you to be fully knowledgeable of the precise limits of your authority?
3. Explain how you would respond to an employee who says to you: "Don't hand me this reengineering stuff. That's just a fancy way of saying you're going to cut staff."
4. Why is it necessary for the organization to have a formal code of ethics? Shouldn't sound personal values be sufficient?
5. Organizations undergoing significant reengineering efforts often engage the services of an outside consultant. Why do you think this is done?
6. How would you handle a situation in which the supervisor of another department approaches you with a strong complaint about one of your employees?
7. Why is it stressed that effective coordination requires persuasive ability?
8. As a supervisor, what would be your response when seriously incorrect information reaches you by way of the grapevine?
9. Why is reengineering often more difficult than expected? Explain, using an example.
10. Who has the broader span of control and can thus effectively supervise more employees: the business office supervisor or the housekeeping supervisor? Why?

Essay Question: Delegation, Authority, and Responsibility

In essay form, describe in detail the appropriate relationship between authority and responsibility in proper delegation. Concerning authority and responsibility, explain why only one of these is truly "delegated," and fully explain why this is so. In doing so, comment on the relationship between authority and responsibility under three possible sets of conditions: authority exceeds responsibility, responsibility exceeds authority, and authority and responsibility are equal. (It will be helpful to briefly research some definitions of the terms involved, especially "delegation.")

Case: Looking for the Limits of Authority

When you accepted the position as supervisor of a housekeeping team, your manager, June Arnold, the assistant director of building services, told you that you would not find a great deal of decision-making guidance written out in policy and procedure form. As June put it, "Common sense is the overriding policy." However, June cautioned you about the need to see her concerning matters involving employee discipline because the organization was presently sensitive to union organizing overtures in the service areas.

Early in your third week on the job there was an occurrence that seemed to call for routine disciplinary action. Remembering June's precaution, you tried to see her several times over a period of 3 days. Being unable to get to her and getting no response to the messages you left, you went ahead and took action rather than risk credibility through procrastination. When you were finally able to see June and explain what you had done, she said, "No big deal. Common sense, like I said."

Some weeks later a similar situation arose. Again you could not get to June, and again you took what you believed to be appropriate action, but this time the problem involved an employee you later learned was a strong informal leader within a contingent of generally dissatisfied employees. The disciplinary action blew up in your face and provided the active union organizers with an issue they immediately inflated for their purposes. June was furious with you. She accused you of intentionally overstepping your authority by failing to bring such problems to her attention as instructed.

Instructions:

1. Explain how you would go about trying to establish the true limits of your decision-making authority.
2. Because the limits of your authority are ultimately those limits set by your manager, the aforementioned June, develop a possible approach to getting June to help you define the limits of your authority.

REFERENCES

1. Longest Jr., B.B. 1984. *Management practices for the health professional*, 3d ed. Reston, VA: Reston Publishing, 179.
2. Smith, B. 1994. Business process re-engineering: More than a buzzword. *HR Focus* 71(1):17.
3. Rollins, R.J. 1994. Patient satisfaction in VA medical centers and private sector hospitals. *Health Care Supervisor* 12(3):44–50.
4. McKenzie, L. 1994. Cross-functional teams in health care organizations. *Health Care Supervisor* 12(3):1–10.

Chapter 5

Position Descriptions and Performance Standards

*No single instrument is as important to effective wage and
salary administration as the job description, yet there is
evidence that it receives far less attention than it requires
to assure either that it is properly prepared in the first
place or that its uses are properly understood or directed.*

— A. R. Brandt[1]

CHAPTER OBJECTIVES

- Introduce the position description (also referred to as job description), and develop an understanding of its importance.
- Review the essential elements of the position description, identifying what must be included in this management instrument and setting forth the reasons for inclusion.
- Highlight those legitimate uses of the position description that are of special significance to the first-line supervisor.
- Explain the effects of the Americans with Disabilities Act (ADA) on present day position descriptions.
- Define the different kinds of performance standards and review the purposes for which they are commonly used.
- Identify the characteristics of an appropriate standard.
- Provide advice applicable in formulating standards for departmental use and identify pitfalls that can hamper the establishment of readily usable standards.

POSITION DESCRIPTIONS

The standards of the Joint Commission on Accreditation of Healthcare Organizations (JCAHO) include specific guidelines for creating and applying job descriptions and performance appraisals.[2] The Americans with Disabilities Act (ADA) of 1990 also focuses on these two functions, with the intent of preventing discrimination against persons having physical or mental conditions that may be considered disabilities.[3]

Job descriptions should be regarded as contracts between employers and employees. In addition to spelling out the manner in which employees are expected to perform, they establish a rational link with performance appraisals. They are versatile documents that are regularly put to more uses than suggested in this chapter. To name only a few additional uses, job descriptions often figure prominently in preparing recruitment advertising, interviewing prospective employees, and training and orienting employees.

Because position descriptions define requirements for jobs as they were done in the past (the recent past, we should hope) and because job responsibilities change rapidly, these documents are out of date a good part of the time. To avoid rapid obsolescence and to provide greater flexibility, managers are becoming less specific about assigned tasks and are making use of more general terminology such as "customer satisfaction" and "willingness to adjust to change."

The fact that far too many employees simply do not fully know what is expected of them is a significant cause of unsatisfactory performance. Professional athletes seldom have written position descriptions, but they know precisely what they must do and how well these things must be done. Institutions use position descriptions and work standards to flesh out these two essentials.

Title and Classification

Job titles are important not only for the convenience of the organization in identifying and classifying jobs but also for employee prestige and self-esteem. Often a title change is accompanied by a pay raise, but even without pay increases most employees appreciate more prestigious titles. In the following list, for example, the title on the right is more likely to be preferred.

Secretary	Administrative Assistant
Technician	Specialist
Technologist	Scientist
Director	Vice President
Salesperson	Sales Associate

Positions are classified as salaried or hourly (exempt or nonexempt) and as part-time or full-time. The classification includes designation of a job grade and wage range. The position classification may note that an employee is permanently assigned to a particular shift or required to rotate shifts. If the employee must occasionally work after hours, take weekend assignments, or be subject to recalls, those requirements should be stated to avoid future disagreements. Verbal promises made prior to hiring have been known to be notoriously inaccurate.

Summary Statement

The summary statement that leads off a position description, also referred to as a position summary, umbrella statement, position purpose or goal, mission statement, or function statement, condenses the responsibilities of the position. This statement is required by the JCAHO. It may include the goals, reporting channel, and other features of the job. For example:

> The incumbent plans, directs, and controls a 10-person hematology section of the laboratory. The major goal of this position is to meet or exceed customer expectations. Our customers include patients, patient's families and visitors, clinicians and other care providers, third-party payers, teammates, students and trainees, and hospital departments or committees served by our department. The incumbent is also responsible for the teaching of students and new employees. The incumbent performs a wide range of hematological procedures. The incumbent reports to the administrative director of the laboratory.

Required Competencies

Competencies or qualifications describe the requirements of the job, not the qualifications of the person holding the job. These competencies include those that the incumbents must have and those you would like them to have. For some positions the basic qualifications can be eliminated because they are detailed in the credentialing process. For example, in the position description for a radiologist, the competency requirement may simply be that applicants must be board certified and hold a state license. This eliminates the need for a long list of tasks that radiologists perform.

In addition to educational and experiential requirements, special skills may be required (for example, a medical transcriptionist will be required to be familiar with medical terminology).

Temperament, traits, and personality are important, as are characteristics such as flexibility, ability to adjust to change, and willingness to learn new skills. However, these are highly subjective, so justification for including them should be provided in the descriptions of duties and responsibilities.

We should always wish to go beyond technical or professional skills and look for people who are willing to walk the extra mile for customers. To assist in the candidate selection process, carefully describe requirements of special importance or sensitivity. Express these in behavioral terms (for example, "is discrete with patient information," "shows composure under stress," "accepts night and weekend assignments," "recognizes or anticipates needs of customers," or "uses tact in personal interactions with customers and staff"). Including "soft skill" items is especially helpful when orienting and training new employees because they express in clear terms the kind of behavior that you expect.

Reporting and Coordinating Relationships

The reporting relationships section of the job description identifies, by position title, an incumbent's immediate superior and others to whom he or she is directly accountable. Many employees must work closely with colleagues in other sections of their department, in other departments, and in outside agencies. Radiology and laboratory supervisors must cooperate with personnel in the surgical suite, the emergency department, and critical care units. Here is an example.

> The radiology supervisor must establish and maintain close working relationships with admissions, the surgical suite, the emergency department, special care units, and the quality assurance coordinator. He or she advises the technical director of the school for radiology technicians and frequently consults with the director of hospital information systems.

Scope of Authority

Delineating levels of authority avoids misunderstandings and embarrassment, especially when supervisors undertake disciplinary actions or incur major expenses. Three levels are recommended for each major responsibility. The level 1 (the highest) designation carries unlimited power to make decisions and to take action without consulting superiors. Level 2 authority has some limitations. For example, a supervisor may be authorized to assign overtime but must inform his or her manager of the action on the next day. At level 3, a supervisor must obtain approval before taking action. A global statement may suffice in some situations. For example, "The supervisor has the authority to discharge all the responsibilities of the job within the constraints of the law, organizational and departmental policy, and the labor contract. He or she has signing authority for up to $1,000 for instrument repair."

Degrees of Independence

Degrees of independence are important in descriptions of nonsupervisory positions. Pertinent questions concerning relative independence include

- Are detailed written instructions always available or only for new or difficult tasks? These instructions may include policy or safety manuals and specific aids such as procedures manuals.
- Does the employee organize his or her daily work and modify it when appropriate, or does the supervisor do this?
- Does the incumbent perform any supervisory or administrative functions? If so, to what extent?

What follows is one such classification.

- Level 1. No responsibility for directing others.
- Level 2. Performs same kind of work as other members of the work group but spends about 10% of time serving as trainer, instructor, or resource person.
- Level 3. Rotates as five-person team leader with five other technical employees, with minimal direction from supervisor.
- Level 4. Permanent team leader. Functions include directing, controlling, assigning, and scheduling. Reports to supervisor. No authority to discipline without approval of supervisor.

Special Demands and the Working Environment

Working conditions include physical space, temperature extremes, and exposure to infectious agents, chemicals, radiation, and other hazards. The position description document may describe the type of safety equipment and attire that are used.

Physical demands have assumed new significance with the passage of the ADA and must be based on the current requirements of actual incumbents. Most professional and technical positions make special demands. Such demands include absolute integrity and accuracy in reporting observations, discretion with patient information, willingness to alter work schedules, and the ability to work under stress.

Responsibilities, Duties, and Tasks

Match each responsibility with a statement that describes the type of behavior or outcome that identifies successful job performance. These descriptors serve as performance criteria. Content validity is thus established because these criteria are based on observable work behavior or results rather than on traits.

Responsibilities describe activities in their broadest sense; tasks describe them in the most specific terms. An example of a responsibility would be "teach radiology students." An example of a duty would be "provide benchwork instruction for twenty 3-hour sessions." Examples of tasks would be "prepare agenda, demonstrate method, grade students." List responsibilities in order of importance or according to the percentage of time needed for each.

The subdivision of duties requires more effort and lengthier documents. However, the effort may be worthwhile when detailed instructions are necessary (for example, jobs filled by individuals who have limited cognitive skills or no previous experience).

Select the best descriptive terminology, using action verbs when possible. Consider the clarification of the duty, the self-esteem of the employee, and the effect of the terminology on the salary classification. Use language carefully. "Makes visitors feel welcome" is better than "greets people;" "evaluates clinical results" is better than "checks records;" and "establishes controls that prevent release of erroneous information" is better than "sets quality controls."

The following list contains verbs useful for position descriptions.

Apply (current knowledge)	Monitor (work of new employees)
Arrange (meeting room)	Perform (tests)
Calibrate (instruments)	Practice (ethical standards)
Design (new work flow)	Process (specimens)
Determine (suitable methods)	Promote (public relations)
Establish (procedures for)	Recognize (errors)
Evaluate (new techniques)	Record (complaints)
Instruct (orientees)	Report (violations)
Maintain (systems for documenting)	Select (new employees)

Effects of the ADA on Position Descriptions

The ADA protects individuals with physical or mental disabilities that limit major life activities. Among those protected by it are persons with acquired immunodeficiency syndrome (AIDS), rehabilitated drug and alcohol abusers, obese persons, and those with cosmetic disfigurement. The law prohibits employers from discriminating against people who have any such limitation when hiring or firing. Generally the law is also relevant to issues of salary, training, promotion, and other conditions of employment for individuals who are considered disabled under its provisions. This legislation has had a major impact on hiring and promotion. People who can otherwise qualify for a job now may not be disqualified because they cannot perform tasks that bear only a marginal relationship to a particular job.

The ADA forces employers to make changes in the work environment to accommodate persons with disabilities. The law specifies that "reasonable accommodations" be provided for physically or mentally challenged employees.

Accommodations may be physical, such as installing ramps, repositioning workstations, widening doors, and installing grab bars in toilet stalls.

Accommodations may also involve deletion of certain nonessential tasks from position descriptions. An example would be to delete a task performed only occasionally and to assign that task to another employee (say if a job calls for occasional driving of an automobile, that responsibility may be assigned to a coworker; or a driver may be assigned to transport the person with the disability). Duties must therefore be designated as essential or nonessential. The essential functions of a job are those that, in the judgment of the employer, constitute business necessity. If a person cannot carry out essential responsibilities, that person is disqualified from the job. Employers are not obligated to lower qualification standards related to the essential functions of a job.

The ADA is concerned with factual determinations of essential functions, such as the percentage of time spent on the function and the consequences of not requiring the incumbent to perform the function. The physical requirements' portion of the position description is critically important in terms of ADA compliance. It must delineate the actual level of physical demands. Information includes kinds and amounts of lifting, types of work surfaces, and any auxiliary devices used, such as ladders. Management must indicate whether the physical demand is occasional, frequent, or constant.

PERFORMANCE STANDARDS

As far as the work itself is concerned, a basic job description states only the required tasks and responsibilities and the qualifications needed to perform them. In addition, performance standards are required. Performance standards have two cardinal purposes; first, to inform employees how well they must do their work and second, to simplify performance evaluations, especially if a pay-for-performance strategy is in place. Without performance standards, employee evaluations are necessarily highly subjective and can lead to charges of discrimination or favoritism.

All employees like to know the following about them and their work, even if they do not articulate these as specific requests.

- "Exactly what is it that you want me to do?"
- "How well and how fast must I perform these tasks?"
- "Show me how to do what I'm presently unable to do."
- "Let me know how I'm doing."

Position descriptions and performance standards address the first two of these queries directly and lay the foundation for responding to the others.

Uses of Performance Standards

Performance standards are used for a variety of reasons, including

- providing guidelines for orienting and training new employees,
- enabling employees to assess their own performance,
- providing a solid basis for performance appraisals, counseling, and disciplinary actions,
- supporting pay-for-performance and promotion selection strategies,
- identifying training and development needs,
- satisfying the requirements of accrediting and licensing agencies, and
- avoiding charges of discrimination and protecting against grievance actions.

Levels of Performance

A few organizations use only two levels of performance: "meets standard" and "fails to meet standard." Significantly more organizations use three levels: (1) does not meet expectations (fails), (2) meets expectations (passes), and (3) exceeds expectations (excels). Two-level systems (pass–fail) seldom aid motivation, except for new employees. Adding an "exceeds expectations" or "superior" level introduces challenge and motivation.

Standards for bilevel and trilevel systems are easiest to administer, but five-tiered systems are also popular. These systems sometimes include a category designated as "meets expectations, but needs improvement." The fifth class is derived by splitting the "exceeds expectations" group into "superior" and "outstanding." A supervisor faced with an indignant overachiever who wants to know why he or she is rated as "superior" instead of "outstanding" appreciates the difficulty inherent in using a five-level system.

Importance of Setting Appropriate Levels

A minimum-level standard provides a pass–fail situation. Performance below that level is unacceptable, signaling a need for remedial or administrative action. If this level is set too low, it leads to the acceptance of poor performance and the accumulation of "deadwood." On the other hand, if the level is too high, there may be frustration and loss of self-esteem when standards are not met.

Compliance Standards

Compliance standards concern obedience to policies and procedures. They relate to attendance, punctuality, appearance, and so forth. These standards need not be duplicated in position descriptions. Dispose of them with a global statement such as "complies with the conditions of employment described in our Personnel Policy and Procedures Manual." While you need not duplicate these criteria, variations from what are prescribed in personnel manuals may be necessary. For example, the dress code for patient care technicians or phlebotomists may be more stringent than that for employees who have no patient contact.

Temperament and Interrelationship Standards

Temperament and interrelationship standards pertain to work habits, initiative, creativity, self-development, reliability, and communication skills. These standards rely on "soft data" because they are highly subjective. Most of them cannot be tied directly to specific tasks and therefore are presented in a special segment of the position description. Although these traits are often omitted from position descriptions, they usually show up on performance evaluation forms and in discussions.

Task Standards

Task standards are based on outcomes and results. They use "hard data" because most of them are objective. Examples are turnaround time, infection rates, and compliance with budget. Task standards have several dimensions.

- Quality (errors, accuracy)
- Productivity (completing daily tasks)
- Timeliness (meeting deadlines)
- Cost-effectiveness (meeting budgets, inventory control)
- Manner of performance (courtesy, cooperation)

Characteristics of a Good Standard

An appropriate performance standard does many things.

- It describes a level below which performance is not acceptable or above which performance is superior.
- It provides a challenge but is attainable by most incumbents.
- It is results based and quantifiable whenever possible.
- It is specific, objective, and measurable.
- It deals with performance over which the employee has control.
- It excludes imprecise words such as professional, suitable, timely, attitude, and ethical unless these words are accompanied by descriptors.
- It limits the use of absolute terms such as never, always, or 100% to actions that are life threatening or serious in other ways (for example, issuing compatible blood for transfusions).

- It is understood and agreed to by both employee and supervisor.
- It does not discriminate against any member of a group protected by the Equal Employment Opportunity Commission (EEOC).
- It directly or indirectly benefits customers.

Practical Approach for Preparing Standards

The simplest approach to preparing performance standards is to list the major task standards, then add appropriate descriptors that represent one or more of the five dimensions listed above. For example:

Task: Answer the telephone.

Standards:

- Provides information sought by callers and ensures that transfers are completed. (Quality)
- Keeps lines open and avoids personal calls. (Quantity)
- Answers calls within three rings. (Timeliness)
- Identifies department and self. Asks "How can I help?" (Manner)
- Uses caller's name frequently. (Manner)
- Closes by thanking caller. (Manner)

Do not be discouraged when you must settle for descriptors that are not as precise as you would like. Periodic modifications dictated by experience are a key to success.

Some General Customer-Oriented Performance Standards

Performance standards that apply to an employee's interactions with customers frequently include the following.

- Uses tact in personal interactions.
- Communicates in an honest, straightforward manner.
- Reports employee concerns to department management.
- Reacts constructively to criticism and to changes.
- Maintains high team spirit and morale.
- Interacts in a positive manner.
- Rarely receives complaints from customers or staff.
- Customer information is always kept confidential.

Examples of Performance Standards for a Specific Position

Performance standards for the position of phlebotomist or patient care technician can be expected to appear as follows, with rare exception.

- Maintains appearance, dress, and decorum that conform to special lab code.
- Greets patients courteously by introducing self and calling patient by name.
- Explains procedure about to be performed.
- Complies with institutional policies and procedures with special attention to isolation procedures.

Quantification When Applicable and Possible

The introduction of numbers or percentages to standards adds objectivity. Employees get a more accurate description of what is required of them. For example, "Answer within three rings" is precise; "answer courteously" is not.

Percentages indicate the amount of tolerance or the number of errors permitted. This can be important. Consider "answer within three rings 90% of the time" and "correctly cross-match blood 90% of the time." This would be appropriate for the telephone rings but would be completely unacceptable for compatibility testing the blood. Often it is not possible or advantageous to apply percentages. Objections to their use have been voiced because one would have to record each episode before percentages could be calculated, converting supervisors into "bean counters."

There is no interpretive problem with terms like "always," "never," or "without exception," but there is a problem of achievement. Even the best employees slip occasionally. Therefore, terms like "with rare exception" are often more appropriate than absolute terms. The adverbs "generally," "ordinarily," and "usually" mean more than 50% of the time; "sometimes," "seldom," and "infrequently" denote occurrences less than 50%.

Tips for Formulating Standards

In developing standards for a particular job, start by updating the position description, particularly the segment on responsibilities. This is the skeleton for the standards. If you have a long list of duties, group theses into segments of related topics. Call these key results areas, significant job segments, or some similar title. For example, for an administrative assistant, all activities that relate to preparing for a meeting can be grouped under meeting preparations. For a nursing unit supervisor, these could consist of the following:

- Personnel functions
- Financial functions
- Operational functions
- Patient care functions
- Professional growth and development[4]

Use a KISS strategy: keep it short and simple. In health care, new technologies, services, and responsibilities translate into frequent changes in position descriptions. If you spend too much time developing comprehensive standards, you'll find yourself spending far too much time back at the drawing board. Most authorities believe that only six or seven major responsibilities of professional or technical specialists need descriptors.

Solicit the help of incumbents when deciding what should and should not be included. Incumbents are also helpful when selecting the degree of difficulty for standards. Contrary to what we may expect, employees consistently peg their expectations higher than do their supervisors.

When working on minimum standards, be sure you know what level of performance is acceptable and what is not. If descriptors are too soft, that is, if standards are too easy to meet, you will find you have accumulated deadwood and cannot get rid of it. To use the old quality assurance cliché, "Do it right the first time." If you subsequently raise those standards, you should negotiate the changes with all the members of the group. Do not forget to raise the same standards for all the other employees who hold the same position.

It is helpful to recall what kinds of problems your borderline performers have had or are having. Perhaps they forget a step in a complicated procedure or have difficulty dealing with certain customers. Composing standards based on such practical knowledge can produce great standards. When pondering descriptors for superior levels, watch one of your best employees at work. What does he or she do that makes the difference? These observations give you clues to good indicators.

Pitfalls

Some pitfalls commonly encountered in standards formulation:

- The list of duties and responsibilities is either incomplete or excessively detailed.
- An average performance level is used rather than a properly established standard. Contrary to much common usage, "average" and "standard" are not identical; average is the average actual performance of a group, and standard is the target for minimum acceptable performance.
- All designated responsibilities are not under the complete control of the employee.
- A standard is based on invalid or unreliable data.
- The expectations established are either too low or too high.
- Too few of the standards are based on outcomes or results.
- The supervisor or the employee is unwilling to renegotiate the level of a standard that appears inadequate.
- There is little or no commitment on the part of the employee.

- There is no input into standard formulation by the employee.
- There is inadequate monitoring of subsequent performance.

For examples of performance standards, see Exhibits 5–1, 5–2, 5–3, and 5–4.

Exhibit 5–1 Sample Format for Duties and Performance Standards for
a Medical Technologist

PERFORMS ROUTINE BACTERIOLOGY PROCEDURES, INCLUDING
READING OF PLATES, IDENTIFICATION, AND ANTIBIOTIC SUSCEPTI-
BILITY TESTING OF SUSPECTED PATHOGENS.
   a) Cultures must be planted on appropriate media within 15 minutes of receiv-
      ing the specimens.
   b) Stat Gram stains must be prepared and interpreted within 30 minutes of re-
      ceiving the specimen.
   c) Plates must be read and necessary tests set up by 3:00 PM.
   d) Must advise technicians on identification workup of unusual isolates.
   e) All procedures in the department must be performed according to laboratory
      specifications.
   f) There shall be no more than three complaints (incident reports) a year from
      physicians or nursing personnel regarding bacteriology results and procedures.

PERFORM ROUTINE AFB WORK, INCLUDING SPECIMEN PROCESSING
AND STAINING.
   a) Process, culture, and prepare smears of specimens within 1 hour.
   b) Interpret stains within 15 minutes, and notify the proper authorities when
      positive.

Note: duties are capitalized. The standards follow in lowercase letters. Reprinted from W.O.
Umiker and S.M. Yohe, *Performance Standards for Laboratory Personnel* p. 99, with permission of Medical Economics, © 1984.

Exhibit 5–2 Sample Format for Coupling of Duties and Performance Standards

Duty	Standards
Orient new employees	Submit schedule and agenda to office 1 week before arrival of new hire.
	Notify trainers at least 1 week before arrival of new employees.
	Complete orientation within 5 workdays.
	Return check-off list to office within 1 week of completion.
	Receive favorable evaluations from indoctrinees more than 90% of the time.

Exhibit 5–3 Performance Standards for Phlebotomists

Duty

Draws blood from patient and returns tubes and requests to clinical laboratory.

Standards

Greets patient by introducing self and calling patient by formal name.

Verifies correct patient by checking name on requisition form against name on patient's wrist band. Explains procedure to patient.

Follows infection prevention instructions in phlebotomist's procedure manual.

Performs phlebotomy. No more than three unsuccessful attempts are permitted. Calls supervisor if help is needed.

Labels blood tubes immediately after blood is obtained by following procedure in manual.

Disposes used needles in accordance with procedure in manual.

Returns tubes and requisitions to the blood collection station within the time allowed by supervisor.

Exhibit 5–4 Sample Format of Behaviorally Anchored Performance Standards

---

I. Quality Assurance

Meets Expectations
Performs required reagent quality control each day; records results, dates, and initials. Notifies supervisor of discrepant results or bad reagents. Changes temperature graphs and charts promptly when needed and makes sure pen and graph are working properly. Performs equipment quality control (QC) according to predetermined time schedule greater than 90% of the time; records dates, initials, and results on proper forms. Notifies supervisor of discrepant results or nonfunctioning equipment. Follows established lab safety regulations.

Exceeds Expectations
Consistently performs reagent QC and temperature checks prior to testing. When there will not be enough reagent to last until the next day, assists other shifts by checking extra bottles. Volunteers to do required equipment QC and follows through without reminders. Completes QC records accurately. Notifies supervisor and/or biomedical department of discrepant results or broken equipment after attempting to identify and fix problem. Follows established lab safety regulations and encourages others to do so.

Fails to Meet Expectations
Forgets to change temperature charts or perform temperature-of-reagent QC more than twice per year. Does not notify supervisor of equipment or reagent problems or discrepant results. Needs reminder more than once per year to perform scheduled equipment QC. Does not follow established lab safety regulations.

II. Result Reporting

Meets Expectations
Efficiently and accurately reports results manually and via computer. Always writes neatly and legibly. Forms always include date, technologist's initials, and completion time. No more than two uncorrected transcription errors (undiscovered before they go into patient records) per year.

Exceeds Expectations
Meets expectations and reports results manually and via computer with no uncorrected transcription errors.

Fails to Meet Expectations
Makes more than two uncorrected transcription errors per year. Reports are found to be illegible or incomplete or lack required information.

Reprinted from *Medical Laboratory Observer*, Vol. 19. pp. 33–39, with permission of Medical Economics, © November 1987.

Think About It

Let's repeat here an extremely important point made in the foregoing chapter. Whether in the expression of performance standards or in the evaluation of employee performance, "average" and "standard" are not equivalent. Standard is minimum acceptable performance; average is the actual average of a group's performance. Because normal processes should weed out substandard performers or improve their performance, the lowest level of performance in the group will be at "standard" and the "average" performance of the group will tend to be higher than "standard."

Questions for Review and Discussion

1. In preparing to write or update a position description, why should the supervisor solicit the participation of the employee or employees presently doing that job?
2. In addition to their important application in assessing employee work performance, how can performance standards be helpful in other ways?
3. What are competencies? Explain and provide two or three examples.
4. Select a job with which you are reasonably familiar and write a summary statement for the position description.
5. Why is it suggested that a title such as "administrative assistant" is generally preferred over one such as "secretary"?
6. Should a proper job description cover absolutely everything the employee could ever be expected to do? Why or why not?
7. What is a "reasonable accommodation" under the Americans with Disabilities Act? Provide an example.
8. Describe in detail at least three important uses of the position description.
9. How would you develop and express a reasonable performance standard when there is no objective means available for measuring task performance?
10. Select a specific task with which you are familiar and develop a brief set of performance standards for that task.

Exercise: Writing a Position (Job) Description

Select a nonsupervisory job with which you are familiar and develop a position description for that job. Follow the early sections of the chapter in creating the sections of your position description, and keep in mind the various uses that your finished description might possibly have to serve.

Case: If It Isn't in the Job Description...

Harry Jones, maintenance supervisor, was troubled about mechanic Dan Wilson. Harry considered Dan a good mechanic based on Dan's consistently good work in completing his preventive maintenance tasks and his success with tough repair jobs. The problem was Dan's apparent lack of motivation to do more or better; he did exactly as told, then waited to be told what to do next. If he had no specific assignment to go to next when he finished a job, he took a prolonged break until Harry found him and gave him a new assignment.

Harry's frustration got the better of him one day when a small plumbing problem got out of hand and became a larger problem. He knew Dan must have seen the leak because it was right next to his most recent assignment, but when Harry asked why he had done nothing about the leak, Dan answered, "Plumbing's not part of my job."

Harry said, "You could at least have reported it."

Dan said, "There's nothing in my job description about reporting anything. I stick to my job description."

"Dan, you're a good mechanic, but you never extend yourself, never reach out to help without being told."

"I'm not paid to extend myself. You're the boss, and I do what you tell me."

Harry responded, "I know, and you always do it right. But I know you're capable of doing more. For some reason or other you're not working up to your capabilities."

Dan shrugged. "I do what I'm told, and if it isn't in the job description, I don't have to do it."

Instructions:

1. Put yourself in Harry's position and consider some possible ways of dealing with Dan. Enumerate a few steps that you might recommend to Harry in an effort to get Dan to perform more in line with his capabilities.

REFERENCES

1. Brandt, A.R. 1972. Describing hourly jobs. In *Handbook of wage and salary administration*. New York: McGraw-Hill, 1–11.
2. Joint Commission on Accreditation of Healthcare Organizations. Vol. 2 of *Accreditation manual for hospital*. Oakbrook Terrace, IL: JCAHO.
3. *Americans with Disabilities Act, U. S. Code 42* (1990), § 12101.
4. Berte, L. 1989. *Developing performance standards for hospital personnel*. Chicago, IL: ASCP Press, 61.

RECOMMENDED READING

L. Berte, *Developing Performance Standards for Hospital Personnel* (Chicago, IL: ASCP Press, 1989).

C.M. Chesser et al. "Job Descriptions and Performance Appraisals." *Health Care Supervisor* 15, no. 4 (1997): 1–34.

S.S. Heatherley, "Key Performance Indicators To Assess Laboratory Operations." *Clinical Laboratory Management Review* 11, no. 3 (1997): 164–170.

R.J. Plachy and S.J. Plachy, *Results-Oriented Job Descriptions* (New York: AMACOM, 1993).

Chapter 6

Policy Making and Implementation

*No organization today can afford to rely on
anything less than a complete and comprehensive
policy guide and expect to stay on top when it
comes to maintaining morale, meeting complex
legal requirements, and attracting the
very best talent in its field.[1]*

CHAPTER OBJECTIVES

- Define policies and describe their overall purpose and function.
- Establish the necessity for comprehensive policies addressing all aspects of the organization's operations.
- Describe the significant uses of policies that establish the necessity for policy observance at all organizational levels.
- Differentiate between organizational policies and department policies, and establish the supervisor's relationship to the latter.
- Identify potential problems concerning policies.

Policies are guidelines established for pursuing goals and shaping behavior. They reflect the mission and values of organizations and are made more specific by procedures and rules and regulations. They are of increasing importance to the modern health care organization because of the growing propensity for litigation of various kinds. Legal, moral, and ethical problems, sexual harassment, discrimination, and patients' rights regularly necessitate reevaluation of existing policies.

Unnecessary or vague policies create red tape and Mickey Mouse rules that frustrate employees and supervisors. Poorly worded policies lead to confusion. Inappropriate, ill-conceived, unfair, or illogical policies are barriers to effective performance, and worse, they necessitate many exceptions.

69

The absence of policies results in management by crisis. Managers waste time making the same decisions and answering the same questions repeatedly. Confusion, uncertainty, and conflict become pervasive.

When practices stray from policies and the procedures that implement them, or when practices turn into unwritten policies, problems arise. Lax and inconsistent adherence to policies may cause legal problems and endanger staff morale.

Although there are always legal risks involved in documenting policies, it is more hazardous not to have an employee handbook than to have a comprehensive set of policies in place. The employee handbook should be understood by all employees and should cover important policies, rules, and regulations. Management must updates policies constantly because of changes in laws, revisions of services, and ever-changing personnel needs. Some policies have received considerable attention in recent years:

- Salary and benefits programs, as employee needs have changed and new laws regulating benefits have been passed.
- Alternative staffing and scheduling practices, such as job sharing, flexible scheduling, and work-at-home programs.
- Smoking and drugs.
- Exposure to hazardous agents; "Right to Know" laws.
- Precautions regarding the care of patients with acquired immunodeficiency syndrome (AIDS).
- Sexual harassment.
- Cultural diversity in both the workforce and customer base.
- Discrimination because of age or disability.
- Employment of persons with disabilities.
- Requirements of accreditation and regulatory agencies.

Policy regarding the use and abuse of e-mail provides an impressive example of why policy manuals are in a constant state of flux. When employers fail to develop appropriate e-mail policies and procedures, they run the risk of legal problems. Significant e-mail problems concern sexual harassment and interference with the privacy rights of employees.

Many state laws require that written policies be distributed to all employees. Therefore, it should be considered mandatory that every organization provide its employees with knowledge of the organization's policies. This is ordinarily accomplished by providing a detailed policy and procedure manual that is available to all for reference and by supplying each employee with a handbook that summarizes all pertinent policies. To reduce exposure to legal liability, employee handbooks include disclaimer language throughout, advising employees that various provisions are subject to change at the discretion of the employer. Also, it is common practice to require each new employee to sign and submit a tear-out page indicating that he or she has received and reviewed the employee handbook.

USES OF POLICIES

Properly formulated policies have a number of important uses. They promote understanding, clarity, and consistency of behavior. Employees who know what is expected of them feel more confident, and they police themselves by following policy. They eliminate repetitive decision making, standardize responses, and save time by providing a standard, repeatable way of addressing issues. Good policies also help in the orientation of newly hired employees. Finally, they provide documented controls as required by licensing and accrediting agencies.

To be effective, policies must be explicit, publicized as well as published, and enforced without favoritism. The first-line supervisor is the chief activator or enforcer of policies. Supervisors must know, interpret, promulgate, and enforce policies. Often supervisors must carry out policies that they have had no hand in developing. They might not comprehend the rationale behind, or agree with, some of these policies, but they still must enforce them. Simply handing out employee handbooks is not enough. Supervisors must understand the purpose of each policy and know how much freedom they have in modifying policies or originating policies independently.

For example: Supervisor Sue says to one of her employees: "Sally, you don't look well. Take the rest of the day off. It won't count as sick time." This is a good-faith action and it is legal, but what is the policy of the organization regarding such an action? Supervisor Sue, as well intentioned as she is, needs to know whether the policies of the organization sanction her action.

Insecure managers attempt to divorce themselves from unpopular policies by saying things such as: "Do not blame me for that stupid policy" or "Management expects you to…" Even worse, they may ignore the policy or depend on others to enforce it. The result is a loss of respect for both the organization and the supervisor who takes this approach. When supervisors feel that a policy is inappropriate or causing problems, they should discuss the problem with their superiors. Usually there is a rational explanation for it. If you find that a policy is hurting morale more than helping a situation, discuss the problem with your manager. Perhaps you have a suggestion on how the policy could be modified. In any event, keep your employees posted on your efforts to change the situation.

There are times when supervisors must bend or even ignore a policy. This is a matter of risk taking. For example, Hospital A has a strict policy that prohibits employees from bringing young children into the clinical laboratory. A blood bank technologist receives an urgent call late one night to return to the hospital because of an emergency. Having no one to care for her 6-year-old daughter, she brings her daughter with her to the laboratory. Should this technologist be reprimanded or thanked for this behavior?

POLICIES FORMULATED BY SUPERVISORS

Common Situations Indicating the Need for a New Policy or a Policy Change

The following situations may require the creation of a policy or the modification of an existing policy.

- The introduction of a new service
- Frequent violations of procedures or rules
- Problems of productivity, quality, schedules, or time
- Frequent complaints from customers or employees
- Legal, ethical, or moral problems
- Behavioral inconsistencies
- Repetitive questions being asked about particular procedures or rules

Your departmental policies must harmonize with those put in place by higher management. These policies must not exceed your supervisory authority. Use plain language; avoid legalistic phraseology or jargon to impress people or to make the policy sound more authoritative. (See Exhibit 6–1 for more information on how to formulate a policy.)

Publish the finished document. Make certain that every employee receives a copy and signs a log acknowledging receipt.

Enforce the policy fairly, firmly, and uniformly. Policies that are not enforced become meaningless. Supervisors often overlook transgressions by their more valued employees, but unfairness of this nature often translates to the filing of grievances. Furthermore, supervisors must make certain that they themselves comply with the letter of the policies. Supervisors always serve as models for their staffs. The old cliché "Do as I say, not as I do" does not work.

Heavy handedness in policy enforcement can be counterproductive. The majority of employees are more skillful in avoiding compliance than managers are in enforcing policies. Sometimes the violation of rules becomes a game, especially when the supervisor is unpopular or autocratic. Be willing to admit when one of your policies turns out to be a dud. Modify or eliminate such policies when appropriate. Never regard any policy as written in stone, forever unchanging. Every policy manual needs an annual checkup.

POTENTIAL PROBLEMS WITH POLICIES

Selection of Job Candidates

Usually the personnel department screens candidates, but the actual employee selection is left to supervisors. This is as it should be; the person who will be a new hire's immediate supervisor is the person who should make the final hiring deci-

Exhibit 6–1 Procedure for Formulating a Policy

1. State the need for, and describe the purpose of, a new policy or a revision of an existing policy.
2. Decide whether the need is great enough to warrant a new policy or a policy change.
3. Consider alternate solutions (for example, a notice on the bulletin board or a memo).
4. Gather data and input from others, especially the people affected by the policy.
5. Check the rough draft of the policy for the following:
   - compliance with institutional philosophy, mission, values, ethics, and established policies, rules, and regulations;
   - completeness, clarity, and understandability;
   - answers to questions of what, when, where, who, how, and why;
   - anticipated acceptance by persons who are affected; and
   - enforcement problems that may occur.
6. Circulate the rough draft, discuss it with others, or both. Get the approval of superiors. Have a legal expert check to determine whether there are liability aspects.
7. Make necessary modifications. Ask whether the policy meets the following criteria.
   - It is needed.
   - It will be understood.
   - It is achievable (workable).
   - It is flexible and fair.
   - It will be acceptable.
   - It can be enforced.

sion. Hazards for inexperienced interviewers—and there are plenty—include numerous questions that cannot legally be asked and the absence of legitimate basis for excluding certain candidates. Also, when job descriptions or performance standards are inadequate or obsolete, even experienced interviewers can be led to select the wrong candidates.

Orientation of New Hires

Personnel departments may be responsible for new-employee orientation and some training, but part of these tasks, especially departmental orientation, is left to supervisors. Supervisors may provide incorrect answers to questions about payroll deductions and benefits packages, so they should not attempt to address such matters.

Faulty orientation or indoctrination policies or negligent implementation of guidelines results in poor work performance and the overrating of poor performers at the completion of their probationary periods.

Schedules

Vague or unwritten policies concerning schedules can destroy morale and lead to the filing of grievances, especially in unionized organizations. Hazards include discrimination in assigning work, vacation, overtime, or call-back schedules.

Safety and Health

Given the dramatic increase in Workers' Compensation claims in recent years, supervisors must be emphatic about reporting, correcting, and following up on suspected safety or health hazards. Failure to follow established policy, including the careful documentation and the prompt handling of injuries, can be costly to the organization. It can also damage the careers of supervisors who have failed in this responsibility.

A touchy situation is presented by the not uncommon presence of AIDS in the workforce. First, there is consideration for the employee who has the disease, and then there is consideration for the coworkers who are concerned about the chances of becoming infected. This is a particularly sensitive issue in health care, where there is an increased risk of workers contracting AIDS from patients and where problems of confidentiality are involved.

The policy should state that employees who have AIDS or who are HIV positive must be treated the same way that individuals with other disabilities are treated. It must explain the rights of both the impaired employees and their co-workers. This information must be known and understood by all employees.

Supervisors should be prepared to cope with workers who object to working with an employee who has AIDS. Training programs for managers and workers are essential. The inadvertent mishandling of an employee with AIDS or who is HIV positive can leave an organization vulnerable to charges of discrimination, invasion of privacy, or unauthorized disclosure.

Handling Problems or Special Employees

Grievances are often filed in protest of disciplinary measures that have been taken. Poor leadership leads to poor followership, which leads to reprimands or other disciplinary actions. This then leads to grievances.

Mishandled severance procedures can be costly in terms of both dollars and feelings. Supervisory botching of charges of sexual harassment or discrimination can be embarrassing and expensive for employers.

Effective resolution of personnel problems begins with sound policies and ends with skillful enforcement of these policies. Concerning sexual harassment, the blanket grievance procedure usually calls for the immediate supervisor to be the first person contacted. However, when allegations of sexual harassment are made, the immediate supervisor may often be the perpetrator. Therefore, a separate policy for reporting allegations of sexual harassment and for confidentially investigating such charges is mandatory.

Also, personnel policy must spell out the limits to be observed with employee drug testing. Is it routine or random testing? Who is to be tested, and how will the potential invasion of privacy issues be addressed?

Special Case: Americans with Disabilities Act

It is necessary to have policies that address the relatively new and complex federal regulations regarding hiring, assigning, promoting, and accommodating people who have physical or mental disabilities, as specified by the ADA. This translates into making changes in position descriptions and performance standards and in the recruiting, testing, and interviewing of candidates.

A particularly sensitive area of concern to supervisors is the occasional need to accommodate a disabled individual. "Reasonable accommodations" under the ADA can include making existing facilities accessible to individuals with disabilities, job restructuring, or job reassignment. Managers may sometimes offer part-time employment or modified work schedules or may grant unpaid leave. Often it is necessary to acquire or modify equipment, provide readers or interpreters, and modify examinations, training materials, or policies.[2]

Reasonable accommodation frequently requires employers to modify examinations, training materials, and policies. Jobs must be restructured so that marginal or nonessential duties that exclude people with disabilities are eliminated when possible. For example, a data entry position requiring $7\frac{1}{2}$ hours at the keyboard and 30 minutes walking around delivering reports might be modified such that someone else does the report delivery. The data entry activities would be the job's "essential function;" the report delivery would not be considered an essential function of a data entry position. (Report delivery surely would be an essential function of the position of interdepartmental messenger.)

Sometimes reasonable accommodations require physical changes in layout, equipment, furnishings, and such. Recognizing potential expenses of renovations, the ADA gives the organization something of an out by saying that such changes need not be made if they impose "undue hardship" (as in potentially spending large sums for renovations). However, there is no workable definition for "undue hardship," giving rise to occasional conflicts over what is or is not reasonable.

Employers must be able to justify exclusionary qualifications or capabilities. Candidates cannot be tested for functions and knowledge that are not essential to the job under consideration. Supervisors should be aware, however, that they will not be required to displace another employee from a position for the sake of hiring a disabled job candidate.

Think About It

The operative word concerning the observance of policies and the application of the procedures that implement them is "consistency." Policies provide a common direction for everyone in the organization to follow.

Questions for Review and Discussion

1. In the chapter it was stated that a policy should be publicized as well as published. What is the difference between these terms, and why would this be said about policies?
2. As a supervisor, what should you do about a policy that is unpopular with your employees or that appears to you to be potentially harmful?
3. Cite an example of one realistic occurrence that could suggest the need for a policy change. Why might the change be necessary?
4. Why be concerned with modeling behavior for employees? The supervisor is the boss—why not simply tell them what to do?
5. What problems might the supervisor be asking for through inconsistent treatment of employees?
6. Explain fully why each employee is asked to sign an employee-handbook receipt to be retained in the employee's personnel file.
7. Explain the essential difference between a policy and a procedure.
8. As a department supervisor, what would you consider to be the primary benefit of having complete, up-to-date organizational policies?
9. Describe a situation in which inconsistent policy adherence could potentially cause legal problems.
10. Provide one fairly detailed example of a reasonable accommodation under the ADA.

Exercise: Writing a Policy

Assume you are supervisor of a sizeable group of employees, both male and female, who work in an office setting. You are to draft a policy governing the use of e-mail in the department, keeping in mind that your draft policy is also to be submitted as a possible model for a policy for the entire organization.

Case: Bending the Break

Assume you are supervisor of a hospital admitting department and also responsible for the reception area and information center (switchboard and main lobby desk). Like other employees, your people are entitled to 15-minute breaks in both morning and afternoon. Most of your employees have some flexibility as to when they can take breaks, but the person who works the switchboard and the one who works the main lobby desk have breaks scheduled for specific times because you have to provide relief for them. You often have no one to spare, so much of the time you provide their relief yourself.

This was a horrible week. Two key people were absent most of the week, admitting activity was up, and a few other problems popped up. You personally had to relieve Alice, the switchboard operator, for morning breaks the entire week. On Monday and Tuesday Alice stayed on break about 20 minutes. Wednesday she was gone 25 minutes, and both Thursday and Friday she stretched her morning breaks to a half hour. With all the work you had to do, you felt you could not tolerate such lengthy breaks, so on Friday you spoke with Alice about her practice of taking longer than the allowed time.

Alice's response was, "I can't help it. The coffee shop is all jammed up most of the morning. Two days last week I didn't get coffee at all, and another day I got it but didn't have time to drink it all so I could get back here in 15 minutes. I know I'm supposed to have only 15 minutes, but the way things are in that coffee shop I can't get served, enjoy my coffee, and get back in time."

You also checked with the employee at the reception desk who echoed Alice's complaint about the coffee shop and added, "What we'd really like is to have our own coffee supply nearby, but you know as well as I do that the big boss forbids coffee pots and cups in office and public areas. Except, of course," she added with a skyward glance, "for the coffee maker in his own office."

You checked with a number of your admitting employees and learned that most of them, not stuck with specific break times had learned how to take advantage of fluctuations in the morning crowd at the coffee shop. However, as far as you were able to determine, the morning coffee break appeared on average to consume 5 or 6 minutes longer than the allotted 15 because of waiting time.

Questions:

1. How might you go about solving the problem of having coffee available to your employees and still accomplish the morning break within the allowed time? What other possibilities might you explore?

REFERENCES

1. *The BBP Personnel Policy Manual,* Bureau of Business Practice, Inc., 1981, p. 9.
2. *EEOC Regulation Pertaining to ADA under Title I Employment* (Title VII, Civil Rights Act of 1964), Federal Register 35 (July 26, 1991): 736.

Chapter 7

Personnel Recruitment and Selection

*The outstanding characteristic of the relationship between
the subordinates and the superior is the superior's
dependence on them for the satisfaction of his needs.*

—Douglas McGregor

*It's a heck of a lot easier to hire the right people to
begin with than to try to fix them later.*

—Brad Smart[1]

CHAPTER OBJECTIVES

- Convey the importance of the employee selection process in building a stable and motivated workforce.
- Profile the kinds of job candidates the supervisor should ordinarily seek to interview.
- Review the significant legal constraints affecting the recruitment and employment process, including designation of the kinds of questions that may not legally be asked on an employment application or in the interview process.
- Review the various sources customarily used for locating appropriate job candidates.
- Review the role of the department supervisor in the recruitment process.
- Provide a systematic review of the employment interview, including sample questions intended to elicit particular kinds of information about job candidates.
- Address the essential follow-up activities that are necessary to complete the interview process, including reference checking.

Finding the right employees in today's fast-changing health care environment is becoming an increasingly important—and increasingly difficult—activity for supervisors. Of all their responsibilities, the selection of new employees ranks near the top in importance. Motivational problems, disciplinary issues, personnel turnover, and susceptibility to unionization can all be reduced by hiring the right people.

Improved selection of new employees is an integral part of improved customer service, team building, successful quality management strategies, and cost control. Poor recruitment and selection are expensive. The eventual cost of a single bad hire may amount to several times that employee's annual salary. Here are some of the expenses associated with a poor hiring choice.

- Cost of training a replacement
- Cost of repeat advertising
- Lost time
- Potential loss of customers
- Reduced productivity
- Possible unemployment compensation expense
- Potential lawsuit

IMPERATIVES OF THE SELECTION PROCESS

Cast a very wide net and carefully sift through what you catch in it.

—Linda S. Goldzimer[2]

Institutions that are known for excellent customer service are careful to hire people who have displayed commendable customer-service attitudes in their previous work and social conduct. Once a person has been hired, it is considerably easier to reinforce good attitudes than to change bad habits. Obtaining the kind of employees we want is governed by three imperatives.

1. A recruiting program that provides a broad choice of good candidates
2. A selection process that can choose the best candidate with a high degree of confidence
3. The ability to persuade the most desirable candidates to accept our offers

If job competencies can be reduced without ill effects, there will be a greater number of candidates to choose from. Separate the must-haves from the nice-to-haves. For example, does the person really need a college degree and 3 years of experience, or will 1 or 2 years experience suffice? Be careful in specifying mandatory qualifications; if your standard is challenged by a candidate from a protected group, would you be able to justify the requirement in court? This risk can be reduced by stating that a particular competency is highly desirable, not mandatory.

DESIRABLE CANDIDATES

Health care institutions are looking for more people who can contribute to the continuous improvement of customer service, productivity, and creativity. Finding candidates with the technical or professional skills needed is easier than finding people who exhibit the types of behaviors that fit into the culture of your organization.

In addition to job expertise, there are other factors that make for success in dealing with customers. These factors include social skills. By social skills we mean being articulate and able to say and do what is necessary to establish and maintain rapport with customers. Other positive attributes include teamwork, cooperation, and collaboration. Unfortunately, the questions most frequently asked of job candidates—and the chief factors in selecting a new employee—relate primarily to work experience and professional or technical skill. The most desirable candidates for the majority of positions are those who

- have a broad technical or professional background,
- are effective communicators and rapid learners,
- can deal effectively with people, and
- are flexible (for example, can easily move among disparate competencies as needed).

When we hire only highly specialized people, we run the risk of falling into the talent obsolescence trap. Because of rapid changes in technologies and services offered by organizations, the qualifications needed of personnel also change rapidly. Job descriptions that are too finely tuned can result in hiring employees who are qualified for today's job but become obsolete when tomorrow's needs arrive.

LEGAL CONSTRAINTS TO HIRING

The primary thrust of federal and state employment legislation is to ensure that hiring, retention, and promotion decisions are made only on the basis of the ability of an employee to do the job.

Affirmative Action

The Civil Rights Act of 1964 and Executive Order 11246 (amended by Executive Order 11375) require employers to identify areas of minority and female underutilization and call for specific numerical hiring and promotion goals and other actions to increase minority and female employment in job classifications where they are currently underutilized. However, most health care supervisors need not be concerned with formal affirmative action plans. Executive Order 11246 requires written affirmative action plans of federal contractors having 50 or more employees and government contracts amounting to $50,000 or more. However, although many health care organizations employ more than 50 people, very few are ever involved with government contracts.

Nevertheless supervisors must be aware of the legal requirements of Equal Employment Opportunity Commission (EEOC) regulations and of their own organization's policies and practices as they relate to EEOC and the Americans With Disabilities Act (ADA). They must recognize and eliminate stereotyping and preconceptions and provide clear and achievable expectations for all their employees.

Unlawful Inquiries

Each state also has its own requirements regarding Title VII of the Civil Rights Act of 1964, and most have some agency, going perhaps by the name of the Division of Human Rights or something similar, that parallels the EEOC at state level. Generally, however, when both state and federal governments address the same issues via regulation and those regulations happen to differ to some extent, the more stringent of the two is assumed to apply.

Under Title VII and various state laws, it is forbidden to ask a job applicant for certain information, whether on an employment application or in a personal interview. If in doubt concerning questions that may be asked, consult your human resources department. Following is a partial list of the kinds of questions that cannot legally be asked of an applicant.

- Any questions intended to elicit age, nationality, or marital status
- One's spouse's occupation or place of employment (or even if there is a spouse)
- Whether one is pregnant or has plans for pregnancy
- Child-care or baby-sitting arrangements (Without asking specifically about children you may ask generally whether the applicant could foresee problems in getting to work at various times or in accommodating call-ins, call-backs, etc.)
- Character of military discharge or service record, except as military experience might relate to job qualifications
- Arrest record (you may ask whether the person has been convicted of a crime but not whether he or she has been arrested)
- Membership in organizations other than those related to one's work or occupation (but not labor unions; no candidate may be asked about union membership or related activities)
- Religious affiliation

- Nature, severity, or existence of physical or mental impairments. Avoid questions about the use of sick leave or whether the individual was ever out on disability or Workers' Compensation. (You may ask how much work time the individual missed as long as the question is not limited to absences resulting from illness or injury.)
- Questions that would be asked only of members of a protected group. For example, if you want to ask women whether they can lift a 50-pound child, you must also ask male candidates that same question.

Recognize that this list could be expanded to encompass literally dozens of specific questions. To be on the safest possible legal ground at all times during an interview, concentrate on learning what the individual knows and has done; that is, knowledge and experience that are relevant to the job in question. By and large the forbidden questions relate to what the person *is* (male, female, spouse, parent, protected group member, religious practitioner, and so on) when the true emphasis should be on what the person knows and can do. If every question you ask relates strictly to the job and its characteristics and requirements, you are on relatively safe legal ground.

Of course some information that cannot legally be requested on an application or in an interview can and must be obtained after the person has accepted an offer of employment. Personal information is of course required for personnel, payroll, and benefits purposes.

Age Discrimination in Employment Act of 1967

As amended in 1986, the Age Discrimination in Employment Act prohibits employers from placing an age limit on candidates for employment and from making retirement mandatory at some designated age. For most hiring purposes, there is but one age-related question that can legally be asked: Are you at least 18 years of age? This lower age barrier exists because of the application of child labor laws below the age of 18. Concerning mandatory retirement, there are exceptions for a few occupations for which age is a *bona fide occupational qualification* (BFOQ) (for example, police officer, firefighter, airline pilot).

Rehabilitation Act of 1973 and the ADA

The major thrusts of the Rehabilitation Act of 1973 and the ADA of 1992 are (1) those dealing with hiring and promotion practices and (2) those that require reasonable accommodation. Again, the cardinal rule is that any question asked of candidates should relate to the job in some way. You can ask whether an applicant can perform all job-related functions and meet attendance requirements. You may not ask about an applicant's current or past medical or health conditions. If an applicant reveals that he or she cannot perform an essential function, do not probe into the medical history. Instead, tailor your questions in an effort to identify how the disability renders the applicant unable to perform the essential functions of the job. Find out what accommodations, if any, would enable the applicant to do the job.

Reasonable accommodation refers to measures that an employer may take to enable a person to perform essential functions. These could be physical changes such as wider doors or magnified displays, or they could be the elimination of some nonessential or infrequently performed tasks. For example, if a job requires occasional typing and the candidate lacks the mechanical ability to type, that activity could be assigned to other employees.

When the ADA became law, the task of interviewing job applicants became more hazardous. Following are five questions that are now illegal.

1. Have you ever filed a Workers' Compensation claim?
2. Do you have any physical problems or injuries?
3. How many days were you sick last year?
4. Are you currently taking any medications?
5. Have you ever been treated for drug abuse?

Under revised guidelines, the EEOC permits employers to ask questions about accommodations at the initial interview stage in a few specific situations. For example, the employer reasonably believes an applicant will need accommodations because of an obvious disability (say the applicant uses a wheelchair or has severe visual impairment) or the applicant voluntarily reveals the need for accommodation during the interview (for example, the person discloses a hidden disability such as diabetes or states the need for breaks to take medication). Except for these circumstances, the law concerning inquiries remains unchanged. All other disability-related inquiries must wait until after a job offer has been made.

RECRUITMENT SOURCES

Employee referrals
Newspaper job listings
Recruitment firms
College recruitment
Direct mail
Employment agencies
Computerized databases
Job fairs

Walk-in applicants
Unsolicited resumés

One of the most effective recruitment methods is employee referral. Your workers have friends and acquaintances who are either working for other employers in your area or actively seeking employment. Employees have their own networks and may encourage their friends to fill out applications. A number of organizations have discovered that a satisfied workforce is a strong recruiter.

The Internet is the newest actively used tool in recruiting. In addition to search engines, such as Yahoo!, there are bulletin board systems, news groups, and job banks (for example, http://www.careercenter@aol.com.). Many organizations have their own recruitment Web sites.

> *If your organization has a reputation as a great place to work, the best people will find you.*

HOW SUPERVISORS CAN HELP IN THE RECRUITING PROCESS

As an individual supervisor, quite likely one of many, you may think that you have no influence on the recruiting practices of your organization. However, you can play an important role in the recruiting process. Do not overlook the possibility of finding good job candidates internal to the organization; be on the lookout for potential candidates in other departments. That young lady in the housekeeping department who always greets you with a smile might do a great job as a receptionist or perhaps could be trained as a phlebotomist or patient care technician. Encourage your staff to serve as unofficial recruiters.

Provide your recruiters with condensed versions of position descriptions that also comment on the attractive features of the job. Recommend what you believe to be the most appropriate publications in which to place advertisements. Obtain a list of technical or professional schools where potential candidates train, and share this list with the employment recruiters. Participate actively in career programs and job fairs.

PERSONNEL SELECTION INSTRUMENTS

Applications and Resumés

Resumés are the public relations handouts of job candidates. As candidates' "balance sheets" they stress—and at times overstress—the assets without mentioning liabilities. We can realistically expect that no job applicants will say anything unfavorable about themselves on their resumés. Unfortunately, we can also expect that a good half or more of the resumés we see are going to contain exaggerations if not outright untruths. As Dortch states, "Some of the best fiction writing in the world is in the form of resumés."[3] Study each resumé carefully, and don't be shy about questioning claims that seem to you to be out of line.

When reviewing applications and resumés, be especially alert to indications of customer service experience (for example, volunteer work and membership in social organizations), teamwork, and responsibilities that exceeded job requirements.

Frequent job changes call for close questioning of candidates. When moves are at best lateral, or to jobs that pay less, involve less responsibility, or require less competency, watch out. Equally significant are job changes attributed to "personal reasons" or covered by explanations like "My boss and I had different chemistries." Other red flags are unexplained time gaps in employment, inconsistencies in salary history, incomplete contact information about previous employers, and vague reasons for leaving previous jobs.

A candidate's outside interests could indicate the presence of certain desirable capabilities, although there could be a risk some of these activities might interfere with attendance or performance. However, the supervisor must proceed with care in questioning a candidate about outside activities or in making an employment decision based on this kind of information; what people do on their own time is their own business.

Avoid the oft-cited halo effect; the success an individual enjoyed in one kind of employment does not ensure his or her success in a different kind of job.

Pay attention to the grammar, spelling, and clarity of expression in the resumé and in any correspondence with the applicant, especially if you seek a meticulous worker.

Credentialing

Confirm all licenses, certifications, and registrations. In most organizations new hires will be required to furnish copies of current licenses.

Preemployment Testing

Preemployment tests can be very revealing, but in general they are underutilized. Employment managers are frequently hesitant to administer certain kinds of tests for fear of violating antidiscrimination laws; employers can be called on to prove that the tests they use possess validity and reliability. However, as long as a test is based on a required skill or on knowledge as documented in the job description, such fears are without foundation. For example:

- Phlebotomist or patient care technician candidates can be tested on making preparations for collecting a blood specimen.

- Clerk-receptionist candidates can take some incoming phone calls.
- Candidates applying for jobs having teaching responsibilities can be asked to deliver a short lecture or perform a demonstration.
- Certain candidates can sometimes be tried in temporary jobs before being hired on a regular basis.
- In one of the most common kinds of preemployment tests, individuals applying for jobs involving keyboarding are often tested on typing skills.

An alternative to these action tests is to ask candidates to tell you in as much detail as possible how they performed certain tasks. Only people who have actually done what they claim can tell you in detail how the work is done.

Questionnaires

Some commercial job-applicant questionnaires purport to measure honesty, loyalty, and positive attitudes, but the jury is still out on the validity of these tools, and many of these instruments are of the kind that can give rise to charges of discrimination.

EMPLOYMENT INTERVIEWS

Most approaches to interviewing and other aspects of recruitment and employment are based on the premise that candidates who have already displayed certain competencies are likely to continue to display those competencies. We are seeking individuals who have done well or seem to be displaying the potential for doing well.

Who Should Conduct the Interviews?

A selection interview is so important that the principal interviewer should be someone who is knowledgeable of interviewing processes and well trained in this essential supervisory skill. One trained interviewer can usually achieve more than a battery of untrained or marginally interested interviewers can.

Experienced interviewers can hold unstructured meetings (no prepared questions) and still maintain fair and legally valid interviews, but they are usually only able to do this because of familiarity gained from conducting many interviews. Inexperienced interviewers should prepare lists of questions in advance, and to ensure fairness and validity they should use the same questions for each candidate interviewing for the same position. Skilled interviewers ask the right questions and listen with their eyes as well as their ears. They show enthusiasm about their organization, their staff, and the job under consideration.

When a team approach is used, one or more of the candidate's future peers should serve on the interview team. Employees have a decided self-interest in seeing who will become their new associates, and they can often spot people they would like to have (or not like to have) working with them.

Computer-Assisted Interviews

Corporations that use expert computer systems report improvement in the quality of new employees and claim beneficial effects on turnover, absenteeism, theft, and productivity. Surprisingly, most candidates seem more willing to feed information into computers than tell it to interviewers. A typical interview program consists of about 100 multiple-choice questions and takes about 20 minutes to complete.

Preparations for the Interview

Following are guidelines to assist in ensuring effective interviews.

- Familiarize yourself with the position description such that you can discuss the position confidently without having to refer to the document. Concentrate on the duties and required qualifications. Make certain that the position description has been updated.
- Study applications and resumés, making sure that everyone applying possesses at least the minimum qualifications.
- Draft a list of questions for the candidates, eliminating those that might raise questions of legality.
- List the positive features of the job, those aspects that are most likely to appeal to the greatest number of applicants.
- Familiarize yourself with the salary and benefits for the position, but be prepared to advise applicants that salary and benefits details will be addressed by human resources.
- Visualize the tour of your facilities that you will provide for applicants, and alert the people you want the candidates to meet.
- Schedule a time and place that ensure privacy and freedom from interruptions.

Two Initial Steps

Breaking the Ice

A nonthreatening introduction can make candidates feel comfortable and relaxed. Be enthusiastic and persuasive, but be honest and sincere. You get only one chance to make a good first impression, so start right. Also, your first impression of each candidate is important. What you see is what future customers will see when they first meet this person.

Be on time and greet interviewees by name. When you introduce yourself, include your title. Thank them for coming. Offer a rest stop or coffee before you get down to talking.

Do not interview from behind a desk. Seat an applicant next to your desk rather than across from you. Do not remain standing or perch on the edge of your desk.

- Make brief small talk as necessary to get interviewees into a talking mode and, just as important, get you into a listening mode. However, even in supposedly off-the-record small talk, take care to avoid questions that could violate EEOC restrictions. Instead, ask how the candidates learned about the job, what their understanding of the job is, whether they had a parking problem on arrival, and about any outside interests mentioned in the resumé.

Review the interview agenda, assuring interviewees that they will have the opportunity to ask all the questions they wish. Ask whether the allotted time poses any problem; they may be scheduled elsewhere after your interview. Then briefly describe the job being offered.

Chronological Review

Have the candidate start with college (high school if there was no college). Inquire about academic standing, study habits, jobs held, attendance record, athletic and social activities, and leadership roles.

Move on to the work history (for example, "Tell me about your jobs. For each job you've held, I'd like to know things like starting and final salary, duties, how you handled setbacks, the most and least enjoyable aspects of your job, reason for leaving, and what your supervisor was like"). Some interviewers like to ask candidates to describe a typical workday.

Ask probing questions using the list you prepared. Finally, market the job, the department, and the organization, and respond to the questions or concerns of the candidate.

QUESTIONS

Kinds of Questions

Whenever possible avoid closed-ended questions, those that can be answered in one or a few words (for example, "Did you like working there?"). Use closed-ended questions only to obtain basic data but not to elicit detailed information. You won't learn much by asking a question like, "Did you like your last supervisor?"

Open-ended questions cannot be answered with only a few words and are better for getting detailed information. Change the above closed-ended question to "Tell me about your last supervisor," and you will learn much more.

Probing questions address the five *W*s: why, what, who, when, and where, plus how. These are excellent, but if overused they may create a dialogue that sounds like interrogation. Here are a few examples of probing questions.

- How did that situation arise?
- Why was that allowed to happen?
- In retrospect, what would you have done differently?

Hypothetical questions include questions such as "What would you do if...?" These situational queries can be very informative when discussing technical or personal skills.

Illegal questions are those prohibited by federal and state statutes. If you do not have a comprehensive list of these, get one from your human resources department before you interview your next candidate.

Leading questions reveal to the applicant the answer you want (for example, "You're willing to serve on committees, aren't you?"). Leading questions should be avoided. Knockout questions address items that automatically eliminate candidates (for example, lack of license or certification, although the employment section should take care to avoid sending candidates who do not have the requisite credentials).

Questions about general responsibilities can be formulated based on the position description and job qualifications. These questions cover education, training, experience, knowledge, and skill. Questions used to evaluate service attitudes and interactive skills are also useful. Novice interviewers ask questions that deal more with technical skills and experience rather than people skills. We want questions that evaluate competence ("can do") and motivation ("will do").

RECOMMENDED QUESTIONS

Questions to Determine Professional or Technical Competency

These questions should be criteria referenced, that is, should be related to duties and responsibilities as documented in the job descriptions. Use hypothetical situations or pose questions along these lines:

- How would you...?
- Describe the technique for...
- If you encountered..., what would you do?
- Tell me about your experience with...
- Explain your role in...
- What aspect of this job would you find most difficult?
- What strengths would you bring to this position?
- What competency would your former boss recommend that you strengthen?

Questions to Assess Motivation

In every department there are clock watchers and other people who could do better if they cared to apply themselves. These questions will help you spot the potential goof-offs.

- What have you done at work that shows strong initiative?
- What did you do to become more effective in your previous position?
- Tell me about a time when you went the extra mile.

Questions to Evaluate Teamwork Potential

Teamwork demands communication skill, congenial relationships, cooperation, the ability to compromise, and a lot of idea interchange. The following questions can help evaluate the ability to work as part of a team.

- Do you prefer responsibility for your own work or do you like to share responsibility with others?
- What kinds of people do you get along with best? What kinds of people do you find difficult? How do you deal with them?
- What other departments did you have dealings with, and what difficulties did you encounter with any of these?

Questions to Evaluate Followership Skill and Attitude

Although you are not looking for a clone of yourself and you want people who complement your strong points, you do not want problem followers. Award bonus points to candidates who speak well of previous employers. Even if an individual's previous employment experience was less than satisfactory, there are diplomatic ways that he or she can relate this without being openly critical of anyone. Beware of the applicant who bad-mouths a previous employer.

These inquiries may help you select a congenial teammate.

- Describe the style of the best boss you ever had. Describe the style of your worst boss. (Watch the applicant's body language while responding to these.)
- What are some issues you and your previous supervisor disagreed about?
- Provide an example of how you handled criticism that you do not believe you deserved.

Questions to Evaluate Resistance to Stress

All of us have different stress thresholds; what one person might be able to take in stride might send another person scrambling up the walls. Also, different jobs generate different amounts of stress. If you consider the position under consideration to be potentially stressful, include questions such as the following.

- When was the last time you got really angry at work? What caused it, and how did you react?
- What was the most difficult situation you faced at work? What feelings did this situation produce, and how did you react to them?
- What are some of your pet peeves concerning work?

Questions to Assess Retention Potential

Because one important objective of personnel selection is to improve employee retention, these questions may be helpful.

- What do you want to be doing 5 years from now?
- What do you think you will be doing 5 years from now?
- How much do you believe you will be earning 5 years from now?
- Let's briefly review your career goals and plans.

Questions for Assessing Customer Service Orientation

- What does superior service mean to you?
- Who do you consider to be our external and internal customers?
- Provide an example of how you made an extra effort to serve a client.
- How do you handle the situation when a caller becomes insulting or abusive on the phone?
- How could your previous employer have provided better service?
- Did you ever provide care for a chronically ill individual? Tell me about it.
- Did you ever work in a nursing home? What was it like?
- Did you ever baby-sit or work in a restaurant? Describe the experience.

CANDIDATES WITH NO PREVIOUS EMPLOYMENT

Most college graduates have held part-time or summer jobs or were employed before attending college. Inquiries into such employment can be worthwhile. The following questions assume greater importance when an applicant's employment history is skimpy or nonexistent.

- Describe a teacher with whom you had problems. How did you handle that situation?
- What were some problems you faced at school or at home? If you had it to do all over, what would you do differently?

- What have you done that shows initiative and willingness to work?
- What are your long-range goals and expectations? How do you plan to fulfill these?

SENSITIVE ISSUES

Be tactful when you probe into what might appear to be soft spots. Start by saying that one way you evaluate maturity is by the ability of people to recognize performance that could be improved. Point out that such people have already taken the first step toward career improvement.

Avoid strong terms such as "weakness" and "deficiency." Substitute phrases such as "area of concern," "need for more experience," and "need to enhance full potential." Use the questions "Is it possible that...?" or "How did you happen to...?"

Clues to Untruthfulness

Not every candidate will be 100% truthful with you (some experienced interviewers may consider this a dramatic understatement). After all, the individual is seeking employment and in doing so will try to present himself or herself in the best possible light. It is fairly common practice for interviewees to "forget" the unfavorable aspects of past employment and dwell only on that which is favorable. At times they may also exaggerate the favorable and even invent experience and qualifications that they believe will make them look good.

One early clue resides in resumés and comments on applications that appear too good to be true. As the old saying goes, If it seems too good to be true, it probably is. That is, if it's perfect, something has likely been invented, masked, or omitted. Always remain aware that a high percentage of resumés contain exaggerations or outright falsehoods, and even more—one might say expectedly so—are favorably slanted.

Watch out for wording that tends to imply more than it actually means. This frequently emerges concerning educational background. For example, some applicants may say "attended" State University and let the casual reader who skims the page infer "graduated" when that is not the case. Saying even less, the individual who writes something like "State University, Business Administration, 2004" is hoping the less-than-careful reader will assume graduation when the person may have had only a semester or so. There are dozens of similar reasons why the interviewing supervisor must read resumés and applications very carefully. Educational achievements are frequently exaggerated or falsified, perhaps because only a minority of employers make an effort to verify the educational records of all job applicants.

You may also be interviewing in the presence of untruthfulness if an applicant's answers to normally challenging questions lack substance. Consider it a red flag if questions bearing on the person's supposed field of interest come across as thin and unconvincing.

Watch also for what an applicant's body language may be telling you. Provide a little slack for applicants who are obviously nervous, especially those who are young and new to interviewing. The ones to be most aware of are those who have apparently been around for a while, have presented themselves in glowing terms on paper, but show signs of discomfort or restlessness when closely questioned. Some avoid eye contact, some blush or perspire noticeably, some experience a change in vocal tone, pitch, volume, or rate of speech; some squirm, fidget, or blink excessively.

Be aware also of inconsistencies between what applicants say in an interview and what their written resumés claim. The more padding or untruth in the resumé, the more difficulty the individual may have remembering everything when questioned.

Finally, when reference checking is done—usually not until a tentative offer of employment has been extended—watch for inconsistencies between what you received from previous employers and what the applicant has claimed.

QUESTIONS FROM CANDIDATES

Some candidates will ask only selfish questions, such as those that deal with salary, benefits, vacation policies, and overtime. Others ask only superficial questions, such as how many employees are on board. Then there are those who do not ask any questions at all. This tips you off that they may not be particularly sharp or have little interest in this particular job.

Questions from candidates reveal insights about their values and goals as well as their professional or technical knowledge. This is especially true of the questions they pose and the interest they show when given a tour of your department. Superior candidates are those who not only ask technical questions but also ask questions such as "How would you describe the personality of your organization?" or "How long have you worked here, and what attracted you to this organization?" Another great question coming from an applicant is "Please describe your mentoring and training programs."

EVALUATION OF CANDIDATES

Interviewers usually have a gut reaction to candidates. Some react impulsively and make poor decisions. Others do their best to ignore these instinctive responses. Skilled interviewers pay attention to these feelings and decide whether these intangible factors are truly job related.

Additional Tips for Evaluating Candidates

In summary, also consider the following points when evaluating a candidate.

- Give negatives somewhat more weight than positives. One or two significant negatives can render a candidate unsuitable.
- Evaluate the candidate's flexibility and ability to adjust to change.
- Watch for strong feelings and beliefs. These often suggest rigidity and intolerance.
- Note the candidate's emphasis. Customer-oriented people talk about service and interpersonal relationships; task-oriented individuals focus on duties. Burned-out workers frequently use the word "stress," and they tend to sigh a lot.
- Avoid leaping to conclusions during the initial phase of the interview.

GETTING CANDIDATES TO ACCEPT JOB OFFERS

Remember that the higher the quality of the candidates, the more competition there is for their services. When you interview outstanding candidates, you will find that they are interviewing you and your organization. They know that you want them, but for the most part they have yet to decide whether they want you. Here are some practical tips that can help sell the job.

- Send a map and directions for getting to the interview site. Include a copy of the position description. These touches display a caring attitude.
- Provide a tour of your facilities. Show off the pleasant environment, efficient arrangements, modern equipment, and access to other departments and facilities. Point out that the personnel smile a lot and do not seem harassed.
- Introduce the candidate to one or two key people (but do not overdo this).
- Create a positive vision in the mind of the candidate by matching what the job offers with what you have learned the candidate wants. Focus on any special features that are attractive to the person.
- If the person has shown a special interest (for example, in research or teaching), discuss what you have to offer. Create a positive picture of the daily routine.
- Do not forget spouses, especially when recruiting from out of town. Frequently spouses cast the deciding vote. It is often wise to have the spouse sit in on part of the interview. How does the spouse feel about the community and the job opportunity? Is this person also looking for new employment? If so, what can you offer or suggest?
- Answer questions completely and honestly. Do not conceal negative aspects of the job. Refer to these aspects as challenges. On the other hand, do not

dwell on the undesirable features or say that it has been difficult to keep people in that position.

- Avoid salary negotiations until ready to make an offer, then do so only through human resources (wage and salary administration). If the person expects more than you are authorized to offer, keep the door open. Say that you will look into it and report back.
- If you have a mentoring program, mention that to candidates. The availability of such programs is an attractive feature to some candidates.

Special Incentives

In addition to cash bonuses, noncash hiring incentives include relocation packages, tuition reimbursement, paid employee training, flextime, and transportation reimbursement.

CLOSING THE INTERVIEW

Ask for the candidate's level of interest (for example, "Although neither of us can make a decision at this point, do you think you're interested in the job?"). Explore doubts or reservations. If the person is noncommittal but appears to be a good candidate, set a deadline for an answer.

State when the selection decision will be made and how you will notify the applicant. Make certain that you have the person's current phone number and address.

Escort the candidate to the next interviewer, to another on-site destination, or back to the employment section of the human resources department, and always remember to thank the candidate for coming.

POSTINTERVIEW ACTIVITIES

Writing and Organizing Your Report

Eyeballing rough notes is not the preferred approach. Match your findings with a written list of criteria you have established. Review information from other sources such as the application form, resumé, and reference reports. If you must use subjective terminology (for example, cocky, pompous, abrasive, personable, ideal, immature, practical, or sarcastic), describe what was said or done that caused you to form those impressions.

Prepare a brief summary of the strengths and weaknesses of the candidate. You may want to use a numerical weighting system to evaluate the major assets and liabilities.

If multiple interviewers participated, compare notes with them. Second interviews with the more promising candidates are often desirable.

Notification and Medical Testing

Do not wait too long before offering the job (24 hours is usually too short, and a month is too long). For jobs for which there are few candidates but many competitors, you must make a decision soon. Have your top choice notified first, and wait for that person's response before moving on to others.

The job offer is usually extended in a formal letter from your human resources department. It may be preceded by a phone call. The candidate should be told how much time he or she has to respond.

Under the ADA, once an employer has made a conditional job offer, the organization is free to ask the applicant to undergo medical tests.

OBTAINING REFERENCES

An employee may fail in one position but perform as a standout in another, so if at all possible references should be obtained from more than one source. Obviously the job that most resembles the one being offered is the most important to check.

Offers of employment are ordinarily extended as tentative offers, contingent on passing the appropriate preemployment physical examination and on the receipt of satisfactory references. Although previous immediate supervisors are often the best sources of information, it is hazardous to deal supervisor to supervisor and organization to organization without involving human resources departments. An increasing number of organizations forbid their supervisors and managers from checking references or giving out reference information themselves and insist that this activity be handled by the human resources department. The reasoning behind this position is that exchanging reference information, whether giving out or receiving, has become such a legal minefield that it is best undertaken by people who are aware of all the pitfalls.

Because of the fear of being charged with defamation for what is said in a response to a request for a reference ("I didn't get this great job I had a good shot at because my last boss said I had a poor attitude!"), many organizations have adopted a policy of limiting all reference responses concerning past employees to job titles and dates of employment. Reference checking has become almost something of a game between organizations, with each organization trying to give out as little information as possible while trying to get as much as they can from other organizations.

Those on one side of the reference issue will argue that it is only former supervisors who know best what kind of worker a person was. This may be so, but it is almost impossible to convey such information to others without being subjective, and it is subjectivity—"poor attitude," "uncooperative," "unmotivated," "crabby," and so on—that causes the trouble. The only information that can safely be exchanged in reference checking is that which can be verified in the record, the record being the individual's personnel file. Thus a human resources practitioner is in the preferred position to address reference checking safely.

Nevertheless numerous supervisors and managers continue to exchange reference information informally with their peers and colleagues throughout the community. This has long been a practice, and it is not likely to disappear completely. Often the reasoning goes that this is colleague to colleague, even friend to friend, nothing is committed to writing, so what's to prevent passing reference information in this fashion?

Look at this scenario, once in a great while faced by some manager. You have decided against an applicant because of what you learned from your counterpart at the previous employer. The applicant has filed a charge of defamation, perhaps only guessing at the reasons for the rejection. It becomes a legal issue, and after much maneuvering you find yourself asked, under oath, if you discussed this applicant with your friend, the applicant's former manager. What will you say? What will the other manager say? This is too great a risk to run on behalf of your employer. Best leave the trading of reference information to the human resources department.

Early in the employment process human resources will have obtained the applicant's signed permission to check with previous employers. Human resources may do this by telephone, letter, e-mail, fax, or some combination of these. All references will be documented and made part of the individual's personnel file if hiring does indeed occur.

Think About It

It has long been felt that the personal interview is not a particularly effective means of determining who will or will not turn out to be a good employee. However, no one has yet managed to come up with a more reliable alternative.

Questions for Review and Discussion

1. A non-question question often used to begin an interview is "Tell me all about yourself." Is this a reasonable request? Why or why not?
2. If age alone is no longer a reason to avoid hiring someone or for forcing one to retire, what is the principal criterion for getting hired or remaining employed?
3. In some (probably very few) organizations, middle management or a personnel department hires employees and simply hands them to the supervisors. What, if anything, is wrong with this practice?
4. How would you proceed to assess the ability of a candidate to fit in with your work group?
5. When interviewing, why is it important to try to fill in the gaps in a candidate's employment history?

6. How would you react if an individual you were interviewing voluntarily revealed forbidden information? What would you do with this information?

7. In only one or two brief sentences, summarize all of the kinds of information you can legally ask for in an employment interview.

8. Is it of any particular importance to sometimes seek new employees for your department from within the organization? Why or why not?

9. It has often been said that the most effective means of filling available jobs is personal networking and referral. Why might this be so?

10. What, if anything, do you believe is wrong with interviewing from behind a desk? Is some other arrangement likely to be more effective? Why?

Case: The Employee Who Didn't Fit

Bob Long was hired by County Hospital as supervisor of engineering and maintenance. Although well experienced in his field, this was his first management job. Soon after Bob's arrival a maintenance helper job came open. This was an important job because of a number of preventive maintenance activities that had to be performed, and Bob recognized the need to fill this job as soon as possible. Bob asked human resources to find some candidates for him to interview.

Bob's manager, general services director Jack Parsons, chose to sit in on the interviews, giving as his reason Bob's newness to management. Jack indicated that because Bob had never interviewed before he should be assisted in the process.

Bob and Jack agreed that given the entry-level nature of the job, they need not look for experience but instead should look for apparent willingness to learn. Together they interviewed five candidates. Of the five, two seemed reasonable choices. One of these, a young man named Simons, was already employed by the hospital as a kitchen helper in food service. The other, a young man named Kelsey, had not worked recently but had had several months experience in the custodial department of a school.

Bob expressed his desire to take on Simons from food service because he appeared to have the aptitude and ability and showed a strong desire to better himself, but Jack disagreed. He told Bob he could do the hiring the next time a job opened and made the decision to hire Kelsey.

As the probation period progressed it became increasingly clear to Bob that Kelsey was not shaping up as a satisfactory employee. Even extending every benefit of the doubt, which he did because Kelsey was the boss's choice, he could conclude only that Kelsey was not going to work out in the long run.

Just before the end of Kelsey's probationary period Bob went to see Jack. He had kept Jack advised all along, so it was no surprise to Jack when Bob said they should cut Kelsey loose and start over.

"Okay," Jack agreed, "let Kelsey go."

Bob hesitated, wondering briefly if he should say anything, then finally said to Jack, "I don't believe *I* should let him go. I didn't hire him."

"He's your employee," Jack said. "Get rid of him."

Questions:

1. Did Jack dodge his responsibility by ordering Bob to get rid of the unsatisfactory employee? Why or why not?
2. What are two other ways in which this situation could have been handled more equitably?
3. What effect might this incident have on the future relationship between Bob Long and Jack Parsons?

Case: Recruiting Inside vs. Outside—Bungled

With adequate notice and with the knowledge of his staff, the manager of information systems left the hospital to take a position elsewhere. Within the department it was assumed that Mr. Smith—"Smitty" to everyone—would move up from his senior position and become manager, but even with the passage of a full week no appointment had been made.

One week became several weeks. The vice president to whom the information systems group normally reported began to make administrative decisions for information systems. To Smitty was left the growing task of overseeing the functions of the group in addition to performing his regular work.

The employees in the department became aware that the hospital was advertising for an information systems manager and that interviews were being conducted at a fairly high level. However, nobody was hired. Finally, after the group had been 6 months without a manager, Smitty was elevated to manager and was immediately authorized to hire a replacement for his old position.

Questions:

1. In a scenario such as that just described, what are the likely effects of leaving a supposedly important position open for so long?
2. What do you believe would be the effects of information systems personnel discovering that apparently "secret" recruiting was taking place?
3. Provide two or three possible reasons why the choice for manager reverted to Mr. Smith, even though external recruiting had been pursued.

REFERENCES

1. Smart, B. 1989. *The smart interviewer.* New York: Wiley, vii.
2. Goldzimer, L.S. 1989. *"I'm First": Your Customer's Message to You.* New York: Rawson, 109.
3. Dortch, C.T. 1989. Job-person match. *Personnel Journal* 68: 46.

RECOMMENDED READING

P. Anderson and M.A. Pulich, "Team-Based Participation in the Hiring Process." *Health Care Supervisor 15*, no. 4 (1997): 69–76.
"Labor News Briefs." *HRFocus* 74, no. 10 (1997): S1–S16.
D. Scotto, "Inventive strategies for Laboratory Recruitment." *Medical Laboratory Observer* 29, no. 7 (1997):50–59.
W.S. Swan, *How To Pick the Right People* (New York: John Wiley & Sons, 1989).
K.J. Yate, *Hiring the Best,* 3d ed. (Holbrook, MA: M.A. Adams, 1987).

Chapter 8

Orientation and Training of New Employees

A sound orientation is the institution's best opportunity to insure a positive employee relations climate while developing productive and knowledgeable workers.

—Martin E. Skolar

CHAPTER OBJECTIVES

- Establish the primary objectives of an employee orientation program, both organization wide and department specific.
- Highlight the general contents of the organizational orientation common to all new employees.
- Establish the means of determining the needs of a department-specific orientation program.
- Convey the importance of affording each new employee a strong, knowledgeable start on the job.
- Enumerate the specific departmental values that must be communicated to all employees early in their employment.
- Review the primary sources of information and assistance used to round out a new employee's introduction to the department.
- Provide a means of evaluating the departmental orientation program in order to maintain its quality and completeness.

At no other time is there a better opportunity to establish open lines of communication with new hires than at new employee orientation. New employees are free from the distortions of peer groups. They have not yet formed strong opinions about the job, the organization, or the boss. They are eager to please.[1]

There are three important considerations governing the design of an orientation program. The first is the need to nudge new employees toward superior customer service. The second is to regard the orientees as our clients because we provide them with our training services. The third is the need to infuse the latest concepts of quality improvement and cost containment. In this chapter we will concentrate on the first two of these objectives. Our vision and mission are to help trainees see their jobs as contributions to the total impact of the organization on the customer and start them out on their pursuit of successful employment.

OBJECTIVES OF AN ORIENTATION PROGRAM

On the first day, make newcomers feel like honored guests. By the second week make them feel like family

We want to get our new employees off on the right foot, and they are most impressionable when they first come on board. In planning for their orientation, you should endeavor to accomplish several things.

- Create a favorable impression of the organization, of the department, and of you, the supervisor.
- Establish responsibilities and accountabilities. Your expectations of their performance must be crystal clear.
- Ensure they learn everything they need to perform their work.
- Provide full information about pay scales, benefits programs, the working environment, and conditions of employment. This includes opportunities for training and advancement.
- Describe policies, rules, and regulations in detail.
- Provide checklists of tasks to ensure that all topics in the orientation process are covered.
- Encourage employee feedback on the effectiveness of the orientation program.
- Emphasize the importance of teamwork, flexibility, innovativeness, and the ability to adapt to change.
- Facilitate satisfaction of their need to be accepted by coworkers and to establish rapport through collegial communication.
- Provide initial experiences that result in early successes. This creates a sense of self-value, instills confidence, and promotes positive attitudes. Most athletic coaches like to begin their seasons against weaker teams for the same reason.
- Identify the kinds of customers to be dealt with and emphasize the importance of satisfying them.
- Initiate the newcomers into the rituals and practices of your work group and your quality improvement program. These rituals and practices may include activities such as team project completion celebrations, customer attendance

at staff meetings, group "brag sessions," and ceremonies for such occasions as special achievements, perfect attendance, and promotions or role changes.

TEN IMPORTANT ASSUMPTIONS

The Corning Glass Works designed a new employee orientation program based on the following 10 assumptions.[2]

1. Early impressions last.
2. The first 90 days are crucial.
3. Orientation begins before the trainees arrive (preparations).
4. Day one is crucial.
5. The new employee is responsible for learning.
6. Teaching the basics comes first.
7. New employees should understand the total company.
8. Information is timed to employees' needs.
9. Informational overload must be avoided.
10. Orientation doesn't work unless the employee's supervisor is involved.

HOSPITAL ORIENTATION PROGRAMS

New employees are usually enrolled in a hospital orientation program conducted by the human resources department or a separate education department, if such exists. Traditionally these programs start with the history, mission, and core values of the organization. Other important topics include information about fire safety, safety in general, infection control, and resuscitation procedures.

However, new employees mostly prefer to receive information that helps them adjust to their new roles. Such information includes when they get paid, where they park their cars, when the snack bar is open, and how they go about requesting educational support and accessing other benefits. However, it is not unusual for many orientees to be dozing off by the time the presenters get to the topics that are most important to them personally.

NEEDS ASSESSMENT FOR DEPARTMENTAL ORIENTATION

The conceptualization of a departmental program starts with an analysis of what is needed by new employees joining the department. Such assessment considers both current and future requirements. The planning and the implementation phases are often slighted because at the time new employees are coming on board, the department is usually understaffed.

Most new employees arrive loaded with questions. Whether or not they are consciously aware of doing so, they are looking for someone to help them to reach a level of comfort and familiarity with this new environment. Orientation planning is facilitated by addressing the following questions before they are actually asked by the new hires.

- Where is my workstation? Where are the cafeteria, restrooms, and parking areas?
- What are my duties and responsibilities?
- How do I answer the telephone, obtain supplies, and operate the computer and all those other gadgets?
- How will I know if I am doing satisfactory work?
- Why do I have to do the things that have been assigned to me?
- Why must we do things this particular way?
- What are my starting and quitting times, when do we get breaks and how long are they, when is payday, and when does my probationary period end?
- To whom do I report? Who will answer my questions, evaluate my work, or be my friend?

PREPARATIONS FOR THE ARRIVAL OF NEW ORIENTEES

There are many ways to prepare for the arrival of new employees.

- Send letters of welcome. Include verification of date, time, and place of reporting, and provide the first day's agenda and any special instructions or suggestions such as what they should bring or wear.
- Arrange your schedule so you can devote most of the first day to the newcomer(s).
- Review the orientation and training check-off lists.
- Prepare an agenda covering the first week.
- Prepare an orientation packet that includes
    1. statement of departmental vision, mission, values, and goals
    2. department organization chart
    3. position description and work standards of the job
    4. personnel policy and procedures manual (employee handbook)
    5. orientation and training schedules
    6. checklists and program evaluation forms
    7. performance appraisal forms
    8. probationary evaluation form (if it is not the same as the performance appraisal form)
    9. safety, infection control, and quality assurance policies, procedures, and rules
    10. names, titles, and locations of trainers
    11. key telephone numbers or a condensed telephone directory

FIRST DAY: WELCOME WAGON

New employees usually report first to the human resources department. Get off to a good start by meeting your new people there. Greet them as you would visiting friends. Have a few well-prepared remarks and deliver them with enthusiasm. For example:

> One reason we selected each of you is that you've shown the kind of attitude we always look for. As you know, the major goal of your position is to meet our customers' expectations. Our customers include patients, the patient's families and visitors, clinicians and other care providers, third-party payers, teammates, students and trainees, and departments served by us. I know you understand the importance of customer service, and you'll soon learn how we want you to deliver that service. You're obviously not allergic to work or to change, and in your past jobs you showed the flexibility and innovativeness we like.

Finally, review the agenda of the orientation program and give the new employees their orientation packets.

"NUTS AND BOLTS" TALKS

On the second day, ask how the first day went. Then establish a dialogue based on the following.

- The mission, corporate values, and goals of the organization (which they probably were not tuned in to during the organization-wide orientation). Explain how the functions of the department focus on supporting the corporate mission, goal, and core values.
- The employee's position description and performance standards. Refer to these documents as contracts that must be honored. Describe the behavior that is rewarded and that which is unacceptable.
- Survival information: work hours, overtime rules, compensatory time, vacation and sick leave policies, assignment of lockers, and completion of personnel data.
- How performance is evaluated and reported.
- Current managerial initiatives. These may include reengineering, new quality improvement or cost-cutting strategies, employee empowerment, or self-directed team building.
- Description of current educational or marketing programs relating to customer service. For example, telephone courtesy, point-of-care testing, cost cutting, or improvements in quality or turnaround time.

- Other information you want them to have. This could include your personal likes and dislikes, your preference in behavior, and whatever else you feel they should know about you and your management of the department. They will not find most such information in formal documentation. It is better to let them know these things up front rather than having to correct them after the fact. You may want to cover:
  1. how you prefer to be addressed (formally or on a first name basis)
  2. that you expect innovativeness of everyone
  3. that you welcome suggestions and insist on hearing about any complaints or other comments from customers (Say, "In this department we don't kill messengers who bring bad tidings, we applaud them.")
  4. things that annoy you (for example, tardiness, abuse of sick leave, chronic lateness for meetings, untidy clothes, or expressions such as "That's not in my job description," "I only work here," or comments suggesting that customers get in the way, such as "I wish those relatives would stop making all those nuisance calls.")
- how each job has a chain-reaction effect on other staffers' ability to do their jobs and, therefore, eventually affects customers
- the list of internal and external customers and the importance of customer satisfaction. Remind them how hard your unit has worked to attract customers and how important it is to keep them. Explain how poor service creates stress for all parties and how they'll gain psychological benefits when they treat customers properly. If true, state, "Your pay and advancement will depend on how well customers are served."
- your interest in the development of their (the employees') potential rather than in their immediate output

Chip Bell offers the following four keys to exceeding customer expectations.[3] Share them now with your new employees.

1. Be a risk taker. Be willing to make tough decisions and take action for customers that may be against policies or rules, provided they are legal, moral, and ethical and represent your best judgment.
2. Be friendly.
3. Be sincere.
4. Relax and have fun.

MAJOR DEPARTMENTAL VALUES

There are essential values that should be shared with all new employees. *Honesty* is not concealing mistakes or blaming others and not calling in sick when you are not. *Integrity* means always doing what you promise to do. Demonstrate *pride* in your appearance and performance, maintaining a tidy workstation. Show *loyalty* by putting in an honest day's work and not bad mouthing management. *Courtesy* means knocking on a patient's door before entering, addressing people by their formal names (not calling them "honey" or "dearie"). Demonstrate your *work ethic* by reporting for work on time, not abusing breaks, or—again—not calling in sick when you are not ill. Finally, *customer service* involves going the extra mile, listening patiently, and exhibiting a can-do attitude.

SHOW AND TELL

Avoid informational overload. Do not try to cover everything during a single tour of the premises; that tends to be confusing. Point out the physical facilities. Do not stop repeatedly to introduce all of the personnel; this can happen later when people are less busy. Show them where the supplies are kept, reports are filed, and paper copies are made.

On a subsequent tour, follow the sequences of various workflows. For example, trace a test request from its point of origin to the physician's receipt of the results. Instruct the orientees to diagram these workflows. Show how customer service is affected by glitches in any step of these workflows.

Devote one session to a discussion of budgets, charges, and costs. As necessary, show orientees how charges appear on patients' bills and how employees can respond to customers' questions about them.

Direct attention to the communication systems, and demonstrate their use. Stress the importance of proper telephone etiquette. Include the intercom, bulletin boards, mailboxes, and message centers. Point out where schedules for work, off-duty assignments, and vacations are posted. Show them how the different shifts communicate with each other. Demonstrate how photocopying and filing are done. Later, discuss the location and use of safety equipment.

After the tours have been completed, ask the new employees to diagram the topography of the department. This should include the identification of each room. Later, have them draw more detailed diagrams of the room(s) to which they are assigned. Have them locate each workstation and major piece of equipment on these drawings.

MEETING COLLEAGUES

It is recommended that you limit the number of introductions during tours of the department. Employees do not like to be interrupted in the middle of their tasks, and their reaction (or lack of reaction) may be misinterpreted by the orientees as signs of unfriendliness. Also, the new folks can become confused by all the faces, names, and titles when these are encountered in rapid succession. Make the introductions during break when people are relaxed and more inclined to be amiable. Also, present newcomers at a staff meeting. Encourage them to talk about their educational and recreational interests at that time.

When you introduce someone, explain how that employee's responsibilities or interests relate to those of the newcomer. An introduction might go like this: "Joyce, I'd like you to meet Sue Smith. Sue is in charge of our main storeroom. If you can't find something there, see Sue." The new employee should meet with each senior member of the staff, preferably in his or her office.

GET HELP FROM YOUR SPECIALISTS

In medium to large departments, certain staff members have special expertise or responsibilities that make them better qualified to cover certain topics. In the absence of these specialists, you are responsible for this training.

Trainer or Educational Coordinator

If you delegate training, have the new employee meet the trainer early in the orientation program. Pick trainers with care. Prerequisites include teaching ability, professional or technical expertise, sufficient time to be thorough, willingness, and loads of enthusiasm. Trainers should be aware of the qualifications and experience of the indoctrinees so they can tailor the training to the particular needs of each individual.

Give trainees folders in which to keep their continuing education records. Most departments have requirements for the number of educational hours required for each job category. Show the trainees how to keep these records, and remind them that it is their responsibility to do so.

Safety Coordinator

Some departments have a safety coordinator who shows new hires the location and proper use of safety equipment and reviews safety policies and regulations. New people often have questions about the dangers of hepatitis, AIDS, and other infectious diseases. The safety expert can allay these fears while explaining the best way to minimize the dangers. When discussing AIDS, the expert must also warn against disclosure of confidential information.

Quality Assurance or Quality Improvement Coordinator

This person may be the chair or the recorder for the quality assurance committee. The coordinator may limit the discussion to the global aspects of the program, leaving specific quality control details for the new employee's immediate supervisor to cover.

Mentors and Buddies

Mentors are experienced employees who willingly share their wisdom or political clout with their protégés. They are unofficial advisors, supporters, and confidants. Encourage new employees to find and to establish alliances with those individuals who go out of their way to please customers. In some departments the buddy system is used; each new arrival is assigned to an experienced employee in the same work section.

> *When new employees complete their orientation, hold a simple celebration.*

TRAINING THE NEW EMPLOYEE

The triple approach to success in customer satisfaction is train, train, train. It is no accident that much of this book is devoted to that subject. Training is especially important during and immediately following the orientation phase because new hires are most open to learning at these times. Initiate good work habits, behavior, ethics, and attitudes before bad ones develop. Assign your best people to do your training. This is a long-term investment that pays off early and continues to pay.

Training during the orientation phase must be tailored to each orientee's needs, and those depend on his or her previous education and experience. At this juncture, list all the skills necessary to handle the job, and prepare check-off lists of tasks to be learned. Divide the individual tasks or responsibilities into those that can be learned on the job, those that must be taught formally, and those that can be self-taught. Prepare a rough timetable for achieving the training goals.

At the completion of the formal orientation or training program, solicit feedback from each participant on the value of the program. See Exhibit 8–1 for an example of an orientation checklist. Get written or verbal comments from each person who helped with the training.

Think About It

One of the surest ways to stimulate unwanted turnover is to turn new employees loose with little or no departmental orientation or personal guidance in finding their places in the group. Even a trained professional can feel abandoned, left to survive alone and unaided, in a new and possibly strange environment.

(more on next page)

Many of those who feel lost or in over their heads early in their employment simply bail out of a disappointing situation.

Exhibit 8–1 Checklist for Evaluating the Orientation Program

Check all of the items with which you agree.
1. On the first day, I was welcomed with enthusiasm.
2. By the end of the first week, I knew I had been accepted by the team.
3. My immediate supervisor spent enough time with me.
4. The entire orientation was well organized.
5. Everyone was patient and encouraging.
6. I quickly learned what was expected of me and how to do my job.
7. The new employee handbook (packet of information) was very helpful.
8. They made it easy and relatively painless to learn about important policies and rules.
9. My fears of infection and other safety factors were alleviated quickly.
10. I was made to feel important.
11. I received much more praise than criticism. When my work had to be corrected, they always explained why.
12. During the first few days, I met not only my colleagues but also important people in other departments.
13. I now understand how my job fits into the big picture of what our organization is all about.
14. I know how the communications systems work and how to make full use of them.
15. I had plenty of opportunities to ask questions and express my opinions.
16. I am familiar with the salary and benefits package and how performance is evaluated.
17. I understand my role in the quality improvement program.

Questions for Review and Discussion

1. Describe how you might try to avoid information overload during a new employee's first few days.
2. Much of the material in the chapter conveys the need to imbue the new employee with a sense of the mission, vision, and values of the organization. Why is this important?
3. Why do we need to offer a relatively formal orientation, complete with checklists of items to cover?
4. Why do we need to bother with individual orientation for a new employee who is a trained specialist hired to perform exactly the same tasks performed at a previous job?
5. Why should we be more interested in developing employee potential than in obtaining immediate output?
6. What do you see as the primary advantages of a strong new-employee orientation? Why?

7. Explain why the chapter states that new-employee orientation begins before the new employees arrive.
8. What are the primary advantages of a mentoring relationship as part of a new employee's orientation?
9. What, if anything, is wrong with the apparently time-honored practice of letting new employees learn by trial and error and by watching others?
10. Why not simply have the department supervisors provide all of a new employee's orientation rather than have a separate organization-wide orientation as well?

Case: No Departmental Orientation?

Assume you have just been hired from outside of the organization to serve as a first-line supervisor in one of the clinical support areas (laboratory, radiology, pharmacy, etc.). Staffing in the department has been lean, with some staff positions having been open for some weeks, but as luck would have it, you were able to fill both open positions during your first 2 weeks on the job.

Being new to supervision and new to this organizational environment, the Friday before the two new employees were scheduled to start work you asked a more experienced supervisor, "Is there anything special I'm supposed to do with these new employees when human resources turns them over to me on Monday?"

The response was simply, "Nothing other than your standard departmental orientation."

You asked each of your employees in turn about their departmental orientation. Their answers were consistent: There was no departmental orientation; they were simply shown their work stations and told where the cafeteria and rest rooms were located. Other than that, nothing.

Instruction:

In written form, describe what you intend to do about (1) the two new employees who start work on Monday and (2) other new employees who join your department in the future.

Case: The Inherited Employee

Soon after she became a supervisor in the building services department, Donna Paine decided that a housekeeping aide named Sally Clark was emerging as a problem employee. An employee of about 4 months, and thus a month past the end of the probationary period, Sally was frequently idle. She seemed always to do exactly what she was supposed to do, if only at a minimally acceptable level, and then do nothing until specifically assigned to another task. Donna grew especially sensitive to the situation when she began to hear complaints from other employees about Sally not doing her share of the work.

Donna pulled the file the previous supervisor had started concerning Sally. There was very little in the file. She set up an appointment with Sally. In opening the discussion Donna said, "I am unable to find your 3-month probationary review. Do you still have your copy?"

The reply was, "What review? I never had one."

Donna then asked, "What about your orientation checklist from when you started in the department? Still have your copy?"

"Never got one. I don't think I had any orientation."

"How did you first learn about your duties and about the department?" asked Donna.

"I watched someone else—Janie, I think her name was—for a couple of hours. But Janie left that week."

At this point Donna dropped her tentative plans to address what she considered Sally's substandard performance. Instead, she thought she had best look into the apparent absence of a probationary review and attempt to determine why Sally had never received an orientation to the department.

Questions:

1. What should Donna do about the departmental orientation that Sally had apparently never received?
2. Sally has apparently gone beyond the end of the standard probationary period without receiving a probationary evaluation. What can Donna do about this, and how might this affect Sally's status?

REFERENCES

1. Werther Jr., W.B. 1989. *Dear Boss.* New York: Meadowbrook, 189.
2. Ideas and trends in personnel. *Human Resources Management* (174) (July 26, 1988).
3. Bell, C. 1994. *Customers as partners: Building relationships that last.* San Francisco, CA: Barrett-Koehler, 86.

RECOMMENDED READING

D. Arthur, *Recruiting, Interviewing, Selecting, & Orienting New Employees.* (New York: AMACOM, 1986).

C.M. Cadwell, *New Employee Orientation.* (Los Altos, CA: Crisp Publishers, 1988).

A. Haggard, *Hospital Orientation Handbook.* (Gaithersburg, MD: Aspen Publishers, 1984).

Chapter 9

Team Building

*There are few, if any, jobs in which ability alone is
sufficient. Needed, also, are loyalty, sincerity,
enthusiasm, and team play.*

—William B. Given, Jr.

CHAPTER OBJECTIVES

- Define the kinds of teams to be found within the organization: those established for specific purposes, departmental teams, and the greater "team" unified by a common goal or directive.
- Enumerate both the benefits and the disadvantages of the use of special-purpose teams.
- Establish the characteristics of an effective team.
- Examine the more common reasons for team failure.
- Describe the interactive forces involved in the formation, assembly, growth, and functioning of most teams, including team rituals and the relative strength of group norms and their role in a team's success or failure.
- Enumerate and discuss the responsibilities of team leadership and explore the implications of leadership style for effective team functioning.
- Suggest how the manager who inherits a team formed under a previous leader can constructively approach the new assignment.
- Briefly consider various means of evaluating and rewarding team performance, recognizing that most evaluation and reward systems focus on individuals, not groups.

As business enterprises of all kinds become more complex, they depend more on the effectiveness of group efforts and cross-functional activities. In health care, no longer do many individuals work as solo practitioners. For example, in the old days an emergency department (formerly referred to as an emergency room) was usually staffed by a physician and a few nurses and aides. Now an emergency department normally features dozens of professionals and technicians with diverse skills and experience who work as a team to save lives.

Various health care institutions are establishing satellite facilities, developing new services, implementing changes to comply with legal and other mandated requirements, and establishing comprehensive quality improvement programs. In the new health care paradigm, cross-functional teams regularly span departmental boundaries, and the third-party payers become senior partners in a health care team.

A team is a group of people who are committed to achieving common objectives. An effective team has members who work well together, enjoy doing so, and who produce high-quality outcomes. Teams have become the utility vehicles of today's organizations.

The term "team" is actually representative of several different kinds of collectives, and it is necessary to know at most times the kind of team to which you may be referring. We regularly encounter special-purpose teams, departmental teams, and the greater team.

Special-purpose teams are groups assembled for a particular purpose, perhaps *ad hoc* (having a specific assignment, after which the group is disbanded) or perhaps a standing team or committee having an indefinite term of existence (for example, a safety committee).

Much that is said about team building is applicable to forging and maintaining a strong *departmental team*, a collection of like-minded people who report to the same manager and cooperatively serve the common purpose of the department.

Frequent reference may be made to "the health care team," essentially all those involved in designing and delivering and paying for health care—the *greater team*. At times, the employing organization and all those it encompasses may be appropriately described as a team.

Regardless of its kind, composition, reason for being, or degree of permanence, however, there is one significant factor that unites the members of any team: common purpose.

BENEFITS OF TEAMS

Health care organizations regularly use teams to handle a wide variety of tasks and problems. They are taking advantage of the following benefits of teams.

- Greater total expertise. Although team formation is not a panacea, it does serve to refine a group's skills and expand its collective ability to solve problems. Teams are especially useful in addressing procedures, relationships, quality, productivity, and problem solving.

- Synergy. The total achievements of teams are invariably greater than what can be achieved by members acting independently.
- Improved morale. The motivational needs of affiliation, achievement, and control are satisfied in the team setting.
- Improved personnel retention. Employees are less prone to leave when they are members of teams, especially teams recognized for their successes.
- Increased flexibility. Team efforts reduce dependence on individuals. Services do not suffer when one member of a team is missing.

DISADVANTAGES OF TEAMS

Teams, however, have their down side. Health care managers must also be aware of the occasionally encountered disadvantages of team activity.

- Teams are not always needed. There are many situations that can be handled as well or better by individuals. Specialists handle specific situations more rapidly and without having to consult others or obtain the approval of other members of a work group. Attempts to introduce work teams in departments where there are no interdependencies are largely a waste of time and effort. However, in most health care departments, people do depend on one another.
- Team building requires start-up time. There is always that period early in the life of a team when effort must be invested in team formation but little if anything specific is being accomplished.
- Teams may become bureaucratic. A once-enthusiastic task force can become a self-perpetuating standing committee, and its business often becomes repetitious and boring.
- When fast action is required, someone—an individual—must take charge and get things rolling. When someone yells "fire," it's not the time to call a meeting.

CHARACTERISTICS OF EFFECTIVE TEAMS

An effective team can be described as follows.

- It is not always limited to a departmental work group or even an interdepartmental collection of members. As is necessary, its members may include vendors, customers, people from other departments, and key support personnel.
- It possesses all the necessary knowledge, skill, and experience required to fulfill its charge and get the job done.
- As a body its members search for excellence in quality, productivity, and customer service. The team removes factors that inhibit quality performance.
- It welcomes innovation, new services, and improved processes and techniques.

- It is democratic. There is an absence of rank or formal authority. It has a leader who refers to his or her coworkers as associates, colleagues, or teammates, not as subordinates.
- It demonstrates effective multidirectional communication and as a group displays openness and candor.
- It remains inspired by a vision of what it is trying to accomplish. Its charge is clear, its goals are clear, and all members are unified in their pursuit.
- It actively constructs formal and informal networks that include people who aid in its mission.
- It possesses power based not on formal authority but on the credibility the team has earned through performance.
- Its members trust each other and are sensitive to each other's needs. They understand their roles, responsibilities, and degrees of authority.
- It addresses and eliminates conflict with other teams or nonteam employees through collaboration, coordination, and cooperation.
- It adheres to strict ethical and moral considerations.
- It conveys optimism, and its members have fun serving.

WHY TEAMS FAIL

There are many reasons why teams fail. Unrealistic mandates from higher management and a lack of purpose and direction are major factors. However, poor leadership is the most common problem leading to team failure. This may be the fault of the person to whom the team reports or the unwillingness of any individual team member to assume a leadership role. Reviews of failed teams almost always reveal a serious breakdown in communication.

Other factors also contribute to team failure.

- Domination of the team by players possessing higher status or greater knowledge or who are more aggressive. Other problem members include the pessimists, negativists, obstructionists, prima donnas, and goof-offs.
- Lack of organizational support (for example, insufficient resources or time, understaffing, or unpleasant work environments).
- Internal politics, hidden agendas, conformity pressures, favoritism, and excessive paperwork.
- The development within the team of cliques that have the effect of isolating the group from the rest of the organization.
- Destructive competition among team individuals for promotions, merit raises, recognition, and access to superiors.
- Unrealistic expectations, resulting in discouragement when there are setbacks.

- Disapproval of a team's output or lack of action on the team's suggestions or recommendations by upper management. Also, failure of a team to respond to the ideas of its individual members can quickly quench enthusiasm.
- Lack of progress, failure to meet deadlines, setbacks, and bad results, any of which may be disheartening.

TEAM DYNAMICS

Team dynamics refers to the interactive forces brought to bear by individuals singly or collectively in a group activity. The success of group dynamics depends largely on how willing team leaders are to share authority, responsibility, information, and resources. Sharing is a large part of what participative management is all about.

Stages in Team Formation and Development

Stage 1: Confusion

This initial stage represents the transition from a group of individuals to a team. Participation is hesitant as members wonder what will be expected of them. Team members may show suspicion, fear, and anxiety, and productivity may suffer.

Stage 2: Dissatisfaction

Some members may display negativity, hostility, bickering, or outright resistance. Infighting, defensiveness, and competition are common at this stage because a number of participants have not yet clearly seen themselves as members of a group. Low productivity may persist.

Stage 3: Resolution

If the team is to be successful, group norms and roles emerge once the dissatisfaction is on the way to resolution. Dissatisfaction and conflict diminish, and a sense of cohesiveness starts to develop. Dependence on strong formal leaders decreases. Cohesion is achieved when individual members feel responsible for the success of the team. Productivity will have attained moderate levels.

Stage 4: Maturation

Productivity is high and performance is smooth. Members have developed insight into personal and collective processes. Team members have learned how to resolve their differences and provide each other with constructive feedback. All of this requires time, and progress is not steady but up and down, in fits and starts. Mature teams experience some turnover in membership, mostly planned or expected. Moreover, priorities change, and a host of other variables constantly affect the nature and makeup of mature teams.

Group Norms

Group norms may be functional or dysfunctional. A functional form is evident when team members defend their team and their organization. A dysfunctional form develops when members feel that their organization is taking advantage of them and they perhaps believe that teams are being assembled only to squeeze more work out of the participants.

In some dysfunctional forms, members struggle so hard to avoid conflict that team decisions suffer. Some conflict is essential to effective problem solving. Cohesion does not mean the complete absence of differences of opinion, arguments, or disagreements. Members of great teams can frequently be heard debating heatedly among themselves.

At the Marine Corps boot camp on Parris Island, drill instructors turn undisciplined men and women into confident leaders. Their group norms are high. The instructors teach a few key lessons and model the behavior they want.

- Tell the truth.
- Do your best, no matter how trivial the task.
- Choose the difficult right over the easy wrong.
- Look out for the group before you look out for yourself.
- Don't whine or make excuses.
- Judge others by their actions, not their race.
- Don't use "I" or "me."[1]

RITUALS AND STATUS SYMBOLS

Certain rituals are important to team success. The truly important positive rituals are mainly expressions of appreciation (eg, trophies, awards, parties, picnics, and special dinners). A negative ritual, largely undesirable but nevertheless a ritual of sorts, is the hazing or taunting of new employees. However, even some positive rituals may change their polarity; for example, the employee of the month award may be regarded with scorn when undeserving candidates are selected or deserving employees are overlooked.

Team status symbols can also be important. Take uniforms for instance. For years the long white hospital coat was worn only by attending physicians and senior house staff members. This is no longer the case; in many units the green scrub suit, complete with stethoscope, has become a uniform of choice of caregivers at all levels. The time-honored nurse's cap has all but disappeared, a sad passing in the view of the old-timers.

TEAM LEADERSHIP

> *A team is like a wheel in which each member is*
> *a spoke. It's the team leader's responsibility to*
> *have enough spokes and to keep*
> *the spokes the same length.*[2]

Many health care managers are unwilling or unable to adopt the concept of the self-directed team or even to take measures that encourage team efforts. Health care leaders must develop dual professional and supervisory skills. Team players must be given opportunities to develop their professional or technical skills (task skills) and skills that pull teams together. The five major responsibilities of team leaders are presented in detail as follows.

First, the team leader must *plan*. Team leaders must know how to make their teams effective and efficient, encouraging them to work smart. This cannot be accomplished without planning. Managers, in concert with their team members, should be able to answer these questions.

- What do our customers want or need?
- What additional information do *we* need?
- What past successes have we had in meeting the wants and needs of our customers?
- What are our strengths, and what needs improving?
- What new objectives and strategies do we need?
- How can we provide customer service faster or at less cost?
- What barriers do we face, and how can they be eliminated?
- Should we learn how others are doing what we're doing?

It is a team leaders job to *develop people*. Members of a work team, like members of an athletic team, have certain competencies, plus the ability to develop additional competencies. After structuring position descriptions and performance standards, team leaders select the best people for the team, then orient, educate, train, coach, and motivate them. Each of these responsibilities is covered in more depth in other chapters. When a team is just getting started, ask all members to share a one-word characteristic each wants to see in a teammate, and relate a scenario in which someone either possessed or lacked that trait. The story rounds out the understanding of the desired characteristic. If all members share a trait they value, the group will develop common ground on which to function.

> *Building a team is like converting a group*
> *of musicians into an orchestra.*

The leader must *build the team*. Team building involves developing relationships, communicating, holding meetings, and interacting on a daily basis. Leaders must create an atmosphere that supports and rewards creativity, openness, fairness, trust, mutual respect, and a commitment to safety and health. There must also be opportunities for career growth. Evaluate your team-building ability by taking the quiz in Exhibit 9–1.

The leader must truly *lead* the team. With the help of the other team members, team leaders prepare mission statements, set goals, develop strategies and plans, design or improve work processes, facilitate, coordinate, and troubleshoot. Leaders must satisfy the affiliation needs of each team member. All employees want to be accepted by their colleagues. Leaders also encourage team members to train and coach each other.

Example of a Simple Departmental Mission Statement

Our department is committed to providing quality care at low cost to inpatients and outpatients. Staff members maintain their expertise through continuing education and development.

The leader must *coordinate* team activities. The team or its individual members often participate in cross-functional activities. Team leaders must coordinate these activities with other departments and services. Leaders must also be ready to serve as followers in some interdepartmental task forces, committees, and focus groups. Typical topics relate to new services, safety, quality management, customer satisfaction, and employee morale.

LEADERSHIP STYLE

The ideal leadership style for team building is based on the perception that personal power is having power with people, not over people. Situational leadership fits that perception. When new employees join a team, the leader uses a directive (paternalistic) style. He or she tells the employees what to do, shows them how to do it, explains why the work is important, and relates how it fits into the big picture. Knowing that workers at this stage are frightened, insecure, and stressed, team leaders are patient and highly supportive at this time. Blanchard and Tager warn against the "leave alone—zap" style in which inexperienced workers are not given enough direction and then are zapped when they make mistakes.[3]

As employees develop confidence in their ability, the leaders back off, give them more latitude, and encourage them to solve their own problems. Some supervisors fail to move on from the initial show-and-tell stage to one that demonstrates confidence in their employees. The result is that employees remain dependent on their leaders or become annoyed with the continual spoonfeeding.

Exhibit 9–1 Rate Yourself as a Team Builder

Check all of the following that you honestly believe describe you as a team leader.
___My teammates help each other and share advice.
___My team functions well when I am not present.
___I hire people who may be able to perform some tasks better than I can.
___I try to avoid hiring people who are just like me.
___Each member of my team learns at least one new skill every year. Each is presently working on a new skill.
___Each member of my team makes at least one suggestion every month.
___I encourage both differences of opinion and suggestions for improvement.
___We resolve rather than avoid conflict and problems.
___Every member of my team can name all our external and internal customers.
___Every member of my team can state the mission of our organization in his or her own words.
___Every member of my team can describe how our quality management program has affected our service.
___Every member of my team follows safety procedures.
___We prefer team over individual competition.
___Every member of my team feels valued and accepted.
___Our team has a can-do attitude. We constantly strive to produce more than we promise.
___Our team has a reputation for cooperating with other teams and individuals.
___I would describe our team attitude as one of optimism and enthusiasm. Negativism and complaining are rare.

Parents encounter the same difficulty when they continue to treat adolescents as though they were still small children. Most employees can advance to a comfortable level of self-confidence or even to a consultative stage in which they participate actively in planning, decision making, and problem solving.

The delegative style, in which team members assume some or many supervisory responsibilities, is appropriate for some team members. In this participative paradigm, the team leader serves as a facilitator and moderator rather than as a manager. Autonomous (self-directed) teams feature a democratic system in which there are no supervisors or first-line managers. The team members select a group leader or leadership is rotated. The characteristics of effective team leaders are listed in Chapter 11.

TAKING ON THE INHERITED TEAM

It is possible you may be assigned to lead a new team, be promoted to a leadership role, or come into such a position as an outsider. If you have been a member of a team, you must make the adjustments discussed in Chapter 1. If you worked previously with the group in a cross-functional activity, put aside old prejudices and stereotypes. Overlook previous areas of friction or irritation.

If you are new to the organization, get as much information as you can about the history, reputation, culture, and rituals of your new employer. Check the leadership style of the previous group leader. How did the group members respond? How effective was that style? You can learn about this from the person to whom you report and from present team members. Hold group meetings to discuss mission, strategy, values, plans, your leadership style, and your previous experience.

Study the position descriptions for every job and the performance reviews of each employee, and hold individual meetings with team members. Find out as much as you can about their aspirations, complaints, and suggestions and about how you can make better use of their services. Prepare an inventory chart of the team's skills.

REWARDING TEAM PERFORMANCE

The increasing focus on teams is changing the way organizations reward people. Traditional reward and recognition systems encourage individual achievement. When traditional merit pay systems are used, team cooperation often suffers. Individual rewards may cause competing employees to withhold information, undermine peers, and hamper cooperation. On the other hand, in the absence of individual rewards there is bound to be some resentment among the high performers, and the slackers have no incentive to improve. This dilemma is resolved by providing for both team and individual rewards. The group recognition builds camaraderie and cooperation. Also, when employees know that their performance ratings are affected by the extent to which they display teamwork, the adverse effects of individual rewards are mitigated.

It is recommended that some of the following be included in your team reward strategy.

- Reward employees who participate in group functions such as serving on committees or working on problem-solving groups or task forces.
- Recognize the entire team when goals are met.
- Arrange for a team to present its special projects to other departments or to higher management.
- Bring in doughnuts or pizza for the team.
- Organize a car-wash day when managers wash employees' cars.
- Make special equipment or publications available.
- Thank the team at a special luncheon or coffee hour.

- Attend some of the team's committee meetings or problem-solving meetings. Comment favorably and encourage them to maintain their excellent performance.
- Display photos of the group in action.
- Broadcast congratulatory news about completed projects, new services, favorable customer comments, or successful cost cutting.
- Spruce up the lounge and provide amenities such as a coffee maker and microwave oven.
- Take practical measures to improve communication systems, and make more information available.
- Eliminate unnecessary meetings and streamline necessary meetings to reduce wasted time.
- Delegate greater authority to the team.

Note: Some of the foregoing suggestions initially appeared in the excellent book by Deeprose, *How to Recognize and Reward Great Employees.*[4]

Think About It

Although there has been much disparaging commentary about teams and committees and other such collectives, few if any forces in business are as potentially creative and productive as a team of honest, fully participating individuals who are united in pursuit of a common objective.

Questions for Review and Discussion

1. What do you believe should be done concerning a team member who monopolizes every meeting? What if this monopolizer is the team leader?
2. Why is shared authority important to proper team functioning?
3. Fully explain why some conflict is essential to effective team problem solving.
4. Many times we have heard that "A camel is a horse designed by a committee." Why have so many committees and teams inspired such cynical descriptions?
5. What do you believe is the primary hazard or significant drawback of a permanent team?
6. What is the "situational leadership" mentioned in the discussion of leadership style? Explain.
7. If you have just inherited a team and must take over today as its leader, how would you go about quickly getting an understanding of the style of the previous leader?
8. How would you suggest that a generally well-functioning team handle a single nonproductive member?
9. What are two significant disadvantages of team action? How can these disadvantages be overcome?
10. What do you believe is meant by the claim that team power is based on credibility? How do a team and its leader go about acquiring this power?

Case: The Quiet Bunch

You learned during your first week on the job as the newly hired Admitting supervisor that each departmental supervisor was expected to lead one of the hospital's numerous quality improvement teams. It came as no surprise that the team to which you were assigned was the team your predecessor, the former Admitting supervisor, had served as leader. Your team, you soon learned, consisted of several of your department's people plus employees from a scattering of other departments.

As you held individual meetings to become acquainted with both your Admitting employees and other members of your team, you were quickly inundated with complaints and other indications of discontent from both Admitting employees and quality team members. There were vocal complaints about the way the department had been run and complaints about the "useless quality improvement team." From a couple of the employees who served both in Admitting and on the quality team you received complaints about "those who shall remain nameless" who regularly "carry tales to administration."

You listened to all the complaints. You detected some common themes in what you were hearing, leading you to believe that perhaps some misunderstandings could be cleared up if some of the issues could be aired openly with each concerned group. You scheduled two meetings, one for your Admitting staff and one for the quality improvement team. You felt encouraged because a number of individuals had told you they would be happy to speak up at such a meeting.

Your first meeting, held with the Admitting staff, was brief; nobody spoke up, even when urged to do so in the most nonthreatening way possible. Your subsequent meeting with the quality team was no better. You got zero discussion going with either group, although before and between the meetings you had been bombarded by complaints from individuals. This left you extremely frustrated because most of the complaints you heard were group issues, not individual problems.

Questions:

1. What can you do to get either or both groups to open up in a group setting about what is bothering them?
2. Can you suggest what might lie in the immediate past that could have rendered these employees unwilling to speak up?
3. Because you have two groups (with overlapping membership) to be concerned with, where would you initially concentrate your efforts?

4. What might you do concerning the charges that someone is "carrying tales to administration?"

Case: The Weekly Team Meeting

Fourteen people from perhaps seven departments make up the long-standing methods improvement team that you were assigned to take over as leader 3 months ago. It has been the practice to hold a meeting at 3:00 PM every second Wednesday, or perhaps we should say you *attempt* to hold it at 3:00 because about half of the team members are more than 5 minutes late, and two or three are usually late by 15 minutes or longer. You have found also that roughly half of the group have not completed assignments they were given at previous meetings.

You have made repeated announcements about being there on time, but to no avail. Come the alternate Wednesday at 3:00 PM, you usually find yourself and the same few punctual members present and waiting for the latecomers.

Questions:

1. What can you do to encourage punctuality at the team meetings?
2. How do you suggest addressing the problem presented by the team members who do not complete their assignments?

REFERENCES

1. Ricks, T.E. What we can learn from them: Lessons from Parris Island. *Parade Magazine* (November 9, 1997): 4–6.
2. Keye Productivity Center. 1991. *How to build a better work team*, 2d ed. Kansas City, MO: Keye Productivity Center, 3.
3. Blanchard, M., and Tager, M.A. 1985. *Working well: Managing for health and high performance*. New York: Simon & Schuster, 50.
4. Deeprose, D. 1994. *How to recognize and reward employees*. New York: AMACOM, 100.

RECOMMENDED READING AND LISTENING

D. Harrington-Mackin, *The Team Building Tool Kit*. (New York: AMACOM, 1994).

A.R. Montebello, *Work Teams That Work*. (Minneapolis, MN: Best Sellers Publishers, 1994).

M. Sanborn, *Team Building: How To Motivate and Manage People* (Boulder, CO: CareerTrack Publishers, 1989), 2 audiotapes.

W. Umiker, *The Empowered Laboratory Team: A Survival Kit for Supervisors, Team Leaders, and Team Professionals* (Chicago, IL: ASCP Press, 1997).

Chapter 10

Safety and Workplace Violence

During the 1990s almost two-thirds of non-fatal workplace assaults occurred in hospitals, nursing homes, and residential care facilities, and in most cases involved patients assaulting nurses.[1]

CHAPTER OBJECTIVES

- Convey an understanding of the apparent principal causes of violence in the health care workplace.
- Review the effects of workplace violence on victims.
- Review the laws and standards pertinent to violence in the workplace, and enumerate the responsibilities of management concerning the maintenance of a safe workplace.
- Outline the essential steps involved in instituting a violence-control program.
- Describe a number of actions the individual supervisor can take to reduce workplace violence.
- Provide guidance concerning the handling of certain violent or potentially violent incidents such as breaking up fights and reacting to bomb threats.

Violence in health care institutions is escalating, and it is not limited to emergency departments and psychiatric units. The leading cause of workplace-related deaths for women is violence. Although violence is more common in facilities located in high-crime areas, it has been steadily increasing in suburban and rural settings.

Employers and managers share responsibility for providing a work environment that minimizes the danger of injury. Medical costs and litigation expenses absorbed by medical institutions because of injuries to or caused by patients and others are considerable. Expenditures for security, Workers' Compensation, and legal services continue to escalate. The goal of management is to decrease the number of assaults and disruptive incidents that occur and to provide protection for all who work within, are served by, or visit the institution.

CAUSES OF VIOLENCE

In our multiracial, multiethnic society we face many situations from which violence may emerge. A list of common predisposing factors is provided in Exhibit 10–1. Exhibit 10–2 enumerates the characteristics of violence-prone individuals.

Violent incidents often involve disgruntled or vengeful employees or former employees. These incidents are frequently the result of real or perceived maltreatment or inept management of conflicts arising in the workplace. The addition

Exhibit 10–1 Factors Predisposing to Violence

Societal factors
- easy availability of weapons
- high crime rate in the community
- catastrophic life events (for example, illness, accident, or death of loved ones)
- distraught or vengeful spouses or other family members

Workplace situations
- layoffs, job outplacements, mergers, reengineering, affiliations, and alliances
- series of threats of violence or aggressive incidents
- jobs that involve handling money, drugs, or valuable property
- employees working alone, especially late at night
- assignments in emergency departments or psychiatric units
- frequent harassment by coworkers or superiors
- weapons brought to the work site
- interpersonal conflicts in the workplace
- chronic labor–management problems or disputes
- frequent grievances or stress-related Worker's Compensation claims filed by employees
- poorly lighted or inadequately monitored parking areas

Management deficiencies
- inept handling of work problems
- inconsistent, inequitable, or insensitive supervision
- failure to recognize and intervene early in the cycle of violence
- lack of responsiveness to the warning signs of a potentially violent situation
- authoritarian management
- lack of staff training in violence prevention

Exhibit 10–2 Characteristics of Violence-Prone Individuals

- History of drug or alcohol abuse
- Reputation as a loner
- Obsession with weapons
- Involvement with racist hate groups
- Tendency to frequently claim unjust treatment; files many grievances
- Does not tolerate criticism
- Low or nonexistent tolerance for frustration
- Dramatic change in personality, behavior, or performance
- History of violence toward animals, women, and others
- Pattern of verbal or physical aggression (threats, intimidation, verbal abuse)
- "Hair-trigger" temper: kicking vending machine, punching wall, throwing chairs, etc.
- Frequent disputes with superiors over policy violations
- Object of criticism or harassment from coworkers, whether real or perceived
- Mentally disturbed, especially paranoid individual who perceives injustice
- Projects responsibility for problems onto others
- Has made statements suggesting feelings of despair about personal or job-related matters
- Is experiencing heightened stress at work or at home
- Obsessive behavior toward coworkers (for example, holding a grudge or having a romantic obsession)

---

of just one more problem, even an apparently minor concern, may push a person over the edge into a violent reaction.

Investigations following violent incidents usually reveal that there were clearly visible warning signs that should have raised concern. Awareness of such signals is a key to violence prevention initiatives.

Overt threats of violence may be absent, but warning signs are usually present. Violence-prone individuals often express bizarre thoughts, fixation with weapons, romantic obsession, depression, or chemical dependence. Offenders may be involved in bitter, repetitive arguments or may issue frequent accusatory memoranda. They often cease to associate with coworkers and even their old friends.

The typical profile of a violence-prone employee is that of a male military veteran who has a quick temper or a short fuse. He suffers from low self-esteem, paranoia, or depression and is a loner who resents authority. He blames coworkers, management, or someone else for any problem that arises. There is often a history of drug or alcohol abuse, a record of criminal assault, or a fascination with weapons. The likelihood of his becoming violent accelerates if there is unresolved conflict and frustration at home or at work.

There are several common events that can predispose some individuals to violence. The person may have recently undergone counseling or have been subject to disciplinary action. He or she may have been passed over for promotion or have become very concerned about job security. Perhaps the individual encountered a series of stressful events or a single but significant emotional shock. There may be extreme frustration or an assault on self-esteem, for example, an employee's request for time off is abruptly denied or a customer is treated shabbily or inconsiderately. One may have been on the receiving end of harsh criticism, a verbal attack, or a threat of physical harm.

EFFECT OF VIOLENCE ON VICTIMS

Employers and managers must be continually sensitive to the effects of violence and the potential danger to their employees. Potential victims include internal customers (eg, caregivers and students) and external customers (eg, patients, physicians, visitors, and blood donors), to name but a few.

After a violent event, victims and their associates are generally less productive; some may become severely depressed and seek treatment for conditions such as anxiety, insomnia, or panic attacks. Family relationships may suffer, and some individuals may turn to alcohol or drugs. Victims may often express rage at employers or managers for failing to protect them. Injured employees may seek to recover lost wages and medical expenses through Worker's Compensation rather than by suing, although employees are protected by law from being discharged for suing their employers.[3]

LAWS AND STANDARDS RELATING TO WORKPLACE VIOLENCE

The Occupational Safety and Health Administration (OSHA) has long held that well-informed workers are less at risk than those who are unaware of the potential dangers. Unfortunately training is often the most overlooked part of compliance with OSHA standards. The general duty clause of the newer OSHA regulations includes many guidelines.[4]

When an employee injures another person, his or her employer may be liable under the doctrine of *respondent superior*. State and federal courts charge employers with the responsibility for ensuring a safe, nonviolent work environment. Simultaneously, employers must not violate the individual rights of employees. These rights include the right to privacy and the right to equal opportunity as provided by the (ADA).[5]

In 1995 the Joint Commission on Accreditation of Healthcare Organizations (JCAHO) added the requirement for all hospitals to conduct security assessments and provide personnel with training in the management of workplace violence.[6]

RESPONSIBILITIES OF MANAGEMENT

Employers must make every effort to avoid hiring individuals who pose risks to employees and customers. When an employer becomes aware of a dangerous employee, that employer has a duty to investigate, and sometimes discharge, the employee.

Although the expense of security measures can be considerable, the lack of such precautions can be considerably more costly. In addition to financial costs, there are many other consequences of frequent violent episodes. These additional consequences include a negative impact on employee attendance, morale, personnel retention, and recruitment.

Employees should be told whom to contact—preferably through a hotline—and be provided with a step-by-step protocol to follow in the event of real or perceived violent behavior or threats.

ESSENTIALS OF A VIOLENCE-CONTROL PROGRAM

Significant Policies

Employer responsibility requires policies, procedures, and protocols that foster workplace harmony and minimize the potential for violence. There must be vigorous implementation of these measures.

An effective initiative begins with a statement of zero tolerance for violence and harassment. This statement includes descriptions of prohibited behavior; for example, banning the use of controlled substances on the job and carrying weapons on the premises. The delineation of possible scenarios of workplace violence is highly recommended so that employees are familiar to some extent with what could play out in a violent situation.

Supervisors must understand the reasons behind any policies relating to violence control and respond effectively to situations that require intervention. Policies should cover the following essentials.

- Employee conduct as part of a formal performance evaluation
- Regulations concerning the use of alcohol and drugs
- When and how workplace searches for drugs or weapons are conducted
- Comprehensive procedures for disciplinary action up to and including termination of employment
- Accommodations for employees with mental impairments and other kinds of disabilities
- Proper means of restraining violent patients and others who may become violent

Improved Screening of Job Candidates

To help eliminate candidates who have histories of workplace violence or whose past behavior suggests the capacity for violence, the screening process may include preemployment psychological testing, background investigations, reference checks, and drug testing.

Preemployment psychological testing may be used at times and under certain circumstances or for candidates for jobs that are considered sensitive or highly responsible. However, there are various laws regulating this kind of testing, and the organization that uses such tests had best be prepared to prove that their tests are statistically validated as nondiscriminatory.

Background investigation, especially for criminal convictions, entail some expense, and in some places there are legal problems relating to privacy and confidentiality issues. Where permitted, however, these background checks can be useful. The individual who checks "no" to the question "Have you ever been convicted of a crime?" when this is not the case has committed an offense that the majority of organizations consider reason for termination: being untruthful on an employment application.

Through reference checks a previous employer has an obligation to inform a prospective employer of violent tendencies of the employee in question if there is a probability of recurrence. Should an employee cause harm to others and there is a history of violence or other major misconduct in the employee's past, the hiring employer could face a negligent hiring charge. To guard against such charges the employer should be in a position to demonstrate that the organization made a good-faith effort to check the references of every employee prior to hiring. This essentially means that a complete record of reference checks be retained for every employee, including—and we might even say especially including—records indicating which previous employers failed to respond to reference requests. For fear of legal entanglements some previous employers will withhold even information concerning severe misconduct; however, they need not fear repercussions if the inappropriate conduct is verifiable with accurate documentation.

Finally, preemployment drug testing has become a relatively common practice in the recruitment process for all levels of staff.

Education and Training of Supervisors and Workers

Supervisors and rank-and-file employees should become thoroughly familiar with the safety rules and procedures of the organization. The employer must

- train interviewers to recognize potential troublemakers during employment interviews,
- teach communication skills that help prevent aggression,

- teach managers and supervisors how to recognize the victims of domestic violence,
- describe how the organization's employee assistance program (EAP) or alternative employee support programs function, including when and how to refer employees and how to handle employees during and after treatment,
- provide periodic staff training and retraining in
  1. prevention and control of violence,
  2. how to recognize early warning signs of potential violence,
  3. conflict resolution and deescalation techniques,
  4. behavior modification,
  5. self-preservation techniques and how to protect bystanders, and
  6. use of telephone number *57 or an alternative system to trace phone calls from harassers or callers who report bomb threats.

Improved Communication

Management is expected to do the following.

- Determine the need for or effectiveness of safety improvement by gathering accurate baseline data, setting precise goals, providing ongoing feedback, and rewarding success.
- Establish a hotline and a confidential procedure for reporting threats, intimidation, belligerence, and other inappropriate workplace behavior. The hotline can also be used to allow disgruntled people to complain.
- Devise special forms and reporting mechanisms for violent incidents.
- Improve collaboration between the institution's security personnel and community law enforcement agencies, similar to working arrangements with fire departments.
- Hold crisis-aftermath sessions.

Modifying Environmental Factors Affecting Susceptibility to Violence

To enhance safety, management can do many things.

They can install bulletproof glass, metal detectors, alarm systems, surveillance cameras, and escape doors in high-risk areas such as the emergency department. They can improve lighting in parking areas and provide security escorts for departing employees. Security can also be provided for threatened individuals, especially for victims of domestic violence.

Identification badges that are easy to read are helpful, as is enforcing their usage, and identifying potentially violent or suicidal patients and flagging their charts is encouraged. When a bomb threat is received, law enforcement officials should be provided with a telephone system for their use.

Finally, improving the availability of EAPs or counseling referral procedures and the formation of violence-response teams to intervene in cases of violence or threats of violence is extremely helpful. In instances involving battered female employees, employers can provide photographs of the violent individuals to security officers, install panic buttons at employee workstations, and provide personal escorts between transportation/parking facilities and the workplace. EAPs should include therapists specially trained in the treatment of domestic violence victims.

SUPERVISORY PRINCIPLES FOR REDUCING WORKPLACE VIOLENCE

The following rules can help supervisors reduce workplace violence.

Avoid hiring problem people. Prior to interviewing job applicants, prepare a list of questions that elicit or can help reveal a tendency toward violence. Here are a few examples.

- What kinds of people do you find difficult to get along with? How do you manage to get along with these people?
- When was the last time you became angry at work? What caused it, and how did you react?
- What was the most difficult situation you faced at work? What feelings did you have, and how did you react to them?
- What kinds of behavior did your boss or fellow workers exhibit that you disliked?

Treat employees with dignity and respect. The administration and management of a health care institution should model behavior that encourages trust, helps open communication, and promotes loyalty.

Maintain open communication. Encourage people to say what is on their minds by using open-ended questions such as "Jess, what is it that's troubling you?" Listen and respond with empathy and sensitivity to employee concerns and grievances. Take the initiative and point out potential problems to superiors and recommend specific additional security measures. Participate in risk management programs, labor–management discussions, and safety committee meetings.

Educate your staff. Train people to recognize symptoms of potential violence, and encourage them to report threats or acts of violence. Assure them that their names will be kept confidential to prevent reprisals. Articulate your expectations of self-control on the job, and make certain that employees know what behavior you expect and what you will not tolerate.

Be alert for potential situational and behavioral problems. Effective personnel control requires cognizance of violence-prone profiles and alertness for internal or external factors that may be propelling an employee in the direction of inappropriate behavior. Be on the lookout for conflict over equipment, space, or services. Associates are usually the first to recognize that something is wrong, but they often find that management does not respond appropriately or promptly to these concerns. When this occurs, workers become frightened and anxious.

Enforce policies that address violence and its control. Violent outbursts can often be prevented when aggressive behavior elicits a quick and appropriate response at the time that behavior first emerges. When aggressive individuals note lack of workplace controls or consequences for their erratic behavior, the potential for unacceptable behavior escalates. Lack of controls or consequences include management denial that a problem exists, lack of investigation or follow-up of violent or potentially violent situations, failure to tell aggressive or threatening employees that they will be held responsible for any inappropriate behavior, and performance appraisals that do not reflect erratic behavior.

Sharpen counseling and disciplinary skills. Be consistent and fair in your disciplinary actions. Document counseling sessions, and follow up on them. Never meet alone with suspected dangerous employees. Do not try to psychoanalyze employees, but do use common sense, reason, and logic. Persuade people that it is to their benefit to resolve conflicts. Do not argue or get caught up in ping-pong repartee such as, "You will do as I say." "No, I won't." "Yes, you will." "No, I won't." Choose your words carefully during counseling sessions. Keep your comments and behavior neutral and nonjudgmental. Be sure the employee knows exactly what behavior you want changed. Avoid referring to yourself (as in, for example, "I think you should…" or "I'm going to recommend…"). This can trigger an explosion of pent-up rage, especially if you do not get along very well with the person. Instead, quote rules or standards (for example, "Hospital protocol is that you contact our EAP"). If the employee begins to lose control, terminate the meeting. If he or she refuses to leave your office, you can leave. Better still, hold such meetings somewhere other than in your office, say in the employee health area or in a readily accessible conference room.

Have the courage to get rid of troublemakers. If termination of employment is required, do it with empathy and compassion, but do it matter-of-factly. Do it in private unless violence is likely. If you feel violence is a real possibility, have someone from the security service nearby or at least on alert. This kind of termination must be done with the greatest of care. Follow mandated procedures to the letter, and thoroughly document each incident leading to the termination. Consult with your superiors or your human resources department at all stages. Firings often require legal advice, especially where possible violations of union contracts or antidiscrimination laws are concerned. Because a person whose employment has been terminated may exhibit aggressive behavior, security, or in some instances perhaps local law enforcement officers, should escort the employee off the premises.

BOMB THREATS

McNerney offers the following sage advice concerning telephoned bomb threats:

- Take every such threat seriously. Tune out all distractions and focus on the caller.
- Keep the caller on the line as long as possible so that the call can be traced. Tracer calls can be activated on most phones by punching *57.
- Collect as much information as possible. Ask where the bomb is, when it will explode, what it looks like, who and where the caller is, and why the bomb was planted.
- Take notes and ask the caller to repeat information.
- Note any unusual phrases used by the caller; this may help identify the caller.
- Listen for background noises such as cars or machinery; such sounds may help determine the origin of the call.[7]

BREAKING UP FIGHTS

Fights usually arise because of attempts to save face, or defend property or territory, or simply because of the propensity to fight of some individuals. The Crisis Prevention Institute recommends the following.

- Be familiar with the policies and procedures of your organization.
- Know your responsibilities and the extent of your authority.
- Consider the safety of everyone in the vicinity of the altercation.
- Be consistent in setting limits.
- Be alert to warning signs.
- Do not underestimate the strength of the combatants. Children, women, and even supposedly ill patients can inflict injuries. Some persons will exhibit surprising strength when angry.
- Obtain assistance in separating the combatants and removing noncombatants from the scene.
- Identify the aggressor.
- Report the incident with thorough documentation.
- As appropriate, bring the combatants back together to determine the cause of the conflict and to discuss the consequences of fighting.[8]

Think About It

The supervisor's primary defense against violence that comes from outside of the work group—whether from patients, visitors, or others—is vigilance and clear procedures for addressing violence when it occurs. But the supervisor's strongest means of preventing violence within the work group is fair, humane, compassionate leadership.

Questions for Review and Discussion
1. Do you believe that an employer served with a charge of negligent hiring might have recourse against the offending employee's former employer? Why might this be so?
2. Why is it important to hold crisis-aftermath sessions? What do we want to accomplish with such sessions?
3. What sort of answers or comments might you hear in an employment interview that might suggest the tendency of an applicant toward violence?
4. What do most of the potential causes of violent behavior have in common? Explain fully.
5. What can we see in the rules and regulations addressing workplace violence in health care organizations that reflects a perceived trend toward increased violence?
6. How much do you believe you may legally ask a job candidate about arrests and convictions?
7. Why might you encounter prohibitions against the use of preemployment psychological testing?
8. Why do you think that a significant proportion of potential perpetrators of workplace violence have in common low self-esteem?
9. In many organizations, carrying weapons or fighting are infractions calling for immediate termination. Why do you believe this is so, and do you agree or disagree with the practice?
10. Why has it become a practice following certain instances of violence to make counselors available even to people who were not directly involved in the violence?

Exercise: What About Lie Detectors?
Although relevant to violence as well as other workplace problems, this particular exercise is going to require a bit of simple research into material that lies outside this chapter.

Lie detectors—polygraphs—were formerly used by numerous employers in the screening of potential employees to assess their personal and employment histories for violent tendencies as well as for honesty. Some employers, usually small firms in which numerous employees handled cash and valuables on a regular basis, even engaged in random polygraph testing during employment.

In essay fashion, thoroughly explain why polygraphs are not ordinarily used today in the manner described in the preceding paragraph. Also, enumerate those instances in which it is probably appropriate to use polygraph testing.

Case: The Employee in the Corner

You are a supervisor in the housekeeping section of the facilities and maintenance department of County Hospital. Your daily activities include a walking tour of all of the sections of the facility within the responsibility of your team.

Early afternoon found you walking along a short third-floor corridor that connected the hospital's surgical wing with one of the larger medical/surgical patient units. It was at a time when about half of the staff assigned to the two areas were still at lunch, and the angled corridor was empty. Or at least it appeared empty until you rounded the bend at the middle of the corridor. You then saw two people at the very end of the corridor in a corner beside the closed double doors that led into the surgical wing.

You stopped in place when you saw the two people. They did not seem to be aware of your presence. At the distance you were from them you could tell that one was a woman. Although you did not recognize her, you could tell she was wearing a hospital uniform. She appeared to be pinned tightly into the corner by the other party, apparently male, whom you could see only from behind. He did not appear to be wearing hospital clothing.

As you hesitated before proceeding, you saw the man place his right forearm across the woman's throat. The woman struggled against the arm; you heard her curse and say, "No, leave me alone!" The man said something that you could not hear but his words apparently made the woman struggle harder.

Instructions:

1. Describe in detail what you would do in this situation. For each decision or action you mention, explain why you are taking this particular step. (It is permissible for you to make a few reasonable assumptions about you and your circumstances, as long as you explain these.)

REFERENCES

1. Group Insurance Agency, Inc., Healthcare Association of New York State. May 1997. *Preventing violence in the workplace*. Albany, NY: Author.
2. Bureau of Labor Statistics, US Department of Labor. 1994. A census of fatal occupational injuries. *News Bulletin 95-288*.
3. McCormick, K., and Stewart, J.D. 1996. Employers confront violence in the workplace of the '90s. *Medical Laboratory Observer* 28: 34–8.
4. Daugherty, D.A. 1996. *The new OSHA: Blueprints for effective training and written programs*. New York: American Management Association, 9–12.
5. McCormick and Stewart, "Employers confront violence," 34.
6. JCAHO. 1995. *Quality improvement standards*. Chicago, IL: JCAHO.
7. McNerney, J.D. 1995. Front-desk security. *HR Focus* 72:18.
8. National Crisis Prevention Institute. 1991. *Nonviolent crisis intervention*. Brookfield, WI: Author. Audiotapes.

RECOMMENDED READING AND LISTENING

M. Minor, *Preventing Workplace Violence*. (Menlo Park, CA: Crisp Publishers, 1995).

C. Tavris, *Controlling anger: How to Turn Anger into Positive Action*. (Boulder, CO: CareerTrack Publishers, 1989). Audiotapes.

M.H. Yarborough, "Responding to a Crisis," *HR Focus* 73, no. 2 (1996): 14.

PART II

Leading People

Chapter 11

Leaders and Managers

Leadership involves remembering past mistakes,
an analysis of today's achievements, and a
well-grounded imagination in visualizing the
problems of the future.

—Stanley C. Allyn

CHAPTER OBJECTIVES

- Explore the relationship between leadership and the culture of the organization in terms of how one has an influence in shaping the other.
- Describe the perceived differences between the popular conceptions of "leading" and "managing."
- Identify the principal characteristics defining the various styles of leadership.
- Identify several special leadership approaches that some leaders have incorporated into their approaches to managing people.
- Discuss some of the primary activities of leadership at the department level that are pursued in the process of getting things done through people.
- Examine in detail the characteristics of effective leaders applicable at all levels of organizational activity and in all organizational settings.
- Identify a number of the more common mistakes made by supervisors in attempting to fulfill their leadership responsibilities.

Leadership is not a process learned in seminars by remembering and following a specific number of steps. Rather, leadership is either intuitive or gained through experience. The best leaders strive to develop the leadership skills of their teammates so that the success of the team does not depend on a single person. Many organizations have failed because charismatic leaders did not develop new leaders, and when they were no longer around, their backups were unable to step up and perform as required.

True leaders can influence people over whom they have no formal authority. This is often referred to as "horizontal management," and it is the mark of a true leader. To meet today's interdepartmental needs for coordination and cooperation, health care managers must possess leadership ability.

The best leaders understand how their own prejudices influence the way they lead. Because they can confront their own prejudices and shortcomings, they can deal with those of others. They censure intolerance and ensure equality of opportunity. They pay special attention to people outside the mainstream culture, knowing that these people can easily feel isolated. They learn about the values and cultural heritage of others and become aware of the differences in communication styles and interpersonal relationships.[1]

> If you are a full-time manager, you are rewarded for what your employees do and for the responsibilities you fulfill, not for the tasks you perform personally.

ORGANIZATIONAL CULTURE

> ### Management Provides
>
> • mission statements (why we do what we do)
> • visions (what it will look like when we get where we want to go)
> • goals (so we know we have arrived)
> • strategies (the journey taken in getting there)
> • values (how we behave on the journey)

Leaders shape the culture of their organization, and to a considerable extent the culture shapes the leaders. Organizational culture can be defined as a "pattern of basic assumptions that has worked well enough to be considered valid and to be taught to new members as the correct way to perceive, think and feel in relation to coping with problems."[2] "A culture in which the leadership style of the manager features coercion and other direct power processes is less effective than a culture characterized by collaboration and participation."[3] In other words, organizational culture is simply the broad-based perception of the way things are done at work.

The health care culture of today demands pervasive and honest communication: openness and authentic interaction in all operations. This translates into the sharing of knowledge, skills, news, experiences, problems, and setbacks. The result is learning at all levels.

To foster a service-oriented culture, supervisors express values that are spin-offs from the mission statement. They put values into action by treating employees as they want customers to be treated. They get personally involved in service activities, and they use periodic meetings of their work groups to inspire and solve problems.

LEADING VS MANAGING

To address apparent differences between leading and managing it is necessary to get beyond dictionary definitions and examine popular perceptions. The definitions in any good dictionary tell us that leading and managing are essentially the same, often to the point of defining one in terms of the other. And any thesaurus we might care to open lists "leader" and "manager" as synonyms for each other. In terms of word meanings on paper, leader and manager are one. When we speak of differentiating between leader and manager, however, we are dealing not with word definitions but with human perceptions. A great many people perceive a difference between the two words, and in the mind of the perceiver, perception is reality.

Decide for yourself how much difference, if any, exists between the two terms. When you hear about leadership do you equate this with management? Or do you perceive a difference between the two, with leadership somehow the more acceptable, indeed the more desirable of the two? Popular perception generally holds that leadership is on a somewhat higher level than management, and it is this perceived difference on which most of what is said here about leadership is based.

The foregoing enables us to say that we have among us many good managers but that we often experience a shortage of good leaders. Business schools develop managers, not leaders, although, unfortunately, some schools readily attach the label of leader to their graduates. Perception, plus observation of such individuals in action, suggests the following differences between leading and managing.

- People obey managers because they must or they expect to; people follow leaders because they want to.
- Leaders envision (for example, Martin Luther King's "I Have a Dream"); managers marshal resources to achieve the visions of others.
- Leaders often rely on their intuition. Although some managers are intuitive, managers by and large rely more on analysis, objectivity, and rationality.
- Leaders generally demonstrate more self-confidence and are willing to take more and greater risks than managers.
- Leaders stress creativity; managers are more likely to stress conformity.
- Managers project power *over* people; leaders project power *with* people.
- Managers strive to satisfy the needs and wants of their customers; leaders endeavor to astonish customers by exceeding their wants and needs.
- The goals of managers usually arise from necessity; the goals of leaders are more likely to arise from desire.

- Managers are more like scientists (methodical, organized); leaders are more like artists (spontaneous, creative).
- Managers say, "I will support you;" leaders say, "Follow me."
- Managers are more concerned with the *how*; leaders are more concerned with the *what*.
- Managers seek obedience; leaders seek commitment.
- Managers control; leaders empower.
- Managers correct problems; leaders prevent problems.
- Managers learn how successful people do things and emulate them; leaders explore new paths.
- Managers may place primary emphasis on system, structure, and process; leaders are more likely to emphasize team building and personnel development.

There have been long-standing discussions concerning whether management is an art or a science; the conclusions drawn usually suggest that it is both art and science. We might further suggest that, if indeed there is a real fundamental difference between management and leadership, it is that management is more science than art while leadership is more art than science.

Certainly managers can be leaders as well. It is most likely that the very best managers are also excellent leaders.

BASIC LEADERSHIP STYLES

Clusters of particular leadership characteristics and behaviors have been described as leadership styles. Like clothing styles, leadership styles come and go; some even return for a while, and others prevail for a time and vanish, never to return.

Authoritarian Leadership

Leaders who use this style are often described as task oriented, paternalistic, or autocratic. They "run a tight ship," and they order or direct their employees. This style is also referred to as top-down or "I" (the leader comes first) management (also referred to as Theory X).

Authoritarian leaders believe that people must be controlled closely and provided with external motivation (for example, pay, benefits, and good working conditions). They are task oriented rather than people oriented. They tell employees what they want but do not necessarily tell them why. They do not invite input from their people and may in fact even discourage input. Autocratic leaders encourage dependency. Employees of authoritarian leaders often exhibit apathy or hostility.

A subset of the pure authoritarian style is the paternalistic approach. Paternalistic managers exhibit either the features of a kind, nurturing parent—call this the benevolent dictator—or those of a critical and oppressive parent or, if you will, a tyrant. A paternalistic approach is appropriate when one is dealing with emergencies in which one must instantly obey without questioning (for example, fire or disaster) and may at times be the best way to deal with inexperienced or insecure employees or hostile people who challenge authority.

"Micromanagement" is a form of authoritarian leadership. Despite nearly universal condemnation of the practice, many supervisors micromanage because they believe their employees are unable to function without them. They feel they must stay on top of things at all times to prevent mistakes or to make sure that the work gets done. They are certain that their staffers are incapable of making decisions. Some simply believe this is what managers are supposed to do. To be successful in the long run, however, these managers must learn to delegate authority and trust their employees.

Participative Leadership

Leaders who use this style are often referred to as people oriented. They run a "happy ship." This style is also described as bottom-up or "we" (all of us together) management (Theory Y).

Participative leaders believe that people want to work and are willing to assume responsibility. They believe that, if treated properly, people can be trusted and will put forth their best efforts. Participative leaders motivate by means of internal factors (for example, task satisfaction, self-esteem, recognition, and praise). They explain why things must be done, listen to what employees have to say, and respect their opinions. They delegate wisely and effectively.

There are several subsets of this style. When in a consultative mode, leaders seek input from their followers before making important decisions. When in a delegative mode, leaders share responsibility with their colleagues.

One simple way to learn whether participative management is in place is to keep track of the number of suggestions each employee makes annually. In many Japanese companies, where participative management flourishes, each employee submits dozens of ideas each year. Equally important is the percentage of suggestions that are acted on by management.

Participative managers can be counted on to articulate two magic phrases: "What do you think?" and "I need your help."

Theory Z Leadership

Unrelated to Theory X and Theory Y, Theory Z was labeled as such primarily to distinguish it from authoritarian leadership. Originated by the Japanese, Theory Z is characterized by employee participation and egalitarianism. It features guaranteed employment, maximum employee input, and strong reliance on team mechanisms such as quality circles.

Bureaucratic Leadership

Terms descriptive of this style include rules oriented, by-the-book management and "they" management (essentially impersonal).

Bureaucratic managers act as monitors or police. They enforce policies, rules, procedures, and orders from upper management. They tend to be buck-passers who take little or no responsibility for directives and who often experience near-paralysis of thought and action when encountering a situation for which no rule exists.

For the most part bureaucrats do not see themselves as bureaucrats. The very term bureaucrat conveys a negative connotation, and few if any people will consciously label themselves that way. Nevertheless, bureaucrats exist in some places in large numbers, and they often play negative, self-serving political games. They advance in stable or static organizations by not making mistakes, reducing risk taking, and blaming others. Government agencies and military services tend to house many bureaucrats, as do occasional other organizations such as major not-for-profits in which employees have found the maximum likelihood of continued employment and minimum likelihood of significant change.

True leadership is incompatible with the stifling character of bureaucracy. However, a bureaucratic style may sometimes be suitable for operations in which tasks must always be performed in the same way (for example, sorting mail or typing reports).

Situational Leadership

Terms used to describe this style include contingency based, flexible, adaptive, and "different strokes for different folks" leadership.

As the name suggests, flexible leaders adapt their approach to specific situations and to the particular needs of different members of the team. As employees gain experience and confidence, the leadership style changes from highly directive to supportive (from task related to people related). For example, two new employees may start work on the same date. If one has had previous experience and the other has had none, different directive styles are needed. A show-and-tell approach is required by the novice, but the same may not be appropriate for the experienced person.

A practical guideline is to consider a consultative or delegative style in reference to areas of expertise and to provide specific direction in areas of weakness. Some managers, in an effort to always be participative, fail to be directive when direction is needed.

Laissez-Faire Leadership

This kind of leadership is described as hands off, fence-straddling, absentee, *Catch-22*, and "not me" management.

Laissez-faire managers avoid giving orders, solving problems, or making decisions. They are physically evasive and are sometimes nowhere to be found when needed. Verbally, they are often masters of double-talk.

A positive form of laissez-faire leadership is the democratic style. Presently in vogue, it features self-directed (autonomous) teams in which leadership is delegated to highly trained work groups. The members of these teams know more about the organization and are better trained, more motivated, and more productive than their counterparts in traditional settings. They solve problems, redesign work processes, set standards and goals, select and monitor new employees, and evaluate team and individual performance.

Clearly this hands-off style of leadership can work extremely well if sufficient leadership has been involved in building the teams and seeing that they are properly charged and appropriately oriented. However, this can also be the refuge of the lazy or incompetent manager who is self-deluded into believing that he or she is backed by strong self-directed teams when this is nowhere near the case.

LEADERSHIP APPROACHES: SPECIAL VARIATIONS

Manipulation

Unfortunately, organizational management includes its share of manipulators. Manipulative managers get people to do their bidding by

- intimidating them, in effect making them fearful of the consequences of not complying,
- engaging in emotionalism: using anger, tears, yelling, or playing to seek sympathy,
- making people feel guilty if they do not immediately do what is wanted of them,
- implying the employees owe them something for past favors, and
- name dropping; for example, "The Director will be very unhappy if this isn't resolved right away" (more or less intimidation-by-proxy).

Management by Crisis

Management by crisis is also referred to as "fire-fighting management," and it is always easy to recognize the people who use this approach. They are surrounded by noise, confusion, and emotional upheavals. Every day is characterized by a series of crises for them. They complain that they cannot get things done because they are too busy putting out fires. They react rather than anticipate; they solve problems instead of preventing them. Their behavior suggests that planning is a concept completely foreign to them. Everything they do is reactive; they are never proactive.

Management by Exception

Managers who have adopted the practice of managing by exception act as facilitators, supporters, and resource people. Their message is "I do not interfere as long as your actions and results remain within broad limits of acceptable performance. Come to me with problems you can't solve or when you need something I can get you." Management by exception is appropriate when leading certain categories of professionals or specialists.

Management by Objectives

Management by objectives (MBO) is considered by many to have been one of the management "flavors of the month," ideas that enjoy immense popularity for a while and then fade away. This particular approach probably remained popular longer than most other special management approaches. Throughout the 1960s and beyond many firms established MBO programs. True, it has lost much of its popularity, but a number of its basic features remain useful. For example, when you are reviewing the performance of an employee, one helpful way to focus on the future is to do so in terms of future performance objectives.

Management by Wandering Around

This particular informal practice discussed in detail in Chapter 12, involves little more than its name implies. At its heart, however, is something of great importance to managers at all levels: visibility. A manager who is "out there" to see and be seen accomplishes much more than the manager who never leaves the office.

CONTEMPORARY LEADERSHIP ACTIVITIES

Leadership has evolved over the ages, and at different periods of time the emphasis has been on different leadership activities. The needs of the times influence the activities in which the leaders of any era are engaged. For example, given the state of health care today, today's leaders are more likely to be concerned with matters of productivity and cost containment than were the leaders of 30 or 40 years ago. For the most part, contemporary leaders are deeply involved in the following activities.

- Team building and group problem solving
- Cross-training for efficiency and flexibility
- Employee empowerment
- Improved quality and customer service
- Cost cutting
- Managing change (new services, products, or facilities)
- Staff reductions or other personnel rearrangements
- Decentralizing activities or establishing satellite activities
- Worker safety and health programs
- Environmental preservation
- Patient home care
- Point-of-care services (for example, expanded bedside services)

FOUNDATION OF LEADERSHIP

One prominent feature of a well-led workforce is the absence of cynicism. Cynicism disappears when employees respect their leaders. They respect their leaders because they perceive them as competent, caring, truthful, and ethical. Those leaders "walk the talk." Their behavior matches their words, and it features integrity and trust. Trust has two parts: being trusting (that is, displaying the ability to believe in others) and being trustworthy (that is, fully deserving others' belief in them). Leadership in its strongest form is leadership by example. Leading is not only walking the talk, it is also talking the walk. Talking the walk is explaining to your employees why you are taking or rejecting certain actions. Your employees must respect what you do and understand why you are doing it. If you achieve that with your employees, you will succeed as a leader.

CHARACTERISTICS OF EFFECTIVE LEADERS

Leaders must be walking mission statements who make their visions come alive by talking about them with enthusiasm and conviction. They must express themselves in attitudes and actions more than in words. Enthusiasm is almost magical; it is a positive and optimistic mindset that generates energy, enhances creativity, builds networks, and attracts other winners. It is especially necessary for the supervisory functions of motivation, communication, delegation, and problem solving.

No matter how you feel, start the day with a burst of enthusiasm. ("Fake it 'til you make it.") Throughout the day, feed positive thoughts into your subconscious mind by saying positive things about your performance. Surround yourself with other optimistic doers. Shun the complaining observers. If you hang around with turkeys, you will never soar with the eagles. Use success imagery; that is, visualize good outcomes in whatever you do. Recharge your energy by relaxing or meditating, especially after setbacks.

Good team leaders use both the helicopter approach and the management-by-wandering-around (MBWA) approach. Like helicopters, they hover over the work area where they can view the total operation. When they spot trouble, they descend for a closer look or to get involved. In the proactive MBWA process, leaders do not wait for people to bring problems into their offices. Instead, they make frequent visits to each workstation. Here they spot potential problems and ask for suggestions. They also seek ideas from vendors and customers.

As will be evident from the following lists, there are a number of factors that figure in the characteristics of an effective leader. It should perhaps be conceded at the outset that only rarely will a particular leader possess every last one of the following characteristics. It is, in fact, possible to point to any number of apparently successful leaders who are clearly lacking several of what we might consider essential characteristics. However, every leader who has succeeded in the job has enjoyed one significant advantage: the followers accepted that person's leadership.

Important Characteristics of Effective Team Leaders

Effective team leaders are competent.

- They possess both professional and team leadership skills, recognizing that the leader must be proficient in both sides of the role.
- People look up to them and respect their expertise.
- Their opinions and advice are sought after by associates both inside and outside their departments.
- They are asked to serve on important committees.
- They work to constantly improve their professional and leadership capabilities.
- They can answer most questions, and when they cannot answer they know where to get the answers.
- They cooperate fully with their counterparts in other departments.

They are emotionally stable.

- They exhibit a relaxed leadership style.
- They remain cool and calm under trying circumstances.
- They handle stress well.
- When they get upset with people, they focus on behavior, not on personalities or individual traits.

They get the job done.

- They provide a sense of direction and set high expectations and standards.
- They expect and demand good performance.
- They are well organized and always prepared.
- They are proactive; they anticipate and prepare for change.
- They focus on important matters; they do not nitpick.
- They place the right people in the right jobs.
- They do not waste their time or that of their followers.
- They stimulate innovativeness and invite ideas.
- They provide all the resources their teams need.
- They get rid of the deadwood.

They are effective communicators.

- They use memos, meetings, and other communication channels effectively.
- They provide clear instructions and request feedback to make sure that their directions are understood.
- They are articulate and persuasive, but they do not manipulate people.
- They are excellent listeners and are easy to talk with.
- They share information but do not repeat gossip.
- They do not withhold bad news, but they deliver it with consideration.
- They are effective teachers.
- They provide feedback, both positive and negative, as needed.
- They criticize behavior, not people or personalities.
- They are quick to praise and to give credit. They praise in public and criticize in private.
- They acknowledge their own mistakes and make sure they learn from them.
- They always seem to know what's going on.

They are unafraid.

- They thrive on responsibility.
- They take risks, and they bend rules when doing so makes sense.
- They are innovative and flexible.
- They chalk up failures to experience.
- They keep their fears to themselves.
- They encourage creativity and risk taking.
- They accept responsibility for failures.

They are credible.

- They are dedicated to telling the truth.
- They carry out their promises and fulfill their commitments.

- They admit their mistakes.
- They do not take credit for the ideas of others.
- They do not play favorites, and their credibility is above reproach.

They develop committed followers.

- They care about their followers, and they show it.
- They are willing to roll up their sleeves and help out when necessary.
- They go to bat for their people.
- They empower employees and encourage autonomy and self-reliance.
- They provide their people with whatever they need to get their work done.
- They allow people freedom in how the work is done, but they insist on getting the results they expected.
- They do not play favorites.
- They are fully as attentive to people below them as to those above them in the organization, perhaps even more so.
- They invite and respect the opinions and suggestions of all their employees.
- They provide opportunities for employees to use newly learned skills or previously untapped skills.
- They encourage and support suggestions, comments, and proposals from all management levels.
- They articulate what they value and back this up with their everyday behavior.
- They reward cooperation as highly as they reward individual achievement.
- They are helpful and anticipate the needs and problems of their team members.
- They defend their people from outside harassment.

They exhibit charisma.

- They maintain a childlike fascination with things and people.
- They make it a point to catch people doing something right . . . and tell them so.
- They hold a warm handshake and smile for a few seconds longer than the other person.
- They use the other person's name often during conversation.
- They project energy and enthusiasm.
- They are good role models.

COMMON SUPERVISORY MISTAKES

Everyone makes mistakes. To do so is human nature. But when someone in a leadership capacity makes a mistake the effect is frequently multiplied through the leader's area of responsibility. A mistake by a supervisor is often visible throughout the immediate work group and beyond. Supervisory errors diminish the effectiveness of the supervisor and, even more so, often negatively affect the effectiveness of the group. Here are some of the more common mistakes made by supervisors.

- They pass the buck and try to avoid accepting accountability, which is directly contrary to what is expected of a supervisor.
- They fail to delegate properly and empower their employees, leaving themselves open to overwork, criticism, and burnout while the employees go unchallenged.
- They take the narrow view of customer service and ignore their internal customers.
- They pay inadequate attention to budgetary concerns and fail to control costs.
- They associate with losers, mindless of the effect on their credibility.
- They use a cookie-cutter approach to managing, as though every problem was solvable by formula.
- They seek to be liked by all instead of seeking respect.
- They tolerate incompetence and fail to set performance standards.
- They neglect their own training and career development as well as the training and development of their employees.
- They recognize and reward only their top performers.

The 12 Commandments of Leadership

1. Know what you want.
2. Take control of your career.
3. Believe in yourself.
4. Go for the goal.
5. Enjoy the game.
6. Be capable.
7. Let your expertise show.
8. Rely on others.
9. Look for opportunities.
10. Learn the ropes.
11. Never stop networking.
12. Get a mentor.

Think About It

As for the best leaders, the people do not notice their existence. The next best, the people honor and praise. The next the people fear; and the next, the people hate. When the best leader's work is done, the people say, "We did it ourselves!"—Lao-tzu

Questions for Review and Discussion

1. Explain what is meant by the following statement: "Leadership cannot be taught, but it can be learned."
2. How is it that true leaders can often influence people over whom they have no formal authority?

3. How does a successful, well-functioning, self-directed, leaderless team get to be that way? Does it *ever* need a leader once it achieves that state?
4. A portion of the chapter addressed perceived differences between the terms "manager" and "leader." What, if any, do you believe are the differences between "manager" and "boss"?
5. Under what kind of leadership would an organization be least likely to change? Why do you believe this is so?
6. The quotation from Lao-tzu cited earlier states that "When the best leader's work is done, the people say, 'We did it ourselves!'" Do you agree with this? Why or why not?
7. Why is failure to delegate thoroughly and properly of particular importance to a group's leader? Provide several possible reasons.
8. As a supervisor, what do you believe you would have to do to become comfortable with managing by exception?
9. Why do you believe teams and team building have enjoyed such increasing popularity in recent years?
10. Why do we claim that leading by example is extremely important? What are some of the problems that can arise when we fail to do so?

Exercise: Examining the Micromanager

Surely most, if not all, readers of these pages are familiar with the term micromanagement. Perhaps some have found themselves in circumstances in which they have been micromanaged and thus will have gained some firsthand understanding of it. Micromanagers often give employees the distinct impression that they do not trust them or think them capable of correctly fulfilling their responsibilities on their own.

In essay form, explain in detail why you believe micromanagers behave as they do and why supervisors who attempt to lead by micromanaging employees are destined for failure in the long run.

Case: That's Her Responsibility, Not Mine

Susan Wilson is the administrative supervisor of Diagnostic Imaging (formerly the radiology department) at Central Hospital. Supervising in an expanding department and coping with steadily increasing outpatient activity, she found her workload increasing to the extent that she felt help was required with some of her duties. Taking a hard look at tasks that she could legitimately delegate, that is, tasks that did not requires supervisory authority, she settled on her monthly statistical report. The report itself was fairly easy to create, but gathering the necessary data consumed a fair amount of time.

She selected employee George Peters to do the report and provided him with all necessary instructions, even to the point of creating a detailed written procedure. She felt that George was capable of doing a thorough job; he had sufficient time available to incorporate the report into his workload, and she further thought that George might appreciate some variety in his work. George expressed no feelings for or against doing the report.

A few days after assigning the report Susan discovered that the current report had not yet been started and that if it were not completed at once it would be late. Susan reminded George; his reply was that other necessary work was delaying the data collection. Susan emphasized the need to get the report done on time, but George seemed in no particular hurry to get into the task.

The following day Susan accidentally overheard a portion of a conversation between George and another employee to whom George was saying: "her lousy statistics. I think she should keep doing it herself. After all, that report's her responsibility, not mine."

Instructions:

1. Identify and describe any actions Susan might have taken incorrectly in delegating the statistical report to George.
2. Decide what, if anything, Susan can do to try to correct the attitude revealed by George in his comments to the other employee.

REFERENCES

1. Rosen, R.H. 1996. *Leading people.* New York: Viking Press, 207, 213.
2. Schein, E. 1990. Organizational culture. *American Psychologist* 45: 109–119.
3. Young, J.A., and Smith, B. 1988. Organizational change and the hr professional. *Personnel* 65: 44.

RECOMMENDED READING

K. Blanchard and S. Johnson, *The One-Minute Manager.* (New York: Berkeley Publishers, 1982).
K. Blanchard and R. Lorber, *Putting the One-Minute Manager to Work.* (New York: William Morrow and Company, 1984).
T. Kent et al., "Leadership in the Formation of New Health Care Environment," *Health Care Supervisor* 15, no. 2 (1996): 27–34.
R.S. Kindler, *Managing the Technical Professional.* (Menlo Park, CA: Crisp Publishers, 1993).
R.H. Rosen, *Leading People.* (New York: Viking Press, 1996).
S.A. Stumpf, "Strategic Management Skills: What They Are and Why They Are Needed," *Clinical Laboratory Management Review* 10, no. 3 (1996): 231–44.

Chapter 12

Coaching

*People have a way of becoming what you
encourage them to be—not what you nag them to be.*

—Scudder N. Parker

CHAPTER OBJECTIVES

- Explore the role of the supervisor as coach and examine the characteristics of an effective coach.
- Identify coaching as an integral part of the daily activities of a supervisor.
- Enumerate the principal reasons behind poor employee performance and describe the role that coaching has in improving performance.
- Expand on the concept of "management by wandering around" as introduced in the previous chapter.
- Describe the role of the supervisor in enhancing employee self-sufficiency through effective coaching.
- Address the supervisor's follow-up in the aftermath of coaching with particular emphasis on dispensing praise and delivering constructive criticism and, in general, providing constructive feedback to employees.
- Identify the pitfalls occasionally encountered by the supervisor as coach.

Coaching is the ongoing process of helping people fulfill their responsibilities and achieve results. It is an integral part of face-to-face leadership. Zemke, a keen observer and prolific author, crystallizes coaching wisdom as follows: "Select the right players, inspire them to win, and show them you care. Tell them where they stand, how much they are improving, and what they could do to improve more."[1]

Coaching goes beyond the activities of instruction. Coaches deal not only with task outcomes but also with attitudes, morale, discipline, ethics, and career development. The effective coach is instructor, cheerleader, counselor, disciplinarian, evaluator, resource person, and troubleshooter.

Coaches are expected to clarify management's expectations of employee performance, modify inappropriate attitudes, instill self-sufficiency, and enhance competencies. Coaches shape values, remove obstacles, build on employees' strengths, stretch worker skills, and build interpersonal relationships.

CHARACTERISTICS OF EFFECTIVE COACHES

Effective coaches are dedicated, enthusiastic leaders who are technically or professionally competent. They push or pull people to their level of capability but not to a level of discouragement.

The organizational goal of every coach is to get work completed on schedule, ensure quality of service outcomes, and satisfy customers. Personnel goals are to get substandard performers up to speed and help the other employees achieve self-fulfillment. Skilled coaches

- exhibit the leadership traits presented in the previous chapter,
- keep workers informed, letting them know what is going on,
- show workers how to get the job done,
- help workers who have problems,
- listen—*really* listen—to the employees,
- direct their negative feedback at performance and results, not people,
- are quick to praise and do so in public,
- set a good example, at all times modeling appropriate behavior,
- provide psychological support,
- pitch in and help with routine work during emergencies and when there is a shortage of staff, and
- are technically or professionally competent in their primary fields of expertise.

Role of the Coach in Improving Performance

There are a number of commonly encountered reasons behind poor employee performance. Some of the more prominent reasons, and the response of the coach to them, are briefly described here.

First, and probably foremost, *employees do not know what is expected of them.* Everyone working at every level must know what is expected in order to perform capably; coaches tell them, coaches remind them, coaches clarify management's expectations of them.

Often, *employees do not know how to do what is expected of them.* Coaches show them how and help them learn.

Sometimes *employees do not know their performance is substandard.* Coaches inform them of this and show them how to achieve standard performance. Also, in some cases, *employees could do better if they tried harder.* Coaches motivate them, encourage them, and cheer them on.

When *employees face obstacles that hinder performance,* coaches remove the obstacles and show them how to clear the barriers that arise in their path.

Employees get discouraged. When this happens, coaches support and encourage them.

Sometimes, *employees feel that their work goes unnoticed or unappreciated.* Coaches are the first to praise, and coaches ensure that others are aware of work well done.

Coaching is an integral part of the daily activity of every supervisor. Coaching begins when a new employee reports to the department for the first time. It begins with orientation and training. From this beginning forward, supervisors coach when someone asks for advice or help, needs assistance, or steps out of line. The more time coaches spend listening to their people and observing what those people are doing, the more opportunities they find to coach. These remarks provide a natural transition into a discussion of management by wandering around (MBWA).

MANAGEMENT BY WANDERING AROUND

One of Tom Peters' appealing contributions is his concept of MBWA. The wandering he espouses includes frequent contacts with people outside of one's own department, for example customers and suppliers, but we will limit this discussion to departmental worksite wandering. Following are the principal features of MBWA offered by Peters and Austin.[2]

- MBWA is meeting people in *their* offices or work areas rather than in yours; it's getting out and visiting.
- MBWA is listening much more than talking.
- MBWA is asking whether employees are having any problems and, if so, offering to help.
- MBWA is asking employees and others for advice and opinions.
- MBWA is catching people doing something right and saying so, not catching them doing something wrong.
- MBWA is carrying a little black book to write down employees' suggestions for improving customer service and to note meritorious performance.
- MBWA is spotting activities, facilities, and problems that need fixing.
- MBWA is calling employees by their names and asking about their families or special interests.

- MBWA, when successful, reduces the number of needed memos and eliminates unnecessary meetings.

As with any particular management strategy, MBWA must be practiced properly to be effective. There are potential problems.

- MBWA can backfire if the "wanderers" are perceived by their staffs as spies, inspectors, critics, or interrupters.
- MBWA is not rambling around smiling and waving or saying, "How are you doing?"
- MBWA does not consist of nitpicking, intruding on peoples' work time for no apparent valid reason, or spreading gossip.

When you supervise people who require a great deal of support, make your visits at the same time each day so they know when to expect you. If some of your people are often not where they should be, vary the times at which you make your rounds.

ENHANCING EMPLOYEE SELF-SUFFICIENCY

Do not overdo the helping-hand role by allowing employees to take advantage of your assistance. For example, consider a nurse who is having a problem hooking up an orthopedic traction setup. Say the nurse calls for help, but instead of staying to watch how the specialist arranges all the ropes and pulleys, the nurse slips off for coffee. The specialist, usually the supervisor, should see that the employee stays at hand and uses the set-up process as a training demonstration.

Do not let employees transfer all of their little problems to you. New supervisors must learn when and when not to solve other people's problems for them. You do not want to be a "Teflon manager" from whom all the cries for help slide off. Neither do you want to be a "Velcro manager" and let all the problems of other people stick to you.

Insist on completed staff work. This term simply means that when employees come to a supervisor with a problem, they must also bring ideas for solving the problem. Once people become aware of this expectation, they will bring you fewer problems, and when they do bring in the problems and their proposed solutions, you may find that their ideas are better than yours.

Do not overdo advising. Try asking first. When someone wants an opinion, respond with "What do you think?" instead of an immediate "Here's what you should do." Finding a solution may take longer this way, but doing so pays off in the long haul.[3]

Encourage people to take small career risks. When they make bad decisions, as we all do from time to time, or fail to pick the best solution, do not punish them for their mistakes. Regard their errors as learning experiences. However, do not tolerate repetition of the same mistakes.

Insist that employees do what they say they will do. Ask for definite commitments. Set deadlines, and, when appropriate, get them in writing.

DEFENDING, FACILITATING, EMPOWERING, AND SUPPORTING

Employees of effective leaders see their coaches as defenders who protect them from outside harassment. A major source of frustration for employees is being attacked by people against whom they are powerless. Coaches are the defenders against such hostility. Baseball managers know the importance of this. To prevent their players from getting thrown out of a game, they rush out on the field to protest an umpire's call, at times even when they know that the call was correct.

Coaches are facilitators who get their teams the personnel, time, and other resources needed to function effectively. At times, supervisors must go to the mat with suppliers or people in other departments to demand that some action be taken.

Coaches empower their staffs and strip away red tape to enable the workers to make decisions and solve customer or operational problems. Simply being authorized to answer customer questions is appreciated by rank-and-file employees.

Coaches should not be afraid of rolling up their sleeves and pitching in to help occasionally. Support also involves providing user-friendly policies, instruments, and procedures and showing respect, fairness, and trust. It is giving a great deal as well as expecting much. It is being available and visible. It is ensuring employee safety and wellness and fighting for employees' rights, benefits, and rewards.

COACHING FEEDBACK

According to the contingency theory of reinforcement, behavior reinforced by positive consequences improves. Behavior that begets negative consequences or is ignored diminishes. We violate this every time we overload our reliable performers and reduce the workload of our goof-offs. We neglect this theory of reinforcement when we fail to provide both positive and negative feedback.

Failure to deliver praise when it is deserved is to overlook one of the most powerful motivators. A simple comment such as "I knew you could do a bang-up job on that important project; I was right" makes even an experienced veteran happy and proud. But delivering undeserved praise consistently reduces the power of positive feedback and makes recipients feel they are being manipulated.

What To Praise

Always praise performance that goes above and beyond the call of duty, performing helpful actions that are not always expected or not usually part of one's regular job. Praise is deserved by the person who

- willingly works extra-long hours,
- substitutes for an absent colleague,
- returns to work after regular hours,
- submits a report ahead of schedule or gets a rush report in on time,
- reports a problem and suggests several good solutions,
- handles a delicate situation diplomatically,
- earns accolades for his or her work unit, or
- receives special awards, achieves an outstanding educational record, or earns an advanced degree.

Praise is also appropriate for performance that may not be outstanding but is consistently acceptable. Praise the person who

- can always be relied on,
- has a good attendance record and is rarely tardy,
- is flexible and willing to adjust to changes, or
- who consistently meets job standards and work objectives.

Also deserving of praise is someone whose substandard performance is improving, even though it may not yet be up to your expectations. So are innovative ideas brought forth by any employee.

Given all that is known about the power of praise, it is surprising to frequently encounter supervisors who say they seldom dispense praise because their people are doing only what they are supposed to do. It would not be surprising, however, to discover that these are the supervisors whose departments experience the highest turnover rates and the poorest productivity.

When Not To Praise

- Do not hand out praise when it is clearly insincere or represents only flattery. Not only is it bad form from a supervisory point of view, employees can usually see through hollow praise in an instant.
- Do not praise when it is not earned. To do so is to diminish the value of all earned praise you might dispense.
- Do not praise when doing so might embarrass you, the recipient, or others.
- Do not dispense praise before you are certain who has really earned it.

Praise Should Not Be Delayed

Praise, much like criticism, is time sensitive. The longer it is delayed after the behavior has occurred, the weaker and less relevant it becomes. If you delay praise, you might forget to deliver it altogether.

If praise is delayed, the recipient is more likely to think that what he or she did is not particularly important or, even worse, might think that you were ignoring praiseworthy performance.

Also, when praise is delayed recipient may be confused about what behavior is being rewarded.

Why Praise Should Be Specific

Recipients should know exactly what it was they did that was appreciated. Misunderstandings are prevented, and the behavior in question is reinforced.

Praise is more believable when it is clearly related to a specific occurrence or result. Also, it is important to avoid conveying the impression that you like absolutely everything the person has been doing, and when your praise is specific, employees know that you know what is going on. Nonspecific praise dilutes the impact of the behavior; specific praise reinforces the particular behavior. It is inappropriately nonspecific to say, for example, "You did a great job last night." But there is strength in specific praise such as "You did a great job of getting that emotional parent calmed down last night."

How To Praise

We have already mentioned that praise should be delivered as soon as possible after the deed, that it should be specific, and that the right person or persons should receive it. The famous 1-minute praisings of Blanchard and Johnson enhance praise by including comments about how the praiseworthy event made you, the coach, feel.[4] These authors also recommend that you pause for a moment after delivering the praise to emphasize its importance. Then shake hands or touch the person to show your support.

Phraseology, such as "great job" or "wow," is important, but the accompanying vocal tone, facial expression, and body language are even more important.

There are sometimes exceptions to the old rule "praise in public." Some people are embarrassed when praised in front of their peers. They may be subjected to harassment from some coworkers, and you may be deemed guilty of showing favoritism. Praise these people privately or in writing. Some supervisors write brief thank-you notes on sticky notes and put them on the outside of people's doors or at their workstations. Do not be surprised when the recipients of these notes leave them on their door for several days.

A thank-you note or memo with copies to the personnel department or to upper management amplifies the effects of a verbal compliment. In selected instances of outstanding accomplishment, get your boss to send a congratulatory note to the person or make a special visit to your unit to thank the employee personally.

Consider submitting a report to the editor of your organization's newsletter or a local newspaper. Put a notice on the bulletin board.

There are very few exceptions to the second part of that old rule: "criticize in private." Under rare circumstances it can be appropriate to air criticism of an employee with others. Say, for example, a glib chronic offender leaves your office after being reprimanded but boasts to coworkers that he was in your office helping you out of a jam. Next time, have a representative witness or two from the group; the offender's behavior will change quickly.

There are other times when witnesses are required. If you are being subjected to sexual harassment, for example, voicing your objections in public is the intelligent thing to do so that you will not stand alone when the allegations are investigated.

How People React To Negative Feedback

Nobody is fond of receiving criticism because it attacks self esteem. Although many will say they welcome constructive criticism, this is not strictly true for most people; criticism, even constructive, still has something of a sting to it. How we react to criticism depends largely on a number of things.

- Who is delivering the criticism
- How legitimate we believe the criticism to be
- Who else hears it
- How fragile our sense of self-worth is
- How high our stress level is at that moment

People may react defensively, counterattack, flee, or become emotional. They may respond by looking for shortcomings in the critic or weaknesses in the criticism itself, or they may reluctantly accept the reprimand and promise to improve. But they may instead try to blame others or strive to change the subject.

How To Criticize While Preserving Self-Esteem

When supervisors encounter employee mistakes, they usually respond in one of four ways.

1. They ignore the situation and hope that someone else will correct it or that the employee will somehow realize it is wrong and correct it without being told.
2. They point out the mistake and ask the person to correct it.
3. They use an indirect approach by asking how things are going, hoping the employee will admit to making the error. If not, they then call attention to it.
4. They use the enhancing-value technique. This technique starts with saying something nice about what the person does and then making specific sug-

gestions for improvement. The basis for this approach is to make the person feel that you are there to help, not to judge or demean. To offer a good example: "Ruth, your report is always on time and I appreciate that. Now, let's try to eliminate those typos, OK?"

If you follow the foregoing statement with another positive statement, such as "I know that I can rely on you to take care of this" or "You're too good an employee to make mistakes like this," you have just used the "sandwich technique." The sandwich technique consists of two slices of praise with a reprimand in between.

Providing Appropriate Constructive Feedback

- Remember always that your goal is to alter behavior, not to castigate.
- Maintain a high ratio of praise to criticism. Aim for about a 4-to-1 ratio; it ordinarily takes at least four positive strokes to neutralize one negative stroke.
- Attack behavior, never personality or character traits. For example, instead of saying "You're too careless," describe what the person is doing or not doing that provoked your criticism.
- Provide feedback as soon as possible after the act but not before you have all the necessary information.
- Avoid critical comments when either you or the employee is emotionally upset. A good rule to remember is never criticize in anger.
- Use "I," not "you," language. For example, instead of saying "You have a bad habit of . . . ," say "I get upset when people . . . " This is less of a blow to one's ego and is less likely to evoke defensiveness.
- Avoid subjective terms such as attitude, work ethic, and professionalism. If you feel that you must use such words, make certain that you qualify them with specific behavioral descriptions or examples.
- Avoid absolute terms such as *always* or *never* (for example, "You're always late for my meetings").
- Do not try to diagnose or read minds. When you say, "The trouble with you is . . . ," you are diagnosing. When you say, "You think what you did is clever," you are trying to get into their heads.
- Don't ask "why?" when you don't expect an answer. For example, instead of "Why did you do such a stupid thing?" say, "That wasn't a very smart thing to do."
- Know when to be tentative. This is usually when you are not sure what happened or who the guilty party is. For example: "I've been told that someone in our unit has been making very critical remarks in the dining room about

upper management. Can you shed some light on this?" Other helpful phraseology includes, "What concerns me . . ." "I'm worried about . . ." or "Perhaps we have a problem with . . ."

- Always give the person a chance to respond without interruption.
- Avoid being too critical or coming down too hard on your people. If you do, they will react by devising ways to keep their mistakes hidden from you rather than trying to avoid making the mistakes.

COACHING PITFALLS

There are several shortcomings the supervisor may encounter from time to time in coaching.

- Using a cookie-cutter approach to coaching all employees, assuming that the same approach fits everyone. Inexperienced or insecure employees often require greater care and more of your time and support. Situational leadership is flexible and more appropriate.
- Believing that you have all the right answers
- Neglecting the coaching process because you do not think you have the time to provide this attention to each employee
- Labeling employees as above or below average or, for that matter, fitting employees with any label that constitutes a stereotype or implies substandard status
- Addressing attitude, personality, or character rather than outcomes or behavior
- Failing to allow some leeway in how things get done
- Overusing criticism or undeserved praise
- Offering excessive amounts of unsolicited advice

Think About It

To any team the coach is, of course, important, but never come to feel that as a coach you are more important than the employees simply because you are a manager. The coach adds much in the way of order to a team and enhances productivity, but the team can function without a coach if it has to—perhaps not nearly as well, but still the team can function. In the last analysis, a team without a coach is still a team, but a coach without a team is unemployed.

Questions for Review and Discussion

1. How would you define or describe the differences between coaching and the fundamental management activity of directing?

2. If it is people who make the mistakes, why are we told specifically to direct our negative feedback at performance or results and not at people?

3. How can a supervisor encourage employees to take risks without allowing them to wander into trouble?

4. What is the contingency theory of reinforcement? Provide a detailed example.

5. Why should we bother to praise performance that is not outstanding in any way but just consistently acceptable?

6. How would you relate MBWA to a supervisor's need to remain visible and available? Explain.

7. Instead of bothering to dispense praise whenever an employee does something deserving of it, why not simply save up all such instances to convey in an outstanding performance evaluation?

8. What do you believe are the fundamental differences between coaching and counseling?

9. Why should a supervisor be concerned with what we have been describing as coaching skills? Shouldn't it be sufficient to have a good grasp of supervisory fundamentals?

10. Describe at least two ways in which a supervisor-as-coach could legitimately remove obstacles for employees.

Case: A Group Problem?

Imagine that you are the supervisor of the transcription group of the health information services department at Community Hospital. Your crew consists of several transcriptionists who handle, in addition to all medical records transcription, all of the dictation from the clinical laboratories and diagnostic imaging and the word processing for several department directors. On a monthly basis you convene a brief meeting of your staff to convey current information and address issues currently affecting the department. At your February meeting you felt you had to air a problem you had seen emerging in recent months: quality was slipping, transcription errors were increasing, and complaints about the group's work were growing more frequent. You stressed that greater care had to be taken to reduce errors. At your March meeting you said, "Transcription quality has not improved since our last meeting; in fact, it has continued to decline. I expect all of you to become more aware of errors and to begin improving immediately."

When the time arrived for your April meeting, it was your best determination that transcription quality had not improved in the slightest.

Questions:

1. Should you continue to deal with the entire group? Why or why not?

2. What would you suggest doing in an effort to identify the real problems?
3. How might you approach the problem of making your criticism more effective?

Case: "She Sticks Like Glue"

"Darla is really a nice girl. I like her, honestly," said housekeeping team supervisor Wendy Smith, "but she's driving me crazy."

"What's wrong?" asked Janis Fredericks, Wendy's friend from nursing service.

Wendy answered, "Her work is all right, but I can't get her to think for herself. She comes to me with questions about every little thing, even all the stuff she ought to be able to take care of herself. She checks with me so often that I might as well be doing her work as well as my own."

Janis said, "Maybe you should be thankful she keeps you informed. I wish some of my gang were better about bringing problems to me. I don't know if there's ever such a thing as too much communication."

"There *is* too much as far as Darla's concerned. Most of what she brings me is simple stuff, stuff she ought to know. And it seems like she *does* know it, but she won't go ahead and do it unless I say so. She's always after me to tell her what to do next. And it seems like every time I turn around, she's there. She sticks to me like glue."

Janis said, "I know you've had the job only 5 or 6 months. Any idea how Darla got along with your predecessor?"

"No idea at all. But some of the folks have told me that their last supervisor was pretty strict and not the easiest person to get along with."

"What are you going to do?" Janis asked.

"At this point I don't know. How can I get her to work more independently without just shutting her out?"

Questions:

1. Why might Darla behave the way she does? Offer two or three possible reasons for her behavior.
2. How would you recommend that supervisor Wendy Smith approach the problem presented by Darla?

REFERENCES

1. Zemke, R. 1996. The corporate coach. *Training* 33(12): 24–8.
2. Peters, T., and Austin, N. 1985. *A passion for excellence.* New York: Random House, 9.

3. Zemke, "The Corporate Coach."
4. Blanchard, K., and Johnson, S. 1982. *The one-minute manager*. New York: Berkeley Publishers, 44.

RECOMMENDED READING

J. Olalla and R. Echeverria, "Management by Coaching," *HR Focus* 73, no. 1 (1996): 16, 17.

M.L. Schack, "Coaching: The Art of Creating Exceptional Results," *Clinical Laboratory Management Review* 11, no. 1 (1997): 28–34.

Chapter 13

Morale and Motivation

*Morale doesn't well up from the bottom; instead,
it trickles down from the top.*

—Eugene J. Benge

CHAPTER OBJECTIVES

- Differentiate between morale and motivation and examine the interrelationship of these two critical forces.
- Identify and examine the significant factors that have a bearing on the state of morale in a given work unit.
- Identify the signs of a morale problem and suggest how to gather pertinent information to use in analyzing such problems.
- Suggest how employing organizations, and particularly first-line supervisors, can support or enhance employee morale.
- Identify the essential nature of motivation and the ultimate source of all motivation.
- Identify strategies, both proactive and reactive, for enhancing the motivational climate of the organization.

Comprehensive employee surveys conducted throughout the 1960s, 1970s, 1980s, and into the 1990s, indicated a steady decline in employee job satisfaction in business in general.[1] In the health care industry the decline in job satisfaction has accelerated. Significant among the apparent reasons for the decline are the changes wrought by the intensifying nursing shortage. This now chronic shortage has forced the adoption of reduced staffing levels and altered patterns of practice for some health care workers, registered nurses in particular. Such changes have demoralized health care workers and led them to discourage others from entering the field.[2]

175

Also, newer technologies and services require a degree of autonomy for professionals that conflicts with traditional bureaucratic hierarchies and divisions between and among departments. Long-established boundaries between functional departments and workstations are rapidly being erased as workflows stream across previously sacrosanct borders and knock down the barriers that formerly protected various territories from intrusion. The result is stress and morale challenges for employees and supervisors alike.

MORALE VS MOTIVATION

Morale is a state of mind based largely on the perceptions of workers toward their work, their employer, their colleagues, and their supervisors. Morale must be differentiated from motivation. Morale relates to overall job satisfaction. If this is high, people are less likely to quit, complain, or become problem employees. Morale factors are those conditions that labor unions fight for: pay, benefits, job security, and work environment; in brief, overall quality of work life.

Morale factors represent the lower three levels of Maslow's hierarchy of needs: survival needs (food, clothing, shelter), safety needs (insurance, job security, pension), and social needs (acceptance by fellow workers).[3]

Motivation is a cognitive drive that occurs when Maslow's two higher-order needs are met. These needs are ego or self-esteem needs (that is, psychological needs) and self-actualization (achieving one's full potential). Unfortunately, high morale does not necessarily go hand-in-hand with strong motivation. Employees may be fully content with the circumstances of employment and yet lack the motivation needed to maximize performance. On the other hand, however, motivation dissipates when morale is low.

MAJOR FACTORS AFFECTING MORALE

Employee Factors

- Basic personality type can strongly influence morale. For example, the natural optimist is surely more likely to enjoy higher morale than the natural pessimist.
- Family situations and other outside factors can influence morale. It is extremely difficult for some people to keep external problems from affecting their work situation.
- The ability to adjust to the job and blend in with fellow workers often has an effect. The individual who can readily fit in is more likely to exhibit higher morale.
- Ease and safety in getting to work, finding a parking space, and getting to the job can influence morale. If the morning commute means a daily traffic jam,

parking is scarce and difficult and perceived as unsafe, and long walks are involved, morale can be adversely affected.

- A mismatch of employee and job is usually a guaranteed morale depressor. This can consist of either being in over one's head and feeling overwhelmed or stuck in a job well below one's capability without challenge or interest. Or it can simply be the wrong person for the job or the wrong job for the person.

Nature of the Job and Job Atmosphere

- Work that is stimulating or monotonous or fulfilling or unrewarding can boost morale higher or drag it down accordingly.
- Greater prestige associated with the job relates to higher morale, and the converse is generally true for the relationship between lack of prestige and lower morale.
- For some employees, the opportunity for promotion or growth is a strong determinant of morale. Lacking such opportunity, some employees see themselves as capped in their present jobs with nowhere to go, thus leading to lower morale.
- Job security is one of the strongest determinants of morale. One who is worried about prospects for continued employment will not be among the happiest or most contented workers.
- The financial status of the organization, economic conditions, and threats of competitors all have their influence on morale in that they are forces beyond the employee's control that also undermine feelings of job security and adversely affect morale.
- The amount of stress experienced on the job and in the organizational setting can, understandably, increase stress and relate directly to reduced morale for some employees.
- The quality, ease, and effectiveness of communication can readily influence morale. This goes for communication both from the top down and from the bottom up. The better information flows up and down the chain of command, the more healthy employee morale in general is likely to be.

Attitude and Behavior of Employer and Management

- How rewards are apportioned can have significant effects on morale. It is extremely demoralizing, for example, to hear of executives receiving generous raises or bonuses while employees are laid off, bypassed for raises, or asked to take salary cuts.
- The frequency with which promotions from within occur has morale effects. More than a few organizations have espoused a policy of development from

within while employees see most of the better opportunities filled from outside.

- The manner in which management adjusts to financial crunches and reacts to fiscal pressure affects employee morale. It is generally demoralizing, for example, for employees to see that the first response to a financial problem is the layoff of rank-and-file staff.

Quality of Supervision

As mentioned in previous chapters, it should go without saying that the quality of supervision—how well and how effectively employees are led and the extent to which employees are treated fairly and with respect and consideration—is a strong determinant of morale. It is not unreasonable to maintain that in many instances the quality of supervision is the primary driver of employee morale.

SIGNS OF A MORALE PROBLEM

Diminishing productivity frequently indicates worsening morale. When morale is low, many employees perform at the minimum level required to simply keep their jobs. When morale is low employees complain about parking, safety, pay and benefits, the organization and its managers, and their assignments. As they become increasingly apathetic or rebellious, they are increasingly likely to voice their complaints in the presence of patients and other customers.

When morale is low employees become more resistant to change than usual, they rarely volunteer, and they seldom pitch in to help without being required to do so. Absenteeism, tardiness, grievances, and turnover are all likely to increase significantly. Employees do not participate at meetings except to voice complaints as they sit in the back of the room scowling, with folded arms. They avoid making suggestions or approving the ideas of others. They fall silent or walk away when managers approach. Cynicism, sarcasm, and belittling conversation flourish.

When morale is poor, conversations and energy are directed away from productive work. Supervisors hear comments like, "Thank God it's Friday," "Don't ask me, I only work here," "We need a union," or "There's no point in knocking yourself out."

Sagging morale prompts some workers to talk about retiring, changing employers, or leaving their chosen fields. They talk of how their friends and relations have better employers. As poor morale persists, the more qualified employees are likely to resign to seek better work environments while the deadwood remains.

Morale improvement begins with the identification of specific morale problems. Severe morale problems are easy to spot; milder forms are more subtle and are harder to detect. Discovery of discontent at an early stage is as important as the early detection of cancer. As with cancer, the longer poor morale is allowed to continue unabated, the more difficult it is to reverse.

METHODS FOR OBTAINING INFORMATION ABOUT MORALE

The management of an organization can gather information about the state of employee morale by several means.

Whenever a morale slippage is suspected, an alert management will often circulate an *attitude survey* and share the findings with all managers. In some organizations, employee attitude surveys are undertaken periodically—once per year is common—whether or not morale problems are evident or suspected.

Exit interviews conducted by specially trained personnel (rather than by the supervisors of the departing employees) are also quite helpful. In many organizations they are conducted by human resources professionals, and in some instances this activity is assigned to outside agencies. All departing employees need not be interviewed, but any sample used should be large enough to yield credible results.

Employee focus groups are best conducted anonymously by external facilitators to whom employees' names remain unknown. Quotes are not attributed to specific individuals. Such focus groups can be especially effective for evaluating morale during or immediately following a major organizational change.

Telephone hotlines and suggestion boxes can be effective if follow-up on complaints and suggestions is timely and visible. (If employees do not see follow-up occurring, these processes can themselves become depressors of morale.)

Finally, *ombudsman programs,* in which ombudsmen mediate employee concerns and report them to management, can prevent problems from getting larger or happening again. Ombudsmen can effectively advocate for employees while enhancing management credibility.

HOW EMPLOYERS IMPROVE MORALE

Employers can sustain or improve employee morale in a number of ways.

- Ensuring timely and visible reaction to employee attitude surveys. Morale is enhanced when employees know that their concerns are heard and addressed.
- Establishing and maintaining a problem-solving culture. Once ingrained, such a culture leads employees to believe—with justification—that emerging problems will be addressed.
- Controlling rumors. No organization will ever rid itself entirely of the grapevine or rumor mill, but management can go a long way in a positive direction by correcting false information that reaches employees by these informal means.

- Sharing financial information with employees. Being kept in the dark concerning the organization's financial condition is demoralizing to many employees.
- Insisting on fair and equitable treatment of all employees. Inequitable and inconsistent treatment of employees feeds discontent and often results in pockets of poor morale throughout the organization.
- Vigorously controlling harassment and discrimination, continuing to ensure that all employees are regarded with respect and that none are singled out for disparate treatment.
- Spending more time where the work is taking place. As noted at numerous points throughout this volume, a manager's visibility and availability mean much to the majority of rank-and-file employees.
- Ensuring that job candidates are carefully screened. This helps new employees fit into the organization as completely as possible and keeps turnover and its attendant demoralizing effects to a minimum.
- Providing timely and thorough supervisory training. This applies not only to a new supervisor's training in basic supervisory skills but also to the continuing education needed to keep each supervisor current and effective.

Compensation and Benefits Systems

Employers generally know what salaries and benefits their competitors offer, and they respond appropriately by upgrading their reward and recognition systems. Often they introduce more flexibility into rules and regulations, modifying practices to reward team as well as individual efforts and outcomes. Some employers offer alternative promotional ladders or parallel path progression systems to allow professionals to remain in their specialties while continuing to advance financially and professionally.

Today more organizations promote and encourage the well-being of their employees, although their purposes are not entirely altruistic. In addition to providing a valuable service, they reduce costs by prescribing special programs that increase wellness and prevent illness. Health promotion initiatives include health education, risk assessment and screening, and special programs such as infertility care; all such employee benefits tend to function as morale boosters. Incentives offered include changes focusing on the family and lifestyles, for example, casual dress, flextime, and earlier quitting times on Fridays during summer months.

HOW SUPERVISORS CAN IMPROVE MORALE

Alert supervisors who enjoy good rapport with their employees become aware of morale problems long before these are recognized by upper management. They respond in a number of ways. Better still, they prevent the slippage in the first place by taking some of the following actions.

- Always treating people as winners or potential winners
- Rewarding and recognizing appropriately
- Ensuring social acceptance of all employees
- Instilling pride through improved orientation of new employees
- Making certain that their employees know the why and how of their tasks
- Maintaining a mindset of optimism and success
- Assigning discouraged workers to teams of go-getters and upbeat individuals
- Getting rid of troublemakers and morale destroyers
- Introducing more flexible work schedules
- Keeping all staff fully informed at all times
- Becoming a change master or change agent, proactive rather than reactive
- Involving employees in decision making and planning
- Helping employees obtain deserved pay increases

Four Techniques for Getting Deserved Raises for Your Employees

The first technique that is useful is to rewrite position descriptions to reflect all of the "creeping changes" that can occur in a job over time. Document the degree of difficulty of all functions and the consequences of errors. Highlight administrative and teaching assignments or anything else that was never reflected in determining rate of pay.

Another useful tactic is to train and mentor your employees to enhance their value to the organization. This will increase their chances of promotion.

If possible, provide employees with more prestigious titles (although this may already be overdone in some organizations).

Finally, never try to retain key people by denigrating their performance or qualifications to others, thus discouraging others from recruiting your employees.

MOTIVATION

All true motivation is self-motivation. Managers cannot motivate employees. Rather, all they can do is change the work ambiance in ways that improve motivation. In other words, managers can create the climate in which employees become more likely to motivate themselves.

All employees are motivated. Unfortunately, the motivational energy of some of them does not always flow into their work. Consider, for example, Steve, who shows little interest in his job or the possibility of promotion but is a talented musician and an effective leader of a local orchestra. Steve has lots of motivation but none that does his employer any good.

Efforts aimed at enhancing motivation are either proactive or reactive. Proactive or anticipative measures precede performance; reactive activities follow performance and serve to reinforce desired behavior or outcomes.

The acronym RAGWAR can help you remember Herzberg's famous list of motivating factors.[4]

R = Recognition
A = Achievement
G = Growth (career)
W = Work itself
A = Advancement
R = Responsibility

We have already noted that although high morale does not motivate, true motivation cannot be achieved until morale deficiencies (Herzberg called these dissatisfiers or hygiene factors) have been eliminated.[5]

PROACTIVE STRATEGIES FOR THE SUPERVISOR

- That which motivates you may not necessarily motivate your employees. Supervisors and employees alike may be subject to the same set of needs, but the mix of needs and their relative strength will vary from person to person. Try to view the work situation from the employees' perspective and think as they might think.
- Define expectations, set goals, delegate, train, coach, counsel, and provide performance feedback.
- Provide for the maintenance and growth of professional skills to avoid employee obsolescence.
- Relax tight supervisory controls, demonstrate trust in employees, and delegate decision-making authority.
- Alter job titles and rewrite position descriptions to make jobs more important or to appear so. This practice can of course be carried too far, but it is highly applicable to entry-level positions. For example, most workers would understandably prefer to be called "building service worker" and not "janitor."
- Recruit and select motivated people, or at least attempt to do so. Never approach recruiting with an attitude, suggesting that "if this one doesn't work out, I can always hire another."
- Improve the job itself to the maximum possible extent. The strongest, most lasting motivation comes from the job itself or, more accurately, from one's perception of the job and its importance. When people like the work but hate the job, watch out!
- Learn as much as you can about your people and their different personalities.
- Do not rely only on salary administration and other corporate mechanisms for rewards and recognition; involve yourself in providing positive feedback on a continuing basis.

- Take your employees into your confidence, seek their advice, and share information. Be fair and consistent.
- Provide support for your employees. Be available to help when they need help, but do not stand in their way.
- Be a respected role model.
- Smile. The presence of smiles and a little good humor goes a long way to creating a pleasant work atmosphere.
- Increase opportunities for education and training (see Exhibit 13–1).

When the going gets tough, the tough lighten up.

The meaningfulness of work is based on how much it affects the worker, other people, and the organization. Jobs that require multiple skills and a variety of activities or skills are usually more satisfying. Most employees also prefer assignments that allow them to complete an entire piece of work. For example, most

---

Exhibit 13–1 How Many of These Questions about Your Educational Program Can You Answer in the Affirmative?

1. Do you have a formal in-house education program?
2. Is this program available to each and every member of your staff?
3. Do you provide sufficient uninterrupted time for your employees to attend the in-house programs?
4. Does each employee have individualized career goals and plans? Are these discussed at annual performance review meetings?
5. Is there financial support for outside education courses? Do you modify work schedules or numbers of work hours to accommodate employees who enroll in these programs?
6. Do employees have the opportunity to cross-train or to learn new skills on the job?
7. Does each of your employees learn at least one new skill each year?
8. Are there real incentives for learning new skills?
9. When your employees attend seminars or workshops, do you discuss the practical value to your unit and to the employee before the meeting?
10. When your employees return from seminars and workshops, do you discuss what they learned and help them put that new knowledge and skill to use?
11. When you attend professional or technical meetings, do you share what you learned with others? Do you encourage your staff to do likewise?
12. Do you include educational topics in your routine staff meetings?
13. Do all of your educational efforts focus on improved customer service?

hematology technologists prefer to investigate a bleeding problem by performing a battery of tests rather than doing only one or two tests of the battery. Most patient-care technicians prefer to provide a range of services for one patient rather than taking the vital signs of all the patients in a unit.

Interesting work and the opportunity to develop skills and abilities, to be creative, and to be challenged are powerful motivators.

A high degree of control over one's work provides a healthy mindset. Lack of operating autonomy leads to frustration and stress. Having control translates into discretionary freedom for scheduling, prioritizing, and selecting methods.

Practical Tips for Increasing the Motivational Value of the Work Itself

- Provide a diversity of experience by giving new assignments, cross-training, or rotating workstations.
- Let people swap assignments. Here you must know the likes and dislikes of each person.
- Assign monotonous tasks or those requiring less expertise to less-qualified employees. Doing so makes two people happy.
- Allow a little time for practical research; special projects; or service on committees, quality circles, or problem-solving groups.
- Permit a few fun tasks.
- Stimulate creativity by talking about new services, products, equipment, or procedures or by sharing publications and handouts from seminars and assigning problems for solution.
- Provide holistic tasks where employees can see the results of their efforts.

To move up a motivational notch, switch from a directive leadership style to a participative style. To help with this, Leeds recommends asking your employees these questions.[6]

- What do you like about what you do?
- How can I help you use more of your skills?
- What do you think you (or we) should do differently?
- How can we carry out your ideas?
- What help do you need from me or from others?

Get employees involved in decisions about their assignments. Consider differences in their motivational needs. Some people have a strong need for control or leadership, others for task achievement, and still others for socializing. For example, Sue gets her kicks when she chairs a committee, Joe is energized when presented with a balky instrument, and Jan is happiest when she can meet new people or work with a group of her friends.

Delegate and empower. Giving ambitious people more responsibility plus the authority they need to discharge that responsibility is empowering, and it is a strong motivator. Most people like to be in charge of something, even when that something is a minor activity.

REACTIVE STRATEGIES

Provide Recognition

When money for rewarding good service is scarce or is no longer the motivator it might once have been, recognition and praise become more important. These factors elevate self-esteem, improve morale, and really motivate if applied skillfully.

A frequent complaint of health care workers is that they do not receive the recognition and respect they feel they are due. Supervisors often misinterpret this to mean that upper management is at fault. Recognition, however, is considerably more than formal ceremonies where accolades, plaques, and certificates are handed out. Such events are too infrequent and too impersonal to have a major impact. Of much greater significance is the day-to-day, person-to-person dialogue in which supervisors express their appreciation in ways that convince employees that they are important. This is what really satisfies the ego needs of the employee.

Your messages, spoken or written, tell employees whether you truly believe in the value of their efforts and their worth. That which gets rewarded informs people of what kind of performance is valued most. Make sure that the recognition is perceived as fair.

In Chapter 14 we will discuss rewards and recognition in more detail.

How To Motivate the Steady but Unspectacular Worker

Managers spend much time devising gimmicks for rewarding their star performers or coping with their problem people. Meanwhile, they neglect those loyal supporters who show up every day, do not make waves, and who live up to all the specifications of their position descriptions. The majority of employees fall into this latter category.

Besides providing the motivators already described, meet periodically with each of these employees to tell them how much you appreciate their efforts.[7] Before each meeting, review the employee's records and update your personal observations. Look for noteworthy behavior, such as excellent attendance or frequent volunteering to substitute for absent coworkers. At each meeting, apologize for not spending more time with the person, and congratulate him or her for whatever it is you singled out to commend. Use the opportunity to ask for suggestions for improving your service or the teamwork. Ask whether there is anything you can do to make his or her job more pleasant. Most employees are more relaxed and willing to talk frankly at these informal sessions than they are at formal performance appraisal interviews.

Think About It

The supervisor cannot motivate employees directly; no one can truly motivate another. Because all true motivation is self-motivation, and the real motivating forces are found in the work itself, the best the supervisor can ever do is establish the conditions under which each employee can become self-motivated.

Questions for Review and Discussion
1. How have organizational mergers and other affiliations affected employee morale, and why do you believe they have had these effects?
2. How can a system for collecting and evaluating employee suggestions become a morale depressor rather than a morale booster?
3. It has been said that the time to think of conducting an employee attitude survey is *not* when there are obvious morale problems. Why is this so?
4. Under what circumstances could morale be high while the motivation to perform is weak or lacking?
5. It has been proven that many employees consider the opportunity for promotion and growth to be important in their organizational environment, and yet only a relative few employees take advantage of this opportunity. Why might this be so?
6. What are the principal differences between the factors affecting morale and those relating to motivation?
7. Why should a departing employee's immediate supervisor *not* conduct the employee's exit interview?
8. Why can it be claimed that the quality of supervision can be the primary driver of employee motivation?
9. How can a worker's stress level be related to the worker's morale? Provide an example.
10. What do you believe are the significant reasons for the decline in the morale among health care workers in recent years?

Case: Surprise!

When the business office employees arrived at the hospital Monday morning, they immediately noticed the apparent absence of the office manager. This was not unusual; the manager was frequently absent on Monday. However, he rarely failed to call the department when he would not be there, and on this day he still had not called by noon.

Shortly after lunch the two working supervisors in the business office were summoned to the administrator's office. They were told that the office manager was no longer employed by the hospital. They, the two supervisors, were told to look after things for the current week and that a new manager, already secured, would be starting the following Monday. All that the two supervisors were told about the new manager was that it was someone from outside the hospital.

The supervisors were not told whether the former manager resigned or was discharged, nor were they told whether anyone within the department had been considered as a replacement.

Questions:

1. What do you suppose would be the reactions and attitudes of the business office staff upon hearing about this change?
2. What circumstances will most likely prevail during this interim week without a manager? Include in your comments consideration of both morale and productivity.
3. With what attitudes do you suppose the business office staff will receive the new manager?

Case: The Artful Dodger

Jane Wilson had considerable difficulty developing the schedule for her nursing unit for the coming 2 weeks. The nursing department was in a marginal position overall as far as available nurses were concerned, so her flexibility was limited. To make matters worse, within hours after Jane issued the newest schedule Alice Johnson, a part-time licensed practical nurse, submitted a request for a personal day on one of the days she was scheduled to work.

The request caused Jane to realize she had been seeing Alice's name in connection with schedule difficulties often in recent months. Looking back over the schedules for the preceding 6 months, she discovered that the current request was the fifth time that Alice had requested time off on a scheduled weekend day. Even more significant was the pattern of Alice's use of sick time. She had called in sick four times, all of these on Saturdays or Sundays. All in all Alice had worked only about half of the weekend days she was scheduled to work over a period of 6 months.

Jane was displeased with Alice's attendance and unhappy with herself for not discovering the problem sooner. She felt she had to talk with Alice about it, but she also felt that her unit could ill afford to lose a nurse. Nevertheless she believed that she could not allow Alice's attendance pattern to continue uncorrected.

Questions:

1. What are the hazards Jane faces in dealing firmly with Alice's behavior or ignoring Alice's absences and saying nothing? Consider the implications for staff morale and motivation as well as staffing level.
2. Assuming that Jane is seriously considering addressing the attendance problem with Alice, how might she best approach the subject?

REFERENCES

1. Doyle, R.J., and Doyle, P. I. 1992. *Gain management*. New York: AMACOM, 9.
2. Schnautz, L. 2003. Viewpoint: Our own worst enemies. *American Journal of Nursing* 103(11): 11.
3. Maslow, A.H. 1954. *Motivation and personality*. New York: Harper & Row.
4. Herzberg, F. 1966. *Work and the nature of man*. Cleveland, OH: World.
5. Herzberg, *Work and the Nature of Man*.
6. Leeds, D. 1987. *Smart questions*. New York: McGraw-Hill.
7. Nail, F.C., and Singleton, E.K. 1986. Common sense survival strategy for nursing supervisors. *Health Care Supervisor* 4: 50–8.

RECOMMENDED READING

D.J. McNerney, "Creating a Motivated Workforce," *HR Focus* 73, no. 8 (1996): 1–6.
J.A. Morris, "How To Motivate High-Achievers," *Training* 33, no. 2 (1996): 74.
R. Davidhizar and A. Vance, "Motivating the Paraprofessional in Long-Term Care," *Health Care Supervisor* 15, no. 4 (1997): 57–64.

Chapter 14

Rewards and Recognition

*Reward people for the right behavior and you get
the right results. That's the simple message of the
greatest management principle in the world.*

—Michael LeBoeuf[1]

CHAPTER OBJECTIVES

- Identify the principles on which an effective reward system should be based, and describe the essential elements of a workable incentive strategy.
- Identify the specific kinds of behavior or accomplishments that are deserving of reward consideration.
- Provide workable guidelines for pursuing an appropriately functioning reward strategy.
- Explore the use of salaries and benefits and other financial rewards in supporting employee motivation.
- Examine the use and potential value of nonfinancial rewards.
- Explore the power of recognition in meeting employees' higher-order needs and thus enhancing motivation, morale, and productivity.

A great many employers tend to believe that they have effective reward and recognition systems in place. However, large numbers of employees disagree. In a national poll, workers were asked, "If you were to improve service quality and productivity, do you believe you would be rewarded accordingly?" The vast majority responded with a resounding "No!"[2] Also, many of these disagreeing employees feel that policies concerning reward and recognition are not administered fairly and that promotions, strongly considered as both reward and recognition, are not fairly apportioned.

To make matters worse, in these times of financial hardship many health care organizations are cutting costs by scaling down their reward and recognition systems. To compensate for losses owing to fiscal belt-tightening, it is imperative for all supervisors to fine-tune their recognition and reward skills and never assume that the paycheck is all that is needed to keep each employee satisfied and productive.

AN EFFECTIVE REWARD SYSTEM

Underlying Principles

An effective reward system must be designed in such a manner that rewards are apportioned principally on the basis of performance outcomes; that is, quality of work, control of costs, customer satisfaction, or other positive contributions to the continued success of the organization.

Rewards should also be based on special behavior, such as acquisition of new skills or knowledge, willingness and the ability to adjust to changes, successful cross-training, and demonstrated teamwork.

Make sure that rewards are available for team performance as well for individual performance.

Also, know that rewards *are* sufficient for retaining personnel.

Designing an Incentive Strategy

An effective incentive strategy must provide employees with clear knowledge of what is expected of them. That is, employees must know precisely what they must do and must know and understand how their performance will be assessed. Incentive strategy design requires (1) ascertaining the needs and wants of customers, (2) setting performance standards or delineating expected results, and (3) measuring performance against these standards or results.

Behavior or Results to Be Rewarded

Employees often deserve to be rewarded when they delight customers. This means not simply leaving customers satisfied to have received what they expected, but rather leaving them surprised and pleased—delighted—at having in some way received more than they expected.

Reward-worthy behavior frequently involves reporting problems and customer feedback and offering suggestions for correcting problems and improving customer service, including actions that may go beyond what the employees would normally be expected to do.

Displays of creativity and assertiveness may also be deserving of reward. Standout employees are often those who are willing to stick their necks out, make difficult decisions, express unpopular opinions, and take actions that may risk their status.

Reward-worthy behavior is often demonstrated by employees who are regularly willing to go above and beyond the call of duty by

1. working extra long hours when needed,
2. willingly substituting for others,
3. returning to work after hours or remaining available for advice by telephone,
4. submitting reports ahead of schedule,
5. volunteering for unpleasant or unpopular assignments,
6. rendering performance you can always rely on as, for example, in showing up during snowstorms, backing you up when you need support, and always remaining ready to help.

Reward System Guidelines

It has been suggested that the supervisor who wishes to maintain an effective and consistent reward system within a department or group do the following:

1. Support and justify deserved pay raises for both the team and its star performers.
2. When selecting a reward for an individual, consider that person's distinctive wants and needs. Ask people what rewards they value.
3. Be consistent and fair in what is rewarded and how it is done.
4. For marginal performers, express appreciation for small improvements, even though outcomes are not yet up to expectations.
5. Reward wanted behavior and outcomes. When people struggle against odds with less than desired results, they still deserve some credit for their efforts.
6. Reward the entire team for a team success, and single out individuals who made special efforts that were recognized by the rest of the team.
7. Reward what supports the values of the organization. Most organizational value statements include terms such as customer satisfaction, innovation, teamwork, career development, and cost control.[3]

COMPENSATION: REWARDS BEARING PRICE TAGS

Wages and Salaries

The point was made in an earlier chapter that compensation that is perceived as inadequate is a dissatisfier but that generous compensation is neither a strong nor a lasting motivator. Although it may be true that the motivational effect of a salary increase is transient and that people are motivated more by their work than by the rewards they earn, the importance of compensation should not be undervalued. Managers can keep telling their employees what great performers they are, but if management fails to support these statements with fatter paychecks, those employees will soon realize that they are being manipulated. In a very real sense, a fatter paycheck can be a scorecard indicating winning performance.

In most instances base pay still reflects the economics of the marketplace, but there have been major changes in corporate compensation strategies in recent years. The old practice of trying to create internal job equity is becoming passé except in unionized organizations.

Compensation systems that provide merit increases have also lost much of their luster, largely because of their negative impact on those who are not selected for raises and thus feel cheated. Strident charges of favoritism and unfairness are commonplace. Even the folks who receive the larger slices of the pie are often left feeling uncomfortable and alienated. A more acceptable option is to reward higher-performing groups as well as individuals. Whatever system is used, however, merit pay must be based on objective data that employ agreed-upon and observable criteria that all concerned employees know and understand.

Broadbanding, which collapses many traditional salary grades into a few wide bands, also may be losing its popularity in favor of competency-based systems. The latter systems reward skills, knowledge, and behavior. Competencies that earn the rewards may include teamwork, technical expertise, and innovation. The centerpiece of many skill-based pay systems is the ability and willingness of employees to perform a wide range of tasks.[4]

For a number of years, compensation in some organizations was based almost entirely on meeting predetermined objectives, this approach being more or less the product of the management-by-objectives paradigm. This has given way to a different kind of outcome-based compensation system in which customer satisfaction is a principal determining factor. By incorporating customer satisfaction measures into their reward systems, employers increase their chances of pleasing their customers. Employees who fail in this effort not only miss out on the rewards, but they also put their jobs in jeopardy.

Whatever compensation system is in effect, supervisors play a pivotal role in explaining and implementing the system for employees.

Employee Benefits

In recent decades the cost of benefits has increased steadily, in some instances dramatically, while their importance to employees has continued to expand. Newer features unheard of 15, 20, or 25 years ago, such as enhanced maternity plans, adoption leaves of absence, and day care for children and elders, keep appearing. Benefits have become problematic for many employers, with employee benefits packages having become so costly that they are often equivalent to as much as 35 to 40 percent of salaries. To control the costs of benefits, employers eliminate some of the more costly offerings or make employees share some of the expenses. Many large organizations have reduced the numbers of their full-time employees and increased their part-time staff because part-time employees receive fewer benefits.

Another currently popular strategy is outsourcing certain operations or departments. This eliminates not only the benefits but also the jobs.

A survey of hospital laboratory supervisors revealed what they perceived as inadequate benefits. Please see Table 14–1 for some of the highlights of that study.

Many organizations have been creative in tying their benefits to the specific physical, psychological, and spiritual needs of their employees. Examples include flextime and other nontraditional scheduling practices, recreational and health club facilities, wellness programs, telecommuting, and even weekly free massages. "Cafeteria plans," in which employees choose from a variety of options, are very popular.

A comprehensive program of employee benefits improves morale, reduces absenteeism and turnover, and increases productivity and customer satisfaction. Caring employers are always open to suggestions for new benefits, especially those that do not carry large price tags.

Being in a position of knowing their individual employees and at least some of their needs and wants, supervisors are in a position to propose new ways of rewarding their employees. Also, they can often pick up useful ideas at their professional meetings and from mentors and personal networks.

Table 14–1 Perceptions of Benefits

Top 5 Benefits Desired/ Not Received	Top 5 Benefits Available/ Deemed Inadequate
Child care	Pension plan
Eye care plan	Paid seminar/workshop expenses
Paid professional membership dues	Paid continuing education
Dental care	Eye care plan
Continuing education	Child care reimbursement

Jahn, M. 1995. Laboratorians speak out on benefits, managed care, and the bottom line. *Medical Laboratory Observer* 27(5): 29–33.

Other Financial Rewards

Beyond wages, salaries, and benefits, there are other forms of monetary reward available.

- Promotions or alternative types of advancement, such as career ladder programs and parallel-path progression systems, that increase salary.
- Bonuses and other cash awards. The Japanese get maximum mileage from their bonus systems. Many Japanese workers receive 25% of their pay as flexible bonuses; in the United States the average is less than 1%.
- Increased compensation for superior customer service, special competencies, and participation in special activities such as process reengineering, teaching, mentoring, or handling tough delegated tasks.
- Financial support for education, training, or personal professional library materials.
- Tickets to entertainment events.
- Awards such as pins, jewelry, and mugs. Although bonuses and salary increases possess an element of recognition, they do not have the same symbolic significance as permanent reminders of their accomplishments.
- Personal offices or expanded work spaces, services of typists or other assistants, and support for educational or professional advancement.
- Professional or technical publications.
- Payment for memberships in professional societies.
- Establishment of funds for research or investigation projects.
- Reimbursement for attendance at professional meetings, workshops, or seminars.

NONFINANCIAL REWARDS

> *It's harder to satisfy employees with money alone.*
> *What were once regarded as rewards are now*
> *considered entitlements.*[5]
>
> —Graham and Unruh

There are many rewards which, at no cost or only nominal cost, can have significant motivational effects. Some of the following may be appropriate in your particular situation.

- Enable employees to attend in-house educational offerings. There is, of course, the hidden cost of employee time, but there is no added out-of-pocket cost, and employee time consumed can be minimized with careful scheduling.
- Delegate activities that individuals perceive as benefiting their careers or providing pleasure.

- Ask the better-performing employees about serving on committees, focus groups, task forces, or cross-functional teams as such assignments may be available.
- Ask for employees' opinions and give them credit for any advice that you use.
- Rotate workstations where possible, varying the work assignments (and avoid rotating a person from one boring job to an equally boring one).
- Create training opportunities for those employees who value them.
- Provide career counseling.
- Assign the better performers to represent you at upper-level or professional meetings when possible.
- Grant additional time off for special events.
- Offer meaningful assignments, diversity of experience, or choice of responsibilities.
- Provide opportunities for employee innovation.
- Provide increased opportunities for challenging work or for the development of new skills.
- Assign significant projects or complex tasks from beginning to end rather than in bits and pieces.
- Bring in a treat for the group or have lunch with your group.
- Increase the amount of information available, giving employees not just what they need to get their work done but also things about which they would like to learn.
- Ask the better performers to consider serving as mentors or trainers for new employees.
- If possible, assign certain employees more or less responsibility and authority according to their individual wishes.
- Provide more prestigious job titles, if allowed. For example, the title of *dietary aide* may be preferred over that of *kitchen helper*.
- Make use of generous doses of recognition (more on this later in this chapter).
- Encourage each employee to become a specialist in some aspect of your unit's activities.
- Help employees develop goals, objectives, and plans.
- Provide assignments that promote and enhance career development.

IMPLEMENTING A REWARD SYSTEM

Establish the goals of your reward system. After reviewing the statements of your organization regarding vision, mission, values, and goals, decide what kind of performance output and behavior support these statements. Consider criteria such as customer satisfaction, work quality and quantity, problem solving, achieving objectives, improving work procedures, attendance, and new skills. Benchmark by noting the systems and techniques used by other leaders who have reputations for high morale and productivity.

Determine what the team and the individual team members regard as rewards. What makes them smile or frown? What kinds of activities do they seem to like doing? What do they talk about during their free time? To avoid making poor choices, try asking people how they feel about a reward before you give it. Give them options. Avoid anything that might embarrass them. Ask their colleagues, friends, or family members for suggestions. Reward everyone who meets the established criteria. Be certain at all times to reward the right outcomes and behavior, not unwanted results.

RECOGNITION

The deepest principle of human nature is
the craving to be appreciated.[6]

—William James, as quoted in Bell

Recognition is our least expensive and most powerful motivational tool. To be effective, it must be earned, specific, sincere, and offered as soon as possible after what the person did or said to earn it.

The principal weakness of customary institutional award ceremonies is that they are too impersonal and are delivered long after the commendatory service. Also, they usually focus on matters such as attendance or length of employment rather than on productivity or customer service. Some rituals make employees feel so demeaned or simply so downright bored that they do not show up at the ceremony.

The philosophical core of recognition is developing self-esteem in the individual. Employees who receive the recognition they deserve have greater self-esteem, more confidence, more willingness to take on new challenges, and more eagerness to contribute new ideas and improve productivity. We all need day-to-day recognition if we are to perform at consistently high levels. Recognition can be as simple as a smile and a sincere "good morning." When provided grudgingly or inexpertly, it is ineffective. Some people find it difficult to deliver praise while others are uncomfortable receiving it. Do not, however, confuse praise with flattery. The latter is insincere, unearned, and usually manipulative.

Recognition Must Be Valued

Recognition is powerful, but the same type of recognition does not work for everyone. Different people require different approaches. Whatever you use must pass the "snicker test." If employees regard an award as having little value, or if they have little respect for its donor, that award will have little effect on the self-esteem or morale of that employee. Salary increases represent a powerful form of recognition, even if their motivational value may be brief.

Features of Effective Recognition

For recognition to be effective, it must exhibit a number of particular characteristics.

- It must be earned. If not earned, it is readily recognized as flattery or manipulation. Meaningful day-to-day recognition comes from supervisors who really know what is going on in their work units.
- It is consistent. Inconsistent recognition confuses recipients, and unequal recognition smacks of favoritism.
- It is timely. The high value of day-to-day recognition lies in its immediacy. The type of reward most preferred by employees is personalized, spur-of-the-moment recognition.[7]
- It is frequent. It takes many positive strokes to neutralize the effects of one instance of criticism.
- It is ubiquitous. Most employees can be recognized for something they do well. It may be something they do not do (for example, avoiding controversy or calmly tolerating the idiosyncrasies of fellow workers). In the case of marginal workers, little steps in the right direction can lead to still more improvement when they receive some positive feedback.
- It is valued by the recipients.
- It is sincere and specific. Telling someone that he or she is doing a good job is not specific. Telling someone that you appreciate how an irate physician was handled a short time before is both specific and timely.
- It does not embarrass. Do not praise in public when it would fluster the recipient.

To enhance the impact of praise, consider the following tactics.

- Praise in public (if not embarrassing to the recipient), and ask one of your superiors to be present.
- Address the person by name, maintain eye contact, and smile.
- State how the action or statement benefited you, the team, the department, or the organization.
- Follow up with a memo. Send a copy to human resources for the employee's personnel file and send one to your superiors.
- Submit the commendation to the institution's newsletter and to the public relations or marketing department.

Other recognition modalities include the following:

- Write a thank-you note and post it on the recipient's office door or workstation.
- Brag about it to colleagues; this is sure to get back to the person.
- Display commendations and pictures on bulletin boards. Place trophies and plaques at the recipient's workstation.
- Attend meetings of committees and other special work groups to thank the members.
- Select an employee of the month (the organization might be doing this over-all, but there's added value in doing it within a department).

Five Cautions About Recognition

1. Avoid saying what behavior or outcomes are wanted while rewarding something else. For example, your values statement may proclaim quality, but recognition goes to people who cut corners for the sake of increased productivity.
2. Avoid sending mixed messages, those containing elements of both praise and criticism. The recipients are likely to become confused or angry.
3. Do not deliver praise that is not merited or is grossly exaggerated. This is not recognition; it is flattery or manipulation. When praising a problem employee, praise only what he or she has done well.
4. Do not overlook anyone. Many employees feel that the only time anyone notices their work is when they do something wrong. Too often recognition is reserved for an elite few.
5. If you have an employee-of-the month program, skip those months during which no person honestly earned the recognition. Do not restrict the award to one person per month. Make certain that the behavior being rewarded is either described in the announcement or is something that everyone in the unit knows. Without such descriptions, the award embarrasses the recipient and fosters charges of favoritism. Ask yourself if your selections pass the snicker test.

Think About It

One of the most important aspects of reward and recognition, perhaps even the single most important feature of these means of providing employees with performance feedback, is reinforcement of behavior. It is fundamental that behavior that is reinforced tends to be repeated; reinforce appropriate performance and behavior, and it will in most instances be repeated.

Questions for Review and Discussion

1. If an employee is continually doing an acceptable job, not excelling but chugging along and producing reasonable results, why should any form of reward or recognition be considered necessary?
2. Why is it considered necessary for recognition to be delivered as soon following the deserving behavior as possible?
3. Why is monetary compensation not necessarily a motivator of improved performance?
4. Explain how a particular reward, specifically a pay increase or a bonus, can have a greater effect as recognition than as a reward.
5. Shouldn't most reward and recognition practices be reserved for outstanding performers only? Why or why not?
6. Why are performance standards critical in an incentive reward system?
7. Provide an example of a potential nonfinancial reward—one that is not listed in the chapter material—and explain the circumstances under which it could be seen as a reward by some employees.
8. Why can it be said that the individual supervisor is the most important person as far as employee recognition is concerned?
9. Describe the fundamental employee needs that reward and recognition processes primarily fulfill.
10. Explain your understanding of a cafeteria-style benefits plan and describe how elements of such a plan can be construed as rewards.

Case: "When I Need Them, They're Nowhere to Be Found!"

Melissa Jones is nurse manager of a 40-bed long-term care unit that is essentially a small nursing home contained within Community Hospital. The unit is almost always fully occupied. A number of the patients spend several hours each day in wheelchairs, but most return to their beds for a couple of hours in the afternoon.

Melissa has a constant concern in that her limited staff is only marginally able to fill the needs of the elderly patients, especially given that some patients who go without visitors for prolonged periods are eager to engage staff members in conversation. Melissa has determined that a number of apparent patient needs, especially the need for socialization, could be met with volunteers, so she developed a volunteer roster consisting of persons who indicated their willingness to help, after which she developed a 30-day schedule for volunteer support.

On the initial day of the schedule three of five scheduled volunteers failed to show up. On the following day, two did not appear. Only one appeared on each of the third and fourth days, and on the fifth day—a Friday with gorgeous summer weather beckoning all to the outdoors—no volunteers were present in the unit. Melissa gave up on her schedule.

Melissa was thoroughly discouraged by the volunteers' lack of dependability. And because she had made no secret of her new volunteer program, a number of patients were similarly discouraged, and several complained that Melissa had not delivered as promised. As Melissa complained to her friend Carol, "I had a couple dozen supposedly willing volunteers on my list, but when I need them they're nowhere to be found!"

Questions:

1. Because volunteers, as unpaid help that essentially supplement the regular staff, may often feel no compelling need to function by the clock, what might Melissa consider doing to encourage a more reliable volunteer presence?
2. How might Melissa have her regular staff assist in encouraging a continuing volunteer presence?

Case: "Whose Job Is It, Anyway?"

As unit supervisor in one of the hospital's service functions you have recently concluded that your workload has been increasing to the point where you need help with certain nonsupervisory duties. One of the first tasks that comes to mind for delegation is a statistical report you are required to submit on the third workday following the end of each month. Creating the report itself is a fairly easy task, but gathering the data is time consuming.

You select an employee to whom you assign the report, and you provide the essentials of the report's preparation in brief form. You pick an employee you believe capable of doing a decent job and who seems to have sufficient time available, and with no discussion beyond the basics of "here's what I want you to do," you made the assignment. The chosen person said nothing to you about the new assignment.

A few days after assigning the task you discovered that data collection for the report had not yet been started. You remind the employee, which gets you a simple nod of acknowledgment and no comment. Shortly thereafter you overhear part of a conversation in which the employee who is supposedly doing the report says to another employee, "the boss's lousy statistics. They're not mine, so why should I do it? Whose job is it, anyway?"

Questions:

1. What was probably done incorrectly in delegating the report to the chosen employee?

2. What should you be trying to do in an effort to correct the employee's attitude and get this person to willingly comply?

REFERENCES

1. LeBoeuf, M. 1985. *The greatest management principle in the world.* New York: Berkeley Books, 11.
2. Barbee, C., and Bott, V. 1991. Customer treatment as a mirror of employee treatment. *SAM Advanced Management Journal* 56: 27–32.
3. Deeprose, D. 1994. *How to recognize and reward employees.* New York: AMACOM, 19.
4. Deeprose, *How To Recognize and Reward Employees.*
5. Graham, J.H., and Unruh, J. 1990. The motivational impact of nonfinancial employee appreciation practices on medical technologists. *Health Care Supervisor* 8: 9–17.
6. Bell, C.R. 1994. *Customers as partners: Building relationships that last.* (San Francisco, CA: BerrettKoehler, 178.
7. Deeprose, *How To Recognize and Reward Employees,* 125.

RECOMMENDED READING

D. Deeprose, *How To Recognize and Reward Employees.* (New York: AMACOM, 1994).
G. Dutton, "Nurturing Employees and the Bottom Line." *HR Focus* 74, no. 9 (1997): 1–4.
Editorial, "Rethinking Rewards," *Harvard Business Review* 71, no. 6 (1993): 37–49.

Chapter 15

Performance Feedback

*Good management is not only the gift of identifying
talent, but the art of selective recognition of
strengths and weaknesses, and the proper
encouragement of the best in any man or woman.*

—Anonymous

CHAPTER OBJECTIVES

- Stress the critical nature of feedback and its importance in employee performance on a day-to-day basis.
- Establish the role of formal performance evaluations in the provision of feedback on employee performance.
- Describe the character and potential uses of multisource feedback systems.
- Provide specific guidelines for the supervisor's conduct of a formal evaluation of employee performance.
- Furnish suggestions to guide the supervisor's conduct of an employee performance evaluation interview.
- Introduce the concept of team evaluation.
- Review the common pitfalls and shortcomings occasionally encountered in employee performance evaluation.

Performance feedback has always been an important responsibility of those who manage the work of others. The rapid and tumultuous changes continuing to unfold in medical care have resulted in employees having to assume greater responsibility and learn new skills. Employees must try to keep up with new organizational initiatives such as managed care, mergers, alliances, reengineering, customer satisfaction, employee empowerment, and team building. These fast-developing changes mandate more daily feedback to employees and more comprehensive appraisals of their performance.

Today's performance appraisals include new duties and new standards because health maintenance organizations and other forms of managed care demand greater customer satisfaction at a lower cost.

In the past, appraisal and reward systems have focused almost exclusively on individuals. However, it is now necessary to evaluate and reward the performance and competencies of teams as well as individuals.

DAY-TO-DAY FEEDBACK

Ideally, new employees learn on a daily basis how well performance expectations are being met, and they receive help in fine-tuning their skills until they can function independently. This coaching is in all likelihood the single most powerful form of feedback. We seek to deliver candid and constructive feedback that is both helpful and enabling, and candid feedback requires saying what we really think. Unless it is helpful, enabling, and honest, feedback does little to help people improve. For more on this critical form of feedback, see Chapter 12, "Coaching."

It must be stressed at the outset of this discussion that feedback to employees concerning their performance and conduct must be provided regularly, in most instances literally every day. In the crush of business that often threatens to overwhelm the supervisor, it is easy to overlook the minor problems and digressions that occur and easier still to ignore the employee who seems to plod along, doing more or less all right. It pays to remain aware that the principal task of the supervisor is to make it possible for the employees to accomplish their work as accurately and efficiently as possible. This suggests that in spite of the conflicting pressures that constantly threaten to divert the supervisor's attention, it is essential that the supervisor maintain a well-working one-to-one relationship with each employee. This can be accomplished only if the supervisor remains in regular contact with each employee.

If the only performance feedback that an employee receives is that which comes with an annual or semiannual evaluation, the relationship between supervisor and employee is seriously flawed.

FORMAL PERFORMANCE EVALUATIONS

A performance evaluation should be an exchange of information and ideas, not simply a report card. Effective interviewers help employees recognize what needs improvement and assist them in exploring ways to capitalize on their strengths. To inculcate job satisfaction and motivation, supervisors serve more as resources and enablers than as actual appraisers. In other words, while performance reviews are evaluative in matching performance with established standards, they are also developmental in that they enhance careers. The evaluative aspect depends on documented standards and verbal reinforcement, while the developmental aspect requires coaching and mentoring.

Effective evaluation combines the features of recognition, self-appraisal, joint problem solving, and management by objectives. Evaluation emphasis is properly focused on the future rather than on the past. The past is only a starting point for a discussion of how the employee can do better in the future.

An evaluation meeting can have a positive or negative impact on employee self-esteem. To boost morale and confidence we must strive to make our associates perceive themselves as winners. A good performance evaluation and planning session results in both parties leaving the room feeling that they have accomplished something. The end product of the performance evaluation is an understanding between the employee and the supervisor that includes the employee's understanding of what is expected of him or her, how the expectations are met, and ways he or she can improve performance.[1]

Purposes of Performance Evaluation

Performance evaluation serves a number of uses. Of primary interest to the supervisor are

- ensuring understanding of performance expectations by both management and employees,
- identifying training and development needs,
- ensuring fair and equitable administration of reward systems,
- providing recognition for past service, and
- assisting employees with career development.

Essentials of Performance Evaluation

Evaluation systems are not all the same, even the more effective ones that are in use. (There are plenty of ineffective or inappropriate systems out there, but fortunately their numbers are dwindling.) Systems may vary according to the kind of organization involved, for example, acute-care hospital vs home-health agency. They may also differ according to the population to be evaluated; for example, the system used to evaluate registered nurses may be different from that used for maintenance personnel. However, there are some broad requirements essential to every evaluation system.

First, it is always necessary to review and clarify performance expectations based on job descriptions, work standards, rules and policies, and previously formulated objectives. All expectations, that is, all tasks, standards, and goals, should be clear and agreed upon. It is fundamental to any fair and equitable evaluation system that the employee has clear and accurate knowledge of everything on which he or she is to be evaluated.

Next, it is necessary to evaluate past performance. The appraisal concerns what was accomplished because the true starting point of a current evaluation should be how the employee performed recently (for example, objectives met, outcomes realized) and how the employee functioned or behaved in the past (for example, teamwork, attendance, policy observance, ethics, etc.). Past performance gets the most attention because the rating process usually deals with previous outcomes and behavior. The key in using the immediate past, however, lies not in delivering praise or criticism of what occurred but in determining, in joint fashion with employee and supervisor if at all possible, where the employee should be going in the future.

Third, the supervisor should express appreciation for what the person has accomplished. This essential step affects self-confidence, self-image, job satisfaction, and motivation, important factors that are all too often omitted or glossed over in evaluations that are founded largely on criticism. It is true that with some employees a certain amount of criticism cannot be avoided, but it is the rare employee indeed about whom the supervisor cannot say something positive at an evaluation interview. Regardless of the negatives that may be present, look for the positives and give them fair hearing.

Finally, develop a plan. Planning moves from the past into the future and directly affects work performance. Honest participative management demands collaboration and promises of support. An honest developmental plan will consist of much more than attempts to correct the deficiencies revealed through the examination of past performance.

Rating the Systems of Performance Evaluation

Little will be said here concerning some of the inappropriate and inadequate systems that were used for many years in many organizations except to advance some precautions concerning the worst of these that might still be encountered here and there.

Beware of what is quite likely the oldest form of performance evaluation, appraisal based primarily on personality characteristics. These systems required the supervisor to "rate" each employee on the likes of "attitude," "cooperativeness," "adaptability," "demeanor," and such. The problem, of course, is that any rating the supervisor might apply is simply the judgment of that supervisor and most likely is no true indicator of performance. Even older criteria that are not quite as "soft" as pure personality characteristics, for example "job knowledge," one that can still be found on many evaluation forms, say nothing about performance (the validity of "job knowledge" lies not with how much of it the employee possesses but in how that knowledge is applied to achieve results). Overall, the more personality judgments required, the more subjective assessments made, the weaker and less defensible the final evaluation.

Other forms of evaluation that are inherently inaccurate and inequitable are the so-called "forced-rating" systems. In such systems the supervisor may be required, for example, to apportion the employees into bands under a normal distribution scheme that calls for a certain percentage to be placed in "superior," an equal percentage in "unsatisfactory," and the remaining employees into two, three, or four bands in between. This by-the-numbers approach completely ignores the reality of the work group and the differences in performance among employees. Consider just one serious flaw in this approach: if the supervisor is doing a decent job at all, "unsatisfactory" employees have individually been helped to improve to a point where their work is acceptable or they have been weeded out, so at any given time there may be few if any "unsatisfactory" employees in the group.

We could fill considerable space describing the inappropriate evaluation systems still in existence here and there. Suffice it to say that to stand a chance of constituting a fair and equitable evaluation approach, a system must be job-description based and must keep required subjective assessments to an absolute minimum.

MULTISOURCE FEEDBACK SYSTEMS

There are many weaknesses inherent in the traditional top-down feedback systems, some of which have already been mentioned. Employees benefit from feedback from their peers as well as from their supervisors. Often peer reviews are considerably more accurate and acceptable and can help to reinforce the emphasis on collective responsibility. Such feedback is especially valuable because the person being evaluated learns how his or her behavior affects the other members of the team.

Evaluating Leaders

In traditional organizations, all of the appraising is accomplished vertically downwards. Yet employees are the recipients of the leadership provided by their superiors, therefore they are customers of the leaders and entitled to evaluate leadership performance. Although in some organizations employees provide such feedback via formal appraisal systems, most employers obtain this information indirectly via employee attitude surveys and, perhaps, other mechanisms such as exit interviews with departing employees.

Multisource Feedback

In the 360-degree multisource feedback system, managers flesh out the evaluation process by obtaining input from colleagues, subordinates, and sometimes customers. This provides a 360-degree view of how people perceive others on the job. Managers may use this kind of system as a developmental tool or as a formal appraisal instrument.

Use of 360-Degree Feedback Systems as Developmental Tools

The majority of people are more likely to modify their self-perceptions in the face of multisource feedback. In this kind of process there is less likelihood that important elements of performance will be overlooked.

In systems intended to provide only employee development guidance, the recipients of the feedback are asked whom they would like included in the battery of evaluators. The data become the sole property of the recipients and are not used in the formal evaluation process. These systems have been garnering favorable comments from many employers. Most of the employees being evaluated find the reports helpful and sometimes surprising.

Use of 360-Feedback Systems in Formal Evaluations

Multisource feedback can make an evaluation system more comprehensive, but employees need to believe that the data is unbiased and objective. Employees must have confidence in the intentions and credibility of the evaluators. The anonymity of the evaluators is usually protected.

Unlike those in the purely developmental approach, these evaluations become the property of management. Evaluators may or may not discuss their ratings with each other prior to releasing them to the person being assessed and to his or her superiors.

There are severe drawbacks to the use of these systems in the formal appraisal process. Lepsinger and Lucia urge a cautious approach.[2] They suggest that management first introduce the 360-degree system to their career development program. Then, if that is successful, a pilot study can be undertaken using the system for formal appraisal.

Drawbacks to Using 360-Degree Feedback in Formal Evaluations

- Recipients may resist feedback that actually affects their salary and chances for promotion.
- When evaluators think they may hurt others by what they report, they are less likely to be completely honest.
- The evaluators may be competitors of those being evaluated for rewards or promotions.

- The organizational culture may not support open, honest feedback.
- It makes an already time-consuming process still more demanding of time.

PREPARATION FOR PERFORMANCE EVALUATIONS OF INDIVIDUALS

The performance evaluation meeting consists of two major components: process and content. The process encompasses the format of the system and the skill of the interviewer. The content is what occurs during the meeting. As with any meeting, advance planning is crucial to success. Too often the interviewer's preparation consists of summarizing the employee's deficiencies while neglecting to look for the person's accomplishments and special efforts.

Review the Evaluation Form

Most organizations design their own evaluation forms, and supervisors rarely have any significant input into the design process. However, this should not prevent the interviewer from introducing additional items, including those that relate to teamwork and customer service. Such items may include

- participation in team efforts,
- willingness to express opinions or assume responsibility,
- willingness to help solve problems,
- ability to adjust to major changes, and
- readiness to take special actions to "delight" customers.

Highlight the criteria on the form that are to receive special attention. Many all-purpose rating forms are deficient in listing the competencies of people in leadership roles. The list provided in Exhibit 15–1 may be helpful.

Obtain Employee Input

An employee scheduled for an evaluation conference should have the following in his or her possession before meeting with the evaluator.

- A copy of the position description, including detailed information about performance standards.
- A copy of the evaluation form used to report the evaluation. If the employee is to hand in a completed form to the interviewer, two copies are provided, and one is retained by the employee.
- A copy of the report of this person's previous formal evaluation.
- Departmental objectives for the current year and the year to follow.
- Instructions on how to prepare for the meeting (see Exhibit 15–2).

Exhibit 15–1 Managerial Competencies

Maintains contemporary professional knowledge and skills
- Keeps up to date in both professional and managerial fields
- Regularly attends seminars and other meetings
- Meets all continuing education standards

Demonstrates initiative and flexibility
- Identifies needs for innovation and change and effectively implements changes
- Solves problems quickly and skillfully

Maximizes the use of personnel and material resources
- Keeps within budgetary limits
- Manages time of self and subordinates effectively
- Evaluates, selects, and maintains equipment and supplies skillfully

Communicates effectively
- Keeps vertical and horizontal channels of communication open and active
- Enjoys good rapport with other team members
- Makes efficient use of meetings and other information systems; has mastered our computer system
- Is skilled in interviewing techniques
- Possesses good writing ability

Shows other leadership abilities
- Coaches, counsels, and evaluates performance well
- Maintains high morale, enthusiasm, and motivation
- Is skilled in selecting, orienting, and training new hires
- Deals promptly and effectively with personnel problems
- Coordinates and cooperates well with other work units
- Delegates and empowers effectively
- Organizes, assigns, and schedules skillfully
- Recognized as a good team builder
- Accomplishes assignments and challenges on time and to the satisfaction of superiors

You may choose to have an employee complete the evaluation form and give it to you before the meeting. There are two advantages to this practice. First, it introduces a spirit of collaboration. Second, it enables the interviewer to note the areas of disagreement or sensitivity. That is, if the evaluator's rating and the employee's self-rating are far apart on any particular criteria, the two of them know at once that these criteria represent items that they need to discuss in depth. But care should be exercised in attempting to get employees to perform self-

Exhibit 15–2 Employee Preparation Instructions

---

1. Review your position description. List any changes since your last review. Pencil in any changes you would like.
2. Scan your previous evaluation. Be prepared to discuss the objectives you achieved and those that were not achieved.
3. Prepare a new list of objectives.
4. Review your current continuing education record.
5. Jot down or otherwise be prepared to discuss the following:
   - How you feel about your performance since the last meeting
   - What you consider your most valuable contribution to the organization since your last review and what gave you the most satisfaction
   - What changes in systems, procedures, equipment, service, cost containment, or quality improvement you suggest we consider
   - Anything that is preventing you from reaching your full potential
   - What frustrates you most at present
   - What supervision can do to help you improve

---

evaluations; some will inevitably be uneasy about doing so, fearing (largely imaginary) consequences should they rate themselves appreciably different from the rating of the evaluator. In some situations it is best to offer self-evaluation as an option.

An employee scheduled for an evaluation conference can be asked to prepare a list of objectives and plans relating to personal improvement needs and career development, including specific requests for assistance needed to achieve the new objectives. Encourage each employee to prepare a list of what he or she considers significant contributions to the organization, and urge each to include those activities that afforded them the most satisfaction.

Review the Personnel File of the Employee

Because the personnel record may relate to performance evaluation, an employee's personnel file should include the following:

- the individual's current position description, complete with performance standards,
- continuing education and attendance records,
- commendations and special recognitions or awards,
- incident reports,
- records of formal counseling or disciplinary actions, and
- copies of previous evaluations.

Schedule a Conference

Set a date, time, and place for the evaluation conference. Give the employee sufficient time to prepare for the meeting. Allow at least an hour for the interview.

Formulate Key Remarks

Select the exact words to use for introductory statements, to criticize, and to confront defensiveness. Anticipate problems. Be prepared to cite specific factual information to support any negative feedback or low ratings; remember to avoid generalizations.

FOUR PHASES OF THE EVALUATION INTERVIEW

First, review and, as necessary, revise the position description and performance standards. This is often a good time to document changes relating to quality improvement, customer service, and empowerment strategies.

Second, discuss the performance ratings using the organization's evaluation form. Begin on a positive note by focusing on criteria that were rated highest by you (and also by the employee, if a self-evaluation is involved). Do not gloss over these with something like "we agree on that." Compliment the person and cite specific instances of outstanding work that led to the high rating. The individual will appreciate hearing why you thought he or she deserved a high rating, especially one that might be higher than a self-rating. Save for last the items that you rated low or for which you and the employee seem far apart in your assessment of performance. Here is where you may encounter defensiveness or where emotional outbursts may occur. Exhibit 15–3 provides suggestions for discussing performance deficiencies.

> *A caveat: Most experienced managers will confess that the biggest mistake they made in the past was to overrate marginal performers. This tendency all too often ends with an embarrassed manager trying to explain to a superior why he wants to fire a problem employee.*

Third, critique the person's accomplishments related to performance objectives formulated at the previous evaluation. Congratulate the person on successes in these areas. Through discussion, decide which of the objectives that were not reached should be retained and which should be abandoned. End this segment by thanking the person for his or her accomplishments since the previous review.

Exhibit 15–3 Suggestions for Discussing Performance Deficiencies

---

1. Limit criticism to one or two significant issues. If there are others, discuss them at another meeting.
2. Offer the employee your support.
3. Save critical remarks for last.
4. Before you criticize, encourage self-criticism.
5. Use all your listening skills.
6. Respond supportively
   - reinforce points of agreement
   - handle disagreement diplomatically
   - use joint problem-solving approaches
   - avoid being defensive
7. Avoid nonspecific terms such as attitude, work ethic, professionalism, weakness, and deficiency.
8. Do not use the global comment "needs more experience" when documenting improvement needs. Spell out exactly what experience is needed.

Finally, discuss future performance. Past performance only provides the basis for planning. Most of the interview time should deal with expectations for the future. The first goal should target activities needed to improve performance. The second should deal with career development; that is, what may be needed to reach one's full potential. Like most New Year's resolutions, goals are meaningless if there is no commitment. Do not accept "I'll try." This is no more than a noisy way of doing nothing. The person who says "I'll try" is simply building excuses for failure. If failure ensues, the person claims to have done what he or she said would be done—try. In this step you jointly develop a list of objectives that are consistent with depart-

---

SCRAM to Recall the Characteristics of Good Objectives

Specific. Specific feedback focuses on concrete and observable behavior, not inferences about traits or personality characteristics.

Challenging. If it is not challenging, it probably is not worth very much.

Relevant. It must be related to the person's responsibilities.

Achievable. It should be challenging but doable. Failures lead to frustration and loss of self-confidence.

Measurable. Statistics and charts are good (hard data), but sometimes behavior is not easy to quantify. Although some words such as caring, respect, and courtesy cannot be meaningfully measured with digits, the key is verifiability.

---

mental goals and objectives. When interviewees have difficulty formulating objectives, help them. Ask them what they think should be done differently in their unit and what role they would like to play in any such change. Do not give up on this too quickly. If the person still comes up empty, suggest a few things you would like the person to do. Then ask what *you* could do to make the work more satisfying.

Conclude the Interview

End the session with an affirmation, an expression of confidence in the ability of the individual to achieve the new objectives. Thank the person not only for what has been accomplished but also for cooperation and participation during the interview.

Postinterview Actions

Make certain that the appraisal form has been filled out completely and includes documentation of new objectives and action plans. Every employee must be given an opportunity to respond both verbally and in writing to adverse comments or unfavorable performance ratings. Do not neglect to

- monitor the person's progress. Provide reminders about their plans and objectives if necessary;
- congratulate the individual on reaching each objective or showing areas of improvement;
- confirm promised support or offer more support when obstacles are perceived by the employee;
- modify, replace, or cancel objectives as appropriate. Conditions change, and objectives must change with them;
- document the employee's achievements.

PERFORMANCE EVALUATION OF WORK TEAMS

Different teams require different approaches to measurement and thus to the evaluation of their work. Teams of floor nurses and their ancillary care providers are evaluated largely based on patient satisfaction. The performance of a laboratory team is usually judged by turnaround time, accuracy, and reliability of test results.

Appraising teams involves the "what" and "how" of team efforts. The "what" refers to the goals, objectives, and key results that the team and each individual achieve. The "how" refers to the performance behavior important in promoting teamwork and achieving the team goals collaboratively.

Teams may be evaluated by team facilitators, with or without the participation of team members. Both individual and team performance is evaluated by members of self-directed teams, except in the early phases of team building when this is still undertaken by the supervisor.

COMMON PITFALLS OF PERFORMANCE EVALUATION

Performance evaluation, or performance appraisal or performance review as it might variously be called, can be a powerful mechanism for employee development when it is applied honestly and conscientiously by a manager who uses it to improve employee performance, expand employee capabilities, and enhance organizational effectiveness. However, performance evaluation is not a favorite activity of many managers because of its time-consuming nature and the shortcomings and weaknesses that are to be encountered both in system design and administration and in the attitudes of managers who may be nearly overwhelmed with work and cannot help but see evaluation as a significant imposition on their time.

Pitfalls commonly encountered relative to evaluation include the following, some of which, if cumulative, can lead to system failure.

- The process is not taken seriously by either manager or employee. This is manifested when there is inadequate preparation by the participants, when the meeting is repeatedly postponed or left until the last minute and then rushed, or when the interviewer tolerates frequent interruptions during the meeting.
- The manager has only superficial knowledge of the employee's performance. It has been truthfully said that the less a manager knows about what a subordinate does, the better chance the subordinate has to do whatever he or she wants to do and how much he or she wants to do (or feels like doing). Perhaps, with increasing spans of control, the supervisor has so many people or the people are scattered over such a broad geographic area that an employee can "get lost" for an extended time. Also, it is common in health care organizations, especially in hospitals where 24-hour-per day, 7-day-per week operations are the rule, that some employees seldom see their supervisors. A supervisor who has direct oversight of an employee's behavior for only short periods may have to rely on only the results of behavior (did the work actually get done?) or on input from others. Reliance on secondhand information weakens the evaluation process. The first, and perhaps most valid, source of performance observation is your own firsthand knowledge.[3]
- Documented, up-to-date, specific work standards or objectives do not exist. This condition gives the supervisor little to measure against, and the resulting evaluation lacks concrete information.
- The evaluation consists of highly subjective assessments (usually because of a weak system or a lazy evaluator), or it lacks honesty altogether. Failure to honestly critique an employee's performance hurts both organization and employee.
- In the evaluation meeting, the evaluator employs excess judging and too little listening.

- There is insufficient positive feedback or respect for the employee's self-esteem. The employee who receives only negative commentary will not truly hear what is being said.
- The evaluation interview consists of generalities; the employee hears little more than "You're doing just fine." Or the evaluator hands out the written evaluation without comment or invites only questions about the report itself.
- The evaluation forms are inadequate (as a great many in active use are). Some evaluators behave as though they are required to write something significant in every space (not so—not every space may be needed for every employee), and some simply write enough to fill a given space even though more should be said. A form—almost any form—seems to establish its own constraints for some users.
- The evaluation "score" is used primarily to allocate salaries instead of to improve performance.
- Primary emphasis is on the past rather than on the future.
- New objectives are nonspecific, inappropriate, or unchallenging.
- The employee has little or no opportunity to participate in formulating objectives or adjusting or resetting standards for future performance.
- Reprimands, criticisms, or performance deficiencies had never been discussed prior to the evaluation meeting, catching the employee by surprise. Few other occurrences place evaluation in a poor light more than a "gotcha!"

Think About It

If you are daunted by or simply dislike the process of performance evaluation, think about why you feel this way. Do you dislike evaluation because it is uncomfortable, or is it uncomfortable because you dislike it? The solution? Just do it, again and again as necessary. Why? Because it is a requirement of the organization as well as outside agencies, but mostly because you and your employees will both benefit from it in the long run. Evaluation may never become your favorite supervisory task, but it will become more tolerable as you gain experience and its value becomes apparent.

Questions for Review and Discussion

1. If we believe that it is inappropriate to evaluate an employee on so subjective a characteristic as "attitude," how then should we address employee behavior that seems to occur because of an attitude problem?
2. Some organizations evaluate all employees at the same time each year; some organizations evaluate employees throughout the year, often using the employment anniversary date. From a supervisor's perspective, explain one significant advantage and one significant disadvantage of each method.

3. Explain what is meant by the statement, "If the relationship between supervisor and employee is all that it should be, the employee's annual evaluation will be a mere formality."

4. There is often very little ongoing contact between a supervisor and those employees who go along quietly doing a passable job and causing no problems. Why can't these employees be counted on to continue working as they have been without constant feedback?

5. Why is it recommended that the initial step toward an evaluation of an employee be the review and update of the job description?

6. It is frequently claimed that an effective objective consists of three elements. One element is *what is to be done* and another element is *how much is to be done*. What do you believe is the third element, and why must all three be present?

7. Consider an acceptably performing employee who has been in the same job for many years, is at the top of the pay scale for that job and can get increases only when the scale itself moves, and has no promotion potential or other advancement possibilities. What will you accomplish by giving this employee regular performance evaluations?

8. In a few brief sentences, write a convincing argument you might use in trying to get a reluctant employee to agree to completing and submitting a self-evaluation (we are assuming that self-evaluation is optional in your evaluation system).

9. In recent years performance evaluations retained in personnel files have often become determining factors in cases of age discrimination involving laid-off employees. Why might this be so?

10. Some organizations have made use of peer-group evaluation in which the several members of a group of similarly situated workers provide input to each others' evaluations. Describe one significant advantage and one likely disadvantage of this process.

Case: "Let's Get This Evaluation Thing Out of the Way"

You stopped by your manager's office to relay a brief message to him. You were later to think that this small act—which you were not obligated to perform—was a mistake on your part, because before you could get away the boss said, "Hey, while you're here, let's get this evaluation thing out of the way. Should've been done 6 weeks ago." He pulled an evaluation form from a stack on his desk and said, "Sit down—this won't take long."

The boss began by asking, "Don't suppose you did a self-evaluation?"

You answered, "No. I didn't know it was expected."

"Well, anyway, we can do without it.

"Now, to get to it. You've done some good work this past year, and I want you to know it's noticed and appreciated. Of course there are always places where some improvement could be made. Starting with the good side, your output has been great these past few months, and I'm especially pleased with the way you handled the implementation of the new billing system. You've got pretty good judgment, and this shows up in your planning. And you did a swell job with the scheduling problem—maybe I told you that at the time.

"But let me tell you where I think you can do better. I know I can speak frankly and right to the point. Your stubbornness is still a problem. I can think of three or four times when I've had to step in between you and the folks in info systems. I'm sure you agree that you haven't shown a great deal of creativity in doing your job, and that's too bad because this is an important area for us to consider when we're picking people for promotion. Another thing I've noticed is that you're too aggressive in dealings with other departments. You know we all have to pull together if this health system is to…"

Instructions:

1. Critique the foregoing portion of the "evaluation meeting" between "you" and the manager. Indicate what you believe to be inappropriate, if anything, and what you believe to be acceptable, if anything. In mentioning something you believe was improperly done, state how it might have been done correctly. In concluding, summarize your reaction to the above passage in a single sentence.

Case: "I'm Not Getting Any Better Than I Was?"

Supervisor Jane was not at all comfortable with the way the performance evaluation meeting with Wilma was going. Wilma was far more uncommunicative than usual; she would speak only when asked something, then answer only briefly. All of Jane's attempts to lighten up the conversation were falling flat.

Except for a brief review 3 months after Wilma's transfer to Jane's unit, this was the first opportunity Jane had had for a thorough review of Wilma's performance. Wilma had initially seemed eager for the meeting, but when they sat down and Jane laid out the completed evaluation forms, Wilma fell silent and seemed to withdraw.

Increasingly frustrated by Wilma's apparent unwillingness to participate, Jane stopped in the middle of trying to make a point and said, "Wilma, something about this evaluation is bothering you. Out with it."

"Nothing's bothering me," Wilma responded.

"I know you well enough to know that you're upset about something. Out with it, so we're not just wasting our time here."

Wilma sat silently for a moment. Then she tapped a fingernail on the evaluation form and said, "It's this—my rating."

"There's nothing wrong with it," Jane said. "It's comfortably above standard performance and very close to the average of the extremely good group of people we have on this unit."

"It's lower than any score I ever got from my last supervisor. I know I've done at least as well here as I did there, but you've given me my lowest score in 5 years."

"Wilma, this is a good evaluation score."

"I can't agree," said Wilma. "All of you who do these use the same forms and pretty much the same job descriptions, and the evaluations ought to be consistent. Compared with Sue, my last supervisor, aren't you telling me that after all my hard work I'm no better than I used to be? That I'm not getting any better than I was? Or even that my performance is slipping because I had a higher score last year?"

Questions:

1. If you were in Jane's position, how would you try to explain the differences in evaluation scores to this employee?
2. What, if anything, do you believe the organization should be doing about its evaluation system?

REFERENCES

1. Metzger, N. 2004. Ch. 6, Human resources management in organized delivery systems. In Lawrence F. Wolper, Editor, *Health care administration,* 4th ed. Sudbury, MA: Jones and Bartlett Publishers, 265.
2. Lepsinger, R., and Lucia, A.D. 1997. 360 Degrees feedback and performance appraisal. *Training* 34(9): 62–70.
3. Lombardi, D.N. 2001. *Handbook for the new health care manager,* 2d ed. San Francisco CA: 294.

RECOMMENDED READING

Chesser et al., "Job Descriptions and Performance Appraisals," *Health Care Supervisor* 15, no. 4 (1997): 1–34.
S.H. Gebelein, "Multi-Rater Feedback Goes Strategic," *HR Focus* 73, no. 1 (1996): 1, 6.
J. Ghorpade and M.M. Chen, "Appraising the Performance of Medical Technologists in a Clinical Laboratory," *Clinical Laboratory Management Review* 11, no. 2 (1997): 132–41.

Chapter 16

Counseling: Preventing Bigger Problems

*Criticism should leave a person with the
feeling of having been helped.*

—Anonymous

A little neglect may breed great mischief.

—Benjamin Franklin

CHAPTER OBJECTIVES

- Define the purpose of employee counseling and identify the principal circumstances under which counseling should be employed.
- Provide guidance for determining whether counseling is appropriate for any given situation, and identify the reasons why employees need counseling and how supervisor sometimes fail to counsel when they should.
- Identify several essential elements of preparation for an employee-counseling interview.
- Provide the supervisor with detailed guidelines for the conduct of an employee-counseling interview.
- Identify the common defensive responses of employees to a counseling situation.
- Establish the necessity for systematic follow-up to every counseling session.
- Identify the common barriers to effective counseling.

There are two kinds of counseling that the supervisor may encounter from time to time. One is career counseling, which involves the supervisor functioning as an advisor or mentor. The other is preventive or remedial counseling, which addresses employee performance or behavior that appears to be straying from es-

221

tablished norms. This chapter focuses on the latter, and from this point through the remainder of the chapter the term "counseling" will be used to mean preventive or remedial counseling.

The goal of counseling is to correct deviant performance or behavior or prevent its occurrence while preserving the self-esteem of the individual employee. A counseling confrontation provides the employee with an opportunity to examine his or her behavior and to decide whether or not to change. The objective should never be to release anger or frustration or to punish.

Unsuccessful counseling, that is, counseling that fails to correct or prevent the deviant performance or behavior, usually culminates in the application of disciplinary measures.

MOST COMMON REASONS FOR EMPLOYEE COUNSELING

The principal reasons for employee counseling include the following:

- Unsatisfactory productivity or diminishing quality of work
- Poor or apparently deteriorating work habits
- Violations of policies, rules, procedures, or ethics or behavior that indicates tendencies in that direction
- Inability to get along with others
- Chronic complaining
- Complaints from customers (whether external or internal)

Deciding If the Need for Counseling Exists

When performance or behavior is borderline, or was once acceptable and is noticeably deteriorating, it is necessary to decide whether action is needed and, if so, what that action should be. In marginal instances in which you are initially unsure if you should proceed with counseling, ask yourself, "What would happen if everyone did that?" or "If I do nothing, what, if any, adverse results are likely to occur?"

If you have a team of overachievers, you may regard the performance of marginal performers as unsatisfactory because it compares unfavorably with that of the overachievers. This sort of trap can be avoided if you measure performance with established standards and do not make comparisons with other employees.

Counseling is not the remedy for all personnel problems. As often as not it is preventive medicine. It can solve small problems before they become big ones that require formal disciplinary action. Figure 16–1 offers a flowchart that can used for this purpose. Note that counseling is usually not the most appropriate remedy.

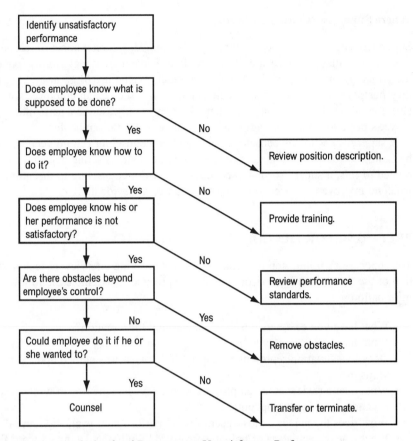

Figure 16–1 Analysis of and Responses to Unsatisfactory Performance

Why Employees Violate Rules

Employees are likely to break rules, violate policies, or ignore procedural requirements because

- they never learned what was required of them or they forgot;
- they see rules, regulations, etc. as meaningless, restrictive, or unfair;
- they are aware that rules are rarely enforced;
- they are influenced by other workers;
- they consider the rewards of misbehavior to be greater than the risks or the penalties; and
- they are misfits or malcontents.

Where Supervisors Often Go Wrong

Supervisors often fail to counsel or apply other remedies for a number of reasons.

First, they may not be aware of the problem. Second, they may simply ignore the problem, with the attitude "If I'm very quiet, maybe it will go away." Third, they postpone action for a "more convenient time," such as an employee's next performance evaluation. Finally, a supervisor may readily ascribe a particular employee's behavior to a "poor attitude" and decide that little can be done.

A supervisor who has conscientiously applied counseling can go very wrong by failing to follow up, that is, failing to monitor postcounseling behavior. And, related to this, a supervisor may fail to escalate from counseling to disciplining when no improvement occurs or frequent relapses are evident.

PREPARING FOR THE COUNSELING INTERVIEW

The supervisor's initial step in preparing for a counseling interview is accumulation of the facts. As a supervisor, you should proceed to assemble the following information:

- What have you or others observed concerning the situation?
- What have you documented?
- Does this situation represent a relapse? If so, what was agreed upon at previous meetings?
- What does a review of the employee's record reveal in the way of written reprimands, customer complaints?
- What does the person's most recent formal performance evaluation reveal?
- What rule or regulation or policy is involved? Study the document word for word.
- What patterns of behavior are evident? For example, concerning absenteeism, individuals may call in sick only on Mondays, Fridays, or on days when scheduled for unpleasant assignments.

Explore the perceived benefit-to-risk ratio of the behavior from the point of view of the employee. For example, when an employee goes shopping on sick days or takes long breaks and is never called on it, the benefit-to-risk ratio is high; that is, the employee has no incentive to reform.

Do not procrastinate. Think about the damage that could be taking place while you hesitate. Also, the more you delay, the harder it will be to convince the person that the matter is important.

If you are inexperienced in these matters and the apparent problem appears to be serious, consult with your manager or with the human resources department.

Schedule a place, date, and time for a counseling interview. The location should be one where there will be no interruptions. Your office might not be the best location if it ordinarily attracts a lot of traffic, so you may need to use an available conference room or an empty office. Hold the meeting in the morning so that you will then have the rest of the day to show by words and behavior that you do not bear a grudge toward the individual, that it is the behavior and not the person that has attracted your criticism. Smile and chat just as you would if you had not held a counseling session.

Mentally rehearse the most important or sensitive aspects of the upcoming meeting, specifically

- your exact opening remarks,
- statements intended to boost the employee's confidence,
- the solution you hope to reach, and
- how you will respond to rebuttals, defensive reactions, anger, tears, or threats.

CONDUCTING A COUNSELING INTERVIEW

This will be a review of your counseling interview with hypothetical employee Joyce, who has exhibited a behavioral problem.

Step 1. The theme of the initial session should be one of helpfulness and caring. Greet Joyce with a smile. You intend to help, not punish, her. Thank her for coming. Do not apologize for calling the meeting; you weaken your position when you start with something such as "Joyce, I hate to bring this up, but..." Equally inappropriate is socking her with an intimidating statement such as "Joyce, we've got to talk about your poor performance." Assume she wants to do a good job, and say so. Affirm that assumption by articulating some specific attribute (for example, "Joyce, I receive many compliments from our medical staff about your gentleness toward patients."). Continue with, "Joyce, I have a problem that I need your help with." (This is true; it really is your problem!)

Step 2. Find out whether Joyce is aware of the problem, especially if a policy or rule is being violated. Describe the situation in specific, nonjudgmental terms. Be tentative if there is some question as to the validity of the charge. Use the words you selected carefully in your preparation. Attack the behavior, not Joyce. Your hope is that Joyce joins you in that attack. The more able you are to move into a problem-solving mode, the more successful the outcome will be.

Step 3. Explain how the behavior affects your department and other people. To convince her that this is important, emphasize how the behavior affects you [for example, "When I see (this happen), I become upset"]. Avoid absolute terms such as "always" and "never." These words are usually inaccurate and invite contradiction. For example, "You're never on time" is countered with "I'm on time most of the time." Avoid sarcasm, kidding, or other put-downs. These elicit resentment and serve no useful purpose. Do not quote from policy manuals unless the employee challenges the authenticity of your charge. Taking refuge in a handbook can make you appear weak. For the same reason, do not say, "Management expects . . ." *Do* say, "I expect . . ."

Step 4. Give Joyce time to respond. Listen until her initial reaction runs its course. Do not interrupt, even if she utters untruths or makes countercharges. Do not become defensive or lose your cool. Respond appropriately. Instead of judgmental responses ("You don't try hard enough") or defensive responses ("That's not true and you know it"), use empathetic responses ("I can understand why you…") and probing responses (when, where, who, why, and how). Paraphrase ("What I hear you saying is…") and summarize ("Then we agree that…"). Jot down key points Joyce makes; you may need to refer to these later.

Step 5. Get Joyce to admit that there is a problem and that she is part of it. This is often difficult, especially if the behavior has been tolerated for an extended period of time. She may respond sarcastically with "Big deal" or some similar remark. Ask her what she thinks the effects of this continued behavior could be on her employment or relationships (for example, the impact on her next performance appraisal). This can force her to reflect on the consequences that are not in her best interest. Empathize with any aired frustration ("You say that you feel like a victim of the system. I can appreciate that").

Step 6. Emphasize that the problem must be solved and that it is up to her to solve it. Add that you are always there to help. Reiterate the point that she should solve her own problem.

Why You Should Avoid Prescribing Solutions

- Quick solutions by you can make the other person feel stupid.
- When your solution fails to work, *you* look stupid.
- The employee may feel obliged to take your advice, even when he or she knows a better solution is available.
- An employee who owns the solution tries harder to make it work.
- An employee can become dependent on you for all solutions.

If you cannot accept Joyce's first offering, keep asking for alternatives until she comes up with one you can live with. Discuss the pros and cons of each suggestion. Avoid directive phrases such as "If I were you…" or "Here's what you should do." Compliment her for coming up with solutions. If the discussion stalls, ask some leading questions to guide her to more options. Do not impose your solution unless absolutely necessary. Offer to help, for example, "Joyce, it's up to you to take care of this. However, I will cooperate. When I notice (such-and-such happening), I'll remind you."

Step 7. Summarize what is agreed upon. Repeat your expectations clearly, and insist on her commitment to the solution. Include a deadline for the problem to be solved. End on a positive note and with an affirmation. Thank her for cooperating, and express confidence in her ability to solve the problem. For example, "Joyce, I appreciate your cooperation. I knew I could depend on you to take care of this. This past performance is way below what I know you are capable of." If it is obvious that despite your best efforts you're not getting near a solution, do not make it a matter of wills. Simply state your position and what you expect, then end the meeting. It is sometimes a good idea to set a date for a follow-up meeting.

Step 8. Document. A common and serious deficiency is the lack of documentation. All too often, counseling is not successful and must be repeated or ratcheted up to disciplinary level. In either instance, you'll be grateful for having the record. The record should include

- the date of the discussion,
- a description of the problem,
- the employee's comments (exact words are best),
- the agreed-upon resolution,
- any warning you delivered, and
- the deadline for resolution of the problem.

Do not include this documentation in the employee's personnel file. If you do so, it can be interpreted as the delivery of a written reprimand, a serious disciplinary step. Simply put this documentation away in your own files, being sure to first supply the employee with a copy. You may have to become a disciplinarian at some later date, but at this stage you are a counselor, and what you have done to this point is informal.

Maintain confidentiality. Keep your personal files locked away, secure from prying eyes. Do not discuss the meeting with anyone other than your immediate superior as may be necessary.

COMMON DEFENSIVE RESPONSES BY EMPLOYEES

Keep in mind that any behavior displayed or comments made by employees during counseling interviews represent behavior that the individual has probably found effective at some time in the past.

Employees may *balk* at any discussion.

- They may say they do not want to discuss the matter at the present time.
- They may deny everything you say.

- They may refuse to listen or keep interrupting.
- They may talk louder and faster.
- They may shed tears.
- They may storm out of your office.
- They may clam up and say nothing.

In these circumstances, the solution is to insist on a dialogue. Respond to loud, angry outcries with something such as "You're starting to yell, Joyce." If Joyce runs out of your office, do not chase after her. Simply wait until later in the day, or the next day, and then send for her again. Start all over. If she cries, hand her a box of tissues and wait for the tears to stop. People who suddenly clam up may be trying to decide whether to say something of a sensitive nature. If you break the silence too soon, you may never know what that was. If the silence persists, say, "Joyce, I thought we were having a conversation." Lean forward and look like you expect a response. If you repeat this without success, sigh or frown and say you will try to establish a dialogue at another time. If a second meeting also ends in failure, you must move on to take disciplinary action.

Employees may try to *minimize* the problem. If a person retorts sarcastically, "OK, I haven't been the employee of the month. I'll try to do better if that'll make you happy," do not accept this. Say you're glad the person recognized there is a problem. Emphasize that this is an important issue and that something definite must be done about it.

Another scenario is that employees may *challenge* you. Joyce may say, "The old boss never said anything about that." If this happens, respond with, "I'm not your old boss." She may say, "If this is so important, how is it that you never said anything about it before?" In this case, respond with "I thought that you would take care of it without my direction" or admit that you should have acted sooner. If she claims that work is not affected ("I get my work done, don't I?"), respond with, "Yes, but you interfere with the work of others and set a bad example for the new employees."

Sometimes employees may *counterattack*. They may threaten to quit or go over your head. They may accuse you of the same behavior ("You have gall, accusing me of that. I've seen you doing the very same thing."). If there is a threat to quit, to go over your head, or to expose something damaging about you, reply that the employee may do so but that you recommend first giving serious thought to the possible consequences of those actions.

Finally, employees may try to *sidetrack* the discussion. They accuse others ("Helen does the same thing. How is it you never say anything to her?"). Or they blame a myriad of personal problems at home. If employees try to sidetrack the discussion, tell them that nothing will be accomplished by accusing others. If they blame problems at home, channel the discussion back to the work situation. If signs and symptoms suggest a serious personal problem, however, recommend professional help. Usually an appropriate comment is "Joyce, I'm not qualified to help you with those kinds of problems. You can confidentially access the Employee Assistance Program or Employee Health can recommend a professional counselor if you like, but for now let's get back to the problem at hand."

FOLLOW-UP

The counseling process never ends with the interview. Supervisors often dismiss the subject from their minds because they are so relieved that the immediate confrontation is over and that the employee has promised to solve the problem.

Appropriate follow-up consists of monitoring performance and reinforcing desired behavior. Positive strokes motivate; negative strokes or the absence of feedback demotivate. Support improvements with smiles and pats on the back. Do not wait until perfection has been achieved. Reinforce each small step with something such as "I know you're making a special effort, Joyce, and I appreciate that."

Identify and address specific concerns that call for exploration or reassurance. When the problem appears to have been solved, hold a commendatory meeting. At that meeting, describe the improvement you've noted and encourage the person to relate how he or she achieved it. At this time you can offer to help with any unanticipated roadblocks. Close the follow-up meeting with expressions of appreciation and an affirmation.

If the undesired behaviors or results persist, you are faced with several choices. You can extend the deadline if there has been some progress, you can begin disciplinary action, or you can counsel again. Most often you will choose to repeat the counseling session, but now you have the initial problem plus a new one—the employee failing to deliver on his or her commitment.

Your objectives in a repeat counseling session are to

- let the employee know that you are aware of the continued problem,
- inform the employee of the risk he or she is taking by repeating the behavior, and
- offer one more chance before you take disciplinary action.

To emphasize the importance of such a meeting to the wayward employee, ask your manager or a representative of the human resources department to sit in. At this session, manifest less patience, and skip the smiles and affirmations. On the other hand, avoid accusatory expressions (which are usually the ones that start with "You didn't try very hard" or "Why did you...?").

Probe for possible roadblocks beyond the employee's control. Most important, insist that the employee come up with a new solution (or resolution), and state what the consequences of another failure will be.

Make certain that you set a target date for resolution.

Seven Key Points to Be Covered in the Repeat Session

1. Review the agreements reached at the previous session.
2. State what you have observed or learned that shows that the agreement has been broached.
3. Ask for an explanation.
4. Insist on a new solution or a renewed effort.
5. State the consequences of continued noncompliance, but avoid threats that you do not intend to carry out.
6. Agree on the new action to be taken and a new follow-up date.
7. State your reluctance to give up on the employee and your belief that he or she can correct the situation.

COMMON BARRIERS TO SUCCESSFUL COUNSELING

The excuse often given by supervisors for failure to counsel is that there were so many other more important things to do that they never got around to it. Often the supervisor is intimidated by the person or fears legal repercussions. Perhaps the supervisor is not trained in interviewing techniques or is hazy about policies or procedures.

Sometimes, the supervisor is dealing with someone who is influential because of seniority, union affiliation, special expertise, or powerful friends. Sometimes one fears loss of friendship, particularly when there had been a peer relationship before one's promotion to supervisor. At other times, a supervisor may feel sympathy for a troubled person and fear making matters worse for that person.

Principles of Successful Interventions

- Initially confront as a friend, not as an antagonist.
- Be direct and honest.
- Listen more than you talk.
- Say how you feel, and ask how the other person feels.
- Select the best time and place for intervention.
- Do not nitpick.
- Expect the other person to come up with solutions.
- Strive for win-win solutions.
- Be willing to compromise.
- Work with facts, not assumptions.
- Be optimistic; expect positive results.

- Preserve the person's self-esteem.
- Do not pontificate or be condescending.
- Do not expect the impossible.
- Look for the good in the person.
- Monitor and reinforce.
- Be specific and consistent.
- Avoid arousing defensiveness.

Think About It

For the busy supervisor it is always a temptation to allow signs of possible problems to go unaddressed, perhaps in the hope that they will correct themselves or simply go away. However, a correlary of the well-known Murphy's Law suggests that "Left unto themselves, things invariably go from bad to worse." An apparent counseling need is a classic case of "Pay me now, or pay me later," and the cost in time, aggravation, and stress is always greater when paying later.

Questions for Review and Discussion

1. How do you believe you would go about deciding if some condition, occurrence, or circumstance suggests the need for counseling or the need to go directly to disciplinary action?
2. When employees seem to be violating the rules, is it always their fault? If not, cite an instance in which the employee may be blameless.
3. Why do you believe some supervisors fail to counsel employees or initiate disciplinary action even when the need to do so is clearly evident?
4. What would you primarily be looking for when following up after an employee counseling session? Why?
5. Often, when you need to counsel an employee you will already have in mind a workable solution to the developing problem. Why not simply mandate the solution and be done with it?
6. Describe one significant barrier to successful counseling. Why do you believe this barrier exists, and what can be done about it?
7. Identify the major similarities and differences between holding an employee counseling session and holding a performance evaluation interview.
8. Why should the supervisor retain documentation of an employee counseling session, and why should this documentation not become part of the employee's permanent record?
9. Explain why it is advisable for the supervisor to counsel an employee when a disciplinary problem seems to be developing. Shouldn't the supervisor simply wait until definite disciplinary action is called for?

10. Why should the supervisor avoid being drawn into discussions of an employee's personal problems?

Case: Negligence or...?

You are nurse manager on a medical/surgical floor of Community Hospital. This morning you walked into the workroom of your unit just in time to see Betty, a nursing assistant whom you considered a usually conscientious and careful worker, commit what appeared to be an act of negligence stemming from horseplay. You felt there was little room for doubt, and Betty's actions resulted in a small tray of supplies being knocked to the floor with a crash.

In addition to Betty, three more of your unit staff were present in the workroom. You felt they had at least witnessed the incident, but you were uncertain as to whether any of them had been actually involved.

Questions:
Should you:

1. Reprimand Betty on the spot, while the incident is fresh and the others can learn a lesson?
2. Counsel or discipline Betty individually? Why or why not?
3. Counsel Betty and the others as a group? Why or why not?
4. Meet with the other three staff to determine what actually happened? Why or why not?
5. Follow some other course of action? If so, what?

Case: Never to Blame

You are the administrative director of clinical laboratories at Community Hospital. One of your section supervisors has come to you with a complaint about a young man named William, one of the laboratory's messengers. The supervisor says:

> I'm nearing the end of my patience with William, and I need your advice. I can't pin him down on anything. No matter what happens or how nearly certain I am that he was involved, when it comes down to assigning responsibility he was never there, he knows nothing about it, he didn't do it, or the other employees are trying to make him look bad. No matter what the situation is he's got an excuse, sometimes a really plausible one, and I can never get him to own up to anything. Even when one of the stops on his rounds gets missed he's got a long,

involved story to account for it, a story I hear only if I learned about what happened and tried to find out more.

To hear William tell it, he's never made a mistake in his life. But if I could believe him for even a minute, then I'd have to believe that the whole world around him fouls up day after day and tries to lay the blame at his doorstep. Tell me—what can I do about him?

Questions:

1. What advice are you going to offer your section supervisor for addressing the problem of the ever-blameless William?
2. As the section supervisor's immediate superior, should you become actively involved in dealing with William? Why or why not?

RECOMMENDED READING

C.R. McConnell, Ch. 11, "Addressing Problems Before Taking Action," in *The Health Care Manager's Human Resources Handbook.* (Vienna, VA: Management Concepts, 2003), 223–41.

Chapter 17

Disciplining: Corrective Action for Behavior Problems

A just criticism is a commendation,
rather than a detraction.

—Henry Jacob

The road to success is usually under construction.

—Anonymous

CHAPTER OBJECTIVES

- Establish the nature of discipline, compare and contrast disciplining and counseling, and introduce the concept of the reward-to-risk ratio as a sometime explanation for employee actions that require discipline.
- Introduce the concept of progressive discipline and review its essential components.
- Address possible employee responses to various forms of disciplinary action.
- Introduce the concept of nonpunitive discipline and describe its operation and potential applicability.
- Review appropriate disciplinary principles and practices available to the supervisor.

Disciplining is not the same as punishing as far as most of the infractions falling under the extremely broad heading of employee misconduct are concerned. There will inevitably come some situations in which the disciplinary result will have the effect of punishment, but the essential purpose of most disciplinary action is correction of behavior. Disciplining is largely intended as an educational process applied to correct inappropriate conduct or behavior. The intent is not to be greasing the slide toward termination of employment but, rather, providing traction with

235

which employees can work to correct deviant behavior. When disciplining is done skillfully, employee self-esteem is preserved.

Discipline should be fair, firm, and fast. Delay only increases tension. If all you do about a troublesome employee is complain, you probably deserve what you get: continued problems and loss of respect of your superiors and the people who report to you. Proper discipline has been likened to a red-hot stove: it provides a warning (in the forms of color or sound), it does not discriminate (everyone who touches it gets burned), and it is immediate, consistent, and effective.

When supervisors treat their employees as they would like to be treated themselves, they have fewer disciplinary problems. They spot potential trouble areas and avoid the need for discipline by using their coaching and counseling expertise. The best discipline is self-discipline, and it is achieved when employees are treated as responsible adults. Some managers treat their employees as children and then are surprised when those employees behave like children.

Supervisors who practice management by intimidation spend much of their time trying to catch people doing something wrong. The employees respond to this kind of management not so much by cleaning up their act as by avoiding being caught. Many grievances are the aftermath of disciplinary actions.

Counseling vs Disciplining

Disciplining and counseling are closely interrelated. Counseling may be regarded as an informal first step in the disciplinary process. It becomes a formal disciplinary step—the oral reprimand—when the employee is warned of the consequences of failure to perform up to expectations or to function according to rules and policies. Most organizations require one or more oral reprimands for the more common and less serious offenses before punitive measures are administered.

Counseling sessions or oral reprimands are not appropriate for certain serious forms of misbehavior that call for immediate suspension or termination. The majority of organizations provide written guidelines for conduct and behavior that designate appropriate responses for various disciplinary infractions. A sample listing of such guidelines appears as Exhibit 17–1.

Reward-to-Risk Ratio

Most employees do not misbehave because they are bad people or because they simply want to harass their superiors. Rather, it is because they derive some benefit, although often an unconscious benefit, from misbehaving.

When supervisors fail to detect violations of rules, policies, or procedures, or they fail to take corrective measures, employees have no incentive to change their

Exhibit 17–1 Guidelines for Disciplinary Action

Class I: Minor Infractions
Discipline
    First offense—Oral warning
    Second offense—Written warning
    Third offense—1-day suspension
    Fourth offense—3-day suspension
Typical Infractions
- Absenteeism
- Tardiness
- Discourtesy to patients, visitors, coworkers, etc.,
- Chronic unsatisfactory work

Class II: More Serious Infractions
Discipline
    First offense—Written warning
    Second offense—3-day suspension
    Third offense—Discharge
Typical Infractions
- Failure to report when scheduled for work
- Unexcused absence
- Performance of personal business on hospital time
- Violation of smoking, safety, fire, or emergency regulations

Class III: Still More Serious Infractions
Discipline
    First offense—Written warning
    Second offense—Discharge
Typical Infractions
- Insubordination
- Negligence
- Falsification of records, reports, or information
- Unauthorized release of confidential or privileged information
- Sexual harassment

Class IV: Most Serious Infractions
Discipline
    First offense—Discharge
Typical Infractions
- Absence without notice for 3 consecutive days ("3 days no-call, no-show")
- Fighting on the job
- Theft
- Using or being under the influence of alcohol or drugs on premises
- Willful damage to hospital property

---

behavior. Consider the ratio of reward to risk. We all play the reward-to-risk game on the road every day. We drive a little faster than the speed limit because we are in a hurry. The reward is getting to our destination quicker. Most of us do not drive at breakneck speed because we know that doing so increases the risk of arrest or accident. Once you recognize the reward an employee derives from inappropriate behavior and what that person fears, you can more readily modify that behavior by decreasing the reward or increasing the risk.

Consider, for example, Ken, who frequently arrives late for work on the evening shift because he knows that the day crew will cover some of his responsibilities. Ken's previous supervisor never said anything to him about his behavior, but his new supervisor quickly becomes aware of the situation and tells the day crew to stop doing Ken's work, thus reducing the reward for this behavior. The supervisor also warns Ken about lateness and tells him to check in with her when he arrives (increased risk).

PROGRESSIVE DISCIPLINE

The commonly used disciplinary process is referred to as progressive because in most instances the disciplinary measures become increasingly severe until there is a resolution of the problem. In its traditional form, progressive discipline typically consists of four steps.

1. Oral warning or oral reprimand
2. Written warning or written reprimand
3. Suspension or probation
4. Discharge

Oral Warning

In delivering an oral warning or oral reprimand, always be conscious of the need to avoid "gunnysacking;" that is, saving up a number of complaints and then, one frustrating day, dumping the entire load on the individual. Deliver warnings as soon as possible after the misbehavior, although not until you have control of your emotions. Keep it confidential. Always reprimand in private. You may have to borrow space for a short while because your office may not be the best location for a private discussion.

Do not be apologetic. Describe what is wrong and how you feel about it. Do not exaggerate. Attack the problem, not the person. Avoid starting sentences with an accusatory "you," and avoid using subjective terms such as attitude, work ethic, professionalism, and the absolute words "always" and "never."

Allow the individual to respond, but cut short any litany of lame excuses that may be forthcoming. Anticipate remarks such as "You're not being fair" or "You can't say things like that to me." Say exactly what you expect the person to do or to stop doing.

If the occasion is a repeat reprimand or if the problem has previously been addressed by counseling, use the counseling technique described in Chapter 16. However, be less empathetic and more formal than when counseling. Show that your patience is running out, and warn of future action if improvement is not forthcoming. For example, "If this is not corrected immediately, it will be necessary for me to…"

If the wayward employee was hired by your superior or was recruited by someone at another higher organizational level, make certain you discuss the problem with your manager. When you discipline employees who are popular with their coworkers, you must rely on the support you have built up within your team. If team members trust you and know that you are fair, they will support your decision.

Written Warning

The written warning or written reprimand frequently leads to discharge with all its legal ramifications, so proceed with caution. Most likely your human resources department has a special form you must use for this purpose. Find out whether you have the authority to issue written warnings by yourself or whether this must be done in concert with human resources or higher management.

Discuss the problem with your manager before generating a written warning. Craft the warning carefully; it is a document with significant legal implications, and it may end up in court. Avoid making statements that you cannot prove. Provide observations and facts, never opinions or hearsay. A list of written warning essentials is presented in Exhibit 17–2.

When you meet with the employee, explain that a written reprimand is a formal warning and will be documented in the employee's personnel file. Review and document any previous counseling sessions or oral reprimands relating to the same problem.

Be specific as to your expectations and the target date for compliance. For example, "If within the next 60 days you are late for work another time without an acceptable excuse, you will be sent home on a 1-day suspension without pay." This may sound juvenile, but sometimes people who fail to act maturely must be treated that way.

Tell the person that after a specified time, for example, 6 months, without further similar kinds of incidents, the record of the disciplinary action will be removed from the personnel file.

Insist that the employee read and sign the written warning. As necessary remind the person that signing does not necessarily mean agreement but is instead a simple acknowledgement that the warning was received and discussed.

Exhibit 17–2 Essentials of a Written Disciplinary Report

Description of the problem
- State facts, never assumptions, hearsay, or opinions.
- Whenever possible provide dates, with examples.
- Record the names of witnesses or involved persons.

Record of previous warnings
- Provide dates.
- Record what was said by both you and the employee.
- Describe resulting changes in conduct, if any.

Record of previous written reprimands or punitive actions
- Attach copies.
- Describe disciplinary measures taken.
- Describe resulting changes in conduct, if any.

Employee's documentation of explanation, denial, or rebuttal
- If the employee chooses to provide documentation, include a copy.
- If the employee provides nothing in writing, describe the employee's stated position as accurately as possible. Note in writing that the employee chose not to prepare such a document.

Record of punitive action presently decreed
- Note in writing that the disciplinary action was explained to the employee.
- Attempt to secure the employee's understanding of the action to be taken.

Description of expected performance
- As appropriate, include a target date for correction.
- Clearly indicate the conduct or behavior that will or will not be tolerated.
- Sign the report.
- Secure the employee's signature. If the employee refuses to sign, call in a witness (preferably another supervisor) and repeat the request; if the employee still refuses to sign, have the witness attest to the refusal.

Inform the person of the right to attach a rebuttal or to confer with your superior.

Suspension or Probation

Some offenses call for immediate suspension or discharge without any antecedent counseling or reprimands. In many organizations supervisors can only recommend such severe action; the actual order has to be approved by human resources or senior management.

If the employee has received oral and written warnings in the past, a formal meeting may not be needed. Your human resources department will provide the necessary form or instruct you on how to prepare the report.

When an individual returns to work after a suspension, treat the person like any other employee. Be businesslike, neither clubby nor aloof. You have already chastised the individual, so consider the matter closed.

Discharges

Today's managers are growing increasingly reluctant to fire people. Many, in fact, feel that it is all but impossible to fire anyone in some particular working environments. They cite all the roadblocks and potential legal backlash that may result from such action. However, if specific standards of conduct, behavior, and performance are in place and mandated procedures are followed, terminations are not especially difficult.

Too often supervisors create the problem by accepting unsatisfactory performance or behavior for an extended period of time and by rating performance as satisfactory when it is not. Robert Townsend claims that purging bad performers is as good a tonic for an organization as rewarding its star performers.[1] One surprising observation is that years after being fired, many people are able to admit that the firing was not only justified but was the turning point in their careers.

Employers protect themselves by providing employee handbooks that state the disciplinary policies of the organization. They avoid any mention of permanent employment and avoid statements to the effect that employees can be terminated only "for cause." These are important precautions because it has been held in the courts time and again that an organization's employee handbook or its policy manual can be interpreted as an implied contract of employment. Employers also warn their managers about the dangers of rating people higher than they deserve; good evaluations can come back to haunt the evaluator when someone who has been dismissed for performance-related reasons protests the action.

Some cautious employers insist that employment lawyers approve discharges before the employees are notified. This is for good reason. Many fired employees file wrongful discharge lawsuits, and these can be expensive and time consuming. Those who sue usually charge that they were fired without cause or for insufficient reasons. Others claim that the termination violated a written or verbal agreement they or their union had with the employer.

To sustain a discharge against legal challenges, an employer must be able to prove the following:

- There are specific and documented work standards and policies, and employees are repeatedly reminded about these.

- What was alleged did indeed take place, involved the employee, and that it warranted the discharge.
- Such behavior had not been condoned in the past or that other workers had been discharged for similar offenses.
- The sequence of discipline followed prescribed policies and procedures.
- The employee made no genuine effort to heed the previous warnings even though he or she had been informed as to potential consequences.
- The firing was based on behavior or results, not on any of the following:
  1. discrimination (gender, race, religion, age, or disability)
  2. whistle blowing related to safety practices, illegal acts, sexual harassment, military or jury duty, or Workers' Compensation claims
  3. violation of implied contract (the employee was promised a permanent job)

Termination Meeting

You may choose not to hold a termination meeting, or you may be required to do so, or you may have no choice in the matter if this chore is customarily handled by the human resources department. There is no perfect time to deliver a discharge. However, if such can be arranged, a Friday afternoon after other employees have departed and shortly after the employee has received written notice from the human resources department could be the best of a number of questionable circumstances.

Never discuss the possibility of reconsideration. All such possibilities should have been exhausted well before this final meeting. You can, of course, say you are sorry things did not work out and wish the person well. If the person gets angry or breaks into tears, remain calm. Do not get drawn into a debate, and do not agree with any charges the person makes. Say that the human resources department will discuss any additional administrative matters such as terminal pay and benefits and will make arrangements for the person's final paycheck.

Tell the person exactly what information will be released to potential employers who request the data and that it will be released only by human resources and only with the employee's signed consent. Your responsibility may include ensuring that the employee has returned keys, identification tags, and other items that belong to the organization. Security codes in computers and keys to secured areas may have to be changed.

EMPLOYEE REACTIONS TO BEING DISCIPLINED

Some employees who are disciplined simply quit. Others quit psychologically but remain on the job because of vested time, unwillingness to look for new work, or lack of opportunity elsewhere. Those who stay often become marginal performers at best. Many disciplined employees file grievances and seek redress via unions, the courts, the Equal Employment Opportunity Commission, the Occupational Safety and Health Administration, or some other governmental agency.

OTHER DISCIPLINARY MEASURES

There are other less formal disciplinary measures available that lie outside of a formal progressive disciplinary system. Innovative supervisors can come up with almost as many punitive measures as their employees can find ways to avoid them. Any number of such measures are commonly applied in the ongoing relationship with some employees. One might, for example, withhold or delay a pay increase for an employee whose performance has been marginal compared with that of others. Surely some of these measures are recognizable as the inverse of actions the supervisor can use to reward employees; that is, that which is extended as a reward can also be withheld as a punishment. These measures include

- withholding or delaying pay increases,
- denying promotions,
- reducing performance ratings to reflect declining performance,
- placing the employee on probation,
- demoting or transferring the employee,
- denying requests for educational support or time off,
- withdrawing special privileges or authority,
- providing unpleasant assignments,
- canceling special projects, and
- removing an individual from teams, committees, or other work groups.

NONPUNITIVE DISCIPLINE

Punishment breeds resistance, encourages subterfuge, and undermines employee willingness to make future contributions to the organization. In many instances the nonpunitive or positive disciplinary approach has been successful in overcoming many of these adverse effects.[2]

The nonpunitive approach frequently works better than the traditional method because it places more responsibility on the employee and thus makes it more difficult for that person to be hostile toward the organization if he or she is eventually terminated. This strategy has reduced the filing of grievances over terminations, decreased involuntary turnover, and improved morale. The principal objections have come from employees' coworkers who resent someone getting a day off with pay while they must do that employee's work.

The theme of the nonpunitive approach is building commitment instead of enforcing compliance. It is congruent with the principle of participative management in that it, too, is treating employees as adults, not children.

Encouragement replaces threats. Rules are redefined as employee responsibilities; oral and written warnings are expressed as suggestions. Discussions are low key with emphasis on problem solving. For example, you tell a person that her performance threatens the success of your unit and her future. When such discussions fail, it is worth considering that there may be a poor fit between employee and job and that a change in employment may be beneficial for all parties.

The most radical departure from the traditional disciplinary approach is the 1-day suspension with pay. The employee is given a day of decision.

Typical Steps in Nonpunitive Discipline

Step 1. Offer the employee an informal, friendly reminder that a work rule has been broken and explain the reasoning behind the rule. Get the employee to agree that his or her behavior is inappropriate and should not be repeated.

Step 2. After a second violation, hold a repeat session, but this time have your manager or a representative of human resources sit in on the meeting.

Step 3. If there is yet another violation, tell the employee that if the rule seems distasteful, perhaps he or she should find another employer. Confirm this conversation in a letter sent to the employee's home. For example:

> Our solutions have not worked. I have serious concerns about whether you want to continue here. I do not want a final commitment right now. Take the rest of the day (or tomorrow) to think over what you want to do, then let me know what you've decided. As a token of our faith in you, and as a sign that we want you to stay with us, you'll receive full pay for the day of decision.
>
> If you want to continue on our team, fine. However, you need to give me a signed, firm commitment that you will fulfill all your responsibilities. If you do not, then we both have failed, and your employment will end. If I do not hear from you by (date, time), your services will be automatically terminated.

If the employee returns to work and agrees to abide by the rules but violates that agreement within a few months, termination is in order.

EIGHT SOUND DISCIPLINARY PRACTICES

1. Make certain your employees know the rules of employment. Periodically review all pertinent rules with all staff, and include each new employee's introduction to the rules as part of new-employee orientation.

2. Do not let misconduct or misbehavior become habitual. The more ingrained such behavior becomes, the more difficult it will be to correct.
3. Do not act before acquiring factual information; never proceed on second-hand information.
4. Always reprimand in private.
5. Do not play "Do as I say, not as I do." Rather, serve as a role model for conduct and behavior.
6. Use punishment only as a last resort, mindful that the primary purpose of disciplinary action is correction of behavior.
7. Use either progressive or nonpunitive discipline according to the policies of the organization.
8. At all times remain aware of your goal in delivering disciplinary action.

DISCIPLINARY PRINCIPLES FOR THE SUPERVISOR

In entering any situation in which disciplinary action is a possibility, you, as the supervisor, should *know*

1. exactly what the unacceptable behavior is and what policy or rule has been violated,
2. any mitigating circumstances,
3. the scope of your authority, and
4. how similar offenses have been handled in the past.

You should *assume* that

1. employees want to do good work,
2. employees are perceiving some benefit from their unacceptable behavior,
3. you or others may be partly to blame, and
4. you ordinarily have multiple corrective options available.

You must *act*

1. quickly once you have the needed information,
2. appropriately by consulting with your superior or the human resources department,
3. consistently and fairly,
4. by using punishment only as a last resort,
5. by selecting penalties that are appropriate for the offenses,
6. by documenting, documenting, documenting, and
7. by having the terminated employee leave the premises as soon as possible.

As a supervisor, do *not*

1. let inappropriate behavior develop into habits,
2. act before all the facts are available,

3. be apologetic,
4. use imprecise terminology such as loyalty, attitude, work ethic, professionalism, or maturity,
5. hide behind "management" in taking necessary action, or
6. trap yourself into a series of oral warnings for the same problem with the same employee.

GETTING RID OF DEADWOOD

Termination may be necessary because of the inability of an employee to meet minimum work standards and the failure of retraining and other corrective efforts. Every once in a while you will encounter an employee who makes the same mistakes or commits the same infractions over and over. He or she may feel bad about it and yet be unable to achieve long-term correction. Bad luck seems to follow these poor souls, who will often admit that they had similar problems at previous jobs. We may feel for such employees, but in health care any number of possible mistakes can jeopardize lives. Therefore, termination becomes necessary.

Before recommending the termination of any employee, make certain that the employee has been amply warned during performance reviews and disciplinary processes and has had abundant opportunities to shore up the deficient performance or correct the offending behavior. Make certain the unsatisfactory work record is adequately documented; even a single laudatory performance appraisal may result in a legal tangle.

There will always come a time when there is no recourse other than termination. However, before electing to label someone as "deadwood" and opting for termination, be certain that you have done everything reasonable that you could possibly do to help the employee succeed. You may find that helping to salvage a single employee who might otherwise be lost can be far more satisfying than firing all of the deadwood you may encounter.

Think About It

> Delivering disciplinary action is among the most dreaded tasks faced by supervisors and managers at all levels. Doing so honestly requires courage and emotional involvement; that is, he or she who disciplines another must feel some uneasiness about performing an unpleasant task the outcome of which can affect a person's employment or career. The supervisor who believes he or she can discipline without feeling should probably not be a supervisor.

Questions for Review and Discussion

1. Provide an example of how a supervisor might positively manipulate the reward-to-risk ratio of a problem situation so as to influence employee behavior.

2. The purpose of disciplinary action has been described as correction of behavior. How is this definition served, if at all, when an employee is terminated for one occurrence of a serious infraction?

3. In what ways do employee counseling and the delivery of an oral warning differ from each other, if at all?

4. Under what circumstances might you go back to the first steps in the disciplinary process when you may have previously advanced to the level of written warning?

5. Most progressive disciplinary systems begin with an oral warning before a written warning but proceed to recommend that oral warnings be documented. Why document that which is defined as "oral?"

6. Why do most disciplinary systems require the supervisor to obtain—or at least try to obtain—employee signatures on disciplinary documentation?

7. Why might nonpunitive discipline work better with some particular employee groups than others? Provide an example.

8. Is it appropriate to advance an employee through the disciplinary process based on multiple offenses? For example, should a written warning for discourtesy follow an oral warning for absenteeism? Why or why not?

9. Under what circumstances might the warnings in an employee's file become legal documentation? What hazards might this present for the supervisor?

10. Why is it appropriate to purge an employee's file of disciplinary documentation after some period of time?

Case: The Know-It-All

Imagine yourself in the position of manager of building services at Community Hospital. One of the people reporting to you is Bill Douglas, supervisor of the maintenance crew. Douglas has come to you with a complaint about Ed Wayne, one of his half-dozen employees. Says Douglas:

> I need some help figuring out how to handle Ed Wayne. I guess his work is OK—he's not the best producer, but he certainly isn't the worst—but he's got such a know-it-all attitude that he drives the rest of the crew crazy.
>
> Ed's assigned to general maintenance, but he's always trying to bust out of this and do all sorts of other things. There hasn't been a job come up in months that Ed hasn't claimed to know how to do, and he's always trying to get his hands on everything new and different that comes along. The others feel that Ed is always trying to crowd in on their territory, and to make matters worse, he's constantly criticizing the others and finding fault with what they do. And he's always quick with an "I told you so" when someone else does something that goes wrong.

The others in the crew have been referring to Ed as "the expert," but they no longer say it kiddingly. One of the others has even asked me to count him out when it comes to teaming him up with Wayne on jobs that take two people. I tell you, I've got to do something about this guy before his behavior destroys the whole crew's morale.

Questions:

1. Do you see any specific grounds for disciplinary action in the behavior of employee Ed Wayne? If so, what are these grounds?
2. Douglas's opening description of the problem refers to Wayne's "know-it-all" attitude. Can you advise Douglas to lean on Wayne concerning attitude? Why or why not?
3. In as many briefly stated steps as necessary, outline the advice you will give Bill Douglas for addressing the problem of Ed Wayne.

Case: Pleasant Dreams

Imagine yourself as night-shift charge nurse on a medical/surgical unit. For several months you have had a problem with a staff nurse whose performance you consider unsatisfactory. She seems to continually take advantage of quiet times during her shift to doze off at the nursing station. You have reprimanded her several times for sleeping on the job, and you have reached the point where you feel you can no longer simply scold her for her conduct. Her position, however, is that "it's no big deal," that she's always certain to hear any call signals as long as she's at the nursing station. (Your hospital has a clear policy concerning written warnings, but policy is relatively loose concerning oral warnings; these can be unlimited and issued at your discretion, so you can deliver as many as you feel necessary.)

For a written warning to become official and be entered into an employee's personnel file, it must be agreed to and countersigned by the unit's nurse manager and the director of nursing. You issued the offending nurse two written warnings; both warnings cleared through the unit manager. However, you feel you can go no further without backing from the office of the director of nursing, and there has been no follow-up from that direction. Meanwhile, the employee continues to be a problem.

Questions:

1. What recourse, if any, do you have in pursuing the disciplinary policy in the manner described in the case?
2. You know the disciplinary policy lists "sleeping on the job" as an infraction. Assuming that you believe the problem to be se-

vere enough to constitute a risk to patients under your care, what can you do about the troublesome employee?

3. If no follow-up from the director of nursing is forthcoming, what might you eventually consider doing to protect yourself?

REFERENCES

1. Townsend, R. 1971. *Up the organization.* New York: Fawcett World Library, 45.
2. Redeker, J.R. 1985. Discipline, part 2: The nonpunitive approach works by design. *Personnel* 62: 7–10.

RECOMMENDED READING

D. Grote, "Discipline Without Punishment," *Training* 33, no. 1 (1996): 129.

J.G. Liebler and C.R. McConnell, Chapter 12, "Authority, Leadership, and Supervision," in *Management Principles for Health Professionals,* 4th ed. (Sudbury, MA: Jones and Bartlett Publishers, 2004), 433–60.

J.L. Raper and S.N. Myaya, "Employee Discipline: A Changing Paradigm," *The Health Care Supervisor* 12, no. 2 (1993): 67–77.

Chapter 18

Cultural Diversity: Managing the Changing Workforce

Diversity is the next step after Affirmative Action.
Now that we have the people, how do
we help them work together to be productive?

—Oliver Brown[1]

What you can't value, you can't lead.

—Lloyd S. Lewan

CHAPTER OBJECTIVES

- Develop an appreciation of the changing composition of the American health care workforce and examine the implications of an employee complement that is increasingly diverse ethnically, socially, and economically.
- Establish cultural diversity as a vital ongoing concern of every supervisor in the health care organization.
- Provide examples of cultural core values that define the kinds of differences that exist between and among groups of varying backgrounds.
- Establish the necessity for congruence of corporate values and personal core values in successfully managing a diverse workforce.
- Describe the essential elements of a diversity management program.
- Address the responsibilities of first-line supervisors in managing an increasingly diverse work group.

THE DIVERSE WORKFORCE

The management of a workforce that is increasingly diverse ethnically, socially, and economically was a topic of steadily increasing concern throughout the decade of the 1990s. The concern for diversity continues to grow in this first decade of the new century, and the implications are inescapable for anyone who manages the work of people in venues in which work groups are likely to be increasingly diverse in their composition.

Diversity management refers to the ways in which managers hire, supervise, use the skills of, and promote or otherwise reassign employees of varied backgrounds. Backgrounds encountered are primarily racial, multicultural, ethnic, and gender oriented, but diversity concerns also include differences in age, education, economic level, organizational tenure, and the presence or absence of disabilities.

The total American workforce is steadily becoming more culturally diverse across all business and industry, but in few if any other settings is increasing diversity being experienced more than in health care. Service workers, such as food service workers, aides, orderlies, attendants, housekeepers, and maintenance workers, are often the most multiracial and culturally diverse components of a health care institution. Also, diversity continues to spread in the professional, technical, and managerial ranks in health care.

The people in each separate work group value their "in-group" more positively than they do any "out-groups." Management and workers have different values and attitudes and often have different political affiliations as well. Managers and professionals usually view the world with different colored glasses than do the rank-and-file employees. Professionals bond more strongly with members of their specialty or profession than they do with other people in the same organization, and their personal networks may show little overlap with others.

Appreciation of cultural differences and appropriate bonding with employees who exhibit these differences can increase the numbers of an organization's customers and job applicants. However, failure to make the necessary adjustments creates resentment, reduces morale, inhibits efficient performance, and increases turnover. Recruitment can suffer severely, and current employees may be more prone to file grievances or create other legal problems.

CULTURAL CORE VALUES

Core values are those beliefs that we hold so strongly that they affect our goals, ethical decisions, and daily behavior. Cultural core beliefs and values affect on-the-job goals and day-to-day behavior.

Different cultures place different values on privacy, courtesy, respect for elders, and the work ethic. These and other values provide the basis for attitudes and behavior. Here are some examples.

In the Philippine Islands and in Arab countries, unequal distribution of power in institutions is highly valued, and status symbols are regarded as deserved and expected. However, in Austria and Sweden, power disparities are anathema.

Many corporations in the United States and Canada adhere to policies that limit the hiring of one's relatives, labeling the practice favoritism or nepotism. In contrast, the cultures of Korea, Pakistan, and Taiwan view the hiring of a relative as desirable, and in some instances even obligatory.

Japan, Austria, Italy, and the United States emphasize assertiveness, competitiveness, and the acquisition of money and material things. In the Netherlands and Sweden, the opposite holds true; there, nurturing and quality of life are more highly valued. Even among American workers, there are great differences in the relative importance of money. Some people never have enough while others are satisfied with just getting by.

Greeks and Japanese minimize the discomfort of risk by adhering to strict laws and rituals, while Jamaicans and Swedes have little aversion to risk.

This list could go on at considerably greater length, but the point is made. There is simply no clear set of core values that holds across all cultures.

CORPORATE VALUES

Corporate values serve as guidelines for employee behavior. Key values are often expressed in slogans such as "The customer is always right," "Quality is number one," or "We aim to please." Some slogans, however, have been so heavily overworked or thrown around so casually and in such obvious conflict with reality ("Our employees are our greatest asset!") that they fail to pass the "snicker test." (Employees are usually quick to decide whether a slogan is sincere or simply a few hollow words.)

Most corporate values and ethical considerations deal with honesty, integrity, and loyalty, the foundation of a moral organizational culture. However, what each person considers ethical or unethical depends on his or her individual value system. This is essentially why ethics, supposedly so simple in concept, can become so murky in practice.

The impact of corporate values quickly dissipates when the behavior people see around them is contrary to the expressed values. This is especially true when it is the leaders who display the inappropriate behavior. The effect of corporate values also plummets when employees who violate those values are not chastised and corrected.

Employees are most impressionable when they are first hired. The majority of orientation programs emphasize the values that reflect the philosophy of the organization. Corporate decisions are often based on these values. But providing a list of corporate values to new employees has little meaning unless the behavioral aspects of each value are described. Trainees understand what you mean by integrity if you tell them that when they make a mistake they must admit it and not blame someone else. Employees know better what you mean by honesty, for example, if you clearly point out that falsifying time records and patient records is grounds for severe disciplinary action up to and including dismissal.

A culture takes its tone and values from its leaders. Effective leaders hold strong values and have the courage to accomplish good works despite great obstacles. They know that improper employee behavior based on faulty value systems can be modified by using the old carrot-and-stick approach. Nevertheless, they prefer to rely on modeling the kinds of behavior they want their followers to copy. Poor role models destroy corporate and personal values. A manager can articulate the importance of integrity and honesty, but the employees recall the many times when the manager broke a promise. Another manager may claim that quality is king, but when the work piles up he forces his staff to hurry, knowing full well they must cut corners to do so.

PERSONAL CORE VALUES

When corporate and personal values are consistent with each other, a team spirit is fostered, and conflicts become less frequent and are easier to resolve. Productivity increases. Teamwork demands a set of values that encourage listening and responding constructively and patiently to views expressed by others. It requires team members to provide support, share knowledge, and maintain high ethical standards.

Our primary personal values are family, career, health, and social or recreational activities. Secondary values include recognition, quality, political affiliation, and ethical considerations. Stress occurs when our behavior does not support our values. For example, when we value our family relationships and activities but spend most of our waking hours tending to our careers, stress results, and problems are likely to arise.

Some employees value friendships. Other employees are loners. The relative importance of family and career also differs widely among workers. Many people are passed over for promotion because they refuse to give up time with their families while others destroy their marriages because they allow career to take precedence over family life.

Americans are increasingly reluctant to take jobs or promotions that involve uprooting and relocating their families. Heier reports that 75% of the employees he interviewed claimed they would not relocate for their employers.[3]

Some managers cannot understand why many professional and technical employees show no interest in becoming managers; again, a matter of values.

Values Modification

Employees who hold values that conflict with corporate values must modify their personal values to some extent. Failure to make that adjustment leads to confrontations, isolation or rejection, and ultimately to loss of employment. Employees whose core values are markedly different from those of other members of their work and social groups find it difficult to develop personal networks.

Values, like attitudes, are difficult to alter. However, behavioral modeling by managers and coworkers can gradually influence individual values. Employees are most susceptible to change when they are first hired. Trainers and managers who earn the respect and trust of trainees have a powerful impact on value modification. The best of these leaders reinforce corporate values by sharing anecdotes of successes and failures and by providing positive feedback.

DIVERSITY MANAGEMENT PROGRAMS

In an ideal workplace complete and unconditional social acceptance is based on merit. Yet even among the most open-minded individuals, stereotypes and subtle prejudices can create difficulties. Managers can seldom change opinions, but they can see to it that all workers are treated fairly. An effective diversity program helps avoid charges of discrimination and enhances creativity.

The goal of a diversity program is to create an environment that allows employees of all backgrounds to reach their full potential and work well together. The people do not all have to be friends, but they must respect each other. Ideally, employees go beyond tolerance to a true appreciation of differences. In such a mutual adaptation paradigm, the parties accept and understand differences and fully adapt to the entire diversity mixture.

The basic strategy is simple: change what is not working, but leave other areas alone. Be certain to abide by all laws, rules, policies, and procedures. Value modification starts with a review of current practices. This review can be accomplished by focus groups or through surveys. The Allstate insurance company surveys all of its employees quarterly on how well it is meeting its commitments. It probes how well employees feel their managers are carrying out their program. Its "diversity index" determines 25% of a manager's merit bonus.[4]

There is widespread dissatisfaction with affirmative action. White males have perceived it as reverse discrimination, and highly qualified members of minority groups are also unhappy with it. They point out that they are stigmatized as people who could not have made it on their own. It is therefore felt in many quarters that affirmative action has had its day and that a conscientious focus on diversity management holds the most promise for the future.

The assimilation approach, in which management attempts to force minorities to become similar to the majority, seldom achieves its goal. Another unsatisfactory technique is the suppression approach in which managers admit to minorities that there is a problem but that the minorities have no choice but to put up with it.

Elements of a Diversity Program

An effective diversity management program will include the following elements.

- Training programs that provide employees with the skills needed to deal with a diverse work force
- Monitoring, with the use of periodic attitude surveys and audits of production and attendance records
- Holding managers accountable for reaching the organization's diversity goals within their units
- Helping employees establish networks or support groups to which minority members can turn in times of stress
- Providing equal assistance to workers who have family problems, such as child- and eldercare needs
- Maintaining communication to reinforce the organization's commitment to diversity and to keep the work force aware of the need to cooperate
- Making mentors available for workers who need support and advice

Diversity Awareness Training

Health maintenance organizations and malpractice insurers recognize the importance of diversity training. One medical malpractice insurer offers discounts on premiums to doctors who attend workshops addressing cultural differences.[5]

Diversity-awareness training is adapted to the culture of the organization. It can vary from a one-time session to a series of training exercises. If people have had limited contact with cultural differences in the past, they feel uncomfortable when faced with them. It is up to each employee to appreciate and value these differences and not to expect that minority customers and employees want to blend in with the mainstream culture. Most employees prefer to maintain their cultural identity while functioning effectively in the work organization.

In these programs workers learn about antidiscrimination laws, cross-cultural communication, respect, and bias. Useful techniques include role-playing, videotapes, and discussions. The training emphasizes the importance of language or dialect, an extremely important cultural variable. For example, a Filipino patient is likely to view caregivers as authority figures and thus remain quiet and subdued in their presence, and certain Asians and others are reluctant to admit that they do not understand instructions; they are concerned that saying that they do not understand might be taken as an insult to your teaching ability. Therefore you must ask them questions to ensure that they comprehend what you have said.

Body language is equally important. For example, Native Americans and some Asians avoid eye contact when conversing. In the United States when you hold up your hand with thumb and forefinger together, you mean "OK." In France it means that you are a zero. In Japan it is a request for some change. In some countries it is an obscene gesture. The "V" gesture in the United States means "victory," but in Australia it is the "middle-finger salute."

Diversity training without follow-up and institutional support is incomplete. Trainers have little or no authority for follow-up or backup outside the training room.

RESPONSIBILITIES OF SUPERVISORS

Higher management can use surveys to detect cultural problems, but it is up to supervisors to make diversity programs work. Supervisors, those managers closest to the rank-and-file workers, are able to check for tensions that may be disrupting harmony or interfering with productivity. They implement the provisions of any diversity program.

Experienced supervisors know that corporate values mean little to employees unless they are explained in behavioral terms. New supervisors quickly learn that what they value is not what many of their employees value. Supervisors are more likely to enjoy challenges, interesting work, recognition, and the sense of having control. Their employees may only want to do their routine work and go home.

Karp warns against reinforcing the role of *victim* of prejudice or discrimination.[6] Victims focus on their pain and weakness. When this occurs during a training program, "suffering contests" may emerge among subgroups in which each group tries to prove that it has suffered the most. People leave these meetings feeling more vulnerable and abused than before they arrived.

Develop programs that reinforce the role of *survivor* of discrimination. This strengthens the individual. Ask employees how it felt and what they did to overcome discrimination. This reinforces individual responsibility for taking care of themselves.

Diversity Management Tips for Supervisors

- Remain ever alert to your own assumptions and those of others.
- Do not allow unfair assumptions to go unchallenged.
- Help new arrivals feel more comfortable by discussing any unwritten rules and practices. These may include appearance, acceptable language, how to disagree or complain, and how to ask for help from others.
- Discuss the importance of cultural diversity at orientation sessions and at staff meetings.
- Do not tell people that they should not feel the way they do when they feel mistreated, but do make it safe for them to have and to express those feelings.
- Challenge stereotypes and assumptions about minority groups. Avoid terms like "yuppie" (young, upwardly mobile professional), "dink" (dual income, no kids), "old," "white male," "subordinate," "honey," and "girl."

- Show interest in people's differences without prying into their personal lives. Seek information regarding various special ethnic observances and events (for example, Chinese New Year, Black History Month, Martin Luther King Jr.'s birthday, Asian/Pacific American Heritage Month, National Hispanic Heritage Week, and Yom Kippur).
- Become more knowledgeable about the religious, family, and food customs of the people with whom you work. Tactfully ask someone from that national culture after establishing appropriate rapport.
- Use humor carefully and always avoid ethnic, sexist, or stereotypical jokes.
- Be familiar with your organization's policy on sexual harassment, and live up to this policy to the letter.
- Involve representatives of all minority groups in the decision-making process.
- Allow minorities to wear their ethnic clothes or hairstyles unless these interfere with their work or offend customers.
- Encourage all employees to get to know the people around them who are different. By embracing differences, we can all make a difference.

ADVANCEMENT FOR WOMEN

We continue to hear much about the glass ceiling and the "old boy network" and the fact that females are still earning less than males for the same kinds of work. Although it remains true that women occupy fewer offices in the executive suites, their numbers are increasing in top management, and they fill many middle hierarchical slots and the majority of supervisory positions in hospitals. Take notice also of the increasing number of women in charge of nursing homes and home care programs. Also, women are highly active in professional societies and increasingly serve as officers in these organizations. For the most part, doors of opportunity for women in health care institutions are wide open. Women who sincerely want leadership roles find the glass ceiling to be illusory in health care. In few if any other lines of endeavor can that claim be made.

More recently men have complained that they are excluded from some informal networks in health care institutions. Others feel that female managers show favoritism toward female employees.

Think About It

Why value diversity? Because, essentially, we have no choice in the face of a changing population. Given existing birth rates and immigration, ethnic and racial minorities in America are growing several times faster than the white population. The demands of the marketplace and the unavoidable competition for

skills and talents demand that the ability to do a particular job be the overriding criterion in employee recruitment. The supervisor has always had to deal with differences between and among employees, and the changing composition of the workforce does no more than add some additional differences to the mix.

Questions for Review and Discussion

1. What do you believe to be the strongest factors in ensuring that a diversity initiative is taken seriously throughout the organization? Why?
2. We have long been admonished to ensure equal treatment of employees. How can we possibly respond to cultural differences among employees in a group without treating some differently from others?
3. What might need to be done with the organization's personnel policies to accommodate workforce diversity? Provide an example.
4. Describe one of the possibly significant risks embodied in a supervisor's lack of sensitivity to diversity issues.
5. Provide at least two reasons why we can state that the total workforce in health care is more culturally diverse than most other lines of business activity.
6. Describe a situation in which the stated values of an organization are in apparent conflict with the values implicit in management behavior.
7. Explain why it is likely that personal values are difficult to alter, and describe how doing so might be accomplished.
8. Describe several of the kinds of legal action that can arise from issues of workforce diversity.
9. Who is likely to be key in ensuring organizational support for a diversity initiative, and to whom will most of the implementation activity belong?
10. Provide an example or two about how assumptions about people can lead a supervisor into difficulty.

Exercise: Your Departmental Diversity Program

Assume you have spent several years as health information management (HIM) supervisor in a relatively small hospital. Your staff of five—four people plus you—consisted of four white females and one Asian female. Your group had been together for several years.

Your hospital recently merged with a considerably larger institution located a few miles away. The other hospital is sufficiently larger that in spite of the frequent use of the term "merger," the prevailing opinion in both organizations is that it is more a matter of the larger absorbing the smaller.

One of the first major changes to occur was the combining of parallel departments under a single supervisor; that is, where before each hospital had a manager of HIM, the new scheme would call for one manager to supervise the HIM groups in both facilities. For perhaps 75% or more of hospital functions, the department manager in the larger institution became manager of the combined department, but in HIM the expanded management role fell to you. The

HIM manager in the larger institution elected to take early retirement rather than manage the combined function.

Now you have acquired, counting full-time and a couple of part-time employees, 12 more employees to manage. The composition of the acquired group is four African Americans, three Hispanics, one Asian, and one Native American. There are three whites, with one of these being the lone male in your newly constituted department.

Your initial observations of the expanded department cause you to conclude that you have a great deal of work to do in bringing these groups together as an effectively functioning unit and securing your acceptance by the employees.

Instructions:

Create an outline of the steps you believe you would consider taking to make your transition to your new role as smooth as possible. Your steps should include consideration of what to look for in familiarizing yourself with the department and what actions you should consider, depending on what you learn. Keep in mind throughout the need to respect each person as a unique individual with unique needs and a cultural background that may differ from yours while also remaining aware of the need for equity and consistency in dealing with employees. (Hint: based on what you learn in the early weeks of your new assignment, your response to the instruction could be anywhere from swift and simple to overwhelmingly complex.)

Case: Opposing Forces

Helen Wilson was hired from outside the hospital to be the new business office manager. She accepted the job, even after hearing that it was something of a hot seat; she would be the fifth person in the position in barely 3 years.

Although Helen did not know reasons for the short stays of her predecessors, it took her very little time to decide that the atmosphere in the department was definitely unhealthy. Her staff appeared to be split among several factions, each of which was clearly at odds with one or more of the others. The groups were divided along the lines of race and national origin, and the members of each group tended to cluster together while working, hang together during lunch times and breaks, and in general behave as though each was a small subdepartment within the larger entity.

From her first day on the job it was apparent to Helen that many of the department's problems were a result of communications barriers among groups. She tried scheduling department staff meetings for the purpose of improving communication, but each such gathering found her frustrated because she could barely get any of the factions to speak with her, let alone talk with the other groups.

After one particularly frustrating meeting Helen was approached by a person who appeared to be an informal leader of the department's largest faction. Said this individual to Helen: "You'll never get anything done this way. There's lots of distrust in the department, and the only way you're going to accomplish anything is to meet with each group separately."

Questions:

1. Would you advise Helen to meet with each group separately, as suggested? Why or why not?
2. How do you suggest that Helen begin an effort to disband the "opposing forces?"
3. Offer a few suggestions for Helen to consider in working with her unhealthily divided department over the coming weeks and months.

REFERENCES

1. American Association of Retired Persons (AARP), Work Force Programs Department. 1994. *How to develop a diversity commitment*. Washington DC: Author, 2.
2. Lewan, L.L. 1990. Diversity in the workplace. *HR Magazine* 35(6): 42.
3. Heier, W.D. 1980. Company loyalty: A zero-based asset? *Management Review* 69(4): 57–61.
4. Wynter, L.E. 1997. Allstate rates managers on handling diversity. *Wall Street Journal,* October 1, 1997, B1.
5. Anders, G. 1997. Doctors learn to bridge cultural gaps. *Wall Street Journal*, September 4, 1997, B1.
6. Karp, B.B. 1994. Choices in diversity training. *Training* 31(8): 73, 74.

RECOMMENDED READING

AARP Work Force Programs Department, *How to Develop a Diversity Commitment*. Washington DC: AARP, 1994.

J.G. Bruhn, "Creating an Organizational Climate for Multiculturism," *The Healthcare Supervisor* 14, no. 4 (1996): 11–8.

J. Notwani et al., "Managing Diversity in the Health Care Industry," *The Healthcare Supervisor* 13, no. 3 (1995): 16–23.

S.M. Paskoff, "Ending the Workplace Diversity Wars," *Training 33*, no. 8 (1996): 42–7.

S.M. Sack, *The Employee Rights Handbook.* (New York: Facts On File, 1990).

R.R. Thomas, Jr., *Redefining Diversity.* (New York: AMACOM, 1996).

Chapter 19

Conflict and Confrontation

The gem cannot be polished without friction,
nor man perfected without trials.

—Confucius

Disagreement is not necessarily disloyalty.

—Wess Roberts[1]

CHAPTER OBJECTIVES

- Identify conflict and confrontation as unavoidable dimensions of communication in a business setting that can prove to be destructive or constructive, depending on how they are used or addressed.
- Identify the primary causes of conflict in the work setting.
- Establish an appreciation of the dangers inherent in escalating or suppressing conflict.
- Present several fundamental working strategies for addressing conflict in the work setting.
- Provide guidelines for the supervisor's constructive use of confrontation in managing an employee group.

CONFLICT AND THE HEALTH CARE ORGANIZATION

Once upon a time, specifically starting in the middle of the 20th century and culminating with the introduction of governmental control over several aspects of health care in the late 1960s, most of health care was seen as a work setting free of stress and strife. Indeed, in the 1940s, 1950s, and early 1960s, health care attracted

263

a significant number of workers, primarily in support activities such as accounting, human resources, building services, food service, and the like, who were escaping the mounting stresses and pressures of other businesses for what was perceived as a considerably calmer environment.

No longer is health care the stress-free environment it was once perceived to be. Now, in this first decade of the new century, the workplaces of health care providers are riddled with tension and strife, and the foreseeable future shows no signs of this changing. If anything, tension and strife will continue to intensify. Conflicts arise under pressure-cooker deadlines, increased workloads, mounting fear of layoffs, and relentless pressures to increase productivity and maintain quality while consuming fewer resources. Conflicts are inevitable in today's health care organization, and for the individual supervisor they are an unavoidable part of the job.

Disagreements can be healthy as long as they culminate in positive solutions that prevent serious mistakes or inappropriate actions, force second looks at questionable situations, and lead to solutions or improvement. When resolved, disputes can foster improved relationships.

Some dysfunctional work groups operate in a manner that suppresses conflict. However, suppressed conflicts fester and eventually disrupt working relationships. Other groups become involved in relationships in which employees compete with each other and with management instead of cooperating. Some conflicts become highly adversarial, characterized by anger, hostility, humiliation, or rancor.

Principal Causes of Conflict

The etiology of any particular conflict is not always apparent. Often there is a covert issue camouflaged by a less important overt factor, that is, a highly visible symptom that obscures a true causal problem. Some conflict situations are simply murky because multiple causes are involved, rendering the central conflict difficult to identify and address.

Unclear Expectations or Guidelines

Employees sometimes do not know what they are supposed to do, how to do what is expected of them, or what outcomes they should achieve. Policies and rules are often ambiguous. For example, a policy forbidding sexual harassment may not clearly or fully explain exactly what constitutes sexual harassment and how it is to be recognized and addressed.

Poor Communication

Conflicts attributed to ill will between and among individuals are frequently the result of communication short-circuits, especially poor listening and, often, hastily scribbled memos or garbled e-mail messages. Faulty perceptions or assumptions cause misunderstandings. Everyone can cite personal examples of hurt feelings and damaged relationships that resulted from distortions or half-truths.

Lack of Clear Jurisdiction

When the limits of power and authority are not clearly defined, disputes erupt. Conflicts can readily arise over funds, space, time, personnel, or equipment. Squabbles involving work and vacation schedules are common.

Differences in Temperaments or Attitudes

Incompatibilities or disagreements based on differences in these areas are often complex conflict situations, frequently influenced by differences of race, religion, nationality, age, politics, ethics, and values. For example, nurses and physicians may disagree about how to deal with dying patients.

Individual or Group Conflicts of Interest

There can be chronic friction or long-standing differences between departments or shifts. Consider, for example, disagreements between a purchasing department charged with serving all departments with limited financial resources and a unit manager who clamors for special consideration. When the perceived objectives of such groups or individuals appear inconsistent with each other, the grounds for conflict are present.

Operational or Staffing Changes

Whenever organizational or functional changes are introduced, conflicts are bound to arise. Some of the most troublesome conflicts encountered in business are those arising because of resistance to change (see Chapter 28).

DANGERS OF ESCALATING OR SUPPRESSING CONFLICT

Unaddressed or suppressed, conflict simply worsens. When it is unaddressed, conflict is essentially being allowed to escalate. No undesirable situation can be ignored in the hope that it will vanish on its own; rather, left to itself it will invariably worsen. When conflict escalates, the involved parties become impatient, angry, or frustrated, and their attention is diverted from problem solving to attacking the other persons who are involved. Blame and threats fly back and forth, and issues multiply. Old grievances come forth to compound the situation, and more often than not relationships are damaged. Bitterness leads to thoughts of how to get even rather than how to solve the initial problem. Eventually the parties may enlist supporters from among bystanders, resulting in the formation of opposing cliques.

When deliberate efforts are made to suppress conflict rather than deal with it, the results usually include chronic complaining, declining productivity, increased absenteeism, decreased morale and loyalty, and increased stress. In a number of worst-case scenarios, serious conflict forcibly suppressed can result in violence or sabotage.

FUNDAMENTAL STRATEGIES FOR COPING WITH CONFLICT

Each of the following strategies is appropriate for certain situations. Face your next conflict by selecting the most appropriate strategy.

Avoidance. Conflict avoidance may involve denying there is a problem, physically escaping the arena of the conflict, passing the buck, or procrastinating. The problem remains unresolved, and, as in the suppression of conflict, the result is usually a buildup of anger that eventually explodes. Avoidance can also be an escape mechanism. For example, when you are challenged by someone in the presence of your manager, you turn to your manager and say emphatically, "I want to respond to that, but not here and now. I'll do that at the next staff meeting."

However, avoidance may be appropriate when:

- The problem is not your problem
- There is nothing you can do about it
- It is inconsequential and thus not worth the effort to face
- You need additional information
- One of you is emotionally upset
- The disruption possible from addressing the conflict outweighs the benefits of resolution
- You can see that the situation will ameliorate if you can wait it out

Fight. There is often the temptation to fight, but there are pitfalls to this approach. First, you can lose. Even if you win a skirmish, your opponents may regroup and return to the fray or wait for another opportunity to retaliate. They may become saboteurs. Use this tactic when quick action is necessary (for example, when someone is violating an important safety regulation). It is also appropriate when you observe severe ethical or legal violations.

Surrender. Nonassertive individuals often succumb to this response, thus building up internal frustration as self-esteem erodes. Nonassertive or passive individuals tend to attract conflict; in effect, they wear "kick me!" signs.

However, surrender may be appropriate when

- You know the other party is right.
- You have no stake in the issue; it does not matter to you.
- Your chance of winning is infinitesimal.

- Harmony and stability, especially important, can be achieved.
- Giving in on a minor item now can mean winning a more important one later.

Compromise. Compromise is a partial-win strategy that you must settle for on occasion. Compromise allows all parties to get part of what they want, so there is some satisfaction for all. Most union–management or international disputes are settled in this manner. On the negative side of compromise, neither faction gets everything it wants. In addition, compromise may involve a certain amount of game playing, with each side pumping up its demands or disguising them. The most frequent mistake made concerning compromise is to adopt this alternative prematurely, without first making a serious effort at collaboration.

Compromise may be appropriate when

- Opposing goals are incompatible, so neither side can realistically expect complete victory.
- A temporary settlement to complex issues is called for.
- Time constraints dictate the need for an expedient solution.
- Discussions have stalled.

Collaboration. The basis for collaboration is established when disputing parties attack the problems rather than each other. Problems are resolved through honest and open discussion. Collaboration builds healthy relationships. It uncovers more information, challenges false assumptions or perceptions, and promotes improved understanding. It leads to better decisions.

This true win-win approach is usually the best alternative, but it customarily requires more creative solutions. The best answer is most often one that neither side had originally considered. An added benefit of this approach is that it builds positive relationships. This strategy is usually the most appropriate one, especially when the issue is too important to be settled any other way or when you must achieve a consensus.

However, there are negative aspects to this approach. Additional time may be required. Decisions may have to be delayed. The parties may become frustrated when no consensus is reached. Although more time is spent seeking solutions, the overall time may be much less because there is less haggling or involvement in side issues. Angry participants can prolong arguments, so it is sometimes necessary to call additional meetings to permit tempers to cool.

CONFRONTATION AND THE SUPERVISOR

Ready, Set...

No individual can long survive in a supervisory role by avoiding confrontation. Whether with employees, peers, or others, the supervisor must confront problems, issues, or disagreements on a daily basis. Many of a supervisor's daily confrontations will not be overly dramatic, but they will nevertheless require a degree of assertiveness on the part of the supervisor.

In preparing to enter a confrontational situation, ask yourself the following questions.

- What do I want to accomplish?
- What is the most I will give up?
- What do I believe the other person wants? Does he or she have covert goals?
- What false assumptions or incorrect perceptions might the other party hold?
- Which strategy should I apply?
- What are my "hot buttons," and what should I do if they are pushed?
- If I plan to use a collaborative approach, what special precautions should I take?

Get psyched up for confrontation with the following three techniques.

Practice success imagery. Visualize a successful confrontation. Picture your body language, hear your words and voice tone, and envision a successful outcome. Athletes and professional speakers have used this technique with great success.

Adjust your self-talk. This is converting negative thoughts to positive ones when talking to yourself. All of us carry on a constant inner dialogue with ourselves. When we are in a passive mode, these internal conversations are negative and pessimistic: our subconscious mind conjures up statements such as "I could never say that" or "She'll just blow me away." Let your positive affirmations take control. Say to yourself, "I'll be in control." Avoid weak statements such as "I'm going to try to stand up to her next time."

Rehearse. After you have selected your dialogue and its appropriate body language, rehearse the anticipated encounter. Do this over and over. Do it in front of a mirror and out loud. Still better, get someone to role-play with you. Do not be satisfied until you have your performance down pat.

...Confront

Confrontations are seldom as bad as anticipated, especially when you go into them thoroughly prepared. Here are some practical suggestions for achieving a collaborative confrontation.

- Avoid sitting across a desk or table from the person; this invites opposition. Sit next to each other. Better still, take a stroll side by side.
- Open the discussion by saying something like "Let's see how we can solve this in a way that satisfies both of us."
- After outlining the problem, move on to areas of agreement. To do this, start with questions you are certain will be answered affirmatively. It is then easier

to get a yes to more controversial questions that come later. For example, "Don't you agree that we must put team goals before our individual agendas?"

- Listen attentively, asking pertinent questions and keying in on what the other person is saying. Be empathetic. Respect the other person's feelings, but still feel free to respond forcibly.

- It often pays to ask the person what he or she wants. You may be pleasantly surprised to find that what is wanted is less than you were prepared to offer. On the other hand, do not neglect to say what it is that you want.

- Let the person know that you hear and understand both the content of what is said and the feelings with which it is said. Validate feelings with something like "As I understand it, you're angry because I asked one of your assistants to give me a hand with my project. Is that right?" Validating has two benefits: it clarifies the problem and lets the person know that what he or she is saying is important.

- Use the person's name frequently. Our own names are the sweetest sounds we humans hear.

- Seek a larger pie instead of dividing up the existing pie. This means finding something more for both of you, a win-win solution.

- Emphasize your inability to change the past and affirm that you want to focus on the present and future.

- Stay cool and avoid rhetorical or emotional escalation. When they become upset, people exaggerate. This increases anxiety and makes it more difficult to solve the problem. When forced into a corner, say, "I find myself getting upset. Let's take a 10-minute break, OK?"

- Let the other party save face. He or she should come away with something.

And to Confront More Effectively...

- Be prepared, just as you would be for a debate.
- Choose the best time and place. Do not meet when your self-esteem is low or when either of you is upset.
- Regard the other person not as an enemy but as a partner in problem solving.
- Clarify the other person's viewpoint as well as your own. Do not proceed further until these viewpoints and the desired outcomes are clear.
- Focus first on a point of agreement, then work from there.
- Be assertive, not aggressive. Use "I" statements (for example, "I get concerned when people approach me like this"). Use nonconfrontational phrases such as "help me understand why..."
- Attack the problem or the behavior and its results, never the other person. Disagree without being disagreeable or trying to prove that the person is wrong.
- Do not cause your opponent to lose face. Do not threaten or issue ultimatums.

- Do not be sarcastic or critical.
- Avoid using the word "you." It is frequently followed by an attack on the person's ego.
- To avoid retaliation, use the straw man technique; that is, set up hypothetical but parallel situations to address.
- Be aware of your body language. Maintain eye contact, sit or stand up straight, and appear relaxed. Do not fidget or squirm. Avoid threatening gestures such as finger pointing, fist making, crossed arms, hands on hips, or scowling. Smile when you agree; remain expressionless when you disagree.
- Control your voice. Keep its volume, pitch, and rate under control. Stop if you find it growing louder, faster, or high pitched.
- Be diplomatic and tentative when facing firm resistance. Use words such as "maybe," "perhaps," or "you may be right."
- When you are cornered or upset, escape by pleading stress.
- Do not get stuck believing that your solution is the only workable one. Simply focus on the benefits of your point of view.
- Promise realistic rewards that you can deliver ("If you will…, then I will…").
- End on a positive note.

When the Person You Are Confronting is Angry

It goes without saying that we sometimes provoke anger in others when we criticize, pressure, threaten, deny, irritate, deride or, in short, do anything that can be perceived as attacking self-esteem. Almost anyone can be provoked to anger if the stimulus is sufficiently intense. However, people differ from each other in terms of their anger threshold. Some associates are overly sensitive; they may exhibit explosive tempers on short fuses. Some people use anger because they have learned through personal experience that it enables them to avoid unpleasant assignments. Sensitive individuals take everything personally. They quickly and angrily charge favoritism or discrimination. Your children are probably already expert at this.

Some people use anger as a defense mechanism, exhibiting anger in defense of viewpoints or positions that they feel, perhaps unconsciously, to be weak, flawed, or incorrect. Anger often provides the shield that holds off further attack. To quote the character Lucy in the comic strip *Peanuts*, "If you can't be right, be wrong at the top of your voice."

Guidelines for Coping with an Angry Person

- Never lose your cool. Never shout or even raise your voice. Avoid any threatening gestures or aggressive body language. Never touch the person. When you are angry, say nothing until your emotions are under control.
- Make no comments about the other person's anger or tell him or her not to be angry ("Why don't you calm down?").

- Do not patronize or lecture.
- When a person approaches you and you sense that he or she is angry, greet the individual as a friend. In most instances the person who speaks first sets the mood for the conversation to follow.
- Ask questions. The person who asks the most pertinent questions controls the agenda and the overall direction of the exchange. The key question is, "What do you want me to do?" Find out exactly what he or she wants and satisfy that want if possible. If you cannot satisfy it, offer your solution.
- Listen to the person's outbursts without interrupting. Doing so can have a powerful calming effect. The person who listens best usually comes out a winner.
- Make certain that you understand the problem.
- Avoid becoming defensive or argumentative.
- Empathize by paraphrasing what you think the person is angry about and why he or she feels that way.
- Assure the person that something will be done.

Negotiation, mediation, and arbitration are special forms of conflict handling that will be discussed in Chapter 36.

Think About It

Occasionally a certain degree of righteous anger can be effective in resolving some difficulty, but for the most part anger is destructive in interpersonal communication. As the level of anger in an interpersonal exchange increases, the chances of effective communication taking place decrease.

Questions for Review and Discussion

1. Why can we claim with a fair degree of certainty that conflict often produces growth and progress?
2. Provide two specific examples of how the interaction between departments or groups can automatically engender conflict.
3. Describe in detail one specific instance of conflict where avoidance might be the appropriate response.
4. Explain why so many individuals in the work environment seem to go out of their way to avoid confrontation.
5. As a supervisor, how are you going to respond when an employee angrily confronts you concerning a mandate handed down by top management?
6. Describe a confrontational situation in which an individual's words seem to be conveying a message opposite from that conveyed by the person's body language. How can you go about determining which is the real message?
7. In some quarters compromise tends to be regarded as an undesirable condition to be avoided. Why might this be so, and what is wrong with this stance?

8. Why might we say that sometimes the best immediate reaction to confrontation by an angry person is to shut down and walk away?
9. Explain in some detail the risks inherent in continually suppressing conflict for the sake of peace and quiet.
10. Why should we want to avoid criticizing another's anger with statements such as "You shouldn't feel that way" or "You have no cause for anger."

Case: Addressing the Squeaky Wheel

You are the supervisor of 20 people in a subunit of one of Central Hospital's service departments. Three of your employees are titled as working group leaders, but they are usually involved in doing the work of the department rather than overseeing others. The busiest of these, a group leader named Sally, is expected to spend 60% of her time on regular work and 40% supervising.

Several times in recent months Sally has mentioned that her group's backlog was growing and that she needed more help. She has never been more specific than saying more help was needed, and her gripes seemed to have been no more than passing remarks offered without preparation or forethought. You have been under pressure from a number of directions, and Sally's complaints seemed to represent no more than chronic grumbling, so you have not felt compelled to add her concerns to your list of worries.

But today, Monday, first thing after starting time, Sally sought you out and confronted you with "I need one more full-time person, and I need her now! I'm tired of waiting and tired of being ignored, and I'm sick of being overworked and taken for granted. If something isn't done about it by Friday, I'm out of here and you can find yourself another sucker."

Instructions:

1. Describe how you will initially address Sally's outburst.
2. Propose two or three possible solutions to the problem and describe the potential advantages and disadvantages of each.
3. The situation places you in something of a trap. Describe this trap, explain why it is a trap, and explain how you might proceed toward a solution in view of the hazards inherent in the situation.

Case: The Artful Dodger

Janet had considerable difficulty developing the schedule for her nursing unit for the coming 2 weeks. The nursing department was in a marginal position overall as far as available nurses were concerned, so her flexibility was limited. To make matters worse, within an hour after Janet developed the new schedule, a part-time licensed practical nurse named Bonnie turned in a request for a personal day on one of the days she was scheduled to work.

The request caused Janet to realize that she had been seeing Bonnie's name in connection with scheduling difficulties often in recent months. Looking back over the preceding 6 months' schedules she discovered that the current request was the fifth time in 6 months that Bonnie had requested time off on a scheduled weekend day. Even more significant was the pattern of Bonnie's use of sick time. She had called in sick four times, all of these on Saturdays or Sundays. All in all, Bonnie had worked only about half of the weekend days she was scheduled to work over a period of 6 months.

Janet was displeased with Bonnie's attendance and unhappy with herself for not discovering the problem sooner. She felt she had to confront Bonnie about the problem, but she also felt that her unit could ill afford to lose a nurse when replacements were so scarce. Nevertheless, she believed she could not allow Bonnie's attendance pattern to continue.

Questions:

1. What are the hazards Janet faces in (a) dealing firmly with Bonnie's behavior and (b) ignoring Bonnie's absences and saying nothing?
2. Assuming Janet decides to confront Bonnie, how should she go about doing so?

REFERENCES

1. Roberts, W. 1990. *Leadership secrets of Attila the Hun.* New York: Warner Books, 17.

RECOMMENDED READING

R.W. Lucas, *Effective Interpersonal Relationships.* (New York: Irwin Publishers, 1994).
D. Tjosvold, *Learning To Manage Conflict.* (New York: Lexington Books, 1993).
W. Umiker, "Collaborative Conflict Resolution," *The Health Care Supervisor* 15, no. 3 (1997): 70–5.

Chapter 20

Employees With Problems

Every difficulty slurred over will be a ghost
to disturb your repose later on.

—Frederic Chopin

Be kind. Remember everyone you meet
is fighting a hard battle.

—T.H. Thompson

CHAPTER OBJECTIVES

- Provide the supervisor with the means of identifying employees whose performance problems and other difficulties might suggest the presence of underlying personal problems.
- Address the commonly experienced problem of absenteeism and suggest how the supervisor can constructively deal with chronic absenteeism among staff members.
- Explore the relationship between personal problems and particular behaviors exhibited on the job.
- Recommend procedures for the supervisor to apply in addressing performance problems that appear to be related to employees' personal difficulties.
- Address special problematic situations such as friction between and among employees and unethical behavior by employees and peers.

THE MARGINAL PERFORMER

It will sometimes seem as though the marginal performer is one of the greatest sources of frustration for the supervisor. This is so because the supervisor often

275

knows an employee to be capable of better performance, perhaps even outstanding performance, but there seems to be no way to get the person to perform to his or her potential. Some marginal performers are that way because they are capable of little more, but many marginal performers have the ability to perform better but for various reasons they are not motivated to do so.

Among the marginal performers who could do better if they so wished are employees who are just putting in time until their retirement and those who regard their present jobs as interim employment before moving on to what they really want. Others just lack motivation for a variety of reasons. The first step in dealing with these people is to get to know them better and, if possible, find their motivational buttons and discover what would encourage them to willingly achieve.

Ask yourself these questions about your marginal performers.

- Are they simply bored with their jobs? If this is so, consider actions such as job enrichment, cross-training, special projects, committee assignments, teaching responsibilities, job rotation, or participation in research; in general, anything that can be done to relieve boredom and stimulate renewed interest in the job.
- Are their social needs being met? Do they prefer to work alone or as part of a group? How do they get along with their peers? Might it be possible to move these employees around so that they work with or around different people?
- If possible, consider transferring marginal performers to faster-moving, more energetic groups or assign them individual work according to their preferences.
- Are their ego needs being met? Do they seem to be getting the attention and respect they think they deserve? And are you making a special effort to provide this attention and respect? Maybe what is needed are status symbols, such as a change in title, a bigger desk, or a personalized nameplate. As possible, provide more recognition.

Never accept unsatisfactory performance. Do not reward poor productivity by transferring some of the work of these employees to the better performers. Do not give satisfactory performance ratings to undeserving employees. Every experienced supervisor has made that mistake and has ultimately regretted it, especially later when they found that "good" evaluations in the personnel file severely complicated an attempt to discharge an employee.

Be especially careful about using marginal employees for orienting and training new employees. A poor attitude can be contagious, as can an attitude toward the work that suggests "just getting by" is enough.

The Older Employee

The majority of older employees are excellent workers who can often run rings around their younger coworkers. However, some older workers lose their spark, allow their expertise to become obsolete, and become unwilling to learn new skills. They may adjust poorly to organizational and procedural changes. The following may be helpful in dealing with older employees.

- Acknowledge their experience by seeking their advice.
- Use them as mentors or involve them in orienting new employees or in providing on-the-job training (select who and what carefully).
- Explain the need for change; get them involved and give them additional training if needed.
- Encourage them to attend professional meetings.
- If they are winding down toward retirement, approve their occasional requests for time off without pay. Hire part-timers to fill the gaps, if necessary, rather than overload their coworkers while they are away.
- Listen to their plans for retirement. Be sympathetic.

Goof-Offs

The goof-offs have poor attendance records. They are all great excuse makers. They always have rational-sounding excuses that invite sympathy (for example, "My wife is sick again," "My son is in trouble with the law," or "My car keeps breaking down"). They waste their time and often the time of others.

Do not allow the goof-offs to trap you into supporting their self-pity or debating the merits of their excuses. Focus on job standards and performance objectives, and the goof-offs will eventually be weeded out as they fail to consistently perform.

Parents of Latchkey Children

Parents of children who come home from school to an empty house are understandably concerned about their welfare. This concern can result in frequent telephone calls and mental distractions that interfere with job performance. You may find these tips helpful.

- Talk with the parent about after-school child care. Your human resources department may be able to say whether assistance is available in the community.
- Explain to the parent that this legitimate concern is affecting job performance, and express your desire to help.
- Consider other solutions:
  1. Rearrange the parent's work schedule, if possible. For example, coffee breaks may be scheduled to coincide with telephone calls to the child.
  2. Assign the employees low-priority tasks at the time their children are getting home from school.

3. Ask parents to limit the length of calls and to restrict calls to important messages.
4. Be tolerant about allowing parents to take time off when crises develop, but know where to draw the line.

You can surely appreciate some of the needs of employees who are concerned about their children during after-school hours, but you can go only so far in accommodating them. In terms of policy application and such, employees with children must be treated in the same manner as employees without children. The supervisor cannot legitimately make personnel decisions that are in any way based on the marital or family status of an individual. To do so is discriminatory.

THE ABSENT EMPLOYEE

It has been estimated that the average American employee takes from 7 to 12 days of unscheduled absence every year. Absenteeism costs American businesses more than $26 billion annually.[1]

When we speak of absenteeism we are ordinarily referring to what we might call external absenteeism, primarily failure to show up for work when expected but also including late arrivals and early departures. Absences may also be internal, however, occurring in the forms of extended breaks or meal periods, absence from the work area without legitimate reason, socializing, and daydreaming (in place but not working).

An absentee rate may be determined by dividing total hours of absence by total paid hours and expressing the result as a percentage. An absentee rate of 3% is considered reasonable by the US Department of Labor. The organization may or may not monitor this statistic for all employees. If an absentee rate is not available for the organization as a whole, it is suggested that the individual supervisor set up a simple scheme for tracking the absentee rate for the department.

There are a number of reasons for employee absence, and legitimate illness is but one of them. In actuality the two most frequent causes of absenteeism are job dissatisfaction and the availability of paid sick leave. It has been repeatedly shown that if sick time is available, it will be used, at least up to a certain point, for reasons other than illness. Consider the experiences of two hospitals located in the same city. At one institution, employees were allowed 12 paid sick days per year; on the average employees actually used about 7.5 days each. At the other hospital employees were allowed 5 paid sick days per year; in this organization the average use was about 3.2 days per person. It has been repeatedly shown in recent years that the greater a sick-time benefit, the greater the use of the benefit.

Although individual supervisors have little control over sick leave policy, there are things they can do that can minimize the abuse of sick time.

- Be certain employees know that sick leave is a benefit, not an entitlement. Like certain other benefits, for example, health insurance, it is there for use when needed.
- Eliminate causes of job dissatisfaction as much as possible. The more satisfied an employee is with the working situation, the less likely the person is to abuse time off.
- Set an example. The supervisor's attendance record should be a visible, positive example for the employees.
- Maintain complete and accurate attendance records, and make no secret of the fact that you monitor absenteeism.
- Be conscious of patterns of absenteeism, for example, weekend stretching by being absent Friday or Monday; absence immediately before or after a holiday or vacation; absence the day following payday; absence at the start of hunting season; and other absences that may fall into patterns.

When an employee calls in sick, try to take the call personally. If a spouse makes the call and the employee is not seriously ill, ask to speak to the employee. Ask if the person has seen a physician, whether he or she is receiving adequate treatment, if there is anything you can do, and when the person might return to work. When an individual returns from an absence of more than a single day, send the person to the employee health service for clearance to work.

When absence becomes excessive and approaches limits spelled out in personnel policy, follow the counseling procedure presented in Chapter 16.

In recent years, as the financial pressures on health care institutions have increased and management has sought ways to reduce costs and boost productivity, straightforward sick-time benefits have begun to shrink or disappear altogether. It is becoming increasingly common to find plans that combine vacation, holidays, personal time, and a modest amount of sick time into paid-time-off (PTO) banks. Under these kinds of plans, a day taken off for "illness" reduces the PTO bank by a day and thus leaves 1 day less for other purposes. Employees tend to think twice about unnecessary absences when they cut into their total time-off benefit.

EMPLOYEES WITH PERSONAL PROBLEMS AFFECTING PERFORMANCE

When it comes to dealing with employees who are experiencing personal problems, the supervisor is often in something of a bind. What goes on in the private life of an employee is just that: private. It is no business of the supervisor what is occurring concerning an employee when that employee is not at work. The supervisor is not permitted to ask about the nature of an employee's personal problem or to probe in any way for information about the person's private life. Although the supervisor cannot dig into the nature of an employee's personal problem, however, the supervisor remains responsible for the performance and output of that employee when on the job.

It is impossible, or at least extremely difficult, to separate the person on the job from the person off the job. Problems at work affect home life to some extent; problems at home and elsewhere affect work life. People vary widely in their ability to keep the two halves of their lives separated, and many people who experience personal problems find that these problems affect their work performance. When work performance is affected, it becomes the supervisor's business.

Personal problems that limit an employee's ability to perform the job as expected commonly include family stress, alcohol abuse, misuse of drugs, emotional disorders, and legal or financial difficulties. Supervisors are responsible for detecting and attempting to correct deteriorating job performance, but they are not expected to diagnose or treat personal problems.

When supervisory efforts do not improve behavior or performance and a personal problem may be the cause of the difficulty, refer the employee to your employee health office, your employee assistance program, or to another source through which professional assistance may be obtained.

The presence of a personal problem that affects performance may be indicated by any of a number of changes in behavior. The more common behavioral changes are

- increased absenteeism, especially important if exhibited by an individual with a history of good attendance;
- frequent absences from the workstation;
- confusion or difficulty concentrating;
- decreased productivity or diminished work quality;
- friction with other employees;
- unusual or atypical behavior, for example, temper tantrums or emotional outbursts;
- becoming accident prone; and
- alcohol on the breath.

You may also have reason to suspect drug involvement when, in addition, an employee

- receives visits from strangers or employees from other areas or meets these people outside of the building (at entrances, in parking lots, etc.);
- is suspected of theft;
- makes secretive telephone calls;
- visits the washroom or locker room for long periods;
- wears dark glasses indoors;
- wears long-sleeved shirts in hot weather;

- has blood stains on the shirt sleeves; and/or
- perspires excessively.

Company Policy Concerning Personal Problems

Every organization should have a well-documented policy and an established procedure for handling employees who have personal problems (see Figure 20–1). Some type of employee assistance program is usually available without charge to the worker. Employees who use the services of the program are guaranteed confidentiality because the information obtained is considered a medical record. Encourage your employees to seek assistance on their own initiative before problems affect their work. Generally, time off for counseling is treated the same as time off for any other disability.

A Recommended Procedure

Hold a frank performance counseling session that lets the employee know that you believe there is a problem.

1. Make certain the employee knows what is expected and that documentation of your observations is complete.
2. Describe the unacceptable behavior or results without stating what you believe the underlying problem to be. Say, for example, "Joe, your daily reports have been 1 to 2 hours late every day for the past week," rather than "Joe, you often have alcohol on your breath; you've got to get off the stuff."
3. Do not accuse the employee of having a personal problem, but encourage such an admission with a statement such as "I've noticed that you seem tense recently. Is something bothering you that we can help with?"

Put the following four questions to the employee.

1. Are you aware that your performance has fallen below the standard for the job? If yes, ask when he or she first observed this.
2. Is it possible that a personal problem may be at the root of this? If yes, ask what he or she has done about it.
3. Are you aware of our employee assistance program?
4. Is there anything I can do to help?

If the employee's performance fails to improve, hold a second counseling session.

1. If the employee still does not admit that there is a personal problem, say, for example, "If you have a personal problem, I suggest counseling help. We

have an excellent employee assistance program here that is completely confidential and free."
2. Emphasize that the person's job may be in jeopardy if performance does not improve.

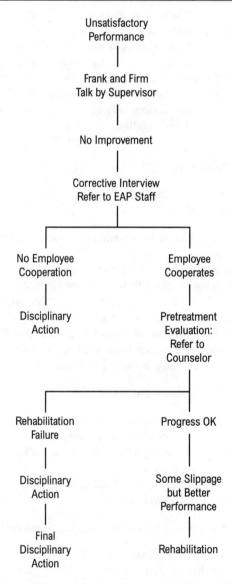

Figure 20–1 Supervisory Procedure for Employees with Personal Problems

If the employee cooperates and progress is satisfactory, continue your support.

1. As with many medical conditions, expect occasional backsliding or relapses.
2. Make sure that you acknowledge good work and noticeable improvement.
3. Resist any temptation to lighten the employee's load. Treat the individual as any other employee, but allow a reasonable transition period after the employee has sought help before expecting job performance to return to an acceptable level.

If the employee refuses all opportunities to seek help or if rehabilitation fails, your final recourse is to take disciplinary action.

Precautions When Addressing Employees with Problems

- Use only job performance to initiate corrective procedures. Your concern is for performance; the reasons that underlie flagging performance lie beyond your authority.
- Never apologize for bringing up performance deficiencies.
- Do not try to be a diagnostician. You are an "expert" only in the area of performance. Other people can better determine the nature of personal problems.
- During your counseling interview, do not discuss personal problems in depth. If the employee volunteers the information, you can listen, but do not ask questions and do not attempt to offer advice.
- Do not moralize. There should be no stigma attached to personal problems.
- Be firm, but do not take punitive action until after counseling has been suggested and declined.

WHEN EMPLOYEES FAIL TO GET ALONG

There are many reasons why some people may not get along with each other at work. Besides cultural, age, political, and gender differences, there may be competition for attention, promotion, recognition, turf, or resources. Personality differences seem to receive most of the blame. However, before you attribute the problem to personality clashes, look for external causes. There may be ambiguous position descriptions that do not show who does what or who has what authority. Sometimes bystanders are provoking disagreements among others.

There are three basic strategies for coping with feuding employees.

First, there is *avoidance*. This is best, not to mention the most sensible, when it is not your problem or when you lack the authority to act.

The second approach is *arbitration*. This consists of analyzing the situation and then taking sides or dictating a solution. This approach often fails because it usually leaves one party satisfied and the other party dissatisfied, and there can be serious side effects.

Finally, there is *mediation.* In this approach you encourage the participants to solve their problem, keep them from exploding, and guide them into mutually agreeable solutions. It is essential that both parties perceive you as neutral. Never take sides.

Sometimes the problem is solved simply by telling the feuding duo that they do not have to like each other to work together and that you expect them to act as adults and to treat each other civilly on the job. If that approach fails to work, talk to each person individually, looking for an underlying cause of the animosity. A solution may emerge during one of these conversations. Job redesign, clarification of limits of authority, or revising territorial boundaries may provide the remedy. If the problem is still not solved, hold a joint meeting with the intent of converting them from adversaries to problem solvers if at all possible. They must understand, however, that you will take whatever action you feel is necessary, up to and including disciplinary action, if their mutual animosity affects job performance or the morale of the department.

A recommended approach to addressing the problems presented by feuding employees consists of the following steps.

1. Caution the employees that if they do not work out a solution, you will take administrative action that may not please either party.
2. Seek some common ground or general area of agreement, for example, "You both agree that our goal is to improve customer service, right?"
3. Listen to both sides impartially. Do not tolerate interruptions, blaming, or name-calling. Make each person summarize what the other person said to clarify any flawed communication.
4. Ask each person what he or she would like to change. Review areas of agreement and disagreement.
5. Discuss the pros and cons of each alternative, and get them to agree to one possible solution.
6. Clarify expected future behavior, for example, "What are we now going to do differently?" or "What are we going to do if...?"
7. Congratulate them on reaching an agreement. Express confidence in their ability to resolve their differences.
8. Follow up. Hold additional sessions if necessary.

If these employees cannot resolve their differences, you must decide whether you can live with the flawed situation. If not, you must take whatever administrative action is necessary, for example, transferring one or reassigning them so they no longer work together.

UNETHICAL BEHAVIOR

Organizational ethics defines the boundaries of acceptable behavior. Ethical considerations may relate to performance appraisals, promotions, and disciplinary actions to cite but a few. They often involve the protection of personal privacy, discriminatory behavior, or the release of information. Nowhere is the practice of ethical behavior more important than in relationships between and among employees, superiors, and colleagues.

Ethics represent what we *should* do but not necessarily what we *must* do. Ethical standards are higher than the standards that apply in civil and criminal laws. The easiest ethical violations to recognize are those that also violate laws. For example, the pilfering of supplies is theft and is therefore both illegal and unethical. More controversial, and within the realm of ethics, is the "borrowing" of workplace equipment for personal use.

Ethical decisions are based on legal, corporate, moral, cultural, and personal values. What we consider ethical depends largely on our core beliefs and values. These are determined early in life and are based on the teachings of parents, teachers, and role models. Life experiences modify or enforce these beliefs about what is right and what is wrong. Complications often arise in the workplace because employees are asked to merge their values with those of the organization. Sometimes these sets of values are discordant. Value differences readily explain why people frequently disagree about what is ethical and what is not.

Here are a number of examples of unethical behavior in the workplace.

- Instructing people to do whatever is necessary to achieve results
- Taking credit for other people's ideas or shifting blame for one's own failures to others
- Playing favorites among staff
- Lying or falsifying records
- Billing for work not performed
- Deliberately making false or misleading statements
- Divulging personal or confidential information
- Failing to report violations of legal requirements
- Failing to report health and safety hazards or accidents
- Stealing or, as it is often euphemistically referred to in policies, unauthorized use or possession of the property of others.

Probably the most common ethical violations are lying, falsifying records, and stealing.

Organizational Climate

Employees are more likely to make unethical decisions when management makes it difficult for them to avoid doing so. Some employees frequently feel pressured to act in ways that violate the codes of behavior of their organization. Again, the likes of "I don't care how you do it, just get it done!" can make an employee feel forced to act unethically in order to stay out of trouble.

Ethics Programs

The majority of ethics programs consist chiefly of "snitch lines" in which people are encouraged to report the perceived violations of others. Experience has shown, however, that most of the calls received concern petty complaints, such as people taking long lunch breaks.

Effective ethics programs include a code of ethical conduct, provide for employee training in the ethics of the workplace, include a monitoring system, and provide an ethics "hotline." The hotline is used less for snitching than for soliciting expert advice as to whether or not something is unethical or on how to respond to certain situations, for example, the appropriateness of accepting a gift from a vendor or hiring a member of one's family. An additional benefit of calls for advice is that they suggest what kind of information should be presented in training programs or discussed at staff meetings. To be effective, calls for advice must be answered promptly and skillfully. Experienced advisors walk the callers through the thought process so they can reach the right decisions by themselves.

The principal reasons people offer for not reporting unethical acts are (1) they doubt that anything will be done, (2) they fear retaliation, or (3) they do not trust the organization to keep the information confidential.

Ethics training may consist of special courses that are given periodically and that are included in orientation programs. In these sessions, case studies involving ethical dilemmas can be presented.

Supervisor Enforcement of Ethical Behavior

With all of the downsizing, restructuring, and reorganizing occurring in health care, and with the increased workloads placed on so many employees, employees often feel pressured to cut corners. Tell your employees to come to you when they are running behind schedule so you can provide them with help or modify their schedules; it is important for them to know that getting the work done honestly and ethically is as important as getting it done at all.

Encourage employees to inform you, in confidence, of their concerns about apparent unethical acts by their coworkers. Tell them that there may be times when they must choose between betraying colleagues and being loyal to the organization.

Make your pronouncements of intolerance of unethical behavior strong, and make your disciplinary reactions fast.

When you observe a colleague engaging in minor unethical behavior, it may be appropriate to tell him or her that you are aware of what is going on and will be obligated to report these transgressions if they continue. If the acts are illegal or represent major ethical violations, go directly to the authorities.

As necessary, discuss individual situations with your superior or a member of the human resources department. Be certain you are familiar with the organization's policies addressing unethical behavior, referring to them before making any waves. If you are a member of a professional organization to which the offending individual belongs, consult with a representative of that organization.

Think About It

Ethical behavior is one of the most important areas in which a supervisor can serve as a role model for employee conduct. Those supposedly "small" ethical lapses, which some are inclined to defend with "Why not? Everybody does it," are far less likely to be considered acceptable if they are visibly avoided by the supervisor. Do not underestimate the power of a strong positive role model.

Questions for Review and Discussion

1. Do you agree that enforcement of ethical guidelines has become more difficult in most settings in recent years? Why might this be so?
2. Why do we frequently say that the supervisor should not give advice to employees concerning their personal problems?
3. Why can we not simply create a special set of conditions to apply just to single parents or parents of latchkey children?
4. Can you envision circumstances under which referral to an employee assistance program should be made a condition of continued employment? When and why?
5. How do paid-time-off programs actively discourage the abuse of sick-time benefits?
6. What do you believe is the most effective way for the supervisor to exert a positive influence on absenteeism? Why?
7. Concerning employee problems, why is it claimed that the supervisor should use only job performance to initiate the corrective process?
8. Why should the supervisor avoid inquiring into the nature of an employee's personal problem?
9. Why do we not simply address all performance problems with a disciplinary process that essentially says "shape up or ship out?"
10. What will you do when one of your employees shows up for work showing signs of being under the influence of drugs or alcohol?

Case: When Jennifer Turned Grouchy

"I'm not trying to tell you what to do," said Mary Stone to Mark Carter, "but as your assistant I feel I've got to point out—again—that we have a problem that's generating lots of grief."

"I know," Mark responded with more than a trace of annoyance. "I'm trying to take it the way you mean it, and I've heard about it from others as well. I know we have a problem with Jennifer, but I don't know how to deal with it."

"But it has to be dealt with. As receptionist she's in a position to make a first and lasting impression on a number of people, and she's generating a trail of complaints from patients and physicians and other staff about her curt, rude treatment of them. It's been going on for weeks, and it's getting worse. Now she's starting to mix up appointments."

Mark said, "I'd hoped that whatever was bugging her would pass, but she's just gone from bad to worse. And it's really too bad; she's been here a long time and this is only recent."

"One of us should talk with her and try to find out what's going on."

Mark said, "I've tried. Last week I gave her a chance to talk in private. I even asked if I could help in any way, but she told me that nothing was wrong. The way she said it, she might as well have told me to mind my own business. But she's wound up tight, and there's obviously something going on in her life that wasn't there a few weeks ago."

"Well, something is certainly wrong," said Mary, "and something's got to be done. Our receptionist has become sullen and ill-tempered, and the department's starting to suffer."

Instructions:

1. Develop a tentative approach to the problem presented by the grouchy receptionist. Be sure to provide reasonable opportunity for correction of behavior and that you account for
   - possible ways to help the employee with the problem,
   - the necessarily progressive nature of any disciplinary action contemplated, and
   - the needs of the department and its customers.

Case: Why Can't They Just Get Along?

Said supervisor Ann Jones, "I'm so frustrated by what's going on in my section that I'm about ready to get rid of two fairly productive employees just for the sake of peace and quiet."

Fellow supervisor and friend Bonnie Smith replied, "I can't see getting rid of good employees for any reason. They're too hard to come by."

"I said fairly good, or at least fairly productive. They both would be practically ideal if I could keep them out of each other's way. But they work in the same office—there are 13 of us crammed into a pretty limited space—and they just don't get along."

"Personalities?"

"Don't know. But if one of them says something's black the other says it's white, seemingly just for spite. When anything's wrong with one's work input or if anything's out of place at one workstation, the other is blamed. They're always competing, and if one thinks the other is gaining favor in any way the jealous behavior becomes intolerable."

Bonnie said, "Maybe they deserve each other. Why not stick the two of them in the farthest corner and leave them be?"

"I can't. They both relate to about half the rest of the staff on any given day, and when they're not getting along the tension affects others. It gets so bad sometimes that these two so-called adults who are supposed to be communicating with each other regularly throughout the day will speak to each other only through a third party."

"Childish."

"Childish indeed, but the effects of their behavior are serious. They have been talked to about it, more than once, in fact, but even though things simmer down a little when they're spoken to, they're back at each other's throats in a week."

Instructions:

1. Describe in detail how you would advise supervisor Ann Jones to proceed in addressing the problem presented by the apparently incompatible employees.

REFERENCES

1. Morgan, P.I., and Baker, H.K. 1984. Do you need an absenteeism control program? *Supervisory Management* 29(9): 1–2.

RECOMMENDED RESOURCES

R. Brinkman and R. Kirschner, *How To Deal with Difficult People.* (Boulder, CO: CareerTrack Publishers, 1988). Two videocassettes.

C. McConnell, Ch 14, "The Problem Employee and Employee Problems" and Ch 16, "Ethics and Ethical Standards," in *The Effective Health Care Supervisor,* 5th ed. (Gaithersburg MD: Aspen Publishers, 2002).

M. Solomon, *Working with Difficult People.* (Englewood Cliffs, NJ: Prentice Hall, 1990).

W. Umiker, *Coping with Difficult People in the Health Care Setting.* (Chicago, IL: ASCP Press, 1994).

Chapter 21

Employees With Negative Attitudes

The great trouble today is that there are
too many people looking for someone
to do something for them.

—Henry Ford

CHAPTER OBJECTIVES

- Address the frequently encountered problems presented by inappropriate employee attitudes, recognizing that it is necessary to always address the results of behavior rather than attempting to deal with attitude itself.
- Provide an overview of the application of coaching and counseling techniques as they relate to behavioral change.
- Identify a number of patterns of employee behavior that manifest themselves as representing forms of bad or poor attitude and suggest how the supervisor might address each of these when encountered.

A MATTER OF ATTITUDE

Most of the time the employees who give supervisors their biggest headaches are not the incompetent ones. There is always a chance that the incompetent ones can be trained. Likewise, the headache producers are not the ones who brazenly violate rules. Rule breakers can be dealt with via disciplinary processes, and if they fail to change their ways they can be fired. Rather, the employees who give supervisors the biggest headaches are the ones who usually meet work standards but make life stressful for supervisors with their idiosyncratic behavior. These are the people who are usually accused of exhibiting an attitude problem: a bad attitude, a poor attitude, a negative attitude, etc. In the following paragraphs we will refer simply to negative attitude.

An employee with a negative attitude may be a chronic negativist, a goof-off, a hothead, or even a disloyal subordinate. We cannot get into the heads of these people to see what a negative attitude really is. We know that this term is universally used to excess and lacks a concise definition. What we do see are various kinds of behaviors that we find annoying. The line between negative attitude and outright disloyalty or unethical behavior, for example, can be fuzzy. We can, however, often infer the presence of a negative attitude by the presence of certain signs. Negative attitudes may be reflected in a number of ways.

- Low or diminishing productivity
- High or increasing error rate and thus diminishing quality
- Repeated minor violations of rules and procedures
- Lack of team spirit or lack of cooperation
- Public criticism of the organization and its management
- Periodic threats of resignation
- Foot-dragging and chronic resistance to change

Supervisors who have the courage and conscientiousness to document what they really think about their employees who display negative attitudes will likely use one or more of the following adjectives in their appraisals of these employees: uninterested, inflexible, pessimistic, complaining, indifferent, change resistant, unenthusiastic, and nonsupportive.

However, the supervisor faces a significant barrier in addressing negative attitudes: attitude cannot be directly addressed by any of the corrective processes available to the supervisor. You cannot, for example, cite "poor attitude" as the reason for issuing a warning and have this hold up under legal scrutiny. This is so because attitude is subjective; it is not a concrete term with a precise definition. It is always open to interpretation, and because it is subjective, it can always be argued because its presence cannot be proven. Therefore, because we are unable to cite negative attitude as the particular offense, we are left with the need to consider what behavior the negative attitude has caused. In some circumstances the supervisor might be on reasonably solid ground in discussing an apparent negative attitude and its effects with an offending employee, but it must always be the noticeable and provable results of behavior to which the corrective or disciplinary processes are applied.

COACHING AND COUNSELING FOR BEHAVIORAL CHANGE

Before taking any action stemming from an apparent attitude problem, take steps to determine if there really is a problem. If there is indeed a problem, how pervasive is it? In the previous chapter we posed a crucial question that comes up whenever we face a difficult person. It is well worth repeating: Does the behavior noticeably affect the department's output, the employee's teammates, or you? If there is no apparent effect and you think you can live with the present situation, your best move may be no move at all.

It is always best to avoid accusing a person of having a negative attitude. If you feel that you must do so, provide specific behavioral examples that led you to that subjective conclusion. Failure to do so will usually elicit defensiveness or anger or, at best, confuse the person. It is not likely to achieve the desired change. What you really want is for some behavioral change to occur. Then if the new behavior meets your standards, you need not be overly concerned about attitude. In the military, for example, it has been repeatedly proven that when you are able to change the behavior of trainees it leads to pride in the service and in themselves, and the negative attitudes disappear.

Often a negative attitude can be modified to a satisfactory extent by vigorous coaching and skillful counseling. Discuss the problem with the person candidly. Explain how the behavior in question affects you, the department, or others. Provide specific examples of how you see the person's behavior affecting services and people, especially customers and coworkers.

When it seems that your coaching and counseling are having no effect, start keeping more detailed performance records. Cutting these folks loose may prove to be the best solution, but you will need concrete proof of how the negative attitude affected performance or other employees. This concrete proof is best retained in the form of factual evidence of the results of behavior.

CHRONICALLY CRITICAL EMPLOYEES

Occasional criticism of the organization or its managers is to be expected from just about every employee, but when it seems that an employee is overdoing it, constantly complaining about the organization and its management, you may have to take a simple step that lets the person know you are aware of the complaining and that you find it inappropriate. A comment from you such as "I can't understand why you would stay with an organization that you seem to think is beneath you" or even "If things are so bad here, why haven't you resigned?" might help put the complaining in perspective. At the very least it may serve to let the employee know you are hearing what is said and that you disapprove.

There are two instances involving complaining in which you must take timely and definitive action before serious harm is done: (1) when the complainers badmouth the organization in the presence of patients, visitors, clinicians, or other customers or (2) when the complaining starts to affect the attitudes and performance of other employees.

These two kinds of situations often justify charges of disloyalty. In most organizations this can be grounds for serious disciplinary action, up to and including discharge (in the disciplinary processes of many organizations this kind of complaining behavior is often included in a broader category of offenses described as "misconduct").

WHEN YOU ARE THE FOCUS OF A NEGATIVE ATTITUDE

There will undoubtedly be times when you must work with a colleague who seems to maintain a negative attitude toward you. This can result in little (and sometimes not-so-little) daily skirmishes that are not conducive to team efforts. Rapport is the key to getting along better. It begins with a genuine desire to improve the relationship.

Throughout this book we mention the importance of risk taking; any situation may present a good example of a risk that is well worth taking. Grab the bull by the horns: ask the other person what it is about you that irritates him or her. You may be in for a surprise. The irritating factor may be as simple as your sending memos or e-mail messages that the other perceives as curt or sarcastic. It may stem from calling the person by a nickname that the individual dislikes.

If you get a frank response, thank the person and promise to modify your behavior. Then ask the person if you can be candid about what change you would like to see on his or her part. Do not unload a stack of complaints, however. This candid approach may fail or it may even make matters worse, but it is often worth the risk.

NEGATIVISTS: PESSIMISTS, CYNICS, AND WET BLANKETS

Negativists may be hard workers who are competent, productive, and even loyal but who harbor a bleak outlook toward most things and people. The negativists lack excitement in life and lack enjoyment at work. If you hang around them long enough, you become infected.

Negativists are convinced that the people in power are self-serving and care for no one but themselves. In meetings when any new idea is proposed, Pessimist Polly can always be counted on to come up with "The trouble with that idea is…," and Wet-Blanket Willie is sure to say, whenever it sounds as though the group is on the trail of a good idea, "Yeah, but what if…?" The "what-if" is of course followed by a litany of reasons why the idea will probably flop. And whatever negative reasons Polly misses, Willie is sure to cover. If there are too many of these people involved, nothing that entails any risk ever gets attempted.

Negativists should not be confused with devil's advocates. Both voice concern or ask challenging questions, but the devil's advocate does so with an open mind and is prepared to join a consensus if convinced. The negativist persists in finding reasons for opposing whatever is being proposed. Even when they lose arguments or are outvoted, they remain unconvinced.

Avoid acceptance of the contrary outlooks expressed by these individuals. Their resistive persuasion not only is depressing and self-defeating, it can be infectious as well. On the other hand, do not dismiss their comments too quickly. On occasion they could turn the group against you. And sometimes—perhaps only once in a great while, but you cannot afford to overlook the possibility—they could be right.

When a known pessimist is present at a problem-solving session, do not rush into offering suggestions. Call on others, including the pessimists; call on *them* first. Some pessimists are silent while a problem is being explored or when decisions are asked for, then spring into action after solutions have been proposed.

Project realistic optimism. Provide examples of past successes of the action now being proposed. Concede that every action carries some element of risk. Using a worst-case scenario, show that the possible consequences are not threatening and that the chances for success are great. Explain that current conditions are not like those that were present at an earlier time when a similar project was unsuccessful.

Avoid arguing with the pessimist. Say that he or she may be right but that you still want to run with the idea. If the person persists, insist that he or she come up with a better alternative. When a person questions the wisdom of a change, assign him or her information-gathering chores relating to the change.

Keep an open mind. Occasionally these employees are right, and sometimes you can use their negativism when you get to discussing pitfalls and contingency planning. Usually they can tell you everything that can go wrong.

If the pessimist is a colleague and the work situation does not demand that you work together, avoid him or her if you want to maintain your optimistic attitude.

KNOW-IT-ALLS

These individuals want you to recognize them as superior. They try to maintain control by accumulating large bodies of knowledge, whether real or assumed. They are condescending if they know what they are talking about and pompous if they do not. If you object to what they say, they take it as a personal affront.

Do not pose a threat to the know-it-all and do not argue. Remain respectful, and avoid direct challenges. Resist the temptation to debate with them. Do your homework. Be certain that you know what you are talking about. Present your ideas tentatively using phrases such as "What would happen if…." or "I wonder whether…"

THE UNCOOPERATIVE SILENT ONES

These people are not those who fail to speak up because they have nothing to say or because they are listening intently. They are not the polite ones who fear that they will say something wrong or will hurt your feelings. The silent ones discussed here are those who reflect fear or suppressed anger by their silence.

Their silence may be preceded by a perfectly congenial conversation until you suddenly touch a sensitive area. You are highly likely to encounter this glum silence during counseling or disciplinary sessions. If you encounter one of these clams in a counseling session, use Bramson's technique.[1] For example, when it is Irene the Clam's turn to speak but she remains silent, lean forward and counter with your own silence plus eye contact and raised eyebrows. Maintain this silent, expectant stare for at least 10 seconds. If she remains silent, say "You haven't answered my questions, Irene. Is there some reason for that?" If her silence persists, say "Irene, I'm still waiting." If there is still no response, state the consequences of her inappropriate silence, perhaps "Irene, you may have a good reason for not talking, but I'm concerned about where this is taking us." If Irene still remains silent, terminate the interview with, "Irene, since we still must resolve this problem, I want to see you here tomorrow at the same time."

SUPERSENSITIVE EMPLOYEES

These individuals take offense at whatever they perceive as a put-down. They are extremely sensitive to criticism, often bursting into tears, shouting, or dashing off to the restroom. When this behavior is effective for them, these people find they have a potent tool for manipulating colleagues and superiors, and they make full use of it.

Handle the supersensitives with care, but do not be manipulated by their reactions. Never withhold negative feedback because of previous overreactions. Do not apologize for what you said or did; avoid the likes of "Gosh, I'm very sorry that I hurt your feelings."

If, when receiving a reprimand, an employee breaks into tears, say something like, "Sue, I find it hard to discuss this when you sob like that. Take a few minutes to compose yourself." Most of the time you can simply hand Sue a tissue and go on with the discussion.

If Sue jumps up and runs out of your office, do not run after her or demand that she return. Instead, reschedule the meeting. At the later meeting make no mention of the previous episode. Sue will have already learned that her inappropriate behavior was not effective.

If an employee loses his or her temper and starts shouting, silently wait for a minute or two while maintaining eye contact. If the employee does not calm down, leave your office.

MOODY PEOPLE

Most people experience some mood swings. It is the degree of the swings and the circumstances that prompt them that are important. Transient moodiness, such as that which occurs during a grieving period, seldom requires supervisory action other than offering a helping hand. A persistent or markedly depressed state, however, calls for professional help. Between these two extremes are a variety of moods manifested by sorrow, sullenness, irritability, or other personality changes.

Ignore mild transient moods. If they persist, ask questions, and listen with empathy. Do not flood these folks with sympathy. Sympathy may prolong the moods or lead to the martyr syndrome. Empathy is more effective than sympathy. If the situation does not improve, suggest professional counseling.

JEALOUS COWORKERS

Jealousy in the workplace is relatively common when employees compete for merit pay, promotions, or recognition. Frustrated people may try to undermine your position by starting unfounded rumors, publicly berating you, becoming a bottleneck, or turning others against you. When any of these disloyal activities occurs, you must take firm action.

First, discuss the problem with your manager and get support. Then confront the envious one. Lay it on the line. Say what you have seen or heard and state that you want it stopped. Describe your future expectations; for example, "I want no arguments in front of staff, patients, or physicians. If you have a gripe, see me in my office." If the undesired behavior persists, remind the person that it is affecting future performance evaluations and can possibly affect continued employment.

GOSSIPS

A little benign gossip is harmless, but when character is attacked or misinformation is spread that affects work or morale, something must be done.

Gossips want attention, so supply it in healthy ways. Spike their misinformation by insisting on validation or by correcting false comments. Explain how their gossiping is affecting the team. Let them know that people are withholding information from them because they fear it will be repeated in distorted forms. Do not encourage gossips by listening intently to their messages. Sometimes it is best to ignore these people.

INCESSANT TALKERS AND SOCIALIZERS

These folks suffer from verbal diarrhea. Monday morning finds them rehashing weekend sports or their recreational activities. They repeat their broadcasts as long as they find listeners. You must know and act when these time wasters become bottlenecks.

Break up the little group discussions in the corridors. Give the verbose ones extra assignments. When they learn that too much talk and too little work result in extra assignments, they will usually modify their abuse of time. If possible, isolate them from willing listeners. Encourage them to do their socializing during breaks. See Chapter 34 for advice on coping with the incessant talkers at meetings.

EMPLOYEES OF QUESTIONABLE APPEARANCE

Be careful how you deal with employees whose appearance—that is, matters of dress and grooming—you personally do not like and of which you disapprove. Before taking any action, ask yourself:

- Is this person's appearance likely to offend customers or interfere with the orderly conduct of business? For example, does how one appears cause people to stop work and stare?
- Does the individual's appearance violate any policy or rule? The supervisor will find this particular issue easiest to deal with if the organization has a dress code included in the personnel policy manual and the person's appearance is in clear violation of the code.
- Is there a safety hazard involved, for example wearing particular kinds of shoes that are proven hazardous in some settings?

Keep appearance in mind when interviewing potential employees. Applicants who show up for employment interviews looking like something the cat dragged in are usually exhibiting the manner in which they customarily appear. When someone appears slovenly and unkempt for an employment interview, you can usually rest assured that the person's appearance will not improve upon hire and may in fact become worse. The best defense concerning employees of questionable appearance is to try to avoid hiring them in the first place.

During new-employee orientation, emphasize the importance of appearance, especially for employees who will have direct contact with customers. Review the dress code and advise them of your personal expectations. Remember that forewarning is proactive; criticizing is reactive.

EMPLOYEES WITH MESSY WORK AREAS

Messiness, like beauty, is in the eye of the beholder. Before you can get employees to clean up their act, you must convince them that there is a problem (parents know that this is not easy). Some fastidious supervisors make a big fuss over a little disorder. The key point is to determine whether a disorderly desk or work area negatively affects performance, coworkers, or customers. For example, the condition of a receptionist's desk in full view of visitors has far more significance than a beat-up desk in the corner of the maintenance department.

There may be barriers to neatness that are beyond the control of the employee. For example, visiting VIPs may drop their coats on a receptionist's chair, or delivery people may place large cartons in doorways. Do what you can to help your staff eliminate such problems. Remember that conditions are always in a state of flux in a normally busy work environment, so do what can be done to keep the worst of it under control, but do not go overboard making a fuss over occasional clutter.

OTHER PROBLEM EMPLOYEES

Hostile individuals, sexual harassers, and chronic complainers will be addressed in subsequent chapters.

Think About It

A supervisor must often address "attitude problems." It is best to remember, however, that attitude, whether negative, sullen, questionable, or otherwise, is not itself a problem that can be addressed via disciplinary processes. It is necessary to look beyond the attitude and address the results of the behavior that occurs because of that attitude.

Questions for Review and Discussion

1. Offer at least two practical suggestions for dealing with constant talkers and socializers. Explain why these could work.
2. What is the principal hazard of having an otherwise productive employee in the group who is constantly critical of organizational policy?
3. What do you believe could be an effective way of dealing with the know-it-all employee, and why might this work?
4. Is it easier to address the negative attitude of an employee or that of a colleague? Why?
5. Suggest how you might deal with an employee who reacts with tears and denial to every criticism regardless of scope or importance.
6. Cite one or two frequently encountered supervisory practices that can have a negative effect on employee attitude.
7. Explain why the supervisor cannot discipline specifically for attitude, and describe the risks inherent in trying to do so.
8. What is the hazard, if any, in judging employee appearance by your own personal standards?
9. What is wrong with the presence of negativists? Should we not always have someone present to point out the hazards and weaknesses in any idea?
10. What can the individual supervisor do about employee appearance if the organization has no dress code that applies to all employees?

Case: The Sensitive Employee

Supervisor Teri Davis was dreading the coming session with clerk Anne James. As Anne entered the office, Teri went through the motions of arranging the papers on her desk for some time before looking up. Teri felt she knew exactly what was coming, and she was determined that this time she would address the continuing problem as well as the current problem.

Teri handed a warning form to Anne and said, "Anne, we have to talk about your excessive absenteeism. This is your second warning. I'm sure you knew it was coming." Anne barely glanced at the warning and dropped it back on the desk. She snapped, "I knew nothing of the kind. There's nothing excessive or unusual about my few days off because I was sick. I'm not accepting any warning."

Teri said, "Anne, you can count the days yourself. Ten sick days in the last six months, and seven of them on Mondays."

"I can't help it if I'm sick a lot."

"Even if you're really ill on those days, and honestly, Anne, it's tough to accept all those Mondays as legitimate sick days, you make it tough to staff the department reliably."

"Why me? Why don't you lean on Donna for a change? She's been out as much as I have."

Teri said, "No, she hasn't, not nearly as much. Anyway, that's strictly between Donna and me. Just like this is strictly between you and me." Teri continued. "You know that you've used up all of your sick time."

"I know. This place made me use vacation the last two times. And that stinks."

"You wanted to get a full paycheck, didn't you?"

Anne glared at her supervisor. "I think it's rotten to make me use vacation when I'm sick."

Teri looked at Anne. Anne's face was stony, her eyes cold, her mouth a thin line. Teri thought: *Any time now. The next thing I say will do it.* Fighting against the knot in her throat, she said, "Anne, you haven't been reliable. I just can't count on you being here when I need you. Your first warning was deserved, and this one is deserved. If you want, you can appeal through proper channels, but the warning stands."

Teri watched Anne's face. Anne's eyes grew round and suddenly filled with tears. She buried her face in her hands and began to sob. If any other employee had been involved, Teri might have felt a measure of sympathy. However, she had been through this several times—in fact every time she had occasion to be critical of Anne. The pattern was always the same: anger and defensiveness, even belligerence, followed by tears and charges of persecution and injustice. And as always, Teri wondered what to do next.

Questions:

1. Although Teri was well prepared with facts about Anne's absences, she might have considered a different opening for the disciplinary dialogue. What opening would you suggest? Why?
2. How did knowing "exactly what was coming" bias Teri in her approach to Anne?
3. What would you suggest as a possible way of dealing with this employee?

Case: Gossip or Information?

One morning as you were enjoying a cup of coffee in the cafeteria shortly before that start of the shift, one of your employees, Ellie West, seated herself across from you without invitation and said, "There's something I have to tell you, and I've simply waited too long."

Ellie proceeded to tell you—"in strict confidence, please, I'm sure you'll understand"—that another of your employees, Mary Gale, has been making many derogatory remarks throughout the department about you and your management style and generally calling your competence into question. You heard a considerable number of "she saids" and "she dids" from Ellie and a smattering of other secondhand tales. However, no incidents that you could identify specifically jumped out at you, and you were too surprised to ask for clarification.

For a good 10 minutes Ellie showered you with criticism of you, your style, and your approach to certain individuals in the department, all attributed to Mary Gale. On finishing her litany, Ellie proclaimed that she did not ordinarily "carry tales" but that she felt you "had a right to know, for the good of the department—but please don't tell her I said anything."

Questions:

1. Should you thank Ellie for her concern and ask her to report anything else she might hear?
2. Should you acknowledge her concern for the department but ask her to bring you no further stories?
3. Should you thank her, ask her to say nothing to anyone else, and decide for yourself to keep an eye on Mary Gale?
4. What would you do instead of, or perhaps in addition to, any of the above three approaches?

REFERENCE

1. Bramson, R.M. 1981. *Coping with difficult people.* New York: Random House, 73.

RECOMMENDED RESOURCES

R.M. Bramson, *Coping with Difficult People.* (New York: Simon & Schuster, 1986). Six audiotapes.

R. Brinkman and R. Kirschner, *How To Deal with Difficult People.* (Boulder, CO: CareerTrack Publishers, 1988). Two videocassettes.

C.R. McConnell, Chapter 11, "Addressing Problems Before Taking Corrective Action," in *The Health Care Manager's Human Resources Handbook.* (Vienna VA, Management Concepts, 2003).

M. Solomon, *Working with Difficult People.* (Englewood Cliffs, NJ: Prentice Hall, 1990).

W. Umiker, *Coping with Difficult People in the Health Care Setting.* (Chicago, IL: ASCP Press, 1994).

Chapter 22

Coping with Hostile People

The real test of education is how we live as individuals and as groups. If we cherish hatred and antagonism, our education has failed. If we learn how to love, our training has been truly successful.

—Dr. Frederick Mayer

CHAPTER OBJECTIVES

- Prepare the supervisor for the inevitable necessity to occasionally deal with hostile people, whether employees, peers, or others.
- Examine the characteristics of the more commonly encountered forms of hostile behavior and suggest how the supervisor might deal successfully with each.

ALWAYS OUT THERE

Hostile individuals are an inescapable part of daily life, whether in the work environment or elsewhere. You might be firmly convinced that people shouldn't be that way, but you do not control their behavior, and you have no control over the feelings that lead them to behave in a hostile or antagonistic fashion.

Your unspoken but assertive message to hostile people is that you respect their right to feel as they feel and to speak their minds but that you also have those rights. In addition, regardless of the rank and power of the person with whom you are in a strained situation, you do not have to listen to profane, intimidating, or obnoxious language.

To achieve freedom of expression, be assertive without being belligerent. If you lack assertiveness, little or none of the advice provided in this chapter will work for you. Passivity will prevent you from using it. Passivity in the presence of hostile or antagonistic people will only get you walked on and pushed around. Fortunately there are many readily available publications, seminars, and audiotapes on the subject of assertiveness.

Bramson identified the "hostile big three" as Sherman Tanks, Exploders, and Snipers.[1] Bramson's terminology will be used throughout this chapter. It is strongly recommend that you read Bramson's original publications or listen to his fascinating tapes (see reference list and Recommended Resources).

SHERMAN TANKS: BULLIES AND DICTATORS

Of the hostile groups, the Sherman Tanks are the most difficult to handle. They often have power, usually are professionally or administratively competent, and they know exactly what they want. Sherman Tanks have usually had years of success at intimidation. Their victims are too numerous to count. Sherman Tanks may be superiors, customers, inspectors, staff coordinators, or even colleagues. Nearly every executive suite and every medical staff has at least one of these characters.

Sherman Tanks have permanently adopted that style because it has proven effective for them. They are sometimes physically intimidating, and they are always psychologically threatening. They are aggressive, abrupt, arrogant, and autocratic. Sherman Tanks are generally contemptuous of their victims.

When Sherman Tanks attack, they expect their targets either to fight back or capitulate. Whichever does not matter, for they usually enjoy a fight, and they always enjoy an opponent's capitulation. The most potentially successful strategy in dealing with these people is to stand up to them but to do so without fighting.

How To Handle Sherman Tanks

When a Sherman Tank launches a tirade, do not become defensive and never try to counterattack. Be sufficiently assertive to get the person's attention. If you are appropriately assertive, you will capture the individual's attention instantaneously, especially if this party is accustomed to dealing with individuals who always cave in at the first strong word. To express your opinions while remaining emotionally neutral, try the following.

- Hear the person out without interruption. Hold your ground. Equalize eye level as much as possible by asking the person to be seated. Stand up if the other will not sit. Much physical intimidation occurs with the intimidator standing over the victim, glaring down. Insofar as possible, try to deny the Sherman Tank the physically higher position.
- Maintain eye contact, but do not try to stare the person down; doing so is not likely to work.

- Hold yourself erect; do not hunch your shoulders or cower. A limp or lack-adaisical posture invites aggression.
- Instead of counterattacking, urge the person to continue, or ask some open-ended questions.
- When the individual starts repeating what has already been said, break in with, "Pardon me." Then deliver your reply, turning up your voice volume enough to be heard, but not quite as loud as the other party's.
- Each time you are interrupted, call the person on it by saying something such as "Please, you interrupted me" or simply "I wasn't finished" and continue.
- Be tentative or noncommittal. Use terms such as "it appears," "it seems," "per-haps," and "possibly." Being absolute simply helps solidify the other party's determination.
- Focus on solving the problems that brought you and the other person to-gether. Remember that the behavior you are facing is designed not only to grind you into the ground but also to resolve a complaint. Because you have taken the fun out of the former, the party is more likely to be ready to deal.
- When the complaints you are hearing are legitimate, apologize briefly and quickly move on to solutions.
- Do not put up with profanity or other offensive language. Walk away. If the person has great influence, tell your manager what you did and why you did it.

EXPLODERS: VOLCANOES, GRENADES, AND BOMBERS

Like Sherman Tanks, Exploders manifest anger, but there are significant differ-ences between the types. Sherman Tanks always exhibit the same overbearing at-titude, whereas Exploders are usually folks who are quiet for stretches between attacks. The anger of Sherman Tanks is largely contrived and under their complete control, while the anger of Exploders is real. They are partially to completely out of control. They sometimes get physical, so handle them with care.

Exploders learned early in life that people often did not take them seriously or give them what they wanted unless they got angry. As children, they often had tem-per tantrums and they continue to do so as adults. These people have a tremendous need for respect. They explode when their self-esteem is threatened. Precipitating episodes may be when they are the targets of jokes, are kept waiting, are pointedly ignored, or when their competency or integrity is questioned.

How To Handle Exploders

Coping is a matter of helping Exploders regain their self-control. Think of them as wind-up toys: if you can wait them out, they eventually wind down. After their ex-plosions, they may become pussycats. Often they become apologetic. Some break down and weep.

If someone is out of control, respond as you would to a hysterical person. In a loud voice call out "Stop! Stop!" or "OK! OK!" or keep shouting the person's name. Try waving your arms to secure attention. While you are going through those motions, gradually move yourself closer to an open avenue of escape just in case in case the Exploder becomes physical.

One useful tactic is to say that you need a piece of paper to write down what the person is saying because you know it is important. This buys still more time for the person to wind down, and it can boost his or her self-esteem.

If the Exploder continues to rant and rave, the speech will likely become louder and more rapid. Say that you cannot write fast enough when the words are coming so fast, then ask if the person would please slow down. When speech slows down, the pitch and volume of the person's voice also diminish. Anger drains energy. Often, the person will now sit for the first time.

Listen carefully for what set the person off—a "hot button" or emotional trigger—and what it is that the person wants. You may hear a word clue repeated multiple times, for example, policy, schedule, recognition, consideration, or fairness.

Never become involved in verbal boxing matches in which accusations or threats swing wildly back and forth without attempts to compromise. Do not try to explain complicated matters while the person is still upset; listening mechanisms are usually out of order at this stage. After the individual has calmed down and become rational, find out exactly what is wanted. If an apology is in order, make it, but make it clear that you get upset when people act as this person just did. Show that you are intent on helping by stating exactly what you intend to do and when. If you learn the nature of an individual's trigger mechanisms, try to avoid them in the future.

If the person remains irrational, say loudly that you want to help but that you cannot do so under the present circumstances. Call a break; for example, "Julie, let's take a 15-minute break. I'll come back after we both have calmed down." Leave immediately if the person becomes abusive. Over your shoulder, offer to meet again later.

Do not forgive the Exploder's behavior, even when the person returns all apologetic. Forgiveness reinforces the explosive behavior. Simply repeat, "I'm always willing to listen to you, but not when you're carrying on like that."

Handling the Employee Who Explodes

The occasional employee has an explosive temper on a short fuse and becomes angry at the slightest provocation. These individuals often are job hoppers; they stay on a job only until they blow up, tell the boss off, and quit or get fired. Emotional immaturity, low self-esteem, and marginal competence are characteristic of these firecrackers. They often harbor intense feelings of frustration, fear, prejudice, or guilt.

A great many potential Exploders can be weeded out during the recruitment process with thorough employment screening and careful reference checking. If you happen to get stuck with any of these powder kegs—perhaps employees who were already in place when you took over the department—keep them away from customers. They can get you into real trouble and can conceivably land you in court.

Never take personally what is said to you in fits of temper. Reply, "I'm sorry you said that. I would think that over if I were you. You've nothing to gain by offending me." If the session continues to degenerate, end it. Do not judge, criticize, or moralize; just break off contact for the time being. Simply say that the meeting is no longer productive and that you will continue later.

Professional counseling is often ineffective in chronic cases, but it is still worth a try, especially when the situation involves an employee who, for one reason or another, you have to retain. If an Exploder resigns during a rage, do not leave the door open to a change of mind.

SNIPERS: FOXES, SABOTEURS, AND NEEDLERS

Like Sherman Tanks, Snipers would like to be in control; however, they lack the necessary boldness. The weapons of the Sniper are sarcasm, snide remarks, and sick humor. Snipers throw snowballs with rocks in them.[2] They have discovered that verbal darts can be thrown without assuming any responsibility. They do most of their dirty work in front of other people, who provide their cover.

Snipers use innuendoes, *sotto voce* remarks, not-too-subtle digs, and not-really-playful kidding. Their remarks often drip with sarcasm. They often talk behind your back, knowing that what they say will reach you. When you respond angrily or call them on it, they often retort, "Can't you take a joke?"

Many victims do not fight back because they do not want to make a scene. They smile weakly, look confused, and later realize they have taken some hits. They lie awake at night thinking of what they should have said or done.

How To Handle Snipers

Your goal is to bring Snipers out into the open and blow them away.[3] Recognize the zingers when you hear them, and say to yourself, for example, "Well, here comes one of Larry's little zingers." Do not laugh, even if what you hear strikes you as funny or if other people who hear it giggle or snicker. But neither should you ignore it.

Bypass your sense of politeness and set some of your normally good manners aside. Stop what you are doing or saying, even if you happen to be in the middle of a sentence. Turn toward the Sniper, and repeat exactly what you heard. These darts lose their zing when repeated.[4] Then add, for example, "Larry, that seemed to be a barb aimed at me. Is that what it was?" or "Are you making fun of what I just said?" In doing so you have just blown his cover. Now he must either confirm what he said or try to weasel out of it with something such as "I was only kidding" or "Where's your sense of humor?" Respond with a sour smile and something such as, "Well, it didn't sound funny to me." If he backs up what he said, you may learn something important. Critical feedback can be worthwhile. If he backs down, you have turned the tables on him.

Alternatively, ask the Sniper what his or her remark has to do with the subject under discussion (the relevance question). Question the purpose of the remark (the intent question). For example, "What do you mean by that?"

Look for help from your associates. When you overhear the Sniper say "What a stupid idea. She's in a dream world," say to the group, "Anyone else see it that way?" If the Sniper gets support, you can search for more information about the situation. When the others do not agree with the Sniper, follow with "I guess there's a difference of opinion" (not "See, you're wrong").[5]

After a dart-throwing episode, take the Sniper aside and make a direct accusation. Snipers do not function well in one-on-one situations; their camouflage is missing. Do not buy their "Oh, you're just too sensitive." Reply that you enjoy a good joke like everyone else but that what you are hearing are not jokes at all, let alone good jokes.

PASSIVE-AGGRESSIVES

Passive-aggressives represent a subset of Snipers. Like Snipers, they conceal their antagonism. Passive-aggression does not mean fluctuations between passivity and aggressiveness. Rather, the behavior is constant. Wetzler aptly calls this behavior sugar-coated hostility.[6] Passive-aggressives are manipulators who pretend to be helpless while they infuriate their superiors and associates.

Passive-aggressives believe that they are getting a raw deal from their supervisors, whom they generally perceive as dictators; this causes them to feel angry and resentful. They lack the confidence to challenge authority directly, so their resistance surfaces indirectly and covertly. They play many psychological games. Typical things they may do to try your patience are showing up late for meetings, submitting late reports, becoming angry with you but refusing to tell you why, or fouling up a procedure.

Passive-aggressives apologize superficially, give you endless excuses, or just clam up. Inwardly they enjoy your anger or discomfort.

How To Handle Passive-Aggressives

You are not likely to change the personality of the passive-aggressive; often they are resistant even to professional psychological help. Your goal should be to insist on behavior that meets your expectations and not to let these people get you upset when they play their mean psychological games. Do not accept their excuses, and never give them the satisfaction of witnessing the anger or frustration you feel when they upset you.

Think About It

In this chapter we have used labels for so-called "types" of hostile individuals, but we have done so only as a matter of convenience in describing kinds of behavior the supervisor may encounter from time to time. Real people, however, frequently cannot be readily or completely described with labels. Use these labels to guide your thinking concerning certain behaviors, but never apply a label directly to an individual in speech or writing. Labels tend to stigmatize, and rarely if ever is the label 100% descriptive of the person.

Questions for Review and Discussion

1. What, if anything, is wrong with engaging in argument with someone who is angry, upset, and whose position on the issue at hand is definitely wrong?
2. How can you arrange your own office or work setting to minimize the chances of unintentionally intimidating others?
3. How would you attempt to stand up to a vocally intimidating individual without engaging in a fight?
4. It has been said that anger is often a shield raised in defense of a weak position. Why might this be so?
5. Why is it a questionable practice to describe individuals by label or type?
6. What do you believe would be your appropriate response to an emotional attack by one of your employees?
7. What is meant by one's hot buttons or emotional triggers? Provide examples.
8. What is it that renders a supervisor's authority completely legitimate in the eyes of the employees?
9. What do you believe is the preferred way of responding to a vehemently angry tirade directed at you by another supervisor?
10. What are the differences between the power of personality and the power conferred by positional authority? Does the successful supervisor need one or the other or both?

Case: The Blindsider

George did not look forward to going to the staff meetings that his middle-manager boss convened once each week. He did not always feel this way about the meetings; in fact, up until 3 months ago he rather enjoyed what he felt were productive and congenial gatherings. What made the difference was one change in the membership of this group of six supervisors: the addition of Charlie, who replaced a usually silent supervisor of one of the building services sections.

Unlike his predecessor, Charlie was anything but usually silent. In fact, it seemed as though Charlie had made it a point to become conversant with every section of their boss's territory, and he almost always had something critical to say about the weekly reports of the other supervisors.

What bothered George most was Charlie's approach to getting his issues or criticisms on the table. Charlie seemed to focus exclusively on problems and weaknesses. As if that in itself wasn't bad enough, what George resented most was Charlie's way of introducing a problem or concern in a way that ensured maximum embarrassment for whoever's area he was commenting on. It was Charlie's practice to openly drop his little bombshells in the staff meeting, where the supervisor whose area was in question first heard of a so-called problem or weakness at the same time the others learned of it.

It seemed to George that Charlie's practice of blindsiding the others in the group was coldly calculated to make himself look better by making others look worse. And George found it even more frustrating to note that their boss did not seem to recognize what Charlie was doing.

Questions:

1. Do you believe there is anything George can do about Charlie's staff meeting behavior? If so, how should he proceed?
2. Do you believe George should take up his concerns directly with Charlie? Why or why not?

Case: The Trouble with Sally

"I've tried to help shape Sally into a good group leader who might even look forward to becoming supervisor someday, but I'm beginning to think I might have made a mistake with her," said supervisor Jane Dawson. "Goodness knows she knows the job inside out, but it's starting to look like her value stops there."

Friend and fellow supervisor Marie Blake said, "I thought Sally was your top performer."

"Well, she was for a long time. And she's always cooperative face-to-face, but lately I've gotten the feeling she's pulling against me most of the time. When I get her going on a project, you know, some idea of mine, she accepts it with little comment, says she'll take care of it, but then I'm hearing—really roundabout—that she's trying to gather staff support for some idea of her own in place of mine."

Marie asked, "But she doesn't disagree with you?"

"No, never, at least not openly. Like I said, she's usually quite cooperative. At least she talks it up that way. And most of the time she's pleasant enough, although once in a while she'll get quiet and kind of distant for a day or two."

"Well," said Marie, "not to tell tales out of school, but since you brought it up—a couple of my people are chummy with some of yours, and it's gotten back to me that your oh-so-cooperative Sally spends quite a lot of time back-stabbing you when you're not around. Seems she doesn't think you're capable of doing justice to the job you hold, and she's doing a lot to convince others of that as well." Marie concluded with, "If I were you, I'd start watching my back around friend Sally."

Instructions:

1. Prepare some advice for Jane to apply in dealing with Sally. Consider what Sally appears to be doing, and make whatever assumptions you need to make in suggesting why Sally is behaving the way she is behaving. Also consider what Jane needs to prepare before confronting Sally and what advice or assistance Jane should seek in addressing the trouble.

REFERENCES

1. Bramson, R.M. 1981. *Coping with difficult people.* New York: Random House.
2. Bramson, R.M. 1986. CD-ROM, *Coping with difficult people.* New York: Simon & Schuster, 26.
3. Brinkman, R., and Kirschner, R. 1987. *How to deal with difficult people.* Boulder, CO: CareerTrack. Video program.
4. Brinkman, R., and Kirschner, R. *How To Deal with Difficult People.*
5. Bramson, R.M., *Coping with difficult people,* 30.
6. Wetzler, S. 1992. Sugarcoated hostility. *Newsweek,* October 12, 1992, 14.

RECOMMENDED RESOURCES

R.M. Bramson, *Coping with Difficult People.* (New York: Simon & Schuster, 1986). Six audiotapes.
R. Brinkman and R. Kirschner, *How To Deal with Difficult People.* (Boulder, CO: CareerTrack Publishers, 1988). Two videocassettes.
M. Solomon, *Working with Difficult People.* (Englewood Cliffs, NJ: Prentice Hall, 1990).
C. Tavris, *Controlling Anger.* (Boulder, CO: CareerTrack Publishers, 1989). Four audiotapes.
W. Umiker, *Coping with Difficult People in the Health Care Setting.* (Chicago, IL: ASCP Press, 1994).

Chapter 23

Complaints and Grievances

These are the times that try men's souls.

—Thomas Paine

*Might as well forget your old troubles;
there are more coming.*

—Anonymous

CHAPTER OBJECTIVES

- Describe the critical role of the supervisor in addressing complaints and provide guidelines for handling employee complaints.
- Furnish the supervisor with specific advice relative to addressing complaints about compensation (wage and salary).
- Review particular circumstances the supervisor is likely to face at times: specifically, dealing with multiple complainers simultaneously, dealing with employees who take their complaints directly to higher management, and dealing with chronic complainers.
- Establish the position of formal grievances in the handling of complaints by the supervisor.
- Address the critical issue of sexual harassment and provide procedural guidance for reporting, investigating, and resolving complaints of sexual harassment.

Complaints represent a significant source of customer feedback. Employees are among our most important internal customers, and these particular customers are usually our greatest source of complaints. Legitimate or otherwise, complaints are signs that somewhere something is wrong and demands attention. Most worker complaints are related to policies and rules, working conditions, compensation and benefits, leadership, and relationships with other employees.

313

ROLE OF THE SUPERVISOR

The role of the supervisor is to respond effectively and promptly to both legitimate and imagined complaints. Doing so avoids formal, and often costly, grievances and legal action. Increasing numbers of lawsuits are being filed by disgruntled employees, often after disciplinary action has been taken against them.

Gripes may be articulated during staff meetings, performance appraisal discussions, exit interviews, and ordinary daily contacts. Observant supervisors suspect potential problems when they note that certain employees are unusually silent, irritable, or depressed. Managers who practice "management by wandering around" often return to their offices with a bag of assorted complaints.

Caring managers engage in naive listening. Naive listening is nothing more than listening as though one is meeting these people for the first time, without preconceived notions. Insightful supervisors readily admit that they have a tendency to tune out long-term patients, loquacious colleagues, or boring supervisors.

Seven Essential Steps for Handling Complaints

1. Listen carefully. The initial complaint is often only a trial balloon to see how you will react. You may have to dig deep to find what is under the surface.
2. Investigate. Is the complaint legitimate? Are there less obvious but more serious problems behind this one? Are other people affected? Is the situation getting better, or is it getting worse?
3. Choose what, if any, action is needed. Get help if you need it. Ask the complainer what he or she would like to accomplish. Make certain that your proposed solution will not make matters worse.
4. Inform the complaining employee about your findings and what you propose to do. Do this without undue delay. If your remedy is not satisfactory to the employee, seek alternatives.
5. Implement your decision.
6. Follow up on implementation, checking the effectiveness of your action.
7. Record what has happened, retaining sufficient documentation to be useful should the particular complaint arise again or if some new action involving the complainant must be taken.

Complaints Concerning Compensation

Every supervisor has received complaints about salary. These surface whenever salary changes are announced or when people in other departments get larger raises than your employees. Also, employees are often well informed as to what local competitors pay their employees and are quick to point that out to their supervisors. And the greater the difference between expected and actual salary increases, the more strident are the voices. Tempers flare, especially when there is a perception of favoritism.

Many pay-for-performance strategies exacerbate salary dissatisfaction. Employees who do not receive the maximum merit increase gripe about their performance ratings. Even more unhappy are those who were told that their work has been outstanding but later found minuscule increases in their paychecks.

For avoiding or addressing salary controversies, take these steps.

- Do not overrate employees or make unrealistic promises.
- Know what competitors are paying (human resources can help with knowledge of pay rates in your area).
- Try to get more pay for your outstanding performers by other means, such as promotions, legitimate title changes, or revision of position descriptions and job upgrading.
- Let employees blow off steam about pay. Be empathetic.
- Refuse to discuss salaries of other employees. An individual's rate of pay is personal information.
- Do not practice favoritism, and try to avoid even the appearance of favoritism.
- Know exactly how salary increases are determined in your organization.

Here is an example of how to cope with a salary complaint.

"Dolores, although salary increases are based largely on performance, other things must be considered. These include market factors such as the availability of certain specialists and what competitors pay. Other considerations relate to how critical each position is to the organization, budgetary restrictions, and projected costs for other activities."

If a raise is not deserved, state the reason very clearly. The person should know exactly why he or she was passed over and how the deficiency can be overcome.

SUPERVISOR "ON THE SPOT"

When Complainers Gang Up on the Supervisor

When confronted with a group of highly vocal complainers, Bernstein and Rozen practice what they call "creative ignoring."[1] The supervisor simply sits quietly and looks thoughtful. This particular response usually gets the group to quiet down and become more manageable. If it is a group of customers or colleagues, the supervisor should ask for each person's individual input before responding, calling on the least hostile person first, if possible. If the group is a bevy of angry subordinates, the supervisor should tell them to pick one spokesperson. The rest must leave. However, the supervisor must be extremely careful in meeting with the single spokesperson. The meeting cannot appear to be a negotiation aimed at resolving the complaint; this would put the supervisor in the position of extending recognition to a "group" through its "representative" (the risk is that of running afoul of the laws governing labor unions). Rather, the supervisor should use this one-on-one meeting to listen and to learn about the complaint in detail.

When Employees Go Over the Supervisor's Head

In the ideal situation the higher manager will send complainers back to the supervisor as soon as he or she realizes that the employee has not given the immediate supervisor an opportunity to respond. Unfortunately, some managers are all too willing to lend an ear to employees who bypass their supervisors, especially when the manager and the supervisor do not get along particularly well.

On becoming aware of one of these occurrences, the supervisor needs to confront the manager and present his or her side of the situation. Before leaving the manager's office, the supervisor needs to suggest that in the future it would be appreciated if the manager would send for the supervisor while the complainer is still in his or her office.

The supervisor needs to let the employee know that what the employee is doing is known and that this "end running" is not appropriate. The employee needs to hear how such activities are counterproductive and can ultimately backfire on him or her.

Chronic Complainers

A characteristic of chronic complainers is that most of their complaints lack validity. These people are more interested in registering feelings than in resolving problems. They rarely participate in finding solutions, and their daily conversations consist predominantly of negative comments. Chronic complainers constantly use absolute words such as "never" and "always." They frequently start their negative comments with "Why doesn't someone...?"

The occasional griper can often be stopped with a "Well, what are you going to do about that?" Unfortunately this does not stop determined chronic complainers. They bounce right back, claiming that they have no influence in the organization and that their suggestions are never taken seriously.

Interestingly, the typical chronic complainer is a conscientious and competent worker. This person's work is usually acceptable, and often it is above average. This makes it all the more difficult to get rid of these annoying people.

Although you seldom cure chronic complainers, with conscientious effort and astute informal counseling, you can often achieve the following:

- The complaining decreases to a tolerable level.
- The complaints brought to you are limited to those about which you can do something.
- Proposed solutions are brought along with the problems.
- The complainers spend more time working and less time griping.
- The complainers develop more confidence in their own abilities.
- The complainers refrain from complaining in front of customers or higher management.

There are some practical suggestions for addressing the chronic complainers.

- Apply active listening. This is essential but not simple. If you ignore their complaints, you may divert the complaining to customers or competitors. If their complaints get to your superiors, your reputation as a leader will suffer.
- Listen to their main points. Write down the complaints in their presence. This is good for their self-esteem. Sometimes simply listening can silence the complainer. Do not agree or disagree with them. Maintain a noncommittal facial expression, avoiding approval nods or sympathetic grimaces.
- Direct your attention more at their feelings than at the object of their complaints. Chronic complainers are usually insecure. They are reassured when their feelings are validated; for example, "I can understand why you're upset about that." Validating feelings is different from agreeing with them; it is simply acknowledging the right to have those feelings.
- Stop them when they start repeating or if they try to move to another topic. Rein in a rambling discussion by asking, "What's your point?" Acknowledge your understanding of what was said by paraphrasing and summarizing their main points.
- Avoid arguments. Trying to argue them out of their negative stance, trying to placate them, or explaining things in detail seldom work.
- Force them to help solve the problem. After acknowledging that a problem exists, move quickly into problem solving. Ask specific, open-ended questions: who, when, where, and how questions. Avoid the whys because they get you into deep water. True chronic complainers are not comfortable with problem-solving questions; they just want you to agree with their complaints.
- Encourage them to research their problems. If they say that they do not have the time, respond with, "Well, if you change your mind, let me know."
- Be honest when you say what you can and will do or what you cannot do. Ask them what it is they want you to do. When they say that what you propose will not work, ask them what's the worst that can happen. Then say you

are not worried about that outcome. Another ploy is to narrow the options to two and ask which they think is the lesser of the two evils.
- When solutions are beyond your control, say so. At times you must make statements such as, "We've simply got to make the best of it."

GRIEVANCES

A grievance is a formal written complaint by an employee for which redress or relief from management is sought. Formal grievance procedures exist to ensure fair treatment of employees, maintain good morale, and avoid costly court litigation.

Employers must abide by certain requirements and limitations placed on them by collective bargaining agreements, antidiscrimination legislation, civil service regulations, and employment contracts. Grievance procedures are included in every union contract. Also, many nonunion organizations have formal grievance protocols, although in places they might be referred to by another name; for example, appeal procedures. Regardless of the name of the process and the authority for its existence, all supervisors must be familiar with its contents.

Supervisors who are vigilant concerning conditions that can induce employee dissatisfaction and who handle gripes expeditiously and fairly seldom have grievances filed against them. When these supervisors are faced with grievances, they can counter the charges effectively because they have documented all exchanges with the involved employees and can justify any measures taken leading to any particular grievance. Often there is a direct correlation between the number of disciplinary actions taken and the number of grievances filed.

When an employee is not satisfied with the response of a supervisor to a complaint, the supervisor should make the employee aware of the appeal process, even though most employees who file charges will have investigated their rights and studied the organization's policy manual before filing the grievance.

Employers frequently lose litigation cases because the involved supervisors have been guilty of inconsistent rule enforcement, unreasonable application of rules, or excessive penalties in terms of policies. Poor documentation is the most common cause of management loss of a dispute brought to the stage of grievance.

SEXUAL HARASSMENT

Sexual harassment is a serious problem because of the legal costs, reduced productivity and morale, and increased absenteeism or turnover that it may cause. However, it is even more serious because its existence indicates that management has been negligent in protecting its employees or others for whom it is responsible.

Sexual harassment can occur in any organization, in any environment. It is especially prevalent in health care institutions because of the many power differences among members (for example, physician and nurse) and the close customer–caregiver contacts (for example, nurse and patient). Most working nurses have experienced or witnessed multiple episodes of harassment.

Major Forms of Sexual Harassment

There are two major forms of sexual harassment. *Quid pro quo* harassment occurs when an employee is expected to give in to unwanted sexual demands to secure some benefit or advantage or to avoid suffering the loss of job or some tangible job benefit for refusing to give in to such demands.

The other form often results in a hostile work environment when an employee is exposed to sexually oriented verbal, visual, or tactile activities. Verbal abuse includes sexual language, innuendoes, epithets, or jokes. Phone calls are frequently mentioned. Visual offenses consist of provocative gestures and sexually oriented posters, letters, notes, or graffiti. Tactile harassment can be sexually oriented touching, patting, pinching, rubbing, or pressing.

Legal Issues

Under Title VII of the Civil Rights Act of 1964, sexual harassment is identified as a form of sex discrimination. The Civil Rights Act of 1991, amending the Civil Rights Act of 1964, gave plaintiffs the right to recover compensatory and punitive damages when discrimination is found to be intentional. Cases can be tried before a jury, or plaintiffs may appeal to state civil rights agencies for relief. Guidelines from the Equal Employment Opportunity Commission (EEOC) in 1980 stated that employers are responsible for the acts of their agents, supervisors, and employees and other people on the premises (for example, patients and visitors).[2]

To prove a case of sexual harassment, plaintiffs must establish that they were subjected to unwelcome sexual conduct that caused them harm.[3]

Organizational Policies and Procedures

The presence and effectiveness of policies and procedures affects the prevalence as well as the control of harassing behavior. These policies must be clear and understandable. Employers and managers must affirm that sexual harassment will not be tolerated and that violations of policy will be treated harshly. Sanctions range from verbal or written warnings to reassignments, demotions, suspensions, or dismissals.

Employers should provide training directed at both potential harassers and victims. This training should include explanations of policies and procedures and illustrations of the kinds of statements or actions that constitute sexual harassment. Confrontational techniques for potential victims are emphasized, and role-playing is recommended.

Role of the Supervisor

Insightful managers are aware of the policies and procedures relating to this form of discrimination. They enforce these vigorously and promptly and with fairness, sensitivity, and confidentiality. They do not forget the rights of the alleged harassers. They find solutions that are satisfactory to the victims. In some cases they provide security for these victims. Supervisors should ensure that the workplace environment is free of sexual humor and inappropriate familiarity. Nursing supervisors should be alert to violations by patients and visitors and should take appropriate actions.

Investigation of Complaints

In some instances victims turn to their immediate superiors. However, if one's immediate superior is the alleged perpetrator or if a victim feels uncomfortable dealing with that person, help can be sought from the superior's manager or a specialist in the human resources department.

The procedure for receiving and investigating complaints of sexual harassment must be prompt, fair, and confidential. For handling a sexual harassment complaint, several steps are necessary.

1. Listen carefully to the complaint. Ask the accuser to put it in writing and to include dates, places, names of witnesses, and the exact statements or behavior of the alleged harasser. Note: if the complainant later decides to withdraw the charge, get that decision in writing.
2. Investigate as soon as possible. Interview witnesses and other alleged victims.
3. Confront the harasser, and inform him or her of the complaint. Listen carefully to the rebuttal. If appropriate, tell the alleged harasser that the offensive conduct must stop immediately. Often you find that they simply were not aware that what they were doing constituted sexual harassment.
4. Document what transpired at the meeting, including the exact words the person used in his or her defense.
5. Get back to the complainant and relate what happened. If no supporting evidence is found, explain this. Reaffirm your own commitment and that of the organization to the preventing of sexual harassment. Tell the complainant to report any further incidents.
6. Report the affair to your superior and to the human resources department.

When You Are the One Harassed

- Do not encourage the person, but do not remain silent.
- Clarify your position and what you expect out of the relationship (for example, "I prefer to keep our relationship on a strictly professional basis").

- If the solicitations continue, review your personnel policy and follow the recommended procedure, or seek the advice of a senior member of the human resources department. If you belong to a union, complain to your union representative.
- Warn the individual that if he or she persists, you will regard the activities as sexual harassment and will report them accordingly.
- Document each episode. Get witnesses, if possible. Remember that a single incident rarely suffices to make a case unless it constitutes blatant behavior.
- If you filed a complaint and it was not handled to your satisfaction, notify the human resources department that you intend to take the complaint to the local EEOC representative, a legal service agency, a state discrimination agency, or an attorney. When legal action is threatened, things usually start happening.
- If you remain dissatisfied, do what you threatened to do!

Think About It

A supervisor once said to a number of peers in great frustration, "My crew seems to get the work out—eventually—but not without enough griping to take up half of my time. I could get some real work done if it weren't for all these nagging employee problems." To this supervisor, and to others who feel the same way, we suggest that listening to and addressing the employees' complaints is a significant and legitimate part of the supervisory role. If we had fewer employee complaints to deal with, we might legitimately need fewer supervisors.

Questions for Review and Discussion

1. What is the critical error being committed when an employee who reports to you takes a complaint directly to your manager and receives resolution?
2. Why is it claimed that sexual harassment is a serious and widespread problem? How did it become that?
3. What do you believe is the one dimension of employee compensation that triggers more complaints than any other? Why?
4. Describe a set of circumstances under which you might legitimately consider disciplinary action for a chronic complainer.
5. Under what circumstances would you consider that one employee asking another for a date could constitute sexual harassment?
6. Why should you avoid dealing with a gang of complainers at one time? Is this not more efficient than meeting with them one at a time?
7. How can you minimize the likelihood of receiving an employee complaint following a disciplinary action?
8. Provide one example of potential *quid pro quo* sexual harassment and one example of hostile environment sexual harassment.

9. Why might some supervisors prefer the presence of a formal grievance procedure over handling all employee complaints as they arise?
10. What is the potential hazard in a consensual intimate relationship between two employees? Between an employee and supervisor?

Case: Where Did the Complaints Go?

As a new supervisor hired from outside the hospital, it took you very little time to learn that morale in the department had been at low ebb for quite some time. As you started getting acquainted with your employees by meeting with them individually, you were quickly inundated with complaints and various other evidence of discontent. Most of the gripes concerned perceived problems with administration and building services, but there were also a significant number of complaints by your staff about other employees in the department and some thinly veiled charges suggesting that a couple of staff members have consistently been complaining about the department to your boss. (Your boss has said nothing to you about this.)

It sounded to you as though a number of common themes ran through the group's complaints, and it seemed to you that a number of differences could be cleared up by airing these issues with the entire group. You planned a meeting for that purpose, instructing all employees to be prepared to air their complaints (except for those directly involving other staff members). Your employees seemed to think this was a reasonable idea, and several led you to believe they would be happy to speak up, but your meeting turned out to be brief. As hard as you tried to get people to air their gripes, nobody spoke. You tried again 2 weeks later, with the same results: no one uttered a word of complaint. Yet all the while the negative undercurrents continued to circulate through the department.

Questions:

1. What can you do, if anything, to get this group off dead center and opened up or otherwise get their complaints out in the open?
2. How might you go about looking into the allegations concerning the employees who are carrying complaints to your boss?

Case: We Need To Talk—Now

A month ago you assumed the role of supervisor of one section of the clinical laboratories of Community Hospital, coming from the outside and taking over leadership of what was obviously a discontented group of employees. It took you very little time to learn that your predecessor was not well liked and that this person's penchant for what a couple of employees referred to as "three Rs"—rigid rules and regulations—was regarded with derision and ridicule. This was not the first time you had entered into a strained situation, and your normal approach was to spend your first 3 months getting to know the people and the procedures before making any significant changes.

On the first day of your second month on the job you were carrying your full lunch tray through the cafeteria toward what you hoped would be a quiet corner when you were approached by four of your employees, three technicians and a receptionist. All four wore scowls and frowns, although one, the receptionist, appeared uneasy to the point of being afraid. One of the technicians said to you, "Look, you've been here long enough to know what we've had to put up with, and we demand to know what you're going to do. Now!"

Standing there holding a full tray, you glanced around at the crowd. A few people were starting to take notice of your little gathering. You quietly asked, "Right this minute? Isn't this a little awkward?"

Sufficiently loud to cause more heads to turn your way, the technician/spokesperson said, "Now!"

Instructions:

1. In the form of either a paragraph or two of essay or an outline of sequential steps, describe how you are going to handle this confrontation with the four employees.

REFERENCES

1. Bernstein, A.J., and Rozen, S.C. 1989. *Dinosaur brains.* New York: Wiley, 74.
2. Discrimination Because of Sex under Title VII of the Civil Rights Act of 1964 as Amended: Adoption of Final Interpretive Guidelines, U.S. Equal Employment Opportunity Commission Part 1604, Federal Register, November 10, 1980.
3. Burns, S.E. 1995. Issues in workplace sexual harassment law and related social science research. *Journal of Social Issues* 51: 193–207.

RECOMMENDED READING

P.J. Decker, "Sexual Harassment in Health Care: A Major Productivity Problem," *The Health Care Supervisor* 16, no. 1 (1997): 1–14.

Chapter 24

Personnel Retention

The deadly enemy of great performance
on the front line is high turnover.[1]

—W.H. Davidow

CHAPTER OBJECTIVES

- Establish the importance of personnel retention in maintaining a stable, committed workforce.
- Examine the shifting role of loyalty, that of both employee to organization and organization to employee, in today's health care environment.
- Consider the principal reasons why employees voluntarily go elsewhere.
- Provide guidance for the supervisor to apply in determining whether a genuine retention problem exists in the department or throughout the organization.
- Enumerate some specifically targeted employee retention incentives.
- Identify a number of critical factors to consider in addressing an organization's apparent employee turnover problem.

As work processes become more complex and employees assume more responsibilities, workforce stability becomes increasingly important. A reasonably stable workforce is essential to long-term organizational success. Vulnerable to the impact of the loss of experienced workers, employers must recognize the importance of personnel retention. People who remain on the job create efficiency and effectiveness by sustaining productive business relationships with customers, suppliers, and associates.

When unemployment rates are low and there is a limited pool of talent to draw from, that is, when it is a "seller's market" in employment, it can be difficult to attract and retain the best people. The people who resign during such a labor market are often among the top performers who are being lured away by what they perceive as greener pastures.

The dollar cost of replacing an individual employee is considerable, often ranging, depending on the character of the position, from half the annual salary to double the annual salary of the person being replaced. This is just the dollar cost of replacement that can be reasonably determined; it is more difficult to estimate the costs resulting from losses in morale, quality, and service continuity. Each departing worker goes away with valuable knowledge, skill, and a piece of a network that may include important contacts within and outside the organization. An angry departing employee can wreak havoc. For example, a terminated employee of an oil company erased a computer database that was worth millions of dollars.[2]

Favorable personnel retention translates into high productivity, fewer mistakes, less stress, greater customer satisfaction, higher employee morale, and significant direct and indirect cost savings.

Formerly, the standard response to personnel shortages was to step up recruiting. However, administrators finally realized that retaining employees is less expensive and less disruptive than replacing them. It was also discovered that the measures taken to improve retention had many other beneficial effects. These effects included increased productivity and customer satisfaction and reduced absenteeism.

A fundamental retention strategy begins at the time of employee selection and continues through to the time an employee attempts to leave the organization.

LOYALTY AND PERSONNEL RETENTION

Needed: A New Paradigm of Loyalty

Corporate loyalty, that traditional bond between an organization and its employees, is rapidly becoming an obsolete concept. Formerly the loyalty of employees was measured in terms of how long they remained with the organization. When workers leave for whatever reason, supervisors complain about the workers' lack of loyalty. When a reduction in force occurs, even one that is undeniably appropriate, employees voice the same complaint against their employers.

Divided loyalties abound in our increasingly complex health care institutions. Employees often find it easier to remain loyal to their professional specialty groups or unions than to their managers. Supervisors, especially, experience a built-in divided loyalty. They are expected to serve both their superiors and their subordinates, and if they lean too far in either direction they are accused of being disloyal by one side or the other.

The first casualty of disloyalty is productivity. Sloppy work, mediocre quality, and poor customer service follow, and apathy takes over. Disloyal employees lower work standards, withhold information, conceal problems, file grievances, and create ill will.

The causes behind loss of loyalty are principally those that destroy morale. Major factors relate to working conditions, compensation, and leadership skills. Other factors are job elimination, limited labor availability in some sectors, and an increasingly mobile workforce.

Almost everyone is loyal to something, be it an organization, a person, a concept, or what have you. Loyalty in the organization may range from resigned acceptance to fanatical commitment, and it is closely related to work ethic and duty, the unwritten contract that requires employees to be faithful to their professions, their employers, and their colleagues.

A New Employer–Employee Model

The new employer–employee model is based on two realities: (1) employers cannot guarantee permanent employment, and (2) resigning from a job is not a sign of disloyalty.

Enlightened executives realize that workers no longer accept the passivity and humility that in the past were regarded as signs of loyalty. They now know that loyalty is founded largely on trust, trust that must be earned. Corporate loyalty is providing a safe work environment and reasonable opportunities for advancement. It is offering first-class benefits, rewards for high performance, and demonstrated respect for ability.

Better organizations replace the career ladders, which disappeared with reengineering and flattened most organizations, with new roles, challenging assignments, and other opportunities for individual growth. They replace job security with new opportunities for their employees. Supervisors earn worker loyalty by effectively representing the interests of workers to higher management.

Supervisory Loyalty

The most important step that supervisors can take is to find a substitute for guaranteed employment. The best substitute for guaranteed employment can be described as the safety net of employability. Managers who encourage employees to learn skills, and who provide the means to accomplish this, lower the rise of unemployment and increase their employees' opportunities for more rewarding careers. Other measures for strengthening loyalty include the following:

- Be honest with employees. Tell them the truth about policies and plans that may affect their jobs.
- Make your expectations clear. Position descriptions, performance standards, orientation, and training are the essential tools for conveying expectations.
- Expect the best. Look for strengths. Either eliminate weaknesses or make them irrelevant.

- Be perceived as a supporter, defender, and facilitator rather than a judge, bottleneck, or nitpicker.
- Be consistent, fair, impartial, and trustworthy. Live up to your promises and earn your coworkers' respect.
- Practice true participative management.
- Show that you value every employee.

Employee Loyalty

Some employees feel guilty offering anything less than absolute loyalty. A more rational approach is to accept the proposition that if employees are reliable and can be trusted and consistently meet their employment obligations, they are loyal. Loyalty is refraining from castigating one's organization, colleagues, or boss, at least in public. Loyalty is not revealing confidential information to competitors or to the press. It is behaving ethically and morally, reducing criticism, and respecting confidences.

Loyalty is making superiors look good and doing everything one can to help them meet departmental goals and deadlines. It is defending superiors against false witnesses or attacks made when those superiors are not present to defend themselves.

Communality is important from a loyalty standpoint. This is a sense of belonging to a work group. It concerns issues of interdependence, mutual respect, and a sense of responsibility for other people. The core of loyalty is genuine caring for the well-being of the others involved in a relationship.

WHY EMPLOYEES SEEK GREENER PASTURES

Employees are often plucked away by competitors who offer higher salaries or better benefits, or so it seems. What management often fails to realize is that many departing employees are not lured away by competitors but leave of their own volition because they cannot stand their supervisors or managers. Other factors driving employees away are boring work, dissatisfaction with career development, or lack of appreciation for their efforts. Many overworked employees feel that they are being taken advantage of, that they are forced to neglect their families because of work, or are experiencing burnout.

In today's culture of job insecurity, employees are looking for the skills, information, and knowledge they can take with them in case of another downsizing. Insightful organizations provide those security blankets, but many hesitate to provide development programs for fear that their employees will leave with their newfound skills and credentials.

Organizations that base their retention initiatives entirely on compensation find themselves in bidding wars with competitors. The more insightful corporate leaders identify morale problems and correct them. They assess the workplace environment and make needed improvements, often based on the findings of their periodic employee morale surveys.

Because supervisors have little control over salaries, they feel absolved of accountability for the departures and identify the employer as the bad guy. Managers often are misled by what they find in letters of resignation or by what comes out of exit interviews. It is easy to challenge the validity of exit interviews. For several obvious reasons, departing employees are reluctant to reveal the real reasons they are leaving. Instead they simply say that they have been offered better jobs elsewhere. Often the real reason for their leaving is how they were treated by their immediate supervisors.

Few employees are assertive enough to confront their superiors. Instead, they sublimate their feelings by directing their ire at top management. When employees say they do not receive recognition, they are usually referring to lack of recognition and praise from the person to whom they report.

ANALYZING A RETENTION PROBLEM

To determine whether a genuine retention problem exists, collect and study information from the following sources:

- Records of actual rates of turnover, grievances, and requests for transfer
- Exit interview documentation
- Recruiters and recruitment-retention committees
- Focus groups
- Employee attitude or morale surveys
- Performance evaluations, coaching and counseling interviews
- Personal observation

Ask yourself several questions. What attracts employees to your organization? What do they like or dislike about their jobs and the workplace? Is there really a problem? If so, when did it start? Are only certain shifts or job categories affected? (Normally, turnover rates are higher for night shifts and nonexempt workers.) How bad is the problem? Is it getting better or worse? Are there manifestations that suggest a general morale problem? What has been our response to date, and how effective have these measures been?

Consider these possible causes that directly contribute to turnover.

- Lack of competitive pay, benefits, or appealing work environment
- Location of facility, parking, and other external factors
- Weak recruiting and selection processes
- Inadequate orientation and training program
- Lack of supervisory support

- Lack of opportunity for promotion, advancement, or education
- Inability to adjust to changes, as in mothers or others who have been away from the work world for some time

RETENTION INCENTIVES

Cash-Oriented Compensation Plans

The retention tools of choice for the majority of organizations are still based on compensation. They include (1) retention bonuses, (2) gainsharing and merit performance pay, (3) premiums for employees consistently working long hours, and (4) salary adjustments or above-market pay for key positions.[3]

Career Development Offerings

Ambitious employees prize career development programs. Many employees leave employers when such programs are lacking. The kinds of programs offered include

- career ladders,
- internal job transfers,
- job posting programs,
- tuition reimbursement,
- a career planning/development center,
- formal succession planning,
- career planning training, and
- outsourcing (outplacement) assistance.[4]

Health-Promotion Initiatives

These initiatives are becoming increasingly important to health care workers. They include (1) health education, (2) health-risk appraisals, (3) health-risk assessments or screening, (4) special programs (for example, smoking cessation, weight loss), and (5) on-site fitness facilities.

RECRUITMENT AND SELECTION FOR RETENTION

Today's health care organizations want employees who share the values and goals of the organization and who best meet the requirements of the positions being filled. Personal referral is an excellent recruiting method; generally, candidates recommended by employees have better retention records.

You can often spot potential quitters by reviewing their past employment histories and by asking provocative questions (refer to Chapter 7). Also, people who have changed jobs frequently are not likely to be with you for a long time either.

FURTHER IMPLICATIONS FOR RETENTION

New Employee Orientation

The skillful orientation of new hires has a powerful positive bearing on employee retention. Texas Instruments reduced its turnover by 40%, and Corning Glass Works slashed theirs by 69% by improving their orientation programs.[5] (See Chapter 8 for more on orientation strategies.)

Coaching

In the absence of competent and compassionate coaching, most retention efforts will falter. In Chapter 12 it was noted that great coaches are out where the action is and where they are needed. Their attitude is "How can I help?" not "You're not doing that correctly." They know the difference between delegating, assigning, and making busywork, and they delegate often. They also know when and how to praise. They cheer loudly and publicly when an assistant comes up with an innovative suggestion. Good coaches support and defend their staffs. They intercede when their coworkers are confronted by angry customers or administrators.

Effective coaching and shared governance are powerful factors in retention efforts. Coaches are able to practice situational leadership because they know the disparate motivational and educational needs of each subordinate and respond appropriately.

Team Building

Personnel retention creates closely knit groups. Because loyalty locks people in place, it follows that team building can be a powerful force in any retention strategy. Two major motivational needs satisfied by team membership are affiliation (social) needs and actualization (achievement) needs. Trainees and employees with limited skills derive much of their satisfaction from team achievements.

Morale

*All other things being equal, the best people will
stay with the company that pays them the most.*[6]
—Frederick F. Reichheld

Critical to any retention program is maintaining high morale. Morale and recognition were discussed in detail in Chapters 13 and 14. Key morale factors in personnel retention include the following:

- Changing management style from command and control to coach, counsel, encourage, and praise

- Treating and compensating employees as professionals
- Carefully selecting benefits and rewards
- Providing a safe and comfortable workplace
- Supporting and encouraging career development
- Keeping employees advised of what is going on in their organization
- Providing flexible and equitable work schedules
- Offering mentoring programs

Think About It

One of the most frequently cited reasons for employees leaving their jobs is the treatment they receive from their immediate supervisor. Regardless of all that can be said about the influence of pay, benefits, and working conditions and such on employee retention, the supervisor who manages fairly, humanely, and honestly, with respect for each individual as both a person and a producer, remains the strongest single factor in employee retention.

Questions for Review and Discussion

1. What do you believe to be the effects, if any, of technological advancement and social progress on organizational and individual loyalty?
2. How will you respond to a supervisor who says, "Just hire the first one who walks in. If that one doesn't work out, we can always get another"?
3. Why, in the present day, are you not likely to see people pursuing careers of 30 or more years with the same employer?
4. How would you structure or arrange exit interviews to maximize the chances of securing reliable information?
5. What is the importance of the opportunity for advancement in employee retention? Will this apply equally to all employees? Why or why not?
6. Do you believe that all turnover is undesirable and to be avoided? Why or why not?
7. Concerning the Reichheld quotation in the final section of the chapter, what are the "all other things" that must be equal? Will this statement always hold true?
8. Where in the health care organization—department, function, occupation, whatever—do you expect turnover to be greatest? Why?
9. Career development opportunities seem to mean a great deal to some employees and little or nothing to others. Why might this be so?
10. What can an individual do to ensure the maximum possible employability in today's health care environment?

Exercise: The Career Ladder

At one point in the chapter the concept of "career ladder" is mentioned without benefit of definition or explanation. You are to do whatever research is necessary to facilitate your understanding of the concept, and explain career ladders and their application in essay form. In your write-up you are to provide at least two examples of multistep career ladders that might be found in a typical health care institution. Your choices of occupation should be appropriate to the use of career ladders; that is, professional or technical occupations rather than entry-level positions or nonspecialized occupations.

Case: "…or Else I Quit!"

You are administrative supervisor of the hospital's department of radiology. The department has been having problems with the special procedures area; you have had considerable difficulty recruiting and retaining special procedures technologists. You presently have your allotted staff of three such technologists, but these people are fully utilized, and at least two of them have recently made comments about staffing being inadequate for the workload.

The senior technologist, Carl Smithers, has been especially vocal in his comments about understaffing. Several times, and as recently as Monday the 7th of this week, he spoke with you concerning his perception of the need for another technologist. Today, Wednesday the 9th, you received the following note from Smithers:

"As I suggested I would do in our conversation of Monday this week, I am going on record notifying you that additional technologist help must be available by Monday the 21st. If you are unwilling or unable to provide the needed help, I will be unable to continue in my present position beyond Friday the 18th."

Questions:

1. Concerning the ultimatum delivered by your employee, should you:
   - Immediately request the added staff in order to retain Smithers? Why or why not?
   - Call his bluff; that is, wait until the 18th to see if he does indeed resign? Why or why not?
   - Take some other approach, and, if so, what should it be?

REFERENCES

1. Davidow, W.H., and Uttal, B.K. 1989. *Total customer service: The ultimate weapon.* New York: Harper & Row, 121.
2. Farnham, A. The trust gap. *Fortune Magazine* (December 1989): 66.
3. Condodina, J., and Erme, L. 1978. Compensation packages changing shape. *HR Focus* 74(10): S1.
4. Davison, B. 1978. Strategies for managing retention. *HR Focus* 74(10): S3.
5. Zemke, R. 1989. Employee orientation: A process, not a program. *Training* 26: 33–40.
6. Reichheld, F.F. 1993. Loyalty-based management. *Harvard Business Review* 71: 64–73.

RECOMMENDED READING

B. Ettorre, "Keeping the Cream," *HR Focus* 74, no. 5 (1997): 1, 45.
Special Report on Recruitment and Retention, *HR Focus* 74, no. 10 (1997): S1–S16.
W. Umiker, "Workplace Loyalty in the 1990s," *The Health Care Supervisor* 13, no. 3 (1995): 30–35.
M. Yate, *Keeping the Best.* (Holbrook, MA: Bob Adams Publishers, 1991.)

PART III

Health Care Cost Control

Chapter 25

Managed Care

Managed care is changing our health care delivery
system as radically as the computer chip has
changed telecommunication.[1]

CHAPTER OBJECTIVES

- Define managed care as an innovating force that has significantly altered the organization and delivery of health care services throughout the United States.
- Highlight the principal features of managed care and briefly describe how they function.
- Review the primary strategies of both health care providers and managed care agencies operating in the managed care environment.
- Introduce the concept of outcomes management.
- Review the common reactions of professional and supervisory employees to managed care initiatives.
- Review the employment opportunities that have been created or expanded concurrent with the advent of managed care.

During the past three decades the nation's health care system has been constantly reinventing itself and continually refining the changes that have been made. Alarmed at the continuing high rate of growth of health care costs and the resulting impact on health insurance premiums—still subject to double-digit annual increases in many parts of the country—employers and consumer groups have mounted major efforts to evaluate how well health insurance plans, hospitals, and physicians provide care. The pervasive growth of managed care has forever altered the lives of consumers and providers alike.

Since its inception managed care has been focused significantly on cost control. The continuing question has been, "Can costs be reduced without adversely affecting the quality and availability of services?" Not a great deal has been heard in the way of answers from the primary accrediting organization for health maintenance organizations (HMOs), the National Committee for Quality Assurance. However, we do know that a great many patients express unhappiness with the availability of care, the lack of choice of providers, restrictions on services, and various other inconveniences. It remains to be determined whether these are simply complaints resulting from change or whether they represent a real decline in benefits.

HMOs frequently boast about their preventive care initiatives aimed at keeping people healthy. This is potentially a real plus for managed care if it can be established that illnesses can be minimized and life prolonged without incurring large medical expenses. However, these preventive measures must consist of more than measures to prevent infections and make maternity care more available, two obvious areas of concentration.

Chronically ill people present managed care with its crucial test. It is the chronically ill and those who need the costlier diagnostic procedures or therapies who are turning to lawyers to help them with everything from interpreting contracts to taking insurers to court when they are denied care. Many patients feel vulnerable and perceive that advocacy can help them.

Because the primary emphasis of managed care is to manage costs, it might have been appropriate to include this topic in the next chapter on cost control. We could also have included it in the chapter on change, because managed care is the most profound change that the health care industry has faced in many years. However, because it involves so many factors in addition to dollars and cents, the topic logically earned a chapter of its own.

FEATURES OF MANAGED CARE PLANS

Managed care is a system of care delivery in which care providers receive predetermined compensation for delivery of services. According to Lohr, managed care plans exhibit some or all of the following features.

- Complex organizational arrangements between institutions and clinicians
- Explicit financial incentives for providers and enrollees
- Defined access to the physician panels and other services
- Strong controls on the use of services, especially the services of health care specialists
- Coordination and integration of services
- Accountability for an enrolled population and for quality of care[2]

Providers strive to reduce utilization rates by offering health promotion programs that target the most costly diseases, such as acquired immunodeficiency syndrome (AIDS), cardiovascular disease, and cancer. They work to limit the use of hospitals in favor of outpatient care and home visits. One result is that many nurses and other health professionals who worked in hospitals now find themselves working elsewhere.[3]

Capitation Reimbursement

One special feature of managed care is capitation reimbursement, a prospectively determined payment system (with capitation meaning "per head" or per person). This approach transfers financial risk from the insurer to the provider based on some anticipated level of activity. The set amount of monthly reimbursement fluctuates only as the size of the enrolled population changes. Providers influence profitability only through controlling costs.[4]

Managed Care Variations

Managed care is found under several different labels for plans or approaches that all essentially have the same meaning and intent: to control health care costs by emphasizing preventive care and by controlling access to various services. A significant feature of all managed care plans is the use of the primary care physician as "gatekeeper" to the health care system. That is, a patient accesses a specialist or obtains other health care services only upon referral by the primary care physician. A person can of course elect to individually obtain any services desired if willing to pay the full cost personally, but the insurers will reimburse providers only if proper referrals have been obtained through the primary care physician.

Managed care variations likely to be encountered include

- HMOs (the aforementioned health maintenance organizations),
- independent practice associations (IPAs),
- preferred provider organizations (PPOs),
- point-of-service (POS) plans,
- physician–hospital organizations, and
- physician management companies.

NEW CHALLENGES

The overriding challenge is to ensure that managed care delivers high-quality service at an affordable price to all enrollees. The organizations that will survive are those whose leaders are able to continually respond to changing needs. The survivors will always know how they are positioned in relationship to competitors; they are knowledgeable about who the customer is and what the customer expects.[5] As rival organizations become more aware of and more responsive to the needs of their enrollees, competition between and among them becomes more intense.

Providers must be skilled administrators of resources while still delivering quality care. To provide quality services within the parameters of fixed budgets, extensive restructuring and reengineering of the delivery systems of care are unavoidable. Simply limiting diagnostic and therapeutic modalities is not enough.

Many services traditionally delivered by physicians are now delivered by clinicians other than physicians. There is active delegation of responsibilities from professional to technical personnel. Technical personnel turn over many of their functions to employees who are less qualified or who have less education. The challenge here is to select these delegates carefully and provide them with the necessary training. Employers seek workers who are proactive, autonomous, and creative and who possess interpersonal skills.

Since the introduction of managed care, there has been a decrease in certain services and an increase in other services. Benge and his associates report a sharp fall in the number of laboratory tests per inpatient.[6] There has been a marked increase in the number of hospitalized patients who are sent home to recover. Although early discharges require more nursing care than they did in the past, insurance agencies are allocating fewer funds for home services. Additional challenging factors include the following:

- Today's patients on average show less trust and less respect for care providers.
- Care providers are more stressed and often display lower morale.
- Work units are forced to adjust to frequent organizational changes.
- "Downsizing" or "rightsizing" and outsourcing have reduced job security.
- Increased errors are anticipated by some observers as emphasis potentially shifts from quality improvement to cost cutting.
- Reductions of space and budgets may restrict services.
- Rapidly growing bureaucracies add to the confusion and frustration.

STRATEGIES OF CARE PROVIDERS

Health care institutions have an obligation to redefine and clarify their missions and values. They must then put in place the kinds of people who can and will carry out those missions and support the values. Their missions should include vigorous efforts to prevent as well as to treat disease.

Successfully making the transition to managed care requires a blend of well-timed and coordinated strategies. Chief executive officers reengineer many of their systems and processes. Initiatives such as bedside testing, expanded computer systems, outsourcing, and modifying locations and hours of service help to ensure economic survival.

Providers display many innovative and diverse modalities for meeting these new challenges. Clinical enterprises are restructured to compete for the managed care dollars and to develop strategies to recapture lost clinical revenue. Sometimes these initiatives are controversial. For example, the practice of using nurse practitioners in place of primary care physicians has come under fire from both patients and physicians.

Providers must overhaul costs and procedures without alienating staff or allowing quality to suffer. This involves reducing numbers of nurses, adding aides, revising treatment procedures to achieve faster discharges from the hospital, and employing more outpatient treatment. Even a simple mechanical change such as pneumatic tubes to shoot laboratory specimens around the hospital saves time.

Hospitals that have purchased physicians' office practices must align the financial incentives of their physicians with their own. They may appoint incentive compensation committees to achieve these alignments.

Clinical Pathways

Clinical pathways are written templates of expected interventions and outcomes for selected groups of patients. Clinical pathways allow health systems to standardize care and to improve the processes and outcomes of care where possible. These pathways provide multidisciplinary health care strategies that optimize patient care by streamlining and coordinating care delivery. Clinical pathways involve collecting patient-treatment data from doctors to compare the cost of service and to devise the best methods for standard treatments. This provides standardized service for specific illnesses or procedures such as pneumonia, hip replacement, and coronary artery bypass surgery.

Patient Focus Care Model

This is a health care delivery structure that seeks to streamline care by restructuring hospitals into delivery units that are more self-sufficient. A premise of this type of system is to provide care to each patient by using fewer providers with a greater number of skills and responsibilities.

Integrated delivery systems put more care into the hands of interdisciplinary teams and coordinate care across many workstations. Computerized clinical assessment systems and automated performance appraisal systems can increase efficiency.

The study of critical patient care paths is essential for managed care environments. Supervisors must know how to develop clinical paths that create excellence in outcomes. There must be emphasis on avoiding errors of both commission and omission. Errors result not only in increased costs because of repeated diagnostic tests and delayed patient discharges but also in less satisfactory medical outcomes. Some of these mistakes can be life threatening.

STRATEGIES OF MANAGED CARE AGENCIES

Managed care agencies and their providers spend considerable time trying to determine what their enrollees want. Responses to what is wanted and what will be paid for result in termination of some services and addition of others.

Insurers resist reimbursement for treatments they deem investigational. Sophisticated drugs and improved disease-monitoring techniques will remain no more than medical-journal jargon if health insurance fails to pay for these advances under the cost-cutting ethic that dominates much of today's health care.

Although the coupling between managed care organizations and their affiliated health care facilities is a loose one and there is little face-to-face communication between these two groups, both parties are now attempting to get to know each other better and to meet each other's expectations.

Managed care has exacerbated the reimbursement wars between insurers and hospitals, physicians, and other care providers. The impact of cost-cutting measures may make the commitment to primary nursing too difficult to maintain. The concept of primary nursing is that each nurse is responsible for a small number of patients.

According to Kongstvedt, managed care has imposed quality management principles of measurement, customer focus, and statistically based decision making. He writes that there are three sets of criteria.

1. Structure criteria, including certification of personnel, licensure of facilities, compliance with safety codes, record keeping, and physician network appointments.
2. Process criteria, used to evaluate the way care is provided. Clinical algorithms, health screening rates, and evaluations against national criteria (benchmarks) are essential.
3. Outcomes criteria, such as infection rates, morbidity, and mortality.[7]

OUTCOMES MANAGEMENT

Relying principally on benchmarking, advocates of outcomes management seek to reduce medical costs while preserving or increasing quality. Outcomes managers develop appropriate descriptors to determine where resources are under- or overutilized and where professional skills need upgrading. Outcomes management depends on quantitative indicators that compare one health care entity against another, that is, benchmarking. The comparisons may be between hospitals or medical staffs. For benchmark comparisons, practitioners of outcomes management usually use financial and administrative data.

There are two types of benchmarking. The first is clinical benchmarking in which physician practice patterns are matched. The second is operational benchmarking, which compares organizations from the standpoint of staff productivity, staffing mix, and the use of space and resources. Clinical benchmarking systems indicate how well one group of physicians performs against other groups. Process indicators such as length of stay, variability in practice patterns, and the impact of clinical pathways are assessed. Quality indicators such as mortality, complications, functional status, and patient satisfaction are tracked.[8]

Operational benchmarking programs are critical tools in reengineering processes in institutions. These programs allow administrators to evaluate the productivity of staff and to determine where the areas of greatest opportunity lie. There are two types of operational comparisons. The first is an internal comparison that follows trends of key indicators over time, for example, cost per billable test. The other operational programs allow for external comparisons, for example, against peer facilities or best-in-class organizations.[9]

EDUCATION

Utilization experts provide practical advice. Physicians and administrators are broadening their focus to include patient education, disease prevention, and health maintenance. Medical staff leaders help management reorient physicians to practice more conservative, cost-effective medicine.

Existing educational efforts must be bolstered and orientation programs upgraded. Educational and training programs should be based on needs assessments in which management determines what supervisors need to know. Appropriate topics include meeting the expectations of enrollees, cost-effectiveness, time management, and personal empowerment.

For employees to feel empowered, they must have the kinds of information that in the past were available only to higher management. Computerized information systems make it a simple matter to summarize and disseminate appropriate information. Supervisors and team leaders should have, at the least, access to the financial data of their unit. All employees should be kept informed of the financial status of their organizations.

At a time when organizations focus on economic survival, patients and employees are all too frequently lost in the shuffle. Management must promulgate a value system of patient service, articulate clear standards of care, and provide practical guidelines. Managers must motivate care providers at all levels to put the patient first and to be personally responsible for maintaining appropriate ethical standards of care.

Managers and supervisors should insist on educational programs on the subject of managed care. Management should provide supervisors with training in developing budgets that reflect clinical realities, cost accounting, and strategic planning.

Examples of Special Training Programs

Cerne reports that small groups of employees in the Henry Ford Health System attend 1-day training programs.[10] These programs cover marketing, human resource needs and strategies, barriers to success, and competitor strategies.

Voluntary Hospitals of America helps its members (nurses, pharmacists, nutritional managers, etc.) by providing satellite programs. These programs cover capital environment, models of managed care, restructuring of clinical care, managing continuous quality improvement, and how to manage change.[11]

REACTIONS OF PROFESSIONALS AND SUPERVISORS TO MANAGED CARE

Organizational and personal survival in these turbulent times is more likely when every employee thinks in terms of what is best for the patients and the payers. It also helps when there are collegial relationships between various care providers, payers, and suppliers.

Employees and their leaders who understand the implications and make the necessary changes are well positioned in this era of managed care. Insightful supervisors develop partnerships. Their partners are in finance, utilization review, human resources, and departments that control the resources needed to manage job performance outcomes.

Health professionals must stay abreast of the dynamic knowledge base within their specialties. They must take responsibility for explaining to their patients the processes and expected outcomes of care. Management must insist on maintaining high standards for licensure, certification, and recertification for all individuals and units.

The challenge for the supervisor is to develop a responsive work group that can change quickly to meet the ever-changing requirements of the health care workplace.

Stucky and Waltrip have listed four competencies that can help providers survive in managed care settings.

1. Clinical management: resource allocation, productivity measurement, disease management
2. Financial management: budgeting, management of variance, cost analysis, statistics

3. Information management: communication flow, medical records, quality improvement
4. Leadership: personnel management, communication skill, team building, time management[12]

EMPLOYMENT OPPORTUNITIES IN THE MANAGED CARE INDUSTRY

Landry and Knox believe that there will still be ample opportunity for health professionals to secure employment in a managed care environment; what will change is the location of the job site and the organizational setting.[13] The hospital will not be the dominant employer.

With focus on the provisions of managed care programs, observers have not paid enough attention to the burgeoning growth of the organizations that control these programs. Like all rapidly growing industries, this one has new buildings, multiple hierarchical levels, internal politics, and the usual growing pains associated with massive change. On the positive side, many opportunities are there for the asking if professional and management personnel look for them and are willing to adjust to new roles and responsibilities.

New opportunities are also available in the hospitals and other provider institutions as they undergo radical changes in their missions, goals, and values. Attractive positions are available for health professionals and supervisors who are multiskilled and willing to master new competencies.

Many employers are looking for multidisciplinary professionals, managers, and supervisors to replace highly specialized personnel in certain settings. Within hospitals, the restructuring process often includes reducing the number of leaders of departments. For example, the technical director of a laboratory may be in charge not only of the laboratory but also of radiology, electrocardiography, and respiratory therapy.

Within the laboratory, the microbiology supervisor may be asked (or told) to direct the histology and cytology sections in addition to the microbiology section. In these instances, the leaders must learn much about services they could ignore in the past.

Many challenging opportunities lie ahead in quality improvement within the managed care systems. Expertise is needed in data management, profiling, administration of patient surveys and satisfaction questionnaires, and other techniques.[14] Health professionals will also fill new positions in case management, utilization review, quality assurance, and programs that emphasize disease prevention. Examples of positions in managed care organizations can be found in the sections that follow.

Case Managers

Case managers are found both in health care institutions and in payer institutions. They function through third party administrators or self-administered programs. They may also work for a patient or family member. Case managers deal with managed care patients who have extensive medical problems or are expected to receive care over an extended period. These managers determine whether the care being received is appropriate for both fiscal and quality assurance purposes.[15] Kongstvedt lists the following activities performed by case managers. They

- coordinate, facilitate, and educate;
- collaborate with physicians, medical equipment providers, home care agencies, therapists, and other providers;
- ensure that patients follow prescribed treatment plans and that the equipment delivered to the home is what was ordered;
- with benefits administrators, pursue alternatives to the plan package in the best interest of the patient and the payer.[16]

Utilization Reviewers

Utilization reviewers are health care administrators and other professionals who conduct evaluations to determine resource usage patterns of patient care. The objective of utilization review is to provide cost control, promote quality of care, and guarantee enrollee satisfaction. These reviewers submit their findings to the appropriate authorities for remedial action.[17]

Advice Nurses

Many plans operate 24-hour nurse advice telephone lines. Nurse advice lines provide members with access regarding medical conditions, the need for medical care, health promotion and preventive care, and many other advice-related activities. These nurses are also called triage nurses.[18]

Enrollees are encouraged (or required) to call nurse advice lines before going to emergency departments. The nurse uses a clinical protocol to evaluate the member's complaints and then renders advice about what the member should do.[19]

Authorizing Authorities

In some PPOs, hospital treatment authorization may require the approval of a primary care physician, the so-called gatekeeper. In other PPOs and in managed indemnity plans, elective hospitalization and various procedures may be authorized by plan personnel rather than physicians. These authorizing personnel are usually nurses.[20]

Marketing and Sales Agents

Marketing staffs gather data on what to sell and how to sell, and they play a role in product development and market research. Sales representatives sell the product and may also serve as service representatives. There are also product specialists who specialize in specific products (for example, HMOs, PPOs, and POSs).[21]

Claims and Benefits Administration Personnel

These employees do not ordinarily require any special medical training, although one who is new to such employment may have a beginning advantage by having some familiarity with the health care environment.

Actuarial Service Personnel

Actuarial services deal with financial risks, budgets, and other financial aspects. The employees set budgetary targets and prepare fee structure analyses and models to determine levels of clinical efficiencies and quality improvement.[22]

Think About It

Managed care has become the predominant approach to health care delivery in the country. Although it continues to change in a number of ways, the changes are directed toward improving and strengthening managed care, not replacing it with something else. Chances are that managed care is not simply a passing fancy and that whatever the approach may be called in the future, it is certain to continue its movement away from fee-for-service reimbursement in favor of some form of reimbursement by capitation. For all practical purposes, the old way of purchasing medical care is gone forever.

Questions for Review and Discussion
1. What do you consider to be the primary objectives of utilization review?
2. Will it ever be possible to return to the free-market approach to health care delivery? Why or why not?
3. What perceived risks are present when all patients are free to select their own specialist providers?
4. What appears to be the primary advantage of using clinical pathways?
5. What can managed care plans potentially do, or what *do* they actually do, to encourage preventive health care?
6. How can a case manager position pay for itself in savings to the health care system?
7. What is the principal advantage of benchmarking? Provide an example.
8. Explain why all managed care plans require the permission of the primary care physi-

cian before a patient visits an emergency room. Under what circumstances is this permission not required?

9. Will straight fee-for-service health care continue to exist at all? Why or why not?

10. What is likely the strongest cost-saving feature of every managed care plan? Why is this so?

Exercise: Comparing Managed Care Plans

Consider the list of six kinds of managed care plans provided earlier in the chapter (HMOs, IPAs, PPOs, POSs, physician–hospital organizations, and physician management companies). Select any three of these plan formats and, in essay form, describe how they appear to be both similar to and different from each other. (A nominal amount of research in sources other than this text may be necessary.)

Exercise: Operational Benchmarking

According to the chapter, operational benchmarking "compares organizations from the standpoint of staff productivity, staffing mix, and the use of space and resources." You are to select one particular health facility department or function, preferably one with which you have some knowledge or familiarity, and develop a benchmarking profile for that department or function; that is, develop a detailed listing of the features or characteristics of the operation that can have a bearing on cost, and indicate what benchmarking data you perceive as necessary or helpful. (You are looking for indicators such as output in units per time period, items processed per person per hour, etc.) As indicated above, consider staff productivity, staffing mix, and the use of space and resources.

REFERENCES

1. Landry, C., and Knox, J. 1996. Managed care fundamentals: Implications for health care organizations and health care professionals. *American Journal of Occupational Therapy* 50(6): 413–6.
2. Lohr, K.N. 1997. Measuring and improving quality and performance in an evolving health-care sector. *Clinical Laboratory Management Review* 11(4): 265–72.
3. Landry and Knox, Managed care fundamentals.
4. Landry and Knox, Managed care fundamentals.
5. Kerfoot, K. 1994. Today's patient care unit manager. *Nursing Economics* 12(6): 340–1.
6. Benge, H. et al. 1997. Impact of managed care on the economics of laboratory operation in an academic medical center. *Archives of Pathology and Laboratory Medicine* 121: 689–94.
7. Kongstvedt, P.R. 1996. *The Managed Health Care Handbook,* 3rd ed. Gaithersburg, MD: Aspen Publishers, 402.
8. Vance, R.P. 1997. Resource utilization and outcomes management: opportunities for the entrepreneurial pathologist. *Clinical Laboratory Management Review* 11(5): 318–21.
9. Vance, Resource utilization.
10. Cerne, F. 1995. Learning to survive. *Hospitals and Health Networks* 11: 47–50.
11. Cerne, F. Learning to survive.

12. Stucky, S., and Waltrip, L. 1995. Managed care: Are your middle managers ready? *Caring Magazine* 14(10): 94–8.
13. Landry and Knox, Managed care fundamentals.
14. Lohr, Measuring and improving quality and performance.
15. Landry and Knox, Managed care fundamentals.
16. Kongstvedt, *The Managed Health Care Handbook*, 274.
17. Landry and Knox, Managed care fundamentals.
18. Kongstvedt, *The Managed Health Care Handbook*, 250.
19. Kongstvedt, *The Managed Health Care Handbook*, 336.
20. Kongstvedt, *The Managed Health Care Handbook*, 470.
21. Kongstvedt, *The Managed Health Care Handbook*, 577.
22. Kongstvedt, *The Managed Health Care Handbook*, 659.

RECOMMENDED READING

P.K. Halverson, A.D. Kaluzny, and C.P. McLaughlin, *Managed Care and Public Health*. (Gaithersburg MD: Aspen Publishers, 1998.)

P.R. Kongstvedt, *The Managed Health Care Handbook*, 3d ed. (Gaithersburg, MD: Aspen Publishers, 1996.)

C. Landry and J. Knox, "Managed Care Fundamentals: Implications for Health Care Organizations and Health Care Professionals," *American Journal of Occupational Therapy* 50, no. 6 (1996): 413–6.

Chapter 26

Budgets and Cost Control

A budget is a practical means of telling
the money where to go—rather than
simply wondering where it went.

—Anonymous

CHAPTER OBJECTIVES

- Introduce the concepts of budgets and budgeting and establish their essential role in the operation of an organization or organizational unit.
- Identify the significant functions and elements of budgets and enumerate the principles and rules of budgeting as they apply to the supervisor.
- Introduce the controlling process as related to budgets.
- Describe a number of significant cost-reducing measures, including right-sizing and reengineering, that the supervisor may encounter when it becomes necessary for the organization to bring expenses down into line with revenue.
- Identify the role of benchmarking in cost control.

The cost-containment measures imposed on health care providers have greatly increased the importance of cost control. Supervisors are key people in the control and reduction of expenses. Essential parts of the supervisory role are participating in the preparation of departmental budgets, suggesting cost-cutting measures, and directing the application of control measures.

FUNCTIONS OF BUDGETS

Planning

The preparation of a budget is part of the planning function. A budget is itself a plan, a financial plan for the conduct of business in the near future. A budget provides a financial map of coming activities. It also contains information vital to the potential determination of new charges and adjustments to various costs of doing business.

Budget planning normally starts at executive levels and trickles down to first-line managers. It should coincide with the review of major policies and the re-assessment of plans and goals.

Controlling

> *A tight budget brings out the best creative*
> *instincts...Put him under some financial pressure.*
> *He will scream in anguish. Then he'll come up with*
> *a plan that, to his own amazement, is not only*
> *less expensive, but is also faster and better*
> *than his original proposal.*
>
> —Robert Townsend[1]

The administration of a budget is part of the controlling function, and the budget itself is the most powerful tool available for controlling. A budget creates a greater awareness of costs on the part of employees, and it also helps them achieve goals within stated cost expenditures.

The finance department usually provides supervisors with weekly or monthly cost reports of expenditures against budget. These reports highlight variances that serve as red flags for remedial action.

Evaluating

Performance appraisals of supervisors usually include the assessment of how accurately they forecast their expenses and how well their expenditures match the monies allocated. Variances can reflect poorly on a supervisor's financial skills unless the deviations result from factors not under his or her control. Staying under budget is not always a cause for celebration. Having funds left over at the end of the year might sometimes indicate efficient management of resources, but it can just as readily result from careless budgeting.

Principles and Rules of Budgeting

- Expenses must always be charged to the department or cost center that incurs the expenditures.
- Every item of expense must be under the control of someone in the organization.

- Supervisors and managers responsible for complying with expense budgets must participate in budget preparation.
- Supervisors must not be held responsible for expenditures over which they have no control.
- Unused budgeted funds may not be carried over from one annual budget to the next.
- Unused funds for capital expenditures may not be transferred to operating expenses or vice versa.
- Requisitions for individual expenditures require approval by some authority.
- "Slush funds" or contingency funds not specifically identified are not permitted, but supervisors should try to allocate some monies for unexpected needs.

Revenue

Depending on the budgeting approach of a particular organization, revenue figures may come from the finance or information services departments. Computerized billing makes it possible to calculate revenue for each department or section and to use these figures to project anticipated future revenue.

Most supervisors are usually not directly accountable for revenues, but they can be helpful in determining charges for the services that their departments render. Without the supervisors' cost data, finance departments have no legitimate basis for figuring out charges or for forecasting profit or loss. In predicting revenue and costs, it is necessary to consider not only historical growth trends but also changes in the anticipated workload because of the introduction of new services, procedures, or equipment.

Preparation of Budgets

A breakdown of expenses charged to a department by categories, such as salaries, benefits, and supplies, is essential (refer to Table 26–1). Expenses should be recorded on an ongoing basis.

A budget cannot be adequately prepared the week before it is due. To prepare an itemization of expenses, collect expense figures for several months. Annualize the figures by dividing the year-to-date expenses by the number of months recorded, then multiply by 12.[2]

During the year, suggestions or proposals may turn up that involve additional expense or cost-cutting opportunities. Record all these. Take into account increases in supply expenses, service contracts, and continuing education expenses when planning a forecast budget.

Table 26–1 Example of a Forecast Budget: Chemistry Section

Item	Annual Expense ($)
Medical/surgical supplies	300
Employee welfare	20,640
Pension	2,112
Postage, freight, express	408
Salaries and wages	281,572
Departmental supplies	367,800
Quality control	28,667
Travel	672
Publications	100
Education	336
Repairs and maintenance	12,000
Total Direct Expense	**714,607**

Capital Equipment

There is usually a separate budget or a section of the overall budget that is set aside for capital equipment. Many organizations project their capital equipment budgets out for 2, 3, 4, or 5 years into the future. This extended capital budget may change from year to year as priorities change and unforeseen circumstances arise, but more often than not capital funds are strictly limited organization-wide, and what one department might want in the short run could have to defer to something another department critically needs. Supervisors who must be knowledgeable of rates of obsolescence of major pieces of equipment often seek this kind of information from manufacturers or suppliers.

Replacement items and new equipment are among the most expensive budgetary items for some cost centers (for example, laboratory or radiology services, where single pieces of equipment can run into the hundreds of thousands of dollars). The capital equipment budget should reflect the costs of these items.

Wages, Benefits, and Overhead

The figures for salaries, benefits, and overhead are not budgeted by the operating departments. These numbers come from elsewhere, primarily from the finance department. However, other areas may be involved; for example, budgeted benefits costs may come from the human resources department. This is appropriate because supervisors have no control over these items and cannot be held responsible for them.

Salaries represent more than 60% of operating expenses for most cost centers in the typical health care organization. Therefore. when administrators want to cut costs, the first area they scrutinize is usually personnel expenses. It is essential to keep detailed records to justify work hours and overtime and make certain that the figures going into the budget are as accurate as possible.

Management is loath to approve requests for additional staff, even when there is a projected increase in the workload, unless the need can be proven on paper. Reports of crises that have occurred because of personnel shortages can help in the justification process. This also holds true for equipment problems and requests for new apparatus.

THE CONTROLLING PROCESS

Always be prepared to defend the budget figures you submit. With or without modifications by higher management, the budget revisits supervisors at least monthly in the form of a responsibility summary (see Table 26–2). This simplified report shows actual expenditures compared with budgeted amounts for the month. The full report received by the supervisor would also show cumulative actual and budget figures for the year to date, so it is possible to track performance against budget in cumulative fashion throughout the year. Variances are shown for each budget category. When variances exceed a certain amount, supervisors generally must submit a written or verbal explanation.

Review these reports soon after receiving them. If an item is not clear or may be in error, seek clarification from finance or information services, whichever division issues the report. Be prepared to discuss the variances with your immediate superior.

CUTTING COSTS

When there is a severe financial crunch, organizations take multiple remedial measures. When drastic action is not imperative, managers introduce changes one at a time to observe the effects of each change before undertaking the next measure.

Cost control involves more than staff reduction and working more efficiently. It involves improved inventory control and seeking price relief from suppliers. Reductions of salary, overtime expenses, and benefits may be necessary but are often counterproductive if made prematurely or without examining their full implications.

Typical hospital responses are the laboratory responses reported by Jahn.[3] These included freezing or limiting expenditures for filling vacancies, capital spending, salary increases, and cutbacks in continuing education. If these were not sufficiently effective, layoffs would follow.

Table 26–2 Responsibility Summary

	Actual	Current Month Budget	Variance
Inpatient revenue	160,414	167,081	6,667*
Outpatient revenue	106,591	78,129	28,462
Total patient revenue	267,005	245,210	21,795
Medical/surgical supplies	207	25	182*
Employee welfare	2,299	1,663	636*
Pension	1,059	1,059	0
Postage, freight, express	31	34	3
Salaries and wages	25,166	23,263	1,903*
Departmental supplies	43,788	30,650	13,138*
Quality control	211	211*	
Travel	118	118	
Publications			
Education	59	59	
Repairs and maintenance	49	1,000	951
Total direct expense	72,810	57,871	14,939*
Total patient revenue	267,005	245,210	21,795
Direct expense	72, 810	57,871	14,939*
Operating gain or loss	194,195	187,339	6,856

*Unfavorable variances (i.e., low revenue or high expenditures).

Rightsizing

Rightsizing is matching staffing to workloads to become more efficient. It differs from downsizing, which is simply laying off people to save money, although more often than not the terms are used interchangeably, along with several other labels for adjusting the size of the workforce. Restructuring, acquisitions, mergers, and financial reverses result in reductions in force (RIFs). Employers can accomplish RIFs through early retirements, attrition, hiring freezes, voluntary separations, or reduced work hours. These measures are often insufficient, however, thus involuntary separations are exercised as the last resort.

The best time to begin this process is before financial constraints demand major staff reductions. The first step for executives is to analyze the workload and find out what can be done to reduce it without decreasing services or turnaround times. The second step is process reengineering or restructuring.[4]

Chief executive officers must decide whether to base furloughing on seniority or on a person's value to the organization. If the latter, supervisors play an important—and often painful—role in the selection process. Also, it is extremely important that whatever scheme is used for determining staff reductions is applied consistently throughout the organization.

Responses to the Call for Reduced Personnel Costs

Initially you should try to determine whether you can increase efficiency or reduce costs by transferring or merging activities within your organizational unit. If you must transfer tasks from professional or highly trained technical employees to less educated workers, insist that the latter be trained first or that they are closely supervised until they have the work fully under control. Tap into the observations and recommendations of the persons who do the work. They have practical ideas on how work flows can be streamlined. When workers participate in the planning, they are less likely to object to changes, even when the changes involve staff reductions.

If the mandate calls for reduction of payroll to a certain level, hold brainstorming sessions with your employees. Get their ideas for reducing salary costs without laying people off. Some senior people may decide that this is a good time for them to end their careers. Some full-time employees may opt for part-time employment, and part-timers may be willing to reduce their hours, especially if they have more schedule options.

Handling Those Who Leave

Supervisors must face the anger of those who leave and the apprehension of those who remain. The reaction of people who are laid off is much like that of patients when they are told that they have cancer. First, there is disbelief, then anger or depression, and finally acceptance. Be tolerant of their anger, bitterness, and hostility, and be empathetic when the tears flow. Console yourself with the knowledge that most of these people will recover and find new and sometimes more satisfying positions. Answer their questions honestly, and make sure that they get the information they need about benefits and eligibility for unemployment benefits.

If outplacement services are available, encourage employees to take full advantage of them. These may include placement services, help with job applications and interview techniques, psychological testing, and training for new vocations. Use your personal network to try to find new jobs for them, or at least to steer them in the right direction. Do not hold out false hopes for recalls. If the likelihood of rehire is high, keep in touch with them.

Handling Those Who Remain

Layoff survivors often feel guilty and depressed because of losing friends and colleagues. They may experience a drop in self-esteem and morale. In the back of their minds is the fear of future layoffs. Remain visible. Do not hide in meetings or bury yourself in paperwork. Share their concern about their friends who are laid off.

Distance yourself from idle gossip, but keep yourself informed. Share that information. Explain the rationale for the changes. Answer questions honestly, and listen to expressions of frustration and fear. Do not wait for staff meetings or newsletters to keep your team informed. Call special meetings whenever you acquire new information.

You and your staff must pick up the slack. Ask for the participation and cooperation of your staff in closing ranks and getting the job done with fewer people. Point out the increased need for teamwork and for everyone to make a special effort. Prepare a list of duties and responsibilities that others must assume. Announce assignment changes, and provide any additional training that may be needed. Use your reward and recognition system to reward your team or individuals who make special efforts.

Process Reengineering

Reengineering may prove to be the most cost-effective mechanism in health care institutions. Without reengineering, cost-reduction initiatives will achieve only modest results. The major savings will not come from departmental reengineering but from those initiatives that address interdepartmental functions and that break down compartmentalization. These include abandoning obsolete systems, forming cross-functional, self-directed teams, amalgamating jobs, discarding old rules and assumptions, introducing new technologies, and creating new principles for task orientation. For more concerning reengineering, refer to the discussion presented in Chapter 4.

BENCHMARKING

Benchmarking is the search for best or preferred practices and is accomplished by comparing current systems or processes with highly successful ones. Your goal is to increase efficiency, cut costs, or improve service. The comparisons may be with standards reported in the literature or with observations at the facilities of recognized leaders. Benchmarking usually leads to some form of process, system, or structural reengineering. It is an essential tool in cost control and quality improvement with improved patient and fiscal outcomes at stake.

A benchmarking strategy usually requires data searches, networking, and creation of cross-functional teams. When national standards are unavailable, your external networks can be crucial to establishing standards. Questionnaires and other survey tools are often employed to locate the best benchmark sources.

The usual approach consists of (1) a data-collection phase that may include literature searches or site visits, (2) an analysis phase, and (3) an action plan. The planning process may involve use of flowcharts and other problem-solving tools; it is frequently necessary to dissect work flows to find problems or weaknesses.

Kreider and Walsh reported a highly successful benchmarking project that ensured decreased ventilator-associated pneumonia and intensive care unit costs.[5]

With a cost-restructuring plan based on benchmark information, one hospital reduced its operating budget by $33 million dollars.[6]

Rotondi et al. benchmarked their preoperative patient routing system. After they identified causes for variation, they created multidisciplinary improvement teams to improve the pinpointed areas.[7]

Mitchell found that the national benchmark for turnaround time between surgical cases was 13.5 minutes, while his hospital's time was 19.9 minutes.[8] A quality improvement team carried out solutions that produced an 18% improvement. The cost–benefit analysis showed a potential revenue enhancement of about $300,000.

Think About It

The best defense against having to make painful reductions at crunch time is to have your unit's cost picture under control at all times. Control consists of more than just monthly budget reports to review. The information comparing budgets to actual expenditures is important, but it is only part of the equation. True cost control is information plus action.

Questions for Review and Discussion
1. Often the productivity of a work group decreases after a layoff, even though there is more work to be done overall. Why might this be so?
2. In budgeting, why are funds for operating expenses and funds for capital expenditures always kept separated?
3. Describe one set of circumstances under which a supervisor may be largely powerless to affect a particular expense charged to the department.
4. Is overtime expense fully controllable, partially controllable, or not at all controllable by the supervisor? Explain.
5. If the numbers say the organization has to reduce 20 positions, and 20 employees leave via resignation and retirement, why might it still be necessary to reduce positions further and even engage in some hiring?
6. How can benchmarking assist the supervisor in determining whether a staff reduction may be necessary?
7. What conditions or circumstances in your own department should you consider before deciding to reduce staff?
8. The term "reengineering" literally means "engineering again." Why is so much so-called reengineering not true reengineering?

9. As a department supervisor, why might you often not get what you have asked for in the capital budget?
10. What information can the department supervisor often supply to finance or information services that can help in developing revenue projections?

Case: Let's Jettison the Deadwood

Two supervisors, call them Robert and Janet, were in charge of sections of the building services department of Central Hospital. They had a fairly close working relationship; they were in a position to cover for each other on occasion and usually did so successfully. Overall, however, they had quite different styles of dealing with their employees.

The long-anticipated word came down that declining admissions and sharp cuts in reimbursement rates necessitated staff reductions. Robert's staff would have to be reduced by three people; Janet's staff was projected to lose two people. On Monday they learned officially of the impending cuts; they had to have names turned in by Wednesday, and layoffs would actually occur Friday. Monday afternoon they found themselves discussing the layoffs.

Robert said, "How is this supposed to be done? I missed the meeting with the boss this morning thanks to a toxic material spill. I got the information secondhand, and all I know is that I've got to dump three people."

"Right," Janet replied. "And I have to lose two. These are the times when I'm almost sorry I took a supervisory job."

"Why? Employees come and go. This just means a few have to go unwillingly. I figure on taking advantage of this to jettison some deadwood."

"How can you do that? You weren't there this morning—it was pretty strongly indicated we should go by seniority. You know, last in, first out. Unless there's some compelling reason to the contrary."

"Compelling reasons I've got lots of," Robert responded. "One of mine who's going is the last in, no trouble there. But the other two are major pains I've wanted to get rid of for a long time."

"Got lots of documentation?"

"Who needs it?" Robert tapped the side of his head. "It's here. Overall I'll be getting rid of the three worst producers in the group. Nobody will have any idea how people are picked for layoff, and, anyway, at least two of these bozos should already figure they're on the way out."

Questions:

1. Is Robert justified in wanting to get rid of "the three worst producers in the group"? Under what circumstances might he be able to do this without creating another kind of problem?

2. What is the possible exposure to the organization and to Robert if he were to go ahead and "jettison the deadwood" as planned?
3. What can you infer from the case about the supervisory styles of both Robert and Janet?

Exercise: The Budgeting Game

There are two common methods for approaching budgeting at the department level. With the more sensible approach, the department supervisor carefully determines the funds needed for each of the group's controllable budget categories and submits as accurate a budget as possible.

The second method, and unfortunately the one used a great deal of the time—perhaps even most of the time—requires involvement in "the budgeting game." In this approach the supervisor calculates an honest budget, then tacks on an additional percentage to each budget category on the assumption that higher management or at least the finance department will assume a certain amount of padding and arbitrarily reduce each category by some unknown percentage. The essence of the "game" lies in being more accurate than the other party in guessing the percentage of padding and thus the percentage of reduction. This sometimes goes back and forth for three or four iterations until the department's total lands where higher management or finance wants it to be.

Instructions:

1. In essay form you are to comment on the validity of the budgeting game, but, most important, you are to describe how you as an individual supervisor might be able to break out of the "game" and submit an honest, accurate, and acceptable budget.

REFERENCES

1. Townsend, R. 1971. *Up the organization.* New York: Fawcett, 173.
2. Sattler, J. 1980. *Financial management of the clinical laboratory.* Oradell, NJ: Medical Economics, 124.
3. Jahn, M. 1995. Laboratorians speak out on benefits, managed care, and the bottom line. *Medical Laboratory Observer* 27(5): 29–33.
4. Medvescek, P. 1997. Rightsizing the right way. *Medical Laboratory Observer* 29(7): 102–6.
5. Kreider, C., and Walsh, B.A. 1997. Benchmarking for a competitive edge. *Medical Laboratory Observer* Supplement (September 1997): S26–S29.
6. Cohen, E., and Anderson-Miles, E. 1997. Benchmarking: A management tool for academic medical centers. *Best Practical Benchmarking in Healthcare* 1(2): 57–61.
7. Rotondi, A.J. et al. 1997. Benchmarking the perioperative process. I. Patient routing systems: A method for continual improvement of patient flow and resource utilization. *Journal of Clinical Anesthesia* 9(3): 159–69.
8. Mitchell, L. 1997. Benchmarking, benchmarks, or best practices? Applying quality improvement principles to decrease surgical turnaround time. *Best Practical Benchmarking in Healthcare* 1(2): 70–4.

PART IV

Developing Employees

Chapter 27

Job Redesign: A Paradigm Shift

*An effective job design meets both the
requirements of the tasks and the social and
psychological needs of the workers.[1]*

CHAPTER OBJECTIVES

- Describe the ongoing shift in the health care paradigm from a technical model to a sociotechnical model; that is, how success of the health care organization is becoming increasingly dependent on human behavior as well as technological advancement.
- Establish the concept of job enrichment and identify its relationship to employee job satisfaction.
- Identify the guiding principles of job redesign and continuing methods of improvement.

This chapter could readily be called the "See Previous Chapter" chapter because, in spite of its brevity, it refers to so many previous chapters. The intent of this chapter is to tie together many different aspects of job design or job modification in a manner that can be helpful for supervisors who ever have occasion to create a new position or change an existing position.

For a number of years health care has been experiencing a paradigm shift from a technical model to a sociotechnical model. Thus today advances in instrumentation and automation are no longer enough. To please our most important external customers, our patients, more high-touch is required. To satisfy our major internal customers, our employees, job enrichment is required. And to appease the third-party payers, lower costs are required.

365

Job enrichment is not a specific project. Rather, it is a continuous process of encouraging employee participation in multiple activities. Job enrichment capitalizes on and makes full use of all available professional abilities and individual skills, and doing so requires taking a second look at how people are assigned and how jobs are designed. Each employee perceives job satisfaction and enrichment a bit differently; one person's meat is another person's poison. It is necessary to know the motivational needs of individual team members (see Chapter 13). For employees who desire more control, we provide delegation and empowerment (see Chapter 31). For those who want greater task satisfaction, we provide training, challenge, and job enhancement. For those who have a strong affiliation (social) need, we provide increased opportunities for team efforts (see Chapter 9).

JOB FIT

Before embarking on cross-training or other job-enrichment measures, first concentrate on placing the right people in the right jobs. If the individual and the job are appropriately matched at the start, short-term changes are far less likely to be required. Begin with accurate position descriptions (see Chapter 5) and comprehensive recruiting and selection of new hires (see Chapter 7). Assign employees tasks that take advantage of their strengths and make their weaknesses irrelevant (see Chapter 4). Ensure that employees are not handicapped by oppressive or restrictive policies and rules (see Chapter 6).

QUALITY OF WORK LIFE

The physical work environment, social relationships, style of supervision, and other morale factors determine the quality of work life. For the most part employees now take these circumstances for granted, and they—and their unions, should they be organized—will fight to maintain them. These essentially generic factors must be favorable before significant sociotechnical breakthroughs can be achieved.

Quality-of-work-life programs and Japanese-style management represent macro models of organizational design. For job redesign it is necessary to turn to micro models.[2]

JOB REDESIGN

The opening quotation in this chapter identifies the essentials of job design as well as could any other words. To be effective any job design must both serve the task and meet the needs of the workers. Common job redesign measures available to many supervisors include

- cross-training;
- rotation of workstations, departments, or shifts;
- job transfer;
- changed work hours (flextime);
- status changes from full time to part time or vice versa;
- deletion or addition of specific duties;
- new locations for workstations;
- improved instrumentation, flow patterns, communication, and methods;
- altered team membership or roles;
- encouragement of creativity and entrepreneurship;
- delegation of more challenging assignments;
- appointments to committees, quality circles, or other work groups;
- involvement in research or development; and
- assignments to teaching or training roles.

When Should Job Design Changes Be Considered?

Anytime! The considerations may be formal or informal, planned in advance or undertaken on the spur of the moment. There may be a number of more opportune times available, such as

- during the latter phases of probationary employment,
- at performance appraisal time,
- when salary discussions are initiated by employees,
- when new services are contemplated,
- when reductions-in-force (layoffs) are necessary, and
- when organizational expansion, merger, acquisition, or other restructuring happens, altering the basic organizational configuration.

Key Questions Affecting Job Redesign

- Does the individual employee want more authority or autonomy?
- Does this employee prefer to work alone or on a team?
- Will the organization and the employee benefit from a change?
- What can be achieved without an immediate change in the job classification?
- Will the budget and current staffing configuration permit changes?
- How will the changes affect work flow and other people?
- Will the results improve customer service, costs or charges, or employee morale?
- Will the changes enhance total quality management (continuous quality improvement) measures?

Guidelines or Cautions for Job Redesign

- Never attempt to use job redesign or job enrichment as a cure-all.
- Tailor the changes to the needs and wants of both the employees and the organization.
- Know the motivational drives of each employee.
- Consider the effects of any change on other people.
- Ensure that the employee endorses the new measures.
- Be certain that the employee has a reasonably good chance to succeed.
- Make the goals and plans flexible and reversible.
- Update position descriptions as appropriate.
- Provide feedback and support.
- Do not promise what you cannot deliver.

Think About It

It is essential to effective job redesign that the affected employees participate in the improvement process. The supervisor may have the stronger overall view concerning how all the pieces of the department's contribution fit together, but when it comes to the inner working details of any particular task, there is no one who knows the job better than the person who does it every day. And it is this expertise that the supervisor must tap in job redesign.

Questions for Review and Discussion

1. Are there any times when job redesign might not be especially appropriate? Why or why not?
2. How would you go about ensuring that the right person is matched with the right job as early in employment as possible?
3. What would you consider to be at least three advantages of successful job redesign? Why?
4. Explain what is meant in the chapter by macro and micro models of job design.
5. What do you believe to be the principal objective of job redesign? Why?

Exercise: A Hypothetical Job Redesign

Select a particular task. It can be something done as part of a job you have performed, or it can simply be a job you are familiar with through observation or perhaps even secondhand description. For this job:

Instructions:

1. Describe the task by naming it and providing a one- or two-sentence description.
2. Identify and describe what might be considered "wrong" about this task or at least weak to the extent of being able to benefit from change.

3. Describe in a series of steps how you might go about redesigning this job.
4. Identify the principal benefits to be gained by adopting your redesign.

REFERENCES

1. Cunningham, J.B., and Eberle, T. 1990. A guide to job enrichment and redesign. *Personnel* 67: 56.
2. Cunningham and Eberle, A guide to job enrichment and redesign. 56–61.

Chapter 28

Adjusting to Change

*Directing and controlling change in
an organization has been likened
to managing in white water.*[1]

CHAPTER OBJECTIVES

- Identify the kinds of change affecting organizational functioning, the essential elements of change in the organization, and the most commonly encountered barriers to successful change.
- Highlight the general concerns of employees concerning change potentially affecting their relationship with their surroundings.
- Identify the essentials of preparation for change potentially affecting the activities and status of employees.
- Enumerate the essentials of the successful implementation of change.
- Describe how the supervisor can help employees through the most stressful stages of change, and review typical employee responses to change.
- Provide workable advice concerning means of addressing and overcoming employee resistance to change.

Nothing in life is as constant as change. Almost weekly we hear about a technological advance or another medical breakthrough. New areas of specialization spring up, and older ones phase out. Acquisitions, reductions-in-force, mergers, reorganizations, and the change to managed care stir tremors throughout the health care industry. In addition, every few years another "revolutionary" management concept surfaces, only to run its course and sputter and die within a few years. Consider, if you will, management by objectives, guest relations, quality circles, and the various permutations of quality improvement such as total quality management and continuous quality improvement.

There are significant differences between the ways that successful and not-so-successful organizations cope with change. A change-oriented culture requires flexibility, rapid responsiveness, and adaptation. Employees must master new technologies and adjust to new systems and procedures.

Effective supervisors are change specialists who know what their clients want and how well these wants are being met. Too many managers at all levels make changes based on their own perceptions of what is best for the customers without finding out what those customers really want or need. There are three general kinds of change encountered in organizational functioning.

1. Organizational changes, in which departments are altered, interdepartmental relationships or reporting relationships are changed, are made or new management takes over.
2. New systems, structures, procedures, or equipment are introduced.
3. Jobs are restructured.

ESSENTIALS OF CHANGE

For change to successfully occur, a number of essential elements must be present and appropriately aligned.

- *Motivation.* Motivating people to change is a major challenge of leadership. Managers must understand why people resist change and cope with that resistance. The presence of appropriate motivation is a significant part of what is required for successful change.
- *Competencies.* These are the technologies, capabilities, and expertise that enable organizations to satisfy customers and meet new standards. Competencies are affected most by hiring and training systems.
- *Creativity.* New, untried, and innovative ideas are required. Brainstorming is often needed to open up new ways of thinking. Change also requires the skills that turn ideas into entrepreneurship.
- *Employee commitment.* Employees must "buy in" for any change to fully succeed.
- *Adaptability.* Retraining and new learning are the orders of the day. Some employees must be completely "recycled."
- *Stability of workforce.* Stability requires low personnel turnover, and the lower the turnover, the greater the chances of successful change implementation.
- *Patience.* While everything seems to be rush and more rush, supervisors must show a modicum of patience with those people who learn or adjust a little more slowly than others. They must couple patience with persistence.

* *Reward and recognition.* People who must adjust to change expect some kind of a payoff for their cooperation and assistance.

BARRIERS TO CHANGE

Positive change may sometimes be forestalled because of the absence of appropriate technology or a lack of financial resources. However, the most numerous and significant barriers to change are the barriers presented by human attitudes and behaviors. Frequently working against change are

* dysfunctional teamwork, typified by individuals pulling in their separate directions instead of acting together;
* satisfaction with the status quo, the absolutely progress-killing attitude that things are OK as they are;
* unjustified pessimism about the ability to change; that is, the feeling that "we can't do this, so why try?";
* ego or personality problems, as evidenced by those who are "always right" and must have their way or be the ones in charge;
* territorial imperatives, which cause much energy to be directed at defending one's boundaries or seeking to annex the territory of others;
* lack of vision or support by upper management;
* inflexible systems, policies, or procedures;
* work overload. As strange as it may sound, some people who recognize the need for change remain too busy trying to stay even with day-to-day activities to take the time necessary to improve their circumstances; and
* lack of confidence in leaders.

EMPLOYEE CONCERNS

Change experts know what may be felt and experienced by employees who are affected by change, and they anticipate a spectrum of emotional responses. Even changes that some individuals hope for can be upsetting when they become reality. For example, a promotion elicits mixed feelings; the pride and the increased paycheck are gratifying, but the altered relationships with former coworkers may be upsetting.

The more a change affects established habits and relationships, the greater the stress produced. Fear is the strongest stressor. There are many kinds of fear that are likely to come into play: fear of the unknown; fear of failure or reduction in one's influence; and fear of job loss, demotion, transfer, or reassignment. It is likely that the most common personal fear is fear of the inability to cope with new tasks or different responsibilities.

Loss of control is another factor. Reactions are more intense when changes reduce employees' control over their daily tasks. People who worked hard to achieve influence are likely to oppose, overtly or covertly, any threat to this status.

Mindsets are significant. People can perceive changes as threats or as opportunities. There may be pervasive perception that the change is either impossible or not practical. This is most likely to occur with employees who have experienced or witnessed failures in the past.

People with low self-esteem and a great need for basic security are reluctant to commit to change. Others balk because they receive too little information or may not have been given the opportunity to participate in the planning process.

PREPARING FOR CHANGE

Role of Supervisors

Supervisors are frequently called upon to carry out changes mandated by upper management or outside agencies, but they also have occasion to introduce some changes of their own. Through networking, they find out as much as they can about current and rumored changes. Then they provide training and support, and they monitor results. If supervisors drag their feet, stonewall, or do much griping, they cannot expect exemplary behavior by their employees or expect to win points with upper management.

Goals and Plans

A well-defined goal is a prerequisite for productive action and arches over four critical objectives:

1. selecting the right people,
2. preparing and motivating people to change,
3. obtaining the other necessary resources, and
4. carrying out the change.

Every successful initiative requires a workable, clearly defined master plan, a plan that must be fully committed to writing. The plan must address the following crucial "W" questions.

What is the proposed change? Is it customer oriented, quality conscious, and cost-effective? What do we hope to achieve? What are the risks, constraints, and barriers? What additional data do we need? What resources are essential? What did we do wrong last time? What additional training will be necessary? What will be the impact on existing power and status relationships?

Will the change fit the existing organizational culture? Will the people affected see a payoff or a setback? Will the change increase or decrease profit, morale, quality, and productivity? Will the change provide an opportunity to use available skills better? Will people have more autonomy over how they do their work? Will the changes make employees' jobs (and mine) easier or harder?

Who wants the change? For what reasons? Who will benefit and who will be affected adversely? Who will resist? Who will be supportive?

When should serious planning begin? Will there be sufficient time? When must we obtain official sanction? When will the work start and when must it be completed?

Where will we find the space, funds, and people?

Assess the compatibility of the proposed change in light of the current organizational culture and goals. The change should not violate cultural norms.

Gather information about previous successes and failures. Experience is still the best teacher. Focus on activities that strongly influenced success and those that were barriers.

Set a timetable complete with checkpoints and completion dates. Install a feedback system so people know how they are doing. Be flexible. Successful plans are usually revised often over the course of implementation.

Test your plan by asking these questions.

- Is it concise and clearly written? Does it include action steps?
- Was it distributed to the right people?
- Has there been sufficient input from others?
- Are there formal and informal networks that can lend credence and support?

Communication

Alert your employees to upcoming changes as soon as possible. Outline the challenges and the opportunities they present. Involve them early while evaluating new technology or new procedures. This also gives them time to adjust to the idea of a major change.

Explain the need for change in pragmatic terms, then patiently listen to them blow off steam. Reassure them about things that are not going to change; usually, what will not change is more extensive than what will change.

When employees report rumors, tell them as much as you are able. Once they know that they know as much as you do, they will gain confidence. The very act of talking about the change reduces fear and resistance, especially if you acknowledge their concerns and anxieties as legitimate. Tell them that what they feel is perfectly normal and that those feelings will pass.

When you must champion a change that you feel is inappropriate, avoid making remarks such as "The idiots upstairs issued these orders." This serves only to increase resentment, reduce morale, and delay implementation. Also, this attitude gains you no points with employees.

The Name of the Game Is Commitment

Obedience is good, but commitment is better. We succeed only when we get commitment from the people who carry out the change or who are affected by it. Ideally, you invite this participation when a change is first contemplated. We all support what we create and may even be ecstatic over our own ideas, but it takes considerably more effort to get enthusiastic over another person's brainchild. When a team lacks ownership of a plan, getting commitment is more difficult. If you demand it, all you get is "lip service."

If it is not possible for employees to participate in the planning sessions, it is even more important for them to be involved in designing or scheduling the implementation process. Follow through on as many of each person's suggestions as possible.

Explain the rationale behind the change. Articulate the reasoning in terms that make sense to the workers. Does it improve customer service, profits, or competitiveness? Detail the shortcomings of the old way. Show them how the change will affect them. What is in it for them if they do well? What happens if they do not?

If the history of change is one of failure, explain the new change fully, and point out how this change is different. Provide examples of how the plans succeeded elsewhere.

Upgrade Your Employee Selection Process

Chapter 7 included a discussion about how to select job applicants. Pick people who have displayed their ability to adjust to change. You want the ones who have the willingness and ability to participate in planning.

Train, Train, and Keep Training

Because fear of the unknown is the source of the most anxiety, eliminate the unknown. The dual approach is to hold enough discussions before the change and to provide sufficient training to ensure confidence.

Clarify training objectives using a thorough needs analysis. Ask the learners what they want, and incorporate their suggestions into the program. Design training that provides the needed job-related skills.

Enlist the highly motivated and influential end-users first. Provide the training just before it is needed and to those who are going to use it first—"just-in-time training"—to ensure that it is fresh in their minds.

CARRYING OUT THE PLANS

It is important to avoid failure at the start. To increase the likelihood of quick and favorable results, introduce changes by using pilot projects and highly motivated teams.

Take change one step at a time. Resist the urge to carry out every aspect of a change at once. Empower employees to make changes happen. Build in incentives for using the change. Stay in touch with workers' daily efforts.

The Seven Keys to Successful Implementation

1. Clarify strategies and plans.
2. Mobilize resources. (Choosing the right people is especially critical.)
3. Introduce new practices slowly.
4. Provide all needed education.
5. Provide and solicit feedback continuously.
6. Run interference for the team members.
7. Do not nitpick or be a bottleneck.

Monitor Progress

Major change efforts require constant monitoring. Things do go wrong. Unexpected situations develop. Some resistance may occur because of certain aspects of the plan that were wrong to begin with or that were carried out poorly. As people are forced to break familiar routines, performance weakens, confusion follows, and job stress increases. People see and hear things that disturb them. They are often disappointed and frustrated by all the problems or bottlenecks that develop.

Some people will hastily conclude that the plan is not working. The grumbling grows louder unless leaders have made it clear that the change will not be trouble free. When employees complain, showcase the benefits or the progress that has been made to date. Make it easy and safe for them to express new concerns.

Talk to people. Track results. Look for symptoms like slippage in timetables, productivity downturns, and increased customer complaints. Be aware of signs of uncooperativeness, complaining, or criticizing the folks in charge. Workers may start regressing to the old way of doing things. If you pay attention, you can address the problems before they get out of hand.

Use weekly meetings to discuss modifications and problems. Continue the group meetings throughout the implementation process. Interactions include give-and-take exchanges. Accept, even welcome, appropriate critical comments. For the first 15 minutes of each meeting, let the complaints and frustrations hang out. Then switch to a brag session where individuals can talk about their little victories. Pay close attention to what is said out in the corridors after the meetings break up.

Monitoring performance and tracking results also enables you to identify the role models who are contributing most to the change effort. Honor them and celebrate their achievements.

Reward

Hanging on to established habits makes sense to employees when their old reward system remains in place. Therefore, try to restructure the way people are compensated. Money may be a limited and transient motivational force, but the lack of a fair compensation system is a strong demotivator.

Autonomy is a powerful reward for some people, so delegate authority to those who show the interest and the ability to use power judiciously. For achievers who relish challenges, the strongest reward may be to get involved in another change, perhaps a bigger or more challenging one. Most employees feel rewarded to some extent if they perceive that the change will enable them to get their work done faster, more easily, or more enjoyably. See Chapter 14 for more about rewards and recognition.

HELPING PEOPLE THROUGH THE STRESSFUL PHASE

Employees are usually relieved when told that their concerns are normal and will pass. The principles of stress management apply here. The earlier you take remedial measures, the better results you will get. Workers appreciate reassurance that their jobs or their teams will not be altered. You may be able to reassure employees whose positions are in jeopardy by:

- Promising new positions, if this is indeed possible
- Offering retraining opportunities
- Recommending early retirement packages
- Reassuring that jobs will be eliminated only by attrition (careful: this must be a strong commitment by higher management)

Vital elements of the coping process to be applied as needed by the supervisor include the following:

- Using active listening skills, isolation avoidance, and empathy
- Legitimizing employees' feelings and expressions
- Ensuring that training measures meet the needs of employees
- Showing understanding but holding firm on the need for the change
- Searching for specific needs and problems and bringing them into the open
- Exploring ways of achieving desired changes through conflict management skills and win-win negotiation

- Displaying technical and managerial expertise pertinent to the situation
- Being patient
- Never promising what you cannot deliver

EMPLOYEE RESPONSES TO CHANGE

Individuals vary significantly in their openness to change. Some thrive on change, but most people do not. Some employees sense that they will be affected; others convince themselves that they will not be involved.

Employees often go through the stages of anticipation, denial, anger, bargaining, depression, and, finally, acceptance. The first opposition to change may take place when news of possible change surfaces.

Although most employees will show some degree of support, others take a wait-and-see attitude, and some actively reject the process. The two undesirable responses are resistance and the development of stress. There may be increased absenteeism and turnover and grievance filing. Hostility, moodiness, and slowed output may result.

Fortunately, most employees eventually settle down and accept the change. Later, many fight to prevent any return to the old system. For example, a computer breakdown that requires a temporary return to the old manual system can cause great consternation in the ranks.

Happy Campers

A few members of any work group, clearly a minority of employees, embrace new marching orders enthusiastically. The better the preparation for change, the larger this percentage of people will be. Alert managers make full use of these eager beavers by assigning them to pilot programs and having them report on successes during the early phases of a new initiative.

Fence Sitters

The majority of employees are fence sitters. Fence sitters are not obstinate or uncooperative, but they do fret about how a change may affect them. Although not hostile to change as such, neither are they enthusiastic. They want proof that the change will work. They ask where the change was tried before and what the outcome was. Most will join in the endeavor when they see colleagues commit themselves and when they witness early successes.

When people believe that they will be unaffected by a change, some of them become amused bystanders. They show little sympathy for the people who are involved. Sometimes they taunt those who are struggling with the new initiative. Do not tolerate snide remarks from supposedly "disinterested" parties.

Cynics

One highly vocal cynic can infect an entire department. Cynics often have some measure of truth to support their pessimism. There may have been failures in the past, or there may be formidable barriers ahead.

When you hear grumbling, investigate the problem and address it without delay. It helps to have some team members relate successes during the early phases of the change.

Rational arguments, such as pointing out that this change is unlike old failed initiatives, may not achieve the desired effect. In that situation the best strategy may be to admit that you also have concerns but decided to risk going ahead with the change. Add that you hope the cynic will also make the same choice. When this does not work, you may have to spend your efforts trying to limit the influence of the cynic on other employees.

Occasionally you can convert cynics by giving them more of the action or getting their ideas for expediting the process.

Resisters

Resistance can be overt or covert, active or passive, well intentioned or subversive. People fight change in ways that best fit their individual personalities, so expect a wide range of tactics at work when resistance emerges.

Managers often mistake the lack of overt opposition for support. Covert resisters disguise their resistance to make it safer or more politically correct. People in this category are cunning. These saboteurs operate undercover, resisting on the sly, fighting change carefully to reduce their chances of being caught. They may claim that they did everything in their power to support the change. Subtle sabotage can be expressed in a number of ways, including

- intentionally "forgetting" to do things,
- inciting the resistance of others,
- doing exactly what the supervisor requests when they know that such action will be detrimental, or
- setting up roadblocks.

Your job is to blow the cover from these saboteurs. Look for signs of passive resistance, such as foot dragging, quiet uncooperativeness, or malicious compliance. When you spot people behaving this way, corner them and give them an earful. If counseling is not effective, consider appropriate disciplinary measures (especially if an employee's resistance goes to the extreme of insubordination).

Among the resisters there may be a few firebrands who are loud and outspoken in their opposition to change. One or two highly vocal critics can rock the boat, so it is hazardous to ignore them. Often you will find it necessary to get rid of such obstructionists. Pritchett expresses the opinion of most of us when he writes, "Make an example of someone who resists. If this sounds ruthless, remember that it is their choice to resist. Something has to suffer, either them or the change effort."[2]

HOW TO OVERCOME RESISTANCE

Resistance to change is not all bad. It can be valuable, sometimes keeping leaders from making critical mistakes. In fact, it can be extremely fortunate for the supervisor to have a couple of loyal employees who will speak up when they see the leader heading for trouble. However, for the most part, resistance is a roadblock that you must remove.

When employees do not accept change, it may be because they do not understand it. They may think that it will be bad for them. Some employees lack confidence in the ability of their leaders or their teams to make it work.

Chances for success decrease when change occurs without proactive analysis, planning, or direction. The likelihood of success increases when you understand how your people react to change and use that awareness to help navigate them through the process.

Participation by Stakeholders

The importance of getting employees involved in the planning and implementation processes has already been discussed. By involving people before specific changes become reality, a leader confronts deep-seated negative attitudes before they become barriers.

Education

Do not overlook the knowledge gap that a change can create. There is usually much to be learned. Make certain that people have the necessary understanding. They must handle new kinds of equipment and face unfamiliar methods. Once workers realize that they will be retrained, their resistance often plummets. When they receive instruction manuals, hands-on training, and the time to use new equipment, they quickly develop self-confidence.

Communication

Earlier we discussed the importance of communication when laying the groundwork for change and when anticipating employee concerns.

In the implementation phase, bring developing resistance out into the open. Make it safe and easy for people to express their feelings. Be patient enough to get beyond superficial answers so you can reach the true issues. Try to understand their positions. Evaluate the legitimacy of their resistance. You might discover that some of their reluctance keeps you from doing something dumb. At the very least, they can educate you about why they are resisting and how you can elicit their support.

When people say that things were better before a change, remind them of the problems that existed then. We tend to forget many of the negative aspects of "the good old days." For example, while people may gripe about the new computer system, few would elect to go back to the old one.

Supervisory Commitment

Your actions speak far louder than your words in this regard, so "walk the talk." Be obvious and passionate in your determination to follow through. Do not try to reduce resistance by softening your position; doing so will only stiffen the resistance. Employees will fully commit only when they trust their superiors, and it is up to every supervisor to earn this trust.

Think About It

In the last analysis there are but three ways to get employees to adopt change: you can tell them what to do, you can convince them of what must be done, or you can involve them in addressing the need for change. The best way, involvement, should be the first one considered, but it may not always be possible. The second-best way, convince them (or "sell them," if you will), is always an option; many will cooperate if they understand why. The first way, tell them, is to be avoided; simply ordering compliance might get some grudging cooperation, but usually it creates resentment and fosters resistance.

Questions for Review and Discussion
1. Why is it that even a successful change implementation plan will probably have to be revised over the course of implementation?
2. It has often been said that change "disturbs an individual's equilibrium" or affects the person's comfort zone. What is meant by this?
3. As a supervisor, how are you going to approach the implementation of a none-too-popular change that is being mandated by your state's Department of Health?
4. It is frequently said that the weakest part of the change implementation process is follow-up. Why?

5. If a particular change that reaches you is of such an urgent nature that you have no time to explain in detail to employees or sell them on what must be done, how would you proceed?
6. Who exercises the ultimate control over whether or not a particular change is successful? Why is this so?
7. If top management is not at all involved in a particular change, is it still important to have their visible support? Why or why not?
8. Why can even a change that is desired or hoped for by employees still be upsetting to them?
9. Is there anything wrong if a supervisor introduces a mandated change with "I don't agree with this, but orders are orders?" If so, what is wrong and why is it wrong?
10. What do you consider to be potentially the most upsetting change that can affect a department or team or other specific work group? Why?

Case: 'Round and 'Round Again

The position of business office manager at Central Hospital has been a "hot seat," frequently changing incumbents. When the position was vacated last June, the four most senior employees in the department were interviewed. All were told that since they were at the top of grade and the salary structure for new supervisors "had not yet caught up with that of other jobs," the position would involve only a miniscule increase in pay. All four declined to interview for the position, but in the process all four were given the impression that they were not really considered qualified anyway. They might, however, be considered at a later date.

That same month a new manager was hired from outside, and the four senior employees were instructed to "show the new boss everything she needs to know." Over the next few months, the finance director, to whom the business office reported, told the four senior employees that they had "come along very nicely" and that they would be considered candidates if the position should open up again.

Barely 8 months after being hired, the manager resigned. However, none of the four senior employees got the job; the process described above was repeated, and again a new manager was hired from outside.

Questions:

1. How are the four senior employees going to feel, having been through this frustrating process twice?
2. What are likely to be the attitudes of the business office staff toward the organization?

3. How are the four senior employees likely to regard their boss's boss, the finance director?
4. What would be your recommendation for attempting to correct (over a period of time) the damage done in the business office?

Case: Who Needs a Boss?

Mrs. Martin is assigned to the reception desk in the lobby of Community Hospital, a small rural facility. Her job also includes sorting incoming mail for distribution and metering and bundling all outgoing mail. She has been the only person doing this job since the hospital opened its doors 16 years earlier. She always worked independently and was never assigned to any particular supervisor. She never appeared on any organization chart, and she considered the hospital's administrator, whom she rarely saw, to be her only "boss."

During a period of growth it was considered necessary to establish the position of business manager. You were hired from the outside to fill this new position. One of the activities placed under your direct supervision is Mrs. Martin's mail and reception area.

You are unable to tell from your initial visit with Mrs. Martin whether her seemingly quiet and stern manner is natural to her or perhaps indicates resentment. Your visit was not preceded by any announcement concerning your arrival and the position you were to fill. All she said when you introduced yourself and told her why you were there was, "Sixteen years I haven't needed a boss, and I certainly don't need one now."

Instructions:

1. In either outline or essay form, develop an approach that will help you get started constructively with Mrs. Martin, recognizing that this significant change affecting her employment was sprung on her without warning.

REFERENCES

1. Boe, G.P., and Hudson, C.G. 1991. Managing change in troubled times. *Medical Laboratory Observer* 23(9): 24.
2. Pritchett, P. 1996. *Resistance: Moving beyond the barriers to change.* Dallas, TX: Pritchett & Associates, 21.

RECOMMENDED READING

J.A. Belasco, *Teaching the Elephant To Dance.* (New York: Crown Publishers, 1990).

A.J. Bernstein and S.C. Rozen, *Dinosaur Brains* (New York; John Wiley & Sons, 1989).

R. Maurer, "Transforming Resistance," *HR Focus* 74, no. 10 (1997): 9–10.

C.R. McConnell, "After Reduction in Force: Reinvigorating the Survivors," *The Health Care Supervisor,* 14, no. 4 (1996): 1–10.

W. Umiker, "How To Prevent and Cope with Resistance to Change," *The Health Care Supervisor* 15, no. 4 (1997): 35–41.

Chapter 29

Encouraging Creativity

*Innovation is the practical application
of a creative thought.[1]*

*A creative person who knows exactly what he
or she is doing is not a creative person.*

—Anonymous

CHAPTER OBJECTIVES

- Define the creative process in simple everyday terms, including the role of intuition in creativity.
- Highlight the behavioral characteristics of creative people.
- Identify the principal characteristics of the innovative supervisor.
- Review the commonly encountered barriers to creativity.
- Suggest how the supervisor can go about stimulating and rewarding creativity in the staff.

Employers who have tunnel vision seem to believe that all worthwhile ideas are generated in executive suites or research departments, but it is the rank-and-file worker who has the best opportunity to see how any particular job can be improved. Employee input results in better cost control, higher quality, greater productivity, and improved customer service.

Organizational infrastructures are shifting to make room for people who are innovative. Those with innovative potential now outrank those with graduate degrees in some progressive organizations. The fundamental driver of continuous quality improvement and cost reduction is innovation. Failure to promote innovation leads to lower quality or more rationing of care, equally undesirable results.

Downsizing, with its adverse impact on morale, has greatly affected employee creativity in many organizations. However, it has also stimulated creativity where economic survival is at stake or competition is keen.

Although workers at all levels have ideas about how to improve things, some are blessed with greater innovativeness, intuition, or entrepreneurship. These creative employees can be among the most valuable members of an organization if their supervisors treat them well. Your goal as supervisor is to keep these people flooding you with ideas—without letting them get out of control.

THE CREATIVE PROCESS

Innovative creativity is the ability to come up with truly new ideas (for example, the artificial lens for cataracts). Inventors use innovative creativity. Just as a kaleidoscope forms new patterns from many disconnected pieces, the creative person forms new patterns from many seemingly unrelated ideas. The process usually starts with a problem. Problems are opportunities in disguise. Edwin Land invented the Polaroid camera after his young daughter asked him why she could not see pictures as soon as she took them.

Adaptive creativity is displayed when people find better ways to do their work. This may be putting old ideas together in new ways or simply putting the creative ideas of others into practice. Entrepreneurs exhibit adaptive creativity. Because creative people are often unable to work out the details of their ideas, we need both types of creative people, the inventors and the entrepreneurs.

When you challenge employees to think creatively about their work, they seek to learn more about their jobs. In the process, they become more competent and more efficient. It is creativity that leads to new services and products.

When supervisors suppress creativity in favor of conformity, the creativity resurfaces outside the workplace in hobbies, recreational activities, and artistic endeavors. Back on the job, stifled operational creativity may be expressed in unique ways to annoy bosses or to bypass policies and rules.

Intuition

Intuition has long been regarded as a mystical power that originates below the conscious level. We refer to it euphemistically as flashes of insight, hunches, and gut reactions. Intuition is knowledge gained without rational thought or logic. Think of intuition as experience stored in the unconscious mind.

> *Intuition + Logic = Common Sense*

Intuition is a sixth sense. Everyone is born with it, but it deteriorates with disuse. The more attention we pay to our intuition, the more useful it becomes. For example, before you sign a contract, make a checklist of pertinent questions, then take time to completely identify feelings about each of those questions. This combination of rational and intuitive decision making is more effective than either process alone. The same holds true for selecting new employees.

CHARACTERISTICS OF CREATIVE PEOPLE

People who are creative possess a sort of restlessness. Confident that there is always a better way of doing things, they challenge systems, processes, procedures, tradition, practices, policies, and rules. Most creative people share many of the following characteristics.

- They possess innumerable bits of information (the pieces in the kaleidoscope) that relate to the focal point of their interest.
- They blot out what to them seems irrelevant or unimportant, sometimes to the annoyance of their supervisors and colleagues.
- They are curious, open, and sensitive to problems. They may bombard their supervisors and others with questions, many starting with "why," "why not," or "what if."
- They are optimistic risk takers who like challenges and rarely talk about failure.
- They often appear preoccupied. At times they work furiously. Their ideas usually come in spurts.
- They dislike rigid routines, monotonous tasks, restrictive policies, and bureaucratic interference.
- They tolerate isolation and ambiguity.
- They value independence and autonomy.
- They often enjoy the innovative process more than the results of the innovation.
- They sense when things are right and when they are not right.
- They bounce ideas off others and build on the suggestions of their associates.
- They are voracious readers.
- They are often nonconformists, regarded by their peers as different. At meetings they are likely to play the role of devil's advocate.
- They may like to hang out with other creative people. Many are loners.

THE INNOVATIVE SUPERVISOR

Effective supervisors strive to increase their own creativity and that of the people who report to them. To avoid job blindness, they occasionally step back and take a new look at processes, systems, and people. They seek fresh insights into nagging problems.

There's a way to do it better—find it.

—Thomas A. Edison

Innovative supervisors

- believe that there is always a better way and are always on the lookout for that better way,
- overcome ideonarcissism, the egotism of thinking that one's own idea is unique,
- view problems as challenges rather than annoyances,
- chalk up failures as learning experiences,
- use brainstorming techniques for making decisions and solving problems,
- are tolerant of ambiguity and the idiosyncrasies of teammates,
- cut red tape when they encounter it,
- set aside some time each day for reflective thinking,
- inject humor into situations (some of the best ideas originate as jokes), and
- are willing to stick their necks out in support of their ideas.

BARRIERS TO CREATIVITY

The following situations and circumstances can stymie creativity.

- Prejudging ideas. We tend to accept ideas more readily from authority figures or people we respect and reject those from marginal performers or individuals below us in the hierarchy.
- Fear of failure. This is a significant inhibitor of creativity.
- Restrictive policies, rules, rituals, and procedures
- Strict controls and limited budgets
- Complex or slow approval procedure for suggestions and projects
- Demands for a consensus
- Understaffing and excessive work group assignments
- Lengthy chain of command
- Group norms
- Disparaging or discouraging remarks

STIMULATING CREATIVITY IN YOUR STAFF

Creativity flourishes only when employees feel secure and free of the fear of failure. Insightful employers establish corporate cultures that support new ideas. To switch from a culture that endorses conformity and compliance to one that fosters innovation is not easy. Here are some suggestions for stimulating creativity in your department or unit.

Identify your innovative people, and strive to know them better. Focus on the unique expertise of each person.

Emphasize creativity during the orientation and training of new employees. Present problems as challenging opportunities. Be alert for and encourage employee statements that begin with "Maybe we could..." or "What if..." These flash the message that a creative idea is about to be born.

Give people a loose rein to *pursue* and *develop* new ideas. Tolerate some daydreaming. They need this to fire up their creativity or to retrieve information stuck in the catacombs of their unconscious minds. Use idea traps, such as quality circles, brainstorming sessions, incentive awards, and suggestion boxes.

Do not nitpick or demand perfection. When employees start to neglect their routine duties in favor of pet projects, you may have to tighten the reins, but do not say, "You can't do that." Instead, say, "You can get back to your project when..."

Let them take some *risks* and make mistakes without risking their jobs. Tolerate failure and mistakes as the cost of innovation and progress.

Provide the necessary *resources* and *psychological boosts*. Give them some discretionary time for nondirected research. The ones who are already spending weekends so engaged are the most deserving.

Expose them to in-house and outside learning, including

- seminars and professional meetings,
- consultants and guest speakers,
- publications, audiotapes, videotapes, and computer programs,
- customer input; and
- vendors and sales representatives.

Protect them. Managers and other employees may harass people who are different.

Expect some creative ideas from everyone and tell them that. Those supervisors who complain that their people never come up with creative ideas should consider this question: If you walked around your department with a roll of $100 bills and offered one for each idea, would you get any suggestions? You bet you would!

Dispense lots of praise and rewards.

Communication Precautions

Do not say yes or no too quickly. A quick no leaves the employee feeling that you have not given his or her idea serious consideration. When you say yes too quickly, you may find yourself in hot water or forced to renege on your promises.

Use the PIC Response to All Ideas

P = Positive: If you find an idea worthwhile, say "Great idea, let's try it" or "What can I do to help?"

I = Interesting: If there may be merit, say "That sounds interesting. Tell me more."

C = Concern: If you cannot find anything of value in the idea, say that you have some concerns, and express those concerns. Avoid killing the suggestion directly.

Avoid statements such as

> You've got to be kidding.
> That would never work here.
> The trouble with that idea is…
> I'm paid to do the thinking.

And substitute the following:

> Keep talking, you may have something.
> How can I help?
> Let's give it a try.
> Can you get me the figures for that?
> Wow!

Rewards for Creativity

Because creativity is usually expressed in bursts, rewards of all kinds are best delivered in bursts. Bonuses that follow specific accomplishments are more motivating than end-of-year bonuses. Do not save recognition for the next performance appraisal.

Base recognition and rewards on outcomes and their value to the organization. These values may relate to teamwork, quality, new services, and customer satisfaction. These systems demand factual and fair performance appraisals.

Give prizes not only for suggestions but also for criticisms that lead to improvements. Creative people are likely to hold reward values that differ from those of their colleagues. For example, they usually value financial support of their projects more than they value salary increases.

Shower them with recognition. Encourage them to publish. Let them attend meetings where they meet other creative people.

Other rewards are

- increased work space, equipment, and resources;
- a personal library;

- appointments to teaching staffs of academic institutions; and
- relief from tedious tasks and bureaucratic time wasters.

Think About It

We have all heard it said again and again that necessity is the mother of invention. If this were strictly true, considerable progress would be coming from some of the most needy places on earth, but we know this isn't so. Invention, rather, as well as discovery, has two parents: intelligence and dissatisfaction. When intelligent people are dissatisfied with the present state of affairs, they are driven to do something about it. Whether for the joy of creating or the satisfaction of making something better, the drive to create will make itself known.

Questions for Review and Discussion

1. Do you believe that everyone is potentially creative to some degree? Why or why not?
2. What is the difference between invention and discovery?
3. In what ways can the structure of the organization stifle creativity?
4. What do you believe is most likely the strongest influence on the potential for creativity of a department's employees?
5. Why should acknowledgment or reward occur as close in time as possible following a creative accomplishment?
6. Write out three "killer statements" or "killer phrases" that are bound to stifle or impede creativity in a work unit.
7. Why is it claimed that employees need to be allowed the freedom to fail?
8. Why is it said that rank-and-file workers are well positioned to find creative ways of improving work methods?
9. What are the usual consequences of swiftly punishing errors when they occur?
10. Provide one fairly detailed example of adaptive creativity.

Exercise: A Simple Paper Clip

Consider one of the most common items in many work areas, the lowly paper clip.

Initially working alone, each person is to spend a maximum of 10 minutes listing as many uses as he or she can think of for a simple paper clip. Approach this activity with a wide-open brainstorming attitude, ignoring the tendency to evaluate and sort alternatives as they arise. Get as many uses on paper as possible in the allotted time.

1. After 10 minutes, get together with at least two other participants and pool your lists. You will have many items in common, but it is almost certain that each person will contribute some uses that the others did not think of.
2. Comment on the principal advantages of bringing together the inputs of multiple persons.
3. While in the act of combining lists, did you and the others think of new uses that none had yet thought of? If so, why might this have occurred and what does this say about individual creativity?

Exercise: Open-Minded Idea Generation

In the foregoing exercise you were instructed to approach idea generation with a "wide-open brainstorming attitude, ignoring the tendency to evaluate and sort alternatives as they arise." You are to comment at whatever length necessary on the likely basis of the tendency to evaluate and sort alternatives as they arise, explaining why many people tend to do this and why this tendency must be overcome if brainstorming-type idea generation is to attain its maximum usefulness.

REFERENCE

1. Filipczak, B. 1997. It takes all kinds: Creativity in the work force. *Training* 14(5): 32–40.

RECOMMENDED READING

R. Davidhizar, "Intuition and the Nurse Manager," *The Health Care Supervisor* 10, no. 2 (1991): 13–9.

A.F. Osborn, *Applied Imagination: Principles and Procedures of Creative Thinking*. (New York: Charles Scribner's Sons, 1953.) (Note: Old, but an absolute classic on the subject of creativity. Osborn was the originator of the term "brainstorming.")

P. Preston, "Breaking Down Barriers to Creativity," *Clinical Laboratory Management Review* 9, no. 6, (1995): 449–55.

W.T. Weaver, "Championing New Ideas: Whose Job Is It?" *HR Focus* 72, no. 1 (1995): 22, 23.

Chapter 30

Staff Development

*Education is a painful, continual and difficult work
to be done by kindness, by watching, by warning,
by precept, but above all, by example.*

—John Ruskin

CHAPTER OBJECTIVES

- Enumerate the benefits of and the necessity for a staff development program.
- Identify the accountability for planning staff education and for creating and promoting the opportunity for career development.
- Introduce the essentials of staff education needs assessment.
- Highlight the elements of an effective staff development program.
- Address mentoring as an especially valuable approach to job-specific staff development.

Throughout the following discussion the terms "staff development" and "career development" will be used essentially interchangeably. They can of course be differentiated by purpose, with one oriented primarily toward supporting and improving skills related to a person's present employment (staff development) and the other encompassing not just one's present employment but one's lifelong work (career development). Even differentiated, however, it is necessary to concede that at any given time staff development is often simply a part of career development.

Career development is a combination of education and experience. Employees may have to reinvent their careers numerous times and must continuously update their technical skills to remain employable. Unfortunately the majority of employers are unable to tell their workers what skills will be needed in the future. Therefore, a paradigm of lifelong education and training must replace short-term consideration of an education completed at the end of college. As Justice Oliver

Wendell Holmes once said, "Your education begins when what is called your education is over."

BENEFITS OF A CAREER DEVELOPMENT PROGRAM

Development programs for employees benefit the employees by making them more eligible for promotion, increasing their self-esteem, and injecting more interest into their jobs. Such programs keep employees abreast of fast-changing skills needs so they can maintain their employability and marketability.

Employers benefit from staff development by having a more talented and flexible workforce. To remain competitive, organizations must help their employees adapt to today's rapid cycle of change. Career development enhances morale and motivation and increases personnel retention, productivity, and service quality. Recruitment is stimulated when candidates learn about the educational advantages offered by the institution.

Some executives express concern over the loss of talented employees who leave for better jobs. This disadvantage, however, is balanced by the enhanced expertise of those who do not leave. There is also the goodwill of the people who have resigned; this often benefits the organization indirectly.

As employees become more highly qualified, supervisors can delegate more to them and therefore have more time to spend on other high-priority responsibilities. They also have the pride and satisfaction that all coaches and teachers derive from watching their charges mature.

THE PLANNING PROCESS

Educational planning is most effective when it is tailored to fit individual needs. Some health care workers seek promotions to managerial positions; others eschew supervisory responsibilities, preferring to climb a professional ladder if it is available. All employees want some growth within their current positions. It adds spice to work and prevents boredom.

Some of you will be reviewing the position descriptions of your employees to ensure compliance with various laws (for example, the Americans with Disabilities Act). This is a good time to consider revisions that will establish the criteria necessary for employee advancement. Such revisions usually address titles, responsibilities, and the amount of supervision that the incumbents require.

When interviewing job candidates, offer a brief explanation of your career development program. This can be a strong incentive for the more ambitious candidates.

Discuss goal changes or modifications at performance review meetings. Action plans for helping the employee work toward these goals should be a major agenda item at these meetings. Affirm your confidence in the ability of the employee to achieve these goals. Employees are motivated more strongly when their desire to move up in the organization is accompanied by an expectation of success.

WHO IS ACCOUNTABLE FOR CAREER DEVELOPMENT?

Top management is accountable for the educational facilities, staff, and resources. Supervisors are partly responsible for developing and implementing the programs for their own units. They share this responsibility with the staff education departments or human resources departments of their institutions.

In the long run, career development is primarily self-development. Many health care professionals complain about not being trained for supervisory jobs before they assume those roles. Most of these people knew for a long time that this opportunity would be available. They often had years to get the necessary training but failed to do so, perhaps assuming that management was responsible for this. This is a hangover from our public education system, in which the programs and schedules are prepared for the students, who quickly learn that if they pass a few tests they will be promoted—and sometimes advanced without even passing the tests.

After accepting supervisory roles, some professionals continue to focus their educational efforts on the clinical aspects of their jobs. They often limit their managerial training to the mandatory programs provided by their organization.

In organizations in which promotions have stalled, supervisors can encourage employees to consider lateral moves or take advantage of cross-training opportunities. These moves have motivational value and increase the marketability of employees.

NEEDS ASSESSMENT

Any training program worthy of the name should be preceded by a needs assessment. This assessment should consider the following:

- The expertise needed by the department, now and in the future. This involves obtaining product- or service-forecasting information from top management. Skills-inventory charts list the employees who are qualified to handle each major job component. These charts are invaluable for planning skills enhancement, cross-training, and workstation rotation.
- What is needed by individual employees to meet or exceed the requirements of their jobs or to be ready to assume greater responsibilities?
- What is needed to bring old-timers up to date? Job obsolescence occurs at an ever-increasing rate, and because women play a major role in health care institutions, many positions are filled by employees who have interrupted their careers to start or raise families.

- What is needed to energize stalled or marginal workers whose interest in work needs rekindling?
- What is needed to make you dispensable? The highest order career development program is succession planning. Supervisors who make themselves dispensable by training capable successors are more eligible for, and worthy of, promotion.
- How does the knowledge of the employees compare with the skills demanded in their field?

Bartsch offers the following tips for determining training needs.

- Ask your human resources department to give you a list of performance deficiencies that are frequently documented in performance appraisal reports.
- Review your department's performance appraisals, looking for specific problems or training needs.
- Observe the behavior of people at work, especially their interactions with customers and coworkers.
- Study patient and employee satisfaction surveys.
- Keep abreast of legal and legislative issues that could lead to performance problems (for example, the Americans with Disabilities Act).
- Review your organization's mission statement and values to find out what kinds of training can contribute to realization of long-term goals.[1]

To assist you in deciding how well your current training program meets basic needs, answer the questions in Exhibit 30–1.

Exhibit 30–1 Questions Related to Skills Enhancement of Your Staff

1. Do you have an in-house educational program for each staff member? Does it include a minimum number of hours of participation or some results evaluation method? Are records kept? Are you satisfied with the results?
2. Are training materials (books, journals, tapes, and other teaching tools) easily available? Do you know how frequently these are used? Are they frequently updated?
3. Is there an ongoing professional and/or management training program readily available?
4. Do your employees have the time to make use of the training materials? To attend lectures, demonstrations, and other educational sessions?
5. Is there financial support for continuing education? Are schedules flexible enough to permit employees to attend programs at educational institutions?
6. Do your employees get intellectual stimulation through problem-solving sessions?

continues

Exhibit 30–1 Continued

---

7. Do your employees have the opportunity to cross-train? To rotate workstations? To assume greater responsibilities? To serve on committees, quality circles, task forces, and other work groups?

8. Do you delegate tasks that provide valued educational experiences for your employees? Do they assume greater responsibilities? Do you empower them sufficiently to carry out these responsibilities?

9. Are educational subjects presented at routine staff meetings?

10. Are there real opportunities for promotion? Do you have dual career tracks? Can your employees be promoted within their current grades?

11. Does each employee have an individualized career growth plan that is jointly formulated?

12. When employees plan to attend outside seminars or workshops, do you jointly establish practical goals for that experience? Are these discussed when the employee returns? Do you provide opportunities to put those new skills to work?

THE DEVELOPMENT PROGRAM

The major goal of any program is self-reliance. Employees are introduced to a lifelong process dedicated to learning and development. Trainers make available a variety of self-assessment instruments such as the Myers-Briggs Type Indicator.

With the guidance of career counselors, employees use benchmarking techniques with which they learn how to identify the best and the brightest in their organization and field and how to determine what makes them successful. They then compare their preferences and skills with those of the top performers. The skills gaps are used to identify development goals when the employees put together action plans for continuous learning. Other available modalities include

- orientation and on-the-job training of new employees,
- in-service education, including the use of guest speakers and consultants,
- workshops and seminars,
- formal programs at educational institutions,
- job rotation and cross-training,
- self-education,
- books, journals, computers, audiotapes, and videotapes,
- participation in any educational endeavor,
- special assignments,
- committees and other special work groups,
- assignments as trainers, instructors, or lecturers,

- duties as coordinators or facilitators (for example, quality assurance, safety, or data processing),
- "horizontal promotions,"
- temporary assignments at satellite facilities or elsewhere, and
- substituting for absent employees.

Practical Career-Building Tips

- Work on easier skills first to ensure early success.
- Ask others to help.
- Maintain a high ratio of praise to criticism.
- Correct errors before they become habits.
- Be patient. Expect plateaus in progress.
- Serve as coach, facilitator, advisor, and cheerleader, not taskmaster.
- Use adult training methods. Employees are not schoolchildren.
- Encourage mentorship.

MENTORING

In mentoring, an experienced or influential person guides and nurtures individuals or small groups of employees. Mentors teach protégés how to survive, thrive, and progress within an organization or a profession to attain their full potential.

Mentoring may begin shortly after a new employee comes on board. During orientation, new hires have an excellent opportunity to spot a manager or senior team member they would like to have as a mentor.

Corporate Mentoring

Some organizations provide formal mentoring programs. They assign mentors to new employees and provide training to mentors and protégés. In the past employers crafted special programs for women and minorities as part of affirmative action. However, today this practice may expose employers to charges of reverse discrimination, so for the present most programs are made available to all employees.

Mentor

A mentor can be someone on the same team, in another department, a retiree, or an outsider. He or she may be a senior manager or an expert in the same field. An employee's immediate supervisor is not the ideal choice because protégés will be more reluctant to ask questions for fear of appearing ignorant or irritating the supervisor.

A *counselor* mentor

- helps protégés make career decisions,
- introduces them to the intricacies of political savvy,
- enhances their sensitivity to organizational culture, and
- helps them enlarge their personal network.

A *coach* mentor is an experienced professional or technical expert who shares knowledge and skills that help protégés fine-tune their expertise.

Mentors teach their protégés how to be successful in a particular organization or profession. They suggest ways to (1) cut bureaucratic red tape and (2) avoid troublesome people, policies, or practices. They point out cultural sand traps, rituals that must be followed, who has the clout, and how decisions are made. They highlight pitfalls such as leaving work before the chief does.

Mentors share visions of the futures of their protégés, perceive their potential, and challenge them when they are not living up to this potential. They detect real and potential hindrances and recommend ways to eliminate or reduce these.

Mentors take an active interest in the continuing education of the employees. They recommend literature and seminars or workshops. They are readily available for questions and are open, authentic, and receptive. They provide appropriate affirmation and offer opinions in a way that promotes feelings of self-worth and competence.

Mentors help individuals enhance their careers by removing obstacles, teaching team skills, advising on career development strategy, and serving as role models. In brief, they may teach, sponsor, advise, coach, counsel, guide, motivate, or critique.

Great mentors are empathetic and inquisitive. They listen more than they talk and avoid excessive direct advice. They avoid remarks such as "Let me give you a piece of advice" or "You ought to…" Instead, they relate their experience (for example, "What I've found helpful in that situation is…").

Mentor–Protégé Relationships

Protégés must respect their mentors and must not disclose confidential information. A little deference is appropriate. Most mentor–protégé affiliations are similar to doctor–patient or attorney–client relationships. Protégés must have a sincere desire to assimilate information and reconceptualize ideas. They should keep their mentors informed of their progress but not make pests of themselves. Associations may end quickly or gradually. Some change into collegial relationships or social friendships.

Recent Developments in Mentoring

With managed care programs and various organizational changes, mentoring programs are showing up with innovative twists. One of these is reciprocal mentorship, in which peers exchange expertise. For example, a laboratory supervisor who has a master's in business administration but lacks laboratory experience may help a lead technologist prepare for a supervisory role. The technologist, in turn, helps the manager understand the intricacies of laboratory procedures.

Another form is team or big-brother mentorship. Here, senior team members offer assistance to struggling junior colleagues.

Group mentorship, where a mentor serves a group of protégés, can save time and elicit broader discussions. The protégés develop the agenda, and the mentor responds to their needs.

Think About It

Education is lifelong, and the person who becomes educated is the person who knows how to find out what he or she wants to learn and how to go on learning it throughout a lifetime. In other words, this is the person who has mastered certain methods of dealing with subject matter; this is the person who has learned how to proceed, who has, in effect, learned how to learn.

Questions for Review and Discussion

1. Why is it stated that career development must largely be self-development?
2. Why would any department supervisor deliberately wish to make himself or herself "dispensable" through self-development?
3. What is meant by the quotation, "Your education begins when what is called your education is over?"
4. What is a significant advantage of a career development program other than the obvious one of stimulating the development of present employees?
5. What are the primary advantages of a one-on-one mentoring relationship? Potential disadvantages, if any?
6. Why is significant emphasis placed on career development? Wouldn't it be more sensible to advise each employee to carefully select a job or occupation or employer and stick with it?

Exercise: Your Career Development Plan

This is an especially personal exercise in that it asks you to plot out a likely career path for the remainder of your working years, subject to the following guidelines:

- Begin with your present working (or student) status, briefly described, stating why you are where you are.
- State where you intend to go next, and where after that, and after that, etc., as necessary.
- For each move you propose to make, indicate what you need to do to make that move (for example, how much education of what kind, experience of what kind, etc.).

- Provide estimates of how much time each step may require (something of a variation on Where would you like to be in five years? Ten years?).

Finally, for each major milestone in your career plan, indicate what you would plan on doing—that is, how your overall plan might change—should any of your critical career milestones prove impossible to attain.

REFERENCE

1. Bartsch, M. 1996. Go beyond surveys to assess needs. *Training* 33(5): 15.

Chapter 31

Delegation and Empowerment

*Make sure the jobs you give your people
are whole and important and that you really give
them the jobs. Ask them not to report unless
they're in trouble. Grit your teeth and
don't ask them how it's going.[1]*

—Robert Townsend

CHAPTER OBJECTIVES

- Delineate the differences between delegating and simply assigning.
- Review the principal reasons why some supervisors are reluctant to delegate.
- Differentiate between proper delegation and "dumping."
- Present an approach to delegation that includes consideration of what to delegate, to whom to delegate, and how to properly implement delegation and monitor progress.
- Briefly introduce the concepts of horizontal delegation, reverse delegation, and hopscotch delegation.
- Address the numerous similarities and parallels between proper delegation and the practice of empowerment as it is understood in today's organizations.

ASSIGNING VS DELEGATING

Assigning is telling a person what to do, how to do it, and when the task must be completed. The tasks are usually of a nonsupervisory nature and for the most part are found in the position descriptions for particular jobs. There may or may not be an assignment of authority. Delegation, on the other hand, is the transfer of authority, responsibility, and accountability. The tasks are activities that the delegator was previously doing or had expected to do should they arise. Delegation is usually negotiable or optional and requires a commitment by the delegate; concerning assignment, the employee need only do what he or she is told to do, usually without question.

WHY SOME SUPERVISORS ARE RELUCTANT TO DELEGATE

There are a number of reasons why some supervisors are loath to delegate.

- They are workaholics or perfectionists.
- They are insecure because they are afraid that (1) the individual will fail, (2) the employee will do it better than the supervisor could do it, or (3) they will be accused of dumping.
- They do not like to turn over tasks they enjoy doing.
- They do not believe their employees are ready or willing.
- They have had unpleasant experiences with delegation.
- They do not know how to delegate properly and effectively.

Supervisors who are reluctant to delegate make statements such as

- "I don't have the time."
- "The last time I tried that it didn't work."
- "If you want things done right, you've got to do them yourself."
- "Why delegate it? I can do it faster and better."
- "When I try to delegate, the employees say that it's not in their position descriptions, or they ask what's in it for them."

WILLINGNESS OF EMPLOYEES TO ACCEPT
DELEGATED ACTIVITIES

The willingness of employees to accept delegated tasks is usually determined by whether or not

- they believe themselves to be qualified,
- their previous efforts have succeeded,
- they are concerned about what their teammates may say or think,
- they believe they have sufficient time available,
- they like the delegated activity or see some reward in it,
- they believe they will have enough authority to get the job done,
- they believe the delegator will support them, and
- they believe they are being manipulated or dumped on.

DUMPING

Delegation is a double-edged sword. It can be the key to increased productivity, better time management, and improved motivation, or it can be a wet blanket that squelches initiative and reduces morale. The latter outcome is usually because the supervisor has been "dumping" rather than delegating.

Dumping occurs when employees are loaded with repetitive, mundane work that has little value to the organization or to their careers.[2] Because dumping is often done on the spur of the moment, the recipient feels like an errand runner, the proverbial "gofer."

The most common responses to dumping are resentment and anger. The perception of being dumped on is just that: a perception. One person's meat is another person's poison. Delegation is more likely to be perceived as dumping when the involved employees

- have poor working relationships with their superiors,
- have been dumped on in the past,
- know that others have resisted undertaking the same task,
- fail to see any personal advantage in carrying out the assignment,
- have not been told that occasionally they will be asked to do things that are not in their position descriptions, or
- see the delegator wasting time while they do all the work.

If you have good rapport with a subordinate and rarely take advantage of your authority, the subordinate will not mind some of the less pleasant or less challenging assignments.

When you assign a task to an employee, and another employee asks, "How come you never ask me to do that?" what you have accomplished is most likely delegation. When an employee says "How come you always stick me with this?" you are most likely dumping.

HOW TO DELEGATE

Four Simple Ways To Pick What To Delegate

1. As you go about your daily routine, just before you tackle a task, ask yourself whether this is something that someone else in your group could do.
2. When you return from a vacation, list your duties that subordinates took care of while you were away. Some of these temporary assignments could become permanent.

3. At performance reviews, when you discuss future career plans for your associates, ask them whether they would like to take over any of your responsibilities.
4. Select tasks from those listed in your position description (see text that follows).

Delegating Using Your Position Description

1. List 10 or more of your tasks, excluding any that cannot or should not be delegated (see list that follows).
2. Select those that someone could assume now and those that a member of your group could learn to do.
3. Prioritize each task according to how much time you would save by delegating the task, how significantly it would benefit or be acceptable to the delegate, and the degree of difficulty. (Usually, you should start with simple tasks, ones that relate directly to the delegate's current assignments or ones that are discrete segments of a complex task.)

What May Not Be Delegated

- *Accountability.* Delegators remain accountable to higher authorities for delegated work; you can delegate the task but you remain accountable for the results.
- *Powers other than task performance authority.* Only formal power, or authority, can be delegated (see Exhibit 31–1 for distinctions among kinds of power).

Exhibit 31–1 Kinds of Power

Authority: Delegated power. "You all report to me because the organization chart says so."

Competency: The power of expertise. "See Louise, she's the only one who really knows this stuff."

Knowledge: The power of information. "Ask Joe, he's on the committee and he has all the figures."

Physical: The power of brute force. "If you want to stay healthy, you'll do as you're told."

Connections: The power of who they know. "His mother is on the board."

Fiscal: The power of who has the bucks. "He who gets grant money gets promoted."

Union: Power conferred by one's peers. "Nora will get action; she's the union rep."

Charisma: Persuasiveness. "He can talk you into anything."

- *Activities forbidden by law, regulation, or policy* (licensure, certification, special training, qualification, or education is required for some duties).

What Should Be Delegated Only Partially and Always with Caution

- Sensitive or high-leverage activities dealing with people:
  1. interviewing, selecting, and orienting new employees (a delegate's best role here is that of making recommendations)
  2. approving new hires (again, it's best for the delegate to be limited to making recommendations to the supervisor)
  3. coaching and counseling (a constructive use of senior employees who can also serve as mentors)
  4. disciplining, evaluating employee performance, and resolving personal conflicts, complaints, or grievances (again largely a recommending role)
- Activities that involve too great a career risk for the supervisor or the delegate
- Activities perceived by the delegate as dumping
- Special administrative responsibilities of the supervisor, such as
  1. formulation of mission statements, goals, objectives, strategies, and plans;
  2. making, publicizing, explaining, and enforcing policies;
  3. presiding over important meetings; and
  4. preparing or approving budgets and reviewing fiscal variances.
- Tasks assigned by your superiors to be done by you personally.
- Some functions that you find very pleasurable.

Select the Delegates and Get Their Acceptance

Select delegates who have the necessary competence and display the willingness to take on the task. The most qualified person for a particular activity may not be the one who will benefit from it most. A less experienced employee may try harder and do a better job in the long run.

Seek cooperation. Avoid petulant or grudging compliance. Consciously or unconsciously, delegates ask you or themselves, "What's in this for me?" If their perception is negative, the delegation is in trouble. Be wary if you hear:

- "Is that an order?"
- "Do I have to?"
- "That's not in my position description."
- "Nobody told me I have to do all that."

People are more willing to take risks if they know for certain what is involved. Perhaps in the past someone took a small step, and Pandora's box opened. Tell them exactly what they are getting into, and give them possible outs. Start by telling them

- why you decided on the change,
- why you picked them,
- whether or not they have a choice,
- what you expect,
- what resources and authority are available to them,
- what you are going to tell other members of the group if they are affected,
- what, if any, modifications there will be in their current assignments, and
- the checkpoints and, when appropriate, a target date or timetable.

When employees object because they do not have the time, agree to share some of the work or apportion some among others. At other times you can relieve them of other responsibilities. Usually you can promise them that the delegation is reversible (for example, you will relieve them of the responsibility with no loss of their prestige). This is seldom necessary if you picked the right task, selected the right person, and prepared the delegate sufficiently.

How to Implement the Delegated Action

- Select the right task and the right delegate.
- If it represents a major change, get permission from your superiors.
- If you are operating in a team mode, discuss the change with your team.
- Provide essential training, resources, and authority.
- Agree on an action plan. Listen carefully to delegates' ideas about how to get it done.
- Set up checkpoints. Checkpoints enable you to monitor progress and to give some pats on the back.

Monitor Progress

Be patient and persuasive, not demanding. Avoid statements such as "Don't worry," "You should have…," or "I wish you had…" Help delegates when they get stuck.

Periodically stop by and ask how things are going. Avoid constantly looking over their shoulders or asking too many questions. Questions should reflect your interest in their approach rather than exhibit nervousness you may have about their ability to finish the job.

WHEN DELEGATION FALTERS

Avoid the temptation to abandon ship when there are problems. Allowing people to make some mistakes is the best way to encourage meaningful growth. Although a delegator accepts responsibility for a failure, confidence in the delegate is not readily restored. When employees have done their best but failed, have them prepare a balance sheet in which they identify what went well and what did not. Always let them criticize themselves first. Ask how you could have helped more, because when your delegate fails, you too have failed.

DELEGATION VARIATIONS

Horizontal Delegation

Truly skilled delegators can delegate to people over whom they have no authority. These individuals may be colleagues or volunteers. Horizontal delegation increases in importance as health care institutions feature more cross-functional activities and make greater use of volunteers. Success depends largely on factors such as

- persuasiveness,
- influence,
- interpersonal skills,
- rapport,
- degree of teamwork,
- past favors done for the other person,
- the strength of one's network, and
- rewards and recognition for past cooperation.

Reverse (Upward) Delegation

Upward delegation is the art of passing along to superiors what employees do not want to do. Employees are often successful in this because their bosses just cannot say no. Managers who seldom delegate are especially susceptible to upward delegation. Drucker and Flower write: "Every subordinate is good at delegating upstairs. It's hard to resist because it's very flattering. You must learn to say 'no.' "[3]

Reverse delegation often follows attempts by a manager to delegate. The delegate reluctantly accepts a task. At the first obstacle he throws up his hands and tries to pass the buck back to the manager. The manager thus becomes the reluctant delegate.

Sometimes upward delegation is necessary. For example, a supervisor may delegate so much work to an assistant that the assistant cannot complete his or her routine work. It is then up to the delegator to consider various options: take back some work, establish new priorities, or transfer some tasks to another employee.

Hopscotch Delegation

When your manager bypasses you and gives assignments directly to your subordinates, that is hopscotch delegation. To correct this, it helps to have good rapport with your superior. If you confront your superior when he or she is in a belligerent mood, you may get a response such as "Well, you're never around when something has to be done." If this shunting of authority rarely happens, it is probably best to ignore it. However, if you feel that a confrontation is necessary, take a positive approach by playing down the issue of authority. As you negotiate with your manager, focus on the advantages of your knowing what he or she wants done or of how your people get confused when they get conflicting orders from different managers.

If you cannot get action through your boss or if you want to avoid a confrontation, try acting through your staff. Instruct them to hold up action on nonurgent orders from other people until they have checked with you. Another tactic is to have your associates ask your boss in a polite way to please make the request directly to you because they are working on a priority item of yours.

If it continues unchecked, hopscotch delegation can be deadly. Every time your superior bypasses you and goes directly to your employees, your boss is violating the chain of command and is thereby undermining your supervisory authority.

EMPOWERMENT

Empowerment is one of the "in" terms to arise in management over the recent couple of decades, prominent in the terminology of the total quality management (TQM) movement. Yet as often as it is used, there remains some confusion as to its real meaning and what it actually appears as in practice. In fact, in any good dictionary or thesaurus, "empowerment" and "delegation" are offered as synonyms for each other. However, it seems that in practice empowerment has taken on the connotation of an activity that is somehow more appropriate and more complete than delegation.

Empowerment is a frequently misunderstood word. It decidedly does not mean that employees may do as they please without orders, monitoring, or control. In practice, empowerment means providing an environment and affording opportunities for employees to enhance their competencies and accept more responsibility. Call it, if you will, total delegation.

External empowerment is giving people the authority to do what they are capable of handling. It encourages people to make judgments, form conclusions, reach decisions, and then act. It liberates workers from rigid oversight and direction.

Internal empowerment or self-empowerment is what individuals generate intrinsically, like they generate enthusiasm or optimism. It reflects competence, experience, assertiveness, character, personality, and charisma.

Benefits of Empowerment

Empowerment enhances feelings of self-efficacy, a state of mind that causes people to believe they can cope effectively with situations and people. Empowerment reduces or eliminates feelings of helplessness. The more that people feel they are in control of their work and their lives, the greater their enthusiasm, optimism, self-confidence, and energy.

With empowered staffs, leaders can mobilize stronger forces when responding to crises and with less risk of chaos. The leaders can also set higher performance goals and standards.

Excellent health care service requires empowered care providers, especially when they interact directly with customers. Patients and other customers want providers who respond with confident empathy, not with calloused indifference, apathy, or plastic smiles.

Empiric Empowering Actions

Employees must know more than how to perform their daily tasks if they are to maximize their contributions. They feel more empowered when they learn about organizational financial matters and their role in providing excellent services.

Ten Steps That Empower

1. Know what each of your employees does and how well the tasks are done. Review position descriptions, performance standards, and previous performance appraisal reports.
2. Decide what additional authority they can handle right now. In their performance reports, look for notes regarding competencies, experience, and training needs.
3. Ascertain what preparation each of your employees needs to achieve the competencies and mental toughness that will empower them. Such preparation may involve training, coaching, psychological support, and incremental delegation.
4. Conceptualize a new supervisory role that reduces micromanaging and matches the level of supervision with the ability, maturity, and motivation of each employee.
5. Ensure that workers know the purpose (mission) of their jobs. Is this stated in their position descriptions and stressed during their orientation? If necessary, clarify each job and your expectations of what outcomes should be.
6. Delegate activities that involve decision making and problem solving.
7. Review your education and training program. Empowered organizations are learning institutions. Design a cross-training and job rotation program so that people become more flexible and more aware of customer problems and their solutions.

8. Make tasks more challenging. Assign complete rather than fragmented tasks. Assign progressively more difficult tasks, starting with ones that ensure success, an essential aspect of situational leadership.
9. Provide sufficient resources, time, and psychological support.
10. Emphasize commitment rather than conformity.

Potential Problems with Empowerment

We previously noted that delegation involves risk. With pervasive empowerment, this risk is even greater. It is also greater than forming autonomous teams because you do not have teammates exerting a tempering effect on other members.

Some empowered employees do silly things; a few abuse their new authority. When employees are ill-prepared, or when they think you have not adequately rewarded them, they may rebel actively or passively.

Many workers are uncomfortable with more power, especially if they are passive or have victim mindsets. They prefer conformity and safety to entrepreneurship and risk. An often-heard comment from these folks is "I just want to do my work and go home."

Employees may lack confidence in their leaders. Those who have been jerked around during a series of failed management initiatives are not likely to join in the celebration of still another program-du-jour. Instead, they hunker down and wait for it to pass as most of the previous ones have.

Some managers simply do not want to share power. They feel they worked hard to earn the power they have and are reluctant to give up any of it.

Think About It

Failure to delegate regularly, honestly, and properly is a major cause of supervisory failure, and if not failure, then it is often the reason why a supervisor may go no higher in the organization. The supervisor who fails at delegation is doing considerable self-damage by limiting his or her chances for growth and is hurting employees by denying them the opportunity to learn and grow. Some employees thus stifled will seek their futures elsewhere, and it is always the ones you should want most to keep who are the first to leave.

Questions for Review and Discussion

1. What do you believe would be the result if your boss consistently practiced hopscotch delegation?
2. What do you consider to be the best way to get a dull, repetitive task accomplished? Why?

3. When is it appropriate for the supervisor to go ahead and do a given task himself or herself rather than delegate it?

4. Why is it said that accountability or ultimate responsibility cannot be delegated?

5. One reason often given for the failure of a supervisor to delegate is fear of competition from subordinates. Instead of fearing competition, why should the supervisor welcome it?

6. What will be your principal response to the employee who says to you, "I don't have to do this—it's not in my job description"?

7. If delegation and empowerment are synonymous in so many contexts, why do they seem to be differentiated so often today?

8. Why is it important for employees who are given a delegated task to know what is in it for them?

9. What does the supervisor need to be most careful of in following up on delegation? Why?

10. What is over-delegation, and what is its principal hazard? Explain.

Case: "Why Should I Do His Job As Well As Mine?"

As unit supervisor in one of the hospital's service functions you have recently concluded that your workload has been increasing to the point where you need help with certain nonsupervisory duties. One of the first tasks that comes to mind for delegation is a statistical report you are required to submit on the third workday following the end of each month. Creating the report itself is a fairly easy task, but gathering the data is time consuming.

You select an employee to whom to assign the report, and you provide the essentials of the report's preparation in brief form. You pick an employee you believe capable of doing a decent job and who seems to have sufficient time available, and with no discussion beyond the basics of "here's what I want you to do," you make the assignment. The chosen person says nothing to you about the new assignment.

A few days after assigning the task you discover that data collection for the report has not yet been started. You remind the employee, which gets you a simple nod of acknowledgment and no comment. Shortly thereafter you overhear part of a conversation in which the employee who is supposedly doing the report say to another employee, " — the boss's lousy statistics. They're not mine, so why should I do it? Whose job is it, anyway?"

Questions:

1. What, if anything, do you suppose was done improperly or incorrectly in delegating the report to the chosen employee?

2. If this same employee behaves in this manner during a second attempt to delegate something to him, how will this affect your future dealings with him?

3. What would you do to try to instill in this employee a feeling of ownership of the statistical report?

Case: Some Delegated Research

You are manager of biomedical engineering at Central Hospital. You are discussing an information need with your superior, general services vice president Peter Gideon. You both agree that your equipment maintenance and repair records are not revealing the kind of information they need to reveal—the nature of breakdowns and failures, maintenance problems, and unique situations encountered—to design an effective preventive maintenance program.

Gideon asks, "Since we started the department year before last, haven't we kept records of all the work done by you and the technicians?"

You respond, "Sure we have, but they won't tell us anything useful without lots of digging. We have nearly 24 months' worth of completed work orders filed in chronological order."

"Could someone sort through the work orders and separate them by kind of work required?"

"I suppose so," you reply, "but I don't have time to do it myself, and both techs are swamped with open work orders. I guess I could always get my secretary, Sharon, to do it. Just tell her what I want and let her go about collecting it in her own way."

Gideon asks, "Does Sharon know the language? All of the work order codes? You might want to provide her with some detailed instructions and maybe even give her a deadline for completion or a schedule for finishing various steps of the project."

You answer, "I don't see much point in delegating the job if I'm going to have to do all that work just to get ready. It ought to be enough for me to give her my objectives, suggest an approach, let her add her own ideas to it, and turn her loose."

"Could this become a regular part of her job?"

"It should," you state. "Hers or somebody's. Then we could monitor the kinds of information we need rather than having to dig for it like we do now."

Gideon states, "Between us we seem to have tossed out three ways of using Sharon on this project." He proceeded to outline the three possibilities as (1) tell her what's wanted and let her do it in her own way; (2) provide her with expected results, a procedure or other instructions, and a schedule or deadline; and tell her what's wanted, recommend an approach, and turn her loose.

Questions:

1. Assuming Sharon is qualified for the project, what should determine whether you do indeed assign the task to her rather than doing it yourself or looking for another way?
2. Identify the advantages and disadvantages of the three possibilities outlined above.
3. Which of the three approaches should you most seriously consider following? Why?

REFERENCES

1. Townsend, R. 1984. *Further up the organization.* New York: Alfred A. Knopf, 55.
2. Werther Jr., W.B. 1989. *Dear Boss.* New York: Meadowbrook, 162.
3. Drucker, P., and Flower, J. 1991. Being effective. *Health Care Forum Journal* 34: 52.

RECOMMENDED RESOURCES

W.C. Byham, *Zapp! The Lightning of Empowerment.* (New York: Harmony Books, 1988).
S.R. Lloyd and T. Berthelot, *Empowerment: A Practical Guide for Success.* (Menlo Park, CA: 1992).
D. Lohr, *How To Delegate Work.* (Boulder, CO: CareerTrack Publishers, 1987). Two audiotapes.
W. Umiker, *The Empowered Laboratory Team.* (Chicago, IL: ASCP Press, 1996).

PART V

Special Supervisory Skills

Chapter 32

Spoken Communication

For good or ill, your conversation is your advertisement. For every time you open your mouth, you let people look into your mind. Do they see it well-clothed, businesslike?

—Bruce Barton

The most difficult obstacle the new technical supervisor needs to surmount is the immediate acquisition of communication skills.[1]

CHAPTER OBJECTIVES

- Introduce the supervisor to the informal communication system of the organization.
- Identify the common barriers to effective spoken communication.
- Emphasize the importance of listening skills and suggest how the supervisor can become a better listener.
- Review the uses of the telephone and its adjuncts—voice mail, answering systems, etc.—and recommend effective means of using the telephone.

As technical experts, supervisors provide scientific information and technical advice, usually by way of speech. As leaders, supervisors use communication skills to discharge their management responsibilities. Communication is by far the most important managerial skill. Without it, all other skills are inoperative. The importance of oral communication in daily work becomes painfully apparent when one experiences acute laryngitis.

Communication systems form the cornerstone of cultural shaping and participative management. To improve quality, customer service, and productivity, we must take a close look at these systems and how we make use of them.

The majority of employees feel that bosses hold back things that employees should hear. Subordinates may withhold important information from their superiors if they dislike or mistrust them or if they fear that the information will adversely affect their relationship.

Effective information sharing must be

- multidirectional, moving up, down, laterally, and diagonally with equal facility;
- objective, factual, and true;
- comprehensive but not excessive;
- credible; and
- timely.

THE INFORMAL COMMUNICATION SYSTEM

There are serious limitations to formal communication systems. These systems depend largely on written messages, formal meetings, and orders or instructions issued orally by higher management. Supervisors who depend entirely on formal sources are soon out of touch with what is going on in the organization. Watered-down newsletters or notices on bulletin boards are not enough. Electronic bulletin boards, voice mail, and one-on-one contact are more effective.[2]

Every organization has a grapevine, and when managers tune in to the grapevine they come to realize that the information they receive via formal systems is often late or incomplete. A common managerial problem is relying too much on the computer. Not all important information gets into the computer, and not everyone knows how to extract all the information that is there.

The informal communication network, or grapevine, flourishes when information is scarce or delayed or when organizational changes take place. The grapevine is rapid, up to date, and pervasive and distributes information quickly. Network senders translate complex directives into understandable language. Like other communicators, the senders add their personal spins to these messages. Managers who tap into the informal communication systems learn what is bothering their employees and how their leadership is perceived by the workers.

On the negative side, much of what is transmitted via the grapevine is rumor and gossip. Rumor mills are subject to distortions and omissions. Many reputations and careers have suffered as the result of misuse of this channel. The grapevine is a major time waster and often sends shock waves through organizations that turn out to be unsubstantiated.

Supervisors must know who the grapevine's principal receivers are and keep tuned into them. Secretaries of VIPs, for example, are excellent sources of current information.

When you hear distorted or false news, put out corrections promptly via both formal and informal channels. This aborts rumors and discredits the rumormongers. Set aside part of each staff meeting to verify, discredit, or clarify rumors.

Use the grapevine to counter misinformation and to distribute good news. You can make pronouncements that are not appropriate for newsletters or memos. You can also test the waters for reactions to controversial projects.

SENDING MORE POWERFUL MESSAGES

> *How well we communicate is determined not by how*
> *well we say things but how well we are understood.*[3]

Effective care providers command respect by displaying self-confidence and poise. Their unspoken message to customers and subordinates is "I can help you because I know what's going on and can make things happen."

This unspoken message is transmitted through words, vocal tone, facial expressions, and body language. Mehrabian, in his studies at the University of California, Los Angeles, found that words convey only 7% of the feeling in spoken messages.[4] Thirty-eight percent comes from voice characteristics and 55% from facial expressions and body language. Every message consists of two parts, the content and the emotional component. When the words do not jibe with the emotional message, the words lose their power. Picture a distraught supervisor yelling at a subordinate with "I'm in control here." The subordinate inwardly grins, knowing that the supervisor has lost control and thus the encounter.

Avoid the assumption that your message has been received and understood. Do not rely on a positive response to your "Do you hear me?" or "Do you understand what I said?" Do not think that because no one asks a question that everyone knows what you said. Although you cannot give a quiz after each communication, you can ask people to paraphrase important things you say or ask for comments on specific points. Watch their body language as they respond. The knitted brow or the blank stare speaks louder than the words.

Practical Tips for Better Messages

- Speak with conviction. Remember the power of voice quality and body language.
- Substitute strong responses for weak ones. Instead of "I wonder if you would send..." say "Please send me..."
- Call a difference between people a misunderstanding rather than a disagreement.
- Say what you can do, not what you cannot do.
- Shake hands with enthusiasm and smile.

- Be assertive. Maintain your right to be recognized and to state what you think.
- Use people's names often and pronounce them correctly. People feel validated when we do that. It says "You're important to me." Insist that your receptionist and telephone answerers use each caller's name at least once.

BARRIERS TO VERBAL COMMUNICATION

Electronic Barriers

Now that we have had them for a while, we could not possibly get along without our computers, electronic mail, faxes, answering machines, and such. However, these can all adversely affect relationships with customers and collegiality with colleagues. Because managers can get masses of data instantly, they often feel that they have a complete handle on things. Unfortunately, not all significant information gets into the computer. Still more gets buried in trivia.

Semantic Barriers

Every day we speak in at least five languages.

1. English
2. Body language
3. Professional and technical jargon
4. Organizational and bureaucratic talk
5. "Computerese"

We often fail to consider the educational, cultural, and mental status of each of our customers and employees. A nurse who uses the same phraseology when conversing with a mentally challenged patient as she does when she talks to a physician confuses the patient or angers the doctor. Garbled messages, jargon, acronyms, and computer language may befuddle even our fellow professionals. Mixed messages, those occurring when words do not match body language, confuse everyone.

The graduates of inferior schools usually need help in basic communication. We must encourage them to eliminate slang, street talk, and fillers like "ya know," "right on," and "ya gotta be kidding."

Psychological Barriers

The psychological barriers are the most pernicious barriers. They include

- interrupting, arguing, blaming, talking down to, kidding, or being sarcastic;
- offering inflammatory utterances, e.g., name calling or threatening;

- using patronizing words or sexist terms such as "you girls";
- making statements indicative of indifference or apathy:
  1. "You have to realize that we're understaffed"
  2. "I don't know" (without offering to find out or refer)
  3. "We can't do that"
  4. "You'll have to…"
  5. "That's not my responsibility"
  6. "That's not our policy"
  7. "It must be a computer error"

LISTENING SKILLS

The majority of people are terrible listeners. Our spouses and children usually will affirm this. If your training program accomplishes nothing more than improving the listening skills of your staff, it will have been well worthwhile.

Body Language

Listening is visual as well as auditory. Make certain that your facial expressions, posture, and movements match your words. You can learn much about a person's thoughts by observing behavior.

Signs of attentiveness or interest include rubbing the chin, rolling the eyes upward and to the right or left, maintaining eye contact, leaning forward, and smiling.

Signs of disinterest or disagreement include touching or rubbing the nose, rolling the eyes straight up, leaning backward, tugging on the ear, folding the arms across the chest, frowning, shaking the head, drumming the fingers, avoiding eye contact, or rearranging papers.

Concealment or deception can be discerned when someone puts the hand partially over the mouth, avoids eye contact, exhibits nervous fingers, blinks the eyelashes quickly, squirms, blushes, or acts like a shirt collar is too tight. When you hear many expressions such as "to tell the truth" or "honestly," be suspicious.

> ***A caveat:*** *Proceed with caution.*
> *People who are just nervous or*
> *insecure may also exhibit these signs.*

Touching Is Tricky

Touching is powerful, but it must be done in such a way that the person cannot interpret the touch as having sexual or aggressive overtones. Important factors in the appropriate use of touching are the anatomic location, the kind of touch, and the context. The safest touch zones are the forearm and elbow. Use light, transient touches. Do not hold, pat, or massage. The context of the conversation is important. The touch should reinforce the verbal response. Touch is especially appropriate when one is expressing appreciation or support.

People like to get handshakes unless those handshakes produce pain (arthritics dread them), are prolonged, or make one think they are handling a dead fish.

Phonetics Count Heavily

How you say something is just as important as what you say. Vocal tone, volume, and rate vary with emotional state. For example, a subordinate may say the words "I'm OK" but actually convey "I feel miserable." Verbal patterns that can reduce your power in an interpersonal exchange include the following:

- Posing questions to make requests or demands: "Would you like to get me a cup of coffee?"
- Using disclaimers: "I know this sounds silly, but..."
- Using weak qualifiers: "sort of," "maybe"
- Tolerating interruptions

Three Keys to Successful Listening

Look as though you are listening. Face the person, and, if sitting, lean forward. Establish eye contact. Good eye contact is not staring down the other person; it is shifting your gaze from the person's eyes to other parts of his or her face or occasionally glancing away entirely. Nod, smile, or frown at the appropriate times. Avoid a poker face. Let your facial expressions show your feelings. Your body language must be congruent with your verbal messages.

Sound as though you are listening. Use expletives such as "please go on," "I see," or "Um-hum."

Provide feedback. This is the most effective of the three. Only when you provide feedback does the speaker know that he or she has sent the right message. Paraphrase what you heard and saw, translating the message content and the associated feelings.

Kinds of Responses

- Defensive: "That's a lie!"
- Judgmental: "You're too sensitive."
- Advisory: "I'll tell you what I would do."

- Questioning: "Can you be more specific?"
- Empathetic: "You seem upset. I can understand that."

Skilled listeners make frequent use of empathetic, that is, supportive, responses and they avoid defensive, judgmental, and advisory ones. Questioning is appropriate unless it sounds like cross-examination. Skilled listeners also listen carefully for underlying feelings.

Avoid the Following:

criticizing	diagnosing	falsely praising
ordering	name calling	advising
moralizing	threatening	cross-examining
diverting	feigned listening	insincerely reassuring

Naive Listening

We often tend to tune out mentally confused patients, orderlies, members of the housekeeping service, and even some colleagues, friends, and family members. To overcome this, stop occasionally and listen as you did the first time you had any contact with that person. This is naive listening, proceeding as though this individual has just entered your life for the first time.

THE TELEPHONE

Telephone etiquette appears to be a low priority item in many health care organizations and physicians' offices. That is unfortunate, because it affects client satisfaction and time management. Managers should be choosy when hiring a receptionist. They should insist that receptionists and others who handle many incoming calls attend a training session on telephone technique, especially matters of courtesy.

How your telephone is answered says much about you and your department. An answering voice may express an affirmative, helpful attitude or convey an I-don't-really-care attitude. Callers mirror how they are treated. If we sound friendly, our callers respond in kind.

A Test for Telephone Etiquette and Helpfulness

Anonymously call your unit after regular hours and ask a complex question about an aspect of your service. Be prepared for a shock.

Tying up telephone lines with personal calls angers callers. So does transferring callers through a series of departments.

Everyone assumes they know how to use the telephone. When you suggest that an employee attend a workshop on telephone courtesy, that employee may become upset. A somewhat manipulative trick is to tell the person that you want someone to attend the training session and then come back and teach what was learned to the rest of the staff. This sensitive issue can be avoided if the organization mandates periodic training programs for the entire staff or includes this training in its orientation protocol. An added benefit is that such group education promotes uniform telephone etiquette, which, in turn, has a reinforcing effect.

What All Telephone Users Should Know

Answering the Phone

Answer within three rings, or apologize for the delay. Sit up straight. Project helpfulness. A smiling face helps; smiles do indeed travel over telephone lines. To remind employees how important customers are, put stickers next to each phone that read "the CEO is calling."

Identify self and unit, then offer to help. Sound enthusiastic and helpful. If the person states his or her name, use it at least once. If the name is not offered, ask for it.

Take messages when appropriate. The message should include the person's full name, organization, phone number, any information they would like to leave, time and date of message, and your initials. (Note: a special phone log is helpful.)

Placing Someone on Hold

Being put on hold is a frequent complaint, especially when a person feels the length of the hold is excessive. Apologize when you cannot connect the person at once. Avoid saying, "Just a second, I'll be right back." This is rarely true and is annoying. Offer a choice of waiting or being called back. When on hold, check every 30 seconds and repeat the offer. If the caller states a preference for calling back, make sure that this is done. Also, avoid use of call waiting. Call waiting forces a choice between which caller is the more important. One or the other is offended.

Screening Calls

If it is necessary to screen calls, do it politely and tactfully. An effective screener helps callers by trying to answer their questions or by directing them to someone who can answer them. To avoid transfers to wrong parties, the screener must be knowledgeable about departmental matters. People who screen calls should know which callers are always to be put through immediately and those who should not be put through at all. They should also know the questions or problems they should handle and the ones they should refer to other people.

The phraseology used is important. Here are some examples of overused or rude phrases:

- "Alice hasn't come in yet."
- "Joe just stepped out."
- "She's in a meeting." (This is used so often that few callers believe it.)
- "I never heard of her."
- "You'll have to call back."
- "What's your name and what do you want?"

By contrast, this is what should be heard:

- "Dr. Jones is out of his office right now. May I ask him to call you?"
- "He's not available at the moment. May I tell him who called?"
- "Doctor, Miss Smith is meeting with our supervisors. The meeting usually ends by 9:00. May I have her call you then?"
- "That name doesn't sound familiar. Can you give me more information?"
- "He's not in right now. I expect him back about 2:00 PM. Will you be available then?"
- "Yes, she's in. May I tell her who is calling?" (Do not ask for callers' names before telling them that their party is not in.)

Some consultants recommend that special customers be given the unlisted phone numbers of key personnel, always with the permission of the latter, of course.

Transferring Calls

Before you transfer a call, ask if you can help or if the caller would like to be called when the person becomes available.

Being transferred from one extension to another is a frequent source of irritation. A courteous transfer requires a brief explanation of why the caller is being transferred. The caller is reassured that his or her questions will be answered. To avoid the consequences of a disconnection, give callers the name, title, and extension number of the person to whom they are being transferred. Do not hang up until the connection has been made.

Taking Messages for Another Person

Walther recommends getting rid of the "little pink slips" in favor of forms that have enough space for the following information:

- Name of caller (phonetic version if the name is difficult to pronounce)
- Caller's organization or department and phone number
- Time, date, and purpose of call
- Impression of caller's mood (for example, angry, unhappy, stressed, euphoric)

- Any promises made to the caller
- Callers' unwillingness to talk to anyone else
- Any known previous important contacts with caller. (If so, it may be appropriate to attach copies of that prior correspondence.)[5]

Telephone Recommendations for All Employees

- Use the caller's name frequently.
- Say what you can do, not what you cannot do.
- Mitigate anger by answering empathetically.
- For outbound calls, state your business first and save the small talk for last.
- Answer promptly and identify yourself.
- Sound enthusiastic and cooperative.
- Keep the person focused on the reason for the call.
- Keep personal calls short and infrequent.
- End conversations on a positive note, and thank the person for calling.
- Make sure that the callers know what you are going to do, and do it promptly.

Forbidden Phrases

"I don't know."
"That's not done in this department."
"There's nothing I can do about that."
"You have to."
"You should have."
"Why didn't you?"
"I'll try."
"You can't have..."
"Our policy is..."

Conversation Ending

In telephone conversations, as in interviews or written correspondence, the beginnings and the endings make the strongest impressions. Conclude calls with a verification of key points covered. You want to be remembered as a pleasant, efficient person to deal with. Therefore take the time to thank the person for calling. Say you were glad to be of service (or sorry that you could not help). End the conversation on a pleasant upbeat note, but refrain from using that tiresome cliché, "Have a nice day" or, even worse, "bye-bye." Instead, say "goodbye" in a pleasant voice or with an appropriate comment such as, "It was nice hearing from you again" or "Thank you for filling me in; I appreciate it." Let the caller hang up first.

Telephone Tag

We all know the frustration of calling people when they are out and when you are not available when the calls are returned. This can go on for hours, even days. It can also be expensive when the calls are long distance ones. Here are some effective ways to avoid phone tag.

- Pick the best time to call. People are most likely to be in their offices just before lunch and late in the afternoon. Ask when it is a good time to call. You can say when you will call again, and ask that this information be placed on the person's desk.
- Ask the person to page your party, or ask if there is another number at which you can reach the person.
- Ask if there is someone else who can answer your question.
- Leave a message.
- Use an answering machine or e-mail.

Tips for Outbound Calls

- Have an up-to-date telephone directory nearby. Keep a list of frequently called persons and their phone numbers. Add the best time to call and any other helpful information.
- Set aside a period each day during which to make outbound calls. If it can be helped, avoid calling before 9:00 AM, after 5:00 PM, or between noon and 1:30 PM.
- Most people do not like to be called at home when the subject is one that can be handled during the workday.
- Keep in mind any time differences when you make long distance calls.
- Plan what you are going to say. Have available any documents you might need.
- Let the phone ring at least five or six times before hanging up. If a secretary initiates the calls, make certain you remain close by. It's irritating to the person being contacted and embarrassing to a secretary who has to hunt for you.
- Start conversations by stating your name. Do not wait to be asked.
- If you are not well acquainted with the person, ask the switchboard operator how the person's name is pronounced, the name of the secretary, and the secretary's extension number in case the first call does not get through.

Voice Mail

Make certain that employees are trained in "technotalk," the languages of e-mail and voice mail, and cellular telephone technology. After all, management has held classes for telephone use for years, so why not teach about these technological variations as well?

Many callers are annoyed by voice mail. Some refuse to leave messages. When used properly, however, voice mail can eliminate frustrations for both caller and call recipient. Deeprose provides the following excellent advice for using voice mail effectively.

- Change your greeting regularly to let callers know your situation (for example, "I'm on another call right now," "I'll be back in my office at noon," or "I'll be out of my office until Monday, February 12").
- In addition to your name, organization, and phone number, state the time and date, the nature of your call, when it is convenient for you to be called, or when you will call back.
- Substitute a message for a request to be called back.
- Suggest a fax response if a response is needed; provide your fax number.
- Let your callers know when you make callbacks (if you screen calls as a time management technique).[6]

Answering Machines

Many people dislike talking to an answering machine, and many refuse to do so. Those who refuse to respond are urged to give the gadgets a fair shake. Using them is like pumping your own gas; as you grow familiar with them, they become less irritating. Answering machines are steadily giving way to voice mail, but some will be with us for some time to come. When properly used, these machines have some advantages over human contacts.

- They force you to be brief.
- You do not get negative feedback or long-winded conversations.
- There is less likely to be misinterpretation because the person can listen to the message as often as he or she likes.
- They're great for minimizing phone tag.
- If you do not want interruptions during interviews or other critical times, the answering machine can be as effective as a secretary.

Think About It

We frequently complain about "no communication" in the workplace, especially when something goes wrong. When we do so, it's not likely that we're talking about ourselves, so we're blaming others for leaving us out of the flow of information. However, we will never improve communication until we recognize that each of us is part of the problem. It pays to remember at all times that each of us is not nearly as effective at communication as we assume we are.

Questions for Review and Discussion

1. What is the greatest shortcoming of the informal communication system, that is, the grapevine? Why is this so?
2. If we are generally aware that face-to-face is the most effective form of interpersonal communication, why do we do use this means today considerably less than it was formerly used?
3. It has been said that effective listening is difficult because we can hear without listening. What is meant by this statement?
4. In the present day, what is the principal hazard in using any degree of touch other than the handshake in interpersonal communication?
5. Why do many employees tend to believe that management is usually holding back important information from them?
6. Which seems to work more readily as far as information flow is concerned: upward communication or downward communication? Why?
7. Why might an employee not ask for clarification, even if he or she has no understanding of what the supervisor has said?
8. What advantages of face-to-face communication are not available in various other means of interpersonal communication?
9. What do you believe the individual supervisor can do to influence the contents of the grapevine and its relative accuracy?
10. As a supervisor, how would you attempt to establish a sound communicating relationship with a superior whose projected attitude seems to say "Don't tell me anything I don't want to hear?"

Case: Why Are They Noisy Alone and Quiet Together?

As a new supervisor hired from outside the hospital, it took you very little time to learn that morale in the department had been at low ebb for quite some time. As you started getting acquainted with your employees by meeting with them individually, you quickly became inundated with complaints and various other evidence of discontent. Most of the gripes concerned perceived problems with administration and building services, but there were also a significant number of complaints by your staff about other employees in the department and some thinly veiled charges suggesting that a couple of staff members have consistently been complaining about the department to your boss. (Your boss has said nothing to you about this.)

It sounded to you as though a number of common themes ran through the group's complaints, and it seemed to you that a number of differences could be cleared up by airing these issues with the entire group. You planned a meeting for that purpose, instructing all employees to be prepared to air their complaints (except for those directly involving other staff members). Your employees seemed to think this was a reasonable idea, and several led you to believe they would be happy to speak up.

However, your meeting turned out to be brief. Hard as you tried to get people to air their gripes, nobody spoke. You tried again 2 weeks later, with the same results: no one uttered a word of complaint. Yet all the while the negative undercurrents continued to circulate through the department.

Questions:

1. Why do you suppose you get only silence from these employees when you attempt to deal with them as a group? Explore possible causes of this frustrating condition.
2. Why might the complaints that several of your employees raised involving administration and building services be a reasonable place to start working on this group's communication problems?
3. How long do you believe it will take to bring this group around to where you need them to be? Why?

Case: Will You Argue with the Boss?

You are at a meeting with your manager, another middle manager, and four other supervisors. The subject of the meeting is the manner in which the supervisors of the organization are to conduct themselves during the present union-organizing campaign.

Your manager makes a statement concerning one way in which supervisors should conduct themselves. You are surprised to hear his statement because earlier that day you read a legal opinion describing this particular action as probably illegal. You interrupt your manager with, "Pardon me, but I don't believe it can really be done that way. I'm certain it would leave us open to an unfair labor practice charge."

Obviously annoyed at the interruption, your manager says sharply, "This isn't open to discussion. You're wrong."

You open your mouth to speak again but are cut short by an angry glance. You are absolutely certain that your boss is wrong; he had inadvertently turned around a couple of words and described a "cannot do" as a "can do." Unfortunately, you are in a conference room surrounded by other people, and the document that could prove your point is in your office.

Questions:

1. What can you do to straighten out this communication problem without prejudicing yourself with your manager any more than necessary?

REFERENCES

1. Shandler, D. 1993. *From technical specialist to supervisor.* Menlo Park, CA: Crisp Publishers, 31.
2. Sonnenberg, F. 1992. The essentials of on-the-job information. *Supervisory Management* 37: 8.
3. Smith, D., and Sutton, H. 1994. *Powerful proofreading skills.* Menlo Park, CA: Crisp Publishers, 29.
4. Walther, G.R. 1986. *Phone power.* New York: G.P. Putnam & Sons, 74.
5. Walther, G. *Phone power,* 50.
6. Deeprose, D. 1992. Making voice mail customer friendly. *Supervisory Management* 37: 7, 8.

RECOMMENDED READING

D. Arthur, "The Importance of Body Language," *HR Focus* 72, no. 6 (1995): 22, 23.
R.W. Lucas, *Effective Interpersonal Relationships* (New York: Irwin Publishers, 1994).
D. Tannen, "The Power of Talk: Who Gets Heard and Why," *Clinical Laboratory Management Review* 10, no. 3 (1996): 209–220.

Chapter 33

Written Communication

Clutter is the disease of American writing.
We are a society strangling in unnecessary words,
circular constructions, pompous frills,
and meaningless jargon.

—William Zinsser

CHAPTER OBJECTIVES

- Provide guidance for selecting the appropriate channels for filling the supervisor's written communication needs.
- Outline the general steps involved in preparing a document.
- Provide step-by-step guidelines for preparing a document of any nature.
- Suggest how the supervisor should approach the editing of an employee's written output.
- Delineate the role of facsimiles and e-mail transmissions in communication via written language.

A significant number of employers are not pleased with the writing ability of today's graduates. Ricks, for example, states, "The secondary schools have disgorged a generation of workers who cannot write a three-sentence memo."[1]

Trainers at health care institutions recognize the importance of helping employees upgrade their writing skills. However, they lack the time to focus on grammatical errors or to search for spelling mistakes. They must limit the little time they have to bare-bones writing competencies. Trainers depend on supervisors to define the writing skills their employees need on the job, for example, in writing memos and preparing reports.

Customer satisfaction is involved when writing skills are addressed. Customers want simple and clear messages they can understand. Many "thank-yous," "pleases," and other stroking terms are less important than tact and helpfulness.

Writers of memos and letters should consider the level of education of their readers. The writer displays a significant measure of courtesy by making it as easy as possible for people to respond. For example, invite readers to return your letter with their responses on the letter, thus eliminating the need to compose and print a new letter.

SELECTING AN APPROPRIATE COMMUNICATION CHANNEL

We find it necessary to select the most appropriate channel of communication on a daily basis. These selections affect efficiency, expense, and client satisfaction. Spoken communication is usually the fastest means because it allows complex exchanges and transmits feelings better than other forms of communication. Use it when you want immediate responses or reactions or when discussion or lengthy questioning is needed.

Written messages can mute hostility or emotion, are permanent, and usually—but not always—are less susceptible to misinterpretation. A significant advantage is that they do not interrupt the recipient's work as face-to-face exchanges and phone calls do. The writing choices include memorandum, letter, facsimile, posted notice, electronic mail, or computer bulletin board.

It is important to know the preferences of one's superiors and clients. Some folks prefer verbal messages; others like everything in writing. We all know people who refuse to leave messages on answering machines; commercial recordings can be irritating, not to mention the oft-encountered music that is guaranteed to annoy some callers. And how often does a recorded voice tell us that our message is very important and then place us on hold for interminable periods?

Letters are for external, private, or formal purposes. Memos—"messages in shirtsleeves"—are more suitable for in-house, less formal messages. Most of these are now transmitted via e-mail. Use a letter when transmitting extensive data or information that will be retained as a permanent record. One simple rule in deciding between memo and letter is that any message that requires a stamp to reach its intended recipient should be a letter.

Anatomy of a Memo

To: Often it is best to send a memo to a position rather than to an individual. If the person is on extended leave, the memo may reside in an in basket for weeks. Use the person's name only if assured the person is available.

From: This is the originator of the message, not the person who types it or an assistant who prepares it for an executive.

Date: The date the memo leaves the department, not the date dictated or typed.

Subject:

Message:

Action: What are you going to do or what do you expect the receiver to do?

Copies: Send copies to everyone you want to take action or be informed.

Attachments: These may be references, copies of previous reports, or special precautions.

Other: Name or initials of the typist may be appropriate.

STEPS IN PREPARING A DOCUMENT

First, *define* the purpose of the message. What do you hope to accomplish? Is the message really needed? Do you expect the receiver to take some kind of action, or do you merely want to inform? What is the best sending channel to use? Must it be typed? Should it be a memo or a letter? Do you have all the information you need?

Freewrite a *rough draft*. Picture the reader sitting across from you. Start with the person's name or with "you." Frontload the opening paragraph with the core of the message. The first paragraph gets the most attention and is what readers remember best. Use a verbal hook to stimulate the reader's interest (for example, "You're going to like what we're doing about your recent suggestion"). Prepare a strong closing statement; the last paragraph gets the next most attention. Do not waste time correcting grammatical errors or spelling in the first draft. Concern yourself only with content and clarity.

Rewrite. Check the rough draft for brevity, clarity, and personal touch. Does it answer what, who, when, where, why, and how? Improve readability by using stroking words (for example, the reader's name, "you" and "we," compliments, or expressions of appreciation) and converting negative or impolite statements into positive, tactful, and courteous ones. For example, change "You receive late reports because your requests are usually late" (bad) to "When we get requests before 0700, our reports are rarely late." (The accusatory "you" has been eliminated, and the focus is on the activity and a solution.) Strengthen vague or abstract wording. Do not use "We're going to try to decrease the turnaround time"; it is imprecise. Use "We're going to decrease the turnaround time by an hour." Use gender-inclusive language. If you want to incur the wrath of females, use all male pronouns. Stereotyping women as secretaries and men as managers is even worse. Although we cannot eliminate "man" from all words (for example, mankind, penmanship, and manager, we can neuter most words or find appropriate substitutes. The simplest way to neuter sentences is to use "he or she," but this gets cumbersome. Substitute titles, such as "the employee," or refer to groups in the plural and use "they." You can also balance the gender by using "he" in one paragraph and "she" in the next.

Edit carefully. Observe the following rules:

- Keep the message simple and specific.
- Check the paragraphs. Keep them short, with one major thought for each.
- Use lists, columns, headings, and alphanumerics.
- Highlight key words or phrases by using different fonts.
- Allow plenty of white space by using wide margins, double spacing, and a limited number of lines per page.
- Check the sentences. Vary their lengths to avoid telegraphic sound; break up the long ones.
- Convert passive to active voice. "Our monthly meeting has been discontinued" is passive. "We elected to discontinue monthly meetings" is active.
- Convert some active to passive voice for diplomatic reasons. It softens statements and avoids finger pointing. "Dr. Jones objected to your appointment" puts Dr. Jones on the spot. "An objection to your appointment was raised" diffuses responsibility.
- Convert "-ion" nouns to verbs: "It is my intention" becomes "I intend."
- Check punctuation, spelling, and grammar. This process has been simplified by the speller, thesaurus, and grammar software now available with most computers.
- Eliminate the following kinds of words and use the substitutes in parentheses:
  - Archaic, pompous, or overused phrases: "Upon receipt of your reply…" ("When we hear from you.") "Please advise us." ("Please tell us.")
  - Unnecessary words, phrases, or modifiers: "The consensus of opinion" ("The consensus"). "It is a gray color and has a round shape." ("It's gray and round.") "Filled to capacity" ("Filled")
  - There are: "There are too many people arriving late." ("Too many people arrive late.")
  - Weak words (substitute strong ones): "We think that we give good service." ("We strive for outstanding service.")
  - Excess pronouns and prepositions: "The decrease in profit is of great concern to us." ("We're concerned about decreased profit.")
  - Slang, jargon, acronyms, buzzwords, or hackneyed phrases: "down the tubes," "out of this world," "belly up," "bottom line."

EDITING AN EMPLOYEE'S WRITING

Do not return an employee's document marked up like it was a school paper, with corrections all over and lacking only a grade to look like a real school assignment. Never use red ink for your comments on an employee's writing; in addition to making errors painfully obvious, this is another practice that marks you as more schoolteacher or critic than supervisor.

Review the document with the person who wrote it. Focus on major defects. Is the piece organized logically and supported by data? Does it clearly state its purpose? Provide specific examples of what you want to see conveyed. If you find too many minor flaws, the employee will think you are nitpicking or will become discouraged. End with an encouraging comment about how the person's reports have improved in content, readability, or promptness.

Of course, you do not want to see glaring language errors in a document that might go outside the department, but your first concern in serving as editor should be clarity of thought and presentation rather than observance of all so-called "rules" of writing.

FACSIMILES

When it is advisable to transmit facsimiles—faxes in today's terminology—avoid sending long or irrelevant documents. Also, a faxed document should contain all the information needed for the recipient to reply. Include your fax number, phone number, and address. Do not fax a confidential document unless confidentiality is assured at the other end, for example, if the recipient is standing by the receiving fax machine or has a secure private fax mailbox. (Like certain other technological advances, the fax machine has improved efficiency but, in doing so, has created security problems.)

ELECTRONIC MAIL

In many respects electronic or e-mail is a marvelous technological advance, but significant risks come with it. Stored messages can become evidence against an organization if it is sued. There have been suits charging sexual harassment, race or age discrimination, and other violations in which e-mail messages have figured. On the other hand, trying to police e-mail can conceivably expose employers to charges of invasion of privacy.

E-mail has put new strength into our open-door policy. E-mail enables all employees to access just about anyone in the organization; they do not even need to knock on the door. On the one hand, executives are sometimes more receptive to e-mail messages because they can read them when convenient. On the other hand, when they return to their offices and find hundreds of messages, they may be less responsive.

Explain your security system to all your employees. They must know what data are sensitive and must restrict e-mail usage to business purposes. It is advisable to express what e-mail should and should not be used for in a formal personnel policy. Also, there should be a procedure for disposing of computer backup after it has served its purpose.

Think About It

Written communication is one of the several subjects addressed in this book that could readily fill a book of its own. Learning to write clearly is an ongoing process that requires practice; one learns to write better by writing and rewriting. It can be said that the most important part of business writing is rewriting—never let a document go out after just an initial pass to get the words on paper. Rather, edit and rewrite, aiming for clarity. As Blaise Pascal is supposed to have said, "I have made this letter rather long because I have not had time to make it shorter."

Questions for Review and Discussion

1. It has been said that the majority of business documents contain from 25% to 100% more words than needed to properly convey their messages. Granted, this makes for longer documents, but what's the harm as long as they contain the correct information?
2. What means would you likely employ to communicate your observation of a serious ethical breach committed by a licensed professional? Why?
3. When you happen to be upset about a particular issue, what are the advantages of responding in writing rather than speaking face-to-face with the other party?
4. What are the primary advantages of communication in writing over face-to-face communication?
5. What are the primary advantages of face-to-face communication over communication in writing?

Exercise: The Smith Letter

Rework the following letter, your objective being to clarify and convey the intended message while reducing the total number of words as much as practical.

Gentlemen:

In reference to the above collection item, which you instructed us to hold at the disposal of the beneficiary, we wish to advise that Mr. Smith has not called on us, nor have we received any inquiries on his behalf.

The above information is provided to you in the event you wish to give us any further instructions in the matter.

Sincerely,

Exercise: What Did He Say?

This is the text of a letter provided by a health care facility's pension-servicing organization in answer to a question asked by a benefits specialist. See if you can deduce the true message and express it with clarity.

Dear (Benefits Manager):

Re: Date of Termination for Retirement Plan Purposes in the Payroll/Personnel System

In connection with your payroll/personnel system, you asked us whether we thought it would be a good idea to have as an additional data item in the payroll/personnel system, beyond an employee's traditional last day worked (i.e., the last day the employee is physically at the Company), the date of termination/retirement for Retirement Plan Purposes (i.e., the date that a terminating or retiring employee's vacation payments are exhausted). For consistency and for administrative ease in having the last day worked and day of termination/retirement needed to determine Retirement Plan benefits all in the same information source, we think it would be a good idea to have both dates for an employee in the payroll/personnel system.

Sincerely yours,

(Hint: The message can be clearly conveyed in one relatively brief sentence. Think about it.)

REFERENCES

1. Ricks, D.M. 1994. Why your business-writing courses don't work. *Training* 31: 49–52.

RECOMMENDED READING

D. Booher, *Send Me A Memo: A Handbook of Model Memos.* (New York: Facts On File Publishers, 1984).

K. Davis, "What Writing Training Can and Can't Do," *Training* 32, no. 8 (1995): 60–3.

W. Strunk, Jr. and E.B. White, *The Elements of Style.* (New York: Macmillan Publishing). (First published in 1959, it has been through multiple editions and numerous printings. Although a small book, it remains a most definitive guide to clear everyday writing.)

Chapter 34

How to Hold More Effective Meetings

One secret of successful conversation is learning to
disagree without being disagreeable. It isn't what
but how you speak that makes all the difference.
Ben Franklin used to remark diplomatically, "On
this point I agree. But on the other, if you don't
mind, may I take exception?"

—Jack Harrison Pollack

CHAPTER OBJECTIVES

- Review the primary purposes of meetings.
- Identify the principal components of a properly structured meeting.
- Review the necessary preparations to be made in advance by the individual who is to chair the meeting.
- Recommend a procedure for the conduct of a meeting.
- Provide advice for meeting attendees to apply as constructive participants.
- Review the various kinds of problem attendees whose behavior threatens to disrupt the meeting, and suggest how the chairperson may cope with non-constructive behavior.

Despite their tainted reputation, meetings are one of our most valuable communication tools. We use them for team building and coordination, cross-functional activities, dissemination of information, training, problem solving, and decision making. Committees, task forces, and focus groups could not function without meetings. Ad hoc problem-solving meetings conducted in a brainstorming mode are often among the most valuable of meetings.

We must, of course, not forget departmental and staff meetings. Essentially every department or departmental subgroup holds regular staff meetings. Indeed, there may be few if any health care institutions that do encounter a shortage of places to meet. It seems that only vehicle parking space is in greater demand than meeting space.

The amount of information flowing out of computers has made meetings even more important because there is an ever-increasing amount of information to be shared and discussed.

Many managers believe they spend too much time in meetings and that most meetings are a waste of time. They are correct on both points. Nevertheless, the higher people rise in the organization, the more time they spend in conferences. Insecure managers call meetings for the sole purpose of getting moral support or sharing responsibility. Perhaps the biggest time waster is the regularly scheduled meeting, often held even when there is nothing important to discuss.

MAJOR PURPOSES OF MEETINGS

Meetings as we know them in organizational life are held to share, exchange, or disseminate information. Specific purposes for holding meetings include

- explaining new policies, laws, services, protocols, systems, or restructuring activities; in general, anything that involves change;
- accepting reports or recommendations;
- making decisions, solving problems, allocating resources, preparing plans, establishing priorities, generating ideas, or assigning tasks;
- persuading or obtaining commitment for an idea, program, or proposal;
- teaching, training, demonstrating, or explaining tasks and procedures;
- congratulating or rewarding.

COMPONENTS OF A MEETING

All properly structured and conducted meetings include the following essential components:

- Purpose: the reason for the meeting
- Input and content: leader, attendees, agendas, visual aids, handouts, meeting room facilities, objectives, facts, and opinions
- Process: presentation, discussion, consensus, voting, negotiation, information exchange, expression of feelings, planning, problem solving, and decision making
- Product: problems solved, decisions made, compromises, commitment obtained, schedules, assignments, priorities, resources allocated, action plans
- Responses and follow-up: actions taken; information provided to meeting constituents and other people affected by the decisions.

ADVANCE PREPARATIONS BY THE CHAIRPERSON

In addition to preparing an agenda and ensuring that meeting space and facilities are available, chairpersons improve their effectiveness by soliciting ideas, opinions, and information before the session. They encourage attendees to submit suggestions for topics. Talking to attendees before a meeting often eliminates the need for that meeting. This is also a technique for getting opinions from passive individuals who may be reluctant to speak up at the meeting. Let the participants know what you expect of them. Designate whom you will call on to discuss certain points.

Morning meetings when everyone is awake and fresh are ideal. After lunch, people fall asleep. Many people find it productive to hold meetings at 4 PM. By that hour, they have taken care of most of their major daily problems and still have a little time to return to their offices for last-minute details after the session.

The selection of attendees is important. You can reduce costs and avoid displeasure if you limit attendance to people you absolutely need and who are willing to serve. The attendees should collectively have the necessary knowledge and experience. They should be the kind of people you can depend on to show up and participate.

The larger the number of attendees, the slower the meeting progress and the more difficult it is to stick to the agenda. A group of five to eight people is ideal for most action meetings. To help reduce meeting size, consider part-time attendance; that is, ask people to be present only when you need them. Encourage them to leave when they have made their contributions (busy people are grateful for this).

If your meetings tend to drag on, schedule them just before quitting time. Many supervisors prefer Friday afternoons because they can review the week's progress. They also prevent the premature departure of folks who like to leave work early on Fridays.

A caveat: You do not win popularity contests with this practice.

Select a Competent and Conscientious Recorder

Meeting records are important, so you want a recorder who takes clear and concise notes. The recorder summarizes and condenses the information into the minutes and submits them to the chairperson for review and approval. Recorders (or chairpersons) often use flipcharts to record progress or to check off agenda items as they are disposed of.

Seating Arrangements

Most meetings are held around a rectangular table. A circular one is preferable, especially if there is no designated leader. Classroom or auditorium arrangements are fine for distributing information, but not for problem-solving or committee meetings. Circular, semicircular, and U-shaped configurations of chairs have their advocates. Seminar leaders and discussion panels like hollow square groupings with the leader or panel on one side.

Do not seat antagonists facing each other at rectangular tables (typical union–management arrangements) where they can glare across the table at each other. If you can, seat them on the same side of the table.

Agenda

Think of the agenda as the rudder of your discussion boat. The agenda is to a chairperson what a recipe is to a cook. Encapsulate the topics in action- or goal-oriented statements. Avoid the word "discuss" when the purpose of the meeting is to recommend action. Discussions that do not lead to actions are usually just a lot of hot air. After each item on the agenda, show the expected kind of result (for example, "to prepare the final draft of our mission statement").

Indicate the time allocated for each topic and the names of the people you expect to report. Use a computer to prepare your personal copy of the agenda. You can leave enough space between each item for notes so you eliminate puzzling over your scribbling in the margins. List everything you want to cover, then cut the agenda in half. Always include a start and end time for each topic. Use action phrases like "to recommend" or "to make a final decision" rather than "to discuss" or "to consider."

Distribute the agenda several days before the meeting. If you issue the agenda too long before the meeting, some of the people will lose their copies and forget the contents. If you do not give them enough time to read and digest the content, they lack time to prepare for the session. You must know where to send each copy. Some people, like members of a board of directors, for example, often prefer to get their agendas at home, while others wish to receive such material only at work. A poor practice followed at some hospitals is for board members to pick up their copies as they enter the meeting room or to have the agendas handed out at the start of the session.

THE MEETING

Get Started

Arrive early to ensure that everything is ready. For quick sessions, remove the chairs and hold stand-up meetings.

Memorize your opening statement, making it clear, concise, and to the point. The opening statement establishes the direction for the meeting.

If this is the first meeting of a particular group, establish some ground rules before any discussions start. Here are some usable guidelines.

- We will begin and end the meetings on time.
- We will listen to others without interrupting.
- We will not allow sarcasm, ridicule, or intimidation.
- Everyone gets a chance to talk and is expected to do so.
- We will seek consensus rather than the majority vote.

Sound and look enthusiastic as you review the highlights of the previous meeting and ask for any comments or corrections. Note any progress made since that meeting.

How to Encourage Participation

- Go around the table, calling on each member by name.
- Respond enthusiastically to all suggestions.
- Split into breakaway groups.
- Let others lead some questioning or chair the session.
- Reinforce participation from reserved members, for example, "Thanks, Erica, for speaking so candidly."
- Use nonthreatening, open-ended questions, such as "How do you think someone opposed to that idea will respond?"
- Withhold your opinion until everyone else has spoken.
- If a person's suggestion cannot be accepted in full, try using part of it.
- Encourage members to build on the ideas of others.
- Preserve the egos of all members.

Avoid the Abilene Paradox

The Abilene Paradox is the inability to manage agreement.[1] It occurs when members approve an action that is contrary to what they really want. This occurs because they fail to express their true opinions and vote for something to which they object but which they feel the group favors. This scenario is common when chairpersons are domineering. When the result turns out unfavorably, members either accuse each other or make lame excuses for not speaking up. This paradox is avoided when participants have courage or when a devil's advocate is present.

Maintain Control

Keep people from going off on tangents. When they stray, say something like, "Jessica, that's interesting. We'll consider that at another time. Now about…"

Summarize progress periodically by using a flipchart or blackboard. Call for a break when things stall.

Force Decisions

Ask if anyone needs more data before a decision is made. Ask a proponent to sum up her view. Do the same for an opponent. Go around the table and ask each person for his or her position; then try to achieve a unanimous decision. Call for a vote only when a serious effort for a consensus has failed or you need a record of how each member has voted.

Ensure that recommendations are phrased in specific terminology. For example, "to improve emergency room service" is too general. "Decrease average waiting time in the pediatric clinic to less than 15 minutes" is more specific.

Close the Meeting

To avoid confusion, summarize the discussion and decisions. Indicate the areas still requiring consideration. Review assignments, and select the date for the next meeting.

When you must leave a meeting that is still in progress, provide a brief explanation and turn the chair over to an alternate. Before you do that, assign any special responsibilities or tasks to members.

Important "Do Nots" for Chairpersons

- Do not try to dominate the meeting.
- Do not state your opinion before others have given theirs.
- Do not tell a participant that he or she is wrong.
- Do not instruct or lecture unless that is the purpose of the meeting.
- Do not argue (disagreeing is acceptable).
- Do not ridicule, kid, or use sarcasm.
- Do not take sides early in the discussion.
- Do not fail to control problem members.
- Do not allow the meeting to run overtime.
- Do not try to accomplish too much at one meeting.

After the Meeting

Notify the convening authority of the outcome, if appropriate. Send thank-you notes to individuals who made outstanding presentations, clarified remarks, supported you, or agreed to carry out post-meeting tasks.

Prepare minutes without delay. Copies should be available within 24 to 48 hours. The minutes should include the following:

- Time started, time adjourned
- Who was present and who was absent
- Statement that previous minutes were read and approved
- Brief discussion or presentation of each item on agenda
- Record of agreement or disagreement, record of vote or decisions made
- Follow-up on actions to be taken
- Date, place, and time of next meeting

TIPS FOR MEETING ATTENDEES

- Ask yourself why you are there, and come prepared to participate.
- Arrive on time.
- Listen thoughtfully to others and try to understand their points of view.
- Look for hidden agendas.
- Ask for clarifications.
- Respect the opinions of those with whom you disagree.
- Offer honest opinions, even when these are unpopular.
- Try to separate facts from perceptions, assumptions, or opinions.
- Disagree without being disagreeable.
- Remain rational and assertive, even when harassed.
- Seek win-win solutions, and be willing to compromise.
- Accept special assignments such as searching the literature or serving as recorder.
- Avoid being a problem attendee.

For Nonassertive Attendees

Some individuals hesitate to speak up at meetings, thus depriving the group of their knowledge and opinions. Ideally, these people should obtain assertiveness training via seminars, workshops, or books.

There are also tactics for bolstering your courage to speak up. One is to come prepared. Another is to use escalating dialogue. Here, you break your silence by asking questions, starting with benign requests for information or clarification, followed by more challenging queries. Finally, you start to express your opinion.

Another technique is to maintain a state of interest and active neutrality during controversies. Opposing members try to convince fence sitters, who then become centers of attention. Simply listening to both sides and asking appropriate questions provides the neutral observer with clout.

Use power language by avoiding discounters like "I know this sounds silly, but…" Do not use clichés like "It goes without saying…" Eliminate those dreadful fillers such as "Ya know" or "Uhhhhhh."

Sound enthusiastic, speaking clearly and forcefully. Do not tolerate interruptions. Say, for example, "I wasn't finished, Lou." Then go on without waiting for an apology.

Support your vocal expressions with appropriate body language. When a speaker looks at you, give a head signal that shows your reaction. If you nod agreement or shake your head, the person will give you more attention.

PROBLEM ATTENDEES

There are all kinds of participants: incisive thinkers, impatient doers, chronic objectors, speech-makers, shoot-from-the-hip decision makers, and ultraconservatives; you can probably name others. Following are descriptions of several who tend to give chairpersons the most difficulty.

Latecomers

It is sometimes best to declare an intermission and brief the latecomer during that interval. Encourage chronically tardy members to arrive on time. Do not reward their tardiness by reviewing what transpired before they appeared. This encourages more tardiness.

Attendees Who Offend Others

No attendee has the right to mock or insult others. The leader should immediately interrupt the errant behavior and apologize to the person who has been ridiculed. Admonish the offender (for example, "Jack, that is uncalled for, and I'm sure the rest here agree. Let's keep this on a professional level").

Intimidators

Intimidation is a common method for trying to force opinions. The three primary intimidation tactics are appearing to be angry, assuming a superior attitude, or employing ridicule. The chair must stop this quickly.

Hostile or Angry Attendees

If you know who these people are, plan what to say to them. Practice by saying it aloud several times before the meeting. Visualize a successful confrontation. At the meeting, encourage venting. The more anger that pours out, the less there is left. Do not interrupt the person, and insist that he or she not interrupt you.

Nonparticipants

Their thoughts are elsewhere. You should not have invited some of these people. Bring their minds back on track by posing questions directly to them or asking for their opinions.

Side Conversationalists

Some private conversation is natural. Timid members may be afraid to speak up, so they whisper to each other. These attendees may be bored or may just be discourteous. If you stop in the middle of a sentence and glare at them, this may work. If not, ask them to share their conversation with the group.

Comics

We all enjoy a little humor, but individuals who overdo this can be disruptive. Stop them in their tracks by not laughing, giving a wry smile as you shake your head, and say that you want to get on with the business.

Motor Mouths

These people are enthralled by their own voices and never seem to run out of gas. Their comments are endless, and their questions are really just more comments.

Jump in when they pause for breath. Say, for example, "Just a minute, Rita, let's hear what others have to say," "We're getting bogged down, Rita, please make your point," or "Please put that in the form of a motion."

Some of these folks cannot get enough air time. They try to engage you in repeated one-on-one conversations, usually by asking many questions. Ask them to stay after the meeting to discuss these; they rarely do.

Destroyers

Some participants become emotionally rather than rationally involved. They play psychological war games and demand attention by criticizing, interrupting, or taking offense at innocent remarks. One of them may say "I resent that" or "If you people approve that, I'm walking out." Ignore their outbursts. Do not argue or get excited. Let them say their piece, and then go on.

COMMITTEE MEETINGS

Committee meetings are subject to the same rules and conduct as other meetings. Standing committees are permanent and meet regularly. The Joint Commission on Accreditation of Healthcare Organizations (JCAHO) requires many of these committees. Standing committees deal with matters such as quality, safety, infections, ethics, and credentials. Bylaws, union contracts, and operational procedures or protocols list the functions and responsibilities of standing committees.

Ad hoc committees are temporary, created to deal with a single issue such as a threat of unionization or a one-time problem. A task force is a special kind of ad hoc committee.

It is unfortunate that so many health care workers dislike committee assignments because committees are constantly growing in number and importance.

Managers at any level can appoint ad hoc committees. When you appoint a committee, be specific about what you expect. Answer the following questions:

- Who is to chair the meeting, and does that person have the power to appoint members, schedule meetings, and prepare agendas? Select the chairperson carefully.
- Is membership voluntary?
- What is the goal or mission of the committee?
- When is a report due? Are there to be interim reports? If so, at what intervals?
- If it is a decision-making committee, what are the alternatives to be considered?
- If it is a problem-solving committee, do you want only what is deemed to be the best solution or do you want a list of all the alternatives?
- Will you carry out whatever the committee recommends, or only the parts you like?
- What facilities and fiscal support are available?
- If the committee is to serve permanently, have terms of tenure and plans for rotation of membership been provided?

TELEPHONE CONFERENCE CALLS

There are disadvantages to these calls. It may be difficult to identify all the voices. Participants lack the opportunity to watch body language, and it is easier for certain individuals to dominate the conversation. Finally, some people are simply not comfortable with this form of communication. Despite all these disadvantages, the use of conference calls has been increasing because of their convenience and the saving of time and expense. They are ideal for obtaining a vote or getting quick opinions from key people.

Think About It

The most important single point about convening and conducting meetings is one to be considered before any of the advice contained in this chapter is applied, and that is: Is this meeting really necessary? Any time a meeting can be avoided with no harm to organizational communication, problem solving, or decision making, it should not be held. What gives meetings their generally bad reputation is the number of them that are held unnecessarily.

Questions for Review and Discussion

1. Why should there be a separate recorder appointed for a meeting? Why not have the chairperson fulfill this function and thus keep down the number of essential attendees?
2. Why should we not seat antagonists facing each other across a conference table?
3. Why and how can the active presence of a devil's advocate help avoid falling prey to the "Abilene Paradox?"
4. What is one form of meeting for which it is appropriate to expect everyone present to actively participate? And one form of meeting where little or no attendee participation is expected?
5. If five to eight people is the ideal range of membership for a group considering various actions, how can a board of, for example, 30 persons effectively do business?
6. When you are convening a meeting, why not make your position, opinion, or recommendation clear at the outset to let attendees know where you stand?
7. Why are so many regularly scheduled meetings wasteful and inefficient?
8. What is the purpose of the practice of setting meeting times at odd hours, for example 9:06 AM?
9. How would you handle a meeting participant who behaves as though he or she knows considerably more about the subject of the meeting than you, the chairperson?
10. Do you believe that meetings in general have a tainted reputation as claimed in the chapter? Why or why not?

Case: The Generalized Quality Problem

You are supervisor of the central transcription service at City Hospital. Your group includes several transcriptionists who handle all the dictation from laboratory and radiology and the typing for several department managers as well as all medical record transcription.

You are in the habit of holding a brief informational meeting with your staff early each month. At your June meeting you felt obliged to point out that quality was slipping and that errors were on the increase and that more care had to be taken with transcription. (Straight typographical errors, such as misspelled words, had dropped to a minimum, thanks to automatic spell-checking programs, but omissions and errors in word choice seemed to have increased.)

At your July meeting you made the following statement: "The overall quality of transcription has not improved at all over the past month; if anything, it has gotten even worse. I expect all of you to begin improving your work quality immediately."

It is now almost time for your August meeting. In your estimation, transcription quality has not improved in the slightest. It is your feeling that as many as half of your employees are contributing to the problem, but you have yet to identify all the offenders by name.

Questions:

1. Should you address this continuing problem with the group at large at your August meeting? Why or why not?
2. Should you do some research aimed at identifying the more troublesome employees and address their quality problems at the August meeting? Why or why not?
3. How would you suggest mobilizing your transcription group to address the quality problem and recommend solutions?

Case: Your Department's Staff Meeting

There are 15 people in your department at City Hospital. It has been your practice to hold a weekly staff meeting at 3:00 PM each Wednesday. Rather, we should say that you *attempt* to hold it at 3:00 PM because about half of your people are more than 5 minutes late, and a couple of them are usually late by 15 minutes or more. And one of these late-late comers can always be counted on to ask, "What have I missed?"

You have made repeated announcements about being there on time, but to no avail. Come Wednesday at 3:00 PM you usually find yourself and the same six or seven punctual attendees present and waiting for the latecomers.

1. Without immediately resorting to disciplinary action (which should always be the last resort), what can you do to improve punctuality in attending your staff meetings?

REFERENCES

1. Harvey, J.B. 1988. The Abilene Paradox. *Organizational Dynamics* 17: 35–80.

RECOMMENDED READING

C.W. Burleson, *Effective Meetings: The Complete Guide.* (New York: John Wiley & Sons, 1990).
G. Carson, *Making Meetings Work.* (Boulder, CO: CareerTrack Publishers, 1992). Two audiotapes.

Chapter 35

Decision Making and Problem Solving

Nothing is impossible: there are ways which lead to everything; and if we had sufficient will we should always have sufficient means.

—Francois de La Rochefoucauld

CHAPTER OBJECTIVES

- Establish the importance of decision making in today's work organizations and outline its implications for the role of the supervisor.
- Present a generalized process for logically approaching and solving large or complex problems.
- Introduce a number of tools that are useful in problem-solving activities.
- Explore the intuitive process and its key role in problem solving.
- Briefly explore the role and potential usefulness of group problem-solving activities.

Problems are inevitable when people work together. The hallmark of a well-managed team is not the absence of problems but whether the team resolves problems effectively. Many managers continue to blame their employees for most of the problems that occur, but all too often the real villains are faulty management decisions.

DECISION MAKING TODAY

The rate of organizational, technical, legal, and operational change constantly increases. Many of the decisions related to these changes have great impact on financial stability or job security, role alterations, assignments, and customer satisfaction.

459

Today's supervisors are forced to make decisions that were less common previously, decisions related, for example, to downsizing, reassigning, cross-training, and replacing professional employees with less qualified personnel. Also, critical shortages of certain specialists demand quick hiring decisions before competitors snap up these scarce resources.

Our society has grown increasingly litigious. Flawed decisions lead to legal nightmares, for example, harassment and discrimination complaints. Employee safety, satisfaction, and ethical issues are becoming more numerous and complex.

People decisions are by far the most important to the supervisor. Hiring, training, disciplining, promoting, and discharging employees all demand careful consideration.

Decision Making and Leadership

Autocratic leaders make decisions without soliciting input from others. Consultative leaders get input from others before deciding. Democratic leaders participate with their staffs in making decisions, and delegative leaders turn the process over to others.

Higher management deals chiefly with decisions that relate to major outcomes or long-range strategies, the *what* of running the organization. Supervisors deal principally with operational processes, *how* day-to-day operations are conducted.

When to Avoid Making Decisions

- The apparent difficulty is not your problem (others will take care of their own problems).
- The problem is likely to correct itself, or interference is likely to make matters worse (in other words, if it ain't broke, don't fix it).
- You or others are emotionally upset or there are serious attention distractions.
- More information or advice is needed before an informed decision can be made.
- The problem is one that should be delegated. Most decisions should be made at the lowest possible organizational level—as close to the scene of action as possible—as long as those delegated to do so are capable and willing.

Essential Trinity for Effective Decisions

An effective decision must be

1. the most cogent decision,
2. timely as to when it is made and when it is implemented. Professionals often procrastinate because they are looking for more additional data; they fall prey to "paralysis from analysis," and
3. acceptable to the people affected. Many managers are adept at making decisions but fail to persuade people to carry them out.

Dual Cognitive Functions

There are two cognitive approaches to decision making and problem solving: analytical and intuitive. Analytical, or left-brain function, provides rational, logical, scientific thinking. Intuitive cognition, or right-brain function, provides creativity and inspiration.

Left-brain thinking is a flowchart process. Analytical people rely on algorithmic processes, plans, reports, computer printouts, and step-by-step procedures. They exercise judgment at each step and exclude anything that is irrelevant. Managers and investigators who treat problem solving as a science often fail to come up with creative ideas because they depend entirely on this rational approach. In an earlier chapter we mentioned that managers tend to use more left-brain thinking and that more effective leaders rely to a great extent on their intuition.

Intuitive thinking depends on data buried in our unconscious minds, which are like computers with almost unlimited memory storage capability. Unfortunately, what we file in these cerebral banks may be difficult to recall; it can be like trying to access a computer program for which we have lost the password. Unlike computer-stored data, brain information is constantly and unconsciously analyzed, synthesized, and reformatted.

Innovative people possess deeper insight or experience stronger gut reactions. They visualize more than their rational counterparts. They prefer diagrams to printouts. They often throw logic out the window. An intuitive thought process can seldom be flowcharted; rather, it is hop, skip, and jump.

> *Common sense is a combination of logic and intuition, the left and right brain working in tandem.*

Coping with Many Minor Problems

Supervisors face innumerable little problems and decisions every day. Much of the time solving problems is the most important responsibility of the supervisor. If there were no problems, we might need no supervisors. Their subordinates bring problems into their offices by the carload. Better training, planning, coaching, delegating, and policy making work wonders in cutting down on the number of these daily interruptions.

The Stop-Look-Listen Approach

Approach these daily questions or problems like you approach a railroad crossing.

- **Stop** what you are doing.
- **Look** interested.
- **Listen** carefully.

If the problem remains unclear, ask pertinent questions. Then ask the folks who bring you the problems what they think should be done. Much of the time they will have thought through the problem and may have a better solution than you can offer on the spur of the moment. If you agree, approve their suggestion and congratulate them. If they keep bringing in the same problem, tell them that they do not need your decision every time.

Tell your people that you expect them to practice completed staff work. Explain to them that the military term, completed staff work, means that a staff member who comes in with a problem must also bring in ideas on how best to solve the problem and perhaps also a recommendation as to which possible solution may be best. Participative management requires much completed staff work.

If the problem is one that only you can solve, provide your answer on the spot or get back to them without undue delay. Follow up when appropriate.

THE LOGICAL PROCESS: KEY STEPS IN SOLVING LARGE PROBLEMS

Step 1. Prepare a problem statement. Diagnosis is often the most important part of problem solving, but it is often the most neglected part. Too often, people offer solutions before they really understand the problem. Poor problem statements can lead people astray. For example, the problem statement "Lack of clear policy relating to sick leave" is not likely to lead to solving a problem of excessive absenteeism that exists because of poor enforcement by the supervisor.

Step 2. Obtain and interpret the facts or data by asking the following questions:

- When was problem first noted?
- How serious is it?
- Is it getting better or worse?
- Is it more complicated than it first appeared? In what way?
- What is the cause? (This is the most important question.)
- How was this handled in the past? What were the results?

Step 3. Generate alternatives (as many as possible).

Step 4. Formulate criteria to evaluate the alternatives. There are two types of criteria. *Absolute* critera must be satisfied by an acceptable solution (for example, "No increase in costs or personnel"). *Differential* criteria are used to compare and contrast the various alternatives (for example, turnaround time, schedule convenience, availability of supplies, and degree of expertise required).

Step 5. Evaluate the alternatives and select the best one.

Step 6. Look for flaws in the choice. Ask many "what ifs." Avoid the jigsaw puzzle fallacy. The jigsaw fallacy is based on the false assumption that there is only one good solution (for example, a jigsaw puzzle must have four straight edges).

Often there are several equally satisfactory solutions: The edges of life's puzzles are seldom straight lines.

Step 7. Develop an action plan.

Step 8. Carry out the plan. If there is hesitation about implementing the plan, ask what would be the worst possible thing that could happen if the plan was carried out. Also ask what the worst possible thing would be if you do not take the risk.

Step 9. Follow up. If what you are doing is not working well, make the needed changes.

USEFUL TOOLS FOR PROBLEM SOLVING

Bar Graphs

Bar graphs (Figure 35–1a) display a series of numbers (for example, the number of patient visits on each day of the month). When a bar graph shows the distribution of a variance, it is called a histogram (Figure 35–1b).

Pareto Diagrams

Pareto diagrams (Figure 35–1c) display the frequency of occurrences listed in order of importance or frequency.

Scattergrams

A scattergram (Figure 35–1d) shows the correlation between two variables.

Run Charts

Run charts (Figure 35–1e) plot data over time. They exhibit trends, cycles, or other patterns in a process (for example, attendance records, turnover, or customer complaints).

Control Charts

Control charts (Figure 35–1f) illustrate values that are either in control or out of control. In Figure 35–1f, the solid horizontal line represents an average or normal value. The spaces between the solid line and the dotted lines are acceptable values, usually plus or minus two or three standard deviations. Any value outside the dotted lines is an out-of-control value.

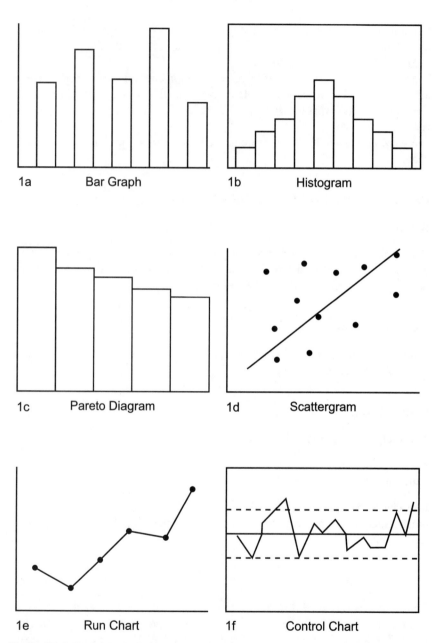

Figure 35–1 Useful Tools for Problem Solving

Flowcharts

A flowchart (Figure 35–2a) represents a series of steps or events arranged chronologically.

Cause and Effect Diagrams

Also known as fishbone diagrams, these devices are useful in an early stage of problem solving or when one is considering potential problems (Figure 35–2b).

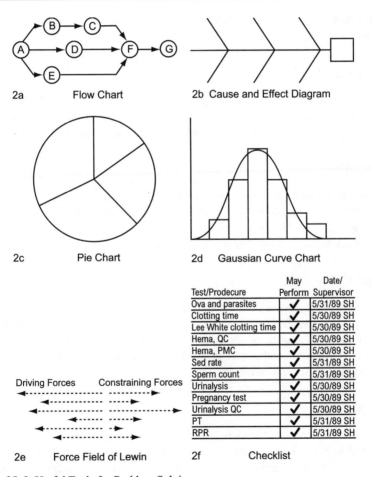

2a   Flow Chart   2b Cause and Effect Diagram

2c   Pie Chart   2d   Gaussian Curve Chart

Test/Prodecure	May Perform	Date/ Supervisor
Ova and parasites	✔	5/31/89 SH
Clotting time	✔	5/30/89 SH
Lee White clotting time	✔	5/30/89 SH
Hema, QC	✔	5/30/89 SH
Hema, PMC	✔	5/30/89 SH
Sed rate	✔	5/31/89 SH
Sperm count	✔	5/31/89 SH
Urinalysis	✔	5/30/89 SH
Pregnancy test	✔	5/30/89 SH
Urinalysis QC	✔	5/30/89 SH
PT	✔	5/31/89 SH
RPR	✔	5/31/89 SH

Driving Forces   Constraining Forces

2e   Force Field of Lewin   2f   Checklist

Figure 35–2 Useful Tools for Problem Solving

A cause and effect diagram forces a focus on potential causes. On each leg (each bone), possible factors are recorded and grouped according to different categories (e.g., process, human, equipment, or policies).

Pie Charts

Pie charts (Figure 35–2c) illustrate relative numbers or percentages.

Gaussian Curve Charts

The bell-shaped curves show frequency distributions. These are among the most common quality control charts (Figure 35–2d).

Force Field Charts

These are useful when considering the advantages and disadvantages of a new service, process, procedure, or piece of equipment. The opposing considerations can be illustrated and quantified by a force field chart (Figure 35–2e).[1]

Checklists

Checklists (Figure 35–2f) are used as reminders or for documentation of activities. Shopping lists, daily "to do" schedules, and validation of records are just a few uses for this ubiquitous tool. Figure 35–2f is a partial list of tests that a new laboratory technician must be qualified to do.

Gantt Charts

The Gantt chart (Figure 35–3) is a graph with activities listed on the vertical axis and time units on the horizontal axis.[2] It is used to find the shortest total time required to reach a goal by showing how much time each activity requires and which activities can and cannot be done simultaneously. In Figure 35–3, note the overlapping of several activities.

PERT Charts

Program Evaluation and Review Technique (PERT) charts (Figure 35–4) were developed to reduce and control the time required for large projects. The PERT chart is composed of activities and events. On the chart, events are represented by circles. Arrows show the time necessary to complete events. When there are steps carried out simultaneously, different times are needed for each of these parallel steps. In Figure 35–4, the lines could represent the following steps:

Weeks

	1	2	3	4	5	6	7	8	9	10	11	12	13	14	15
1	x	x													
2			x	x											
3					x	x	x	x							
4					x	x									
5							x								
6								x							
7									x						
8									x						
9									x						
10										x	x	x	x		
11														x	
12												x			
13															x

Activities

Total time: 15 weeks

Figure 35–3 Gantt Chart

A-B = time for a request to reach a workstation
B-C = time for blood collection and delivery to a laboratory
C-D = time for serological testing
C-E = time for immunohematological testing
E-F = time for delivery of blood product to patient

The critical path represents the sum of the times for individual steps in the path that require the most time. In Figure 35–4, the critical path is A-B-C-D-F because it takes longer to do the serological tests than to do the routine compatibility tests.

Break-Even Charts

This chart is a scatter diagram (or scattergram) in which the Procedures and the Expenses—variable and fixed—are plotted with diagonal lines representing total

---

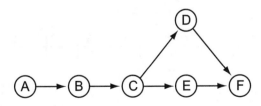

Figure 35–4 PERT Chart with Critical Path

revenues and total costs (Figure 35–5). The point at which the diagonal lines cross represents the financial break even point. The number of procedures performed below that crossing show a loss; those above that crossing show a profit.

Likert Charts

Likert charts (Figure 35–6) are useful when one is comparing and contrasting multiple factors of performance at two different times (e.g., before and after a change).[3]

Computer Applications

For as long as they have been in practical business use computers have been used to file data, reassemble information into new formats, and perform logical operations and calculations. An exciting trend evident in computer problem solving is in the growth in the applicability of expert systems. These rely on stored facts and rules of thumb to mimic the decision making of human experts. This has been successful when applied to narrowly defined tasks, but we still lack a system that possesses common sense.

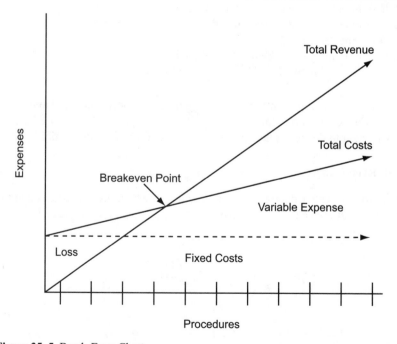

Figure 35–5 Break-Even Chart

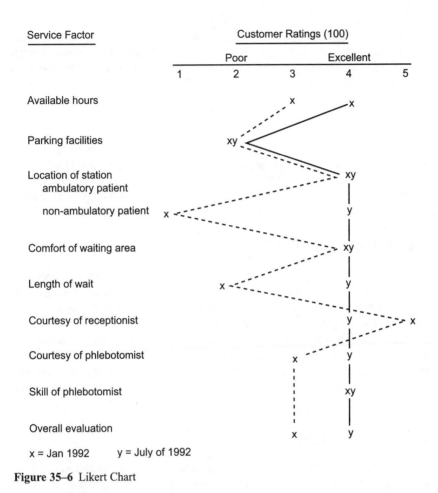

Figure 35–6 Likert Chart

YOUR INTUITIVE PROCESS: KEY TO CREATIVE PROBLEM SOLVING

Give your intuitive process time to act. Set aside some think time each day. Capture thoughts as they occur, like the ringing of a muted telephone. These are most likely to pop up when your logical thought process is on hold. Turn off conscious cerebration to let your cerebral energy flow into your unconscious mind. Daydreaming, relaxation, and meditation help. Walking, jogging, and other kinds of exercise increase cerebral blood flow, and this improves the thought generation process. Solitude can be effective, particularly when it is enhanced by listening to ocean sounds (real or recorded) or background music.

Pay attention to the nagging doubts you feel when you are trying to make a decision. They may represent experience stored in your unconscious mind. A strategy espoused by Dr. Joyce Brothers, the well-known television psychologist, is to think about a problem just before dropping off to sleep.[4]

A Simple Way to Stimulate Your Intuitive Process

Document your problem at the top of a sheet of paper. Under this heading, number the lines 1 through 20. Now force yourself to write down 20 solutions. The first few will come easily (these are usually the ones that you have already considered and discarded). Subsequent alternatives surface with increasing difficulty and are more likely to have originated in your unconscious mind and are more inspirational.[5]

GROUP PROBLEM SOLVING

A problem of any appreciable scope is like a world globe. From any one spot, you cannot see all of the globe. Neither does any one person have an all-encompassing view. In group problem solving, more ideas are generated. An added bonus is that a group is more likely to support the choice it made.

Group discussions increase the likelihood of serendipity, the fortuitous result of two or more elements or events accidentally coming together to create an opportunity. When people put their heads together, they come up with more solutions than when they work individually. With this synergy, one plus one can readily equal three.

Importance of Consensus

A group often makes decisions before all the opinions of the members have been explored. Participants who are not heard from may leave a meeting angry. They

---

The Basics of Consensus Decision Making

- Ensure that each person expresses his or her viewpoint fully.
- Avoid hasty conclusions or agreements.
- Explore the positive features of each alternative.
- Expose and analyze the negative features of each alternative.
- Resolve disagreements.
- Avoid techniques of voting, averaging, or bargaining.
- Insist that each member agree that he or she can live with the solution. If any member balks, you do not have a consensus.

may not support the implementation of the decisions. A few will even sabotage the initiative. A consensus prevents such occurrences.

A consensus is a genuine meeting of the minds. It is not reached by voting. Even a unanimous vote does not represent a consensus if some members are denied an opportunity to speak up. With a consensus, some members may prefer different solutions, but after full and fair discussion, they agree that they can live with what the group decided.

Be wary of the possibility of the Abilene Paradox described in Chapter 34.

CREATIVE PROBLEM-SOLVING GROUPS

Unstructured Brainstorming Groups

Unstructured meetings are little more than beer-and-pretzel gabfests, typically lots of talk, lots of wandering off the topic, and not much action. All too many committee meetings degenerate into these kinds of sessions. There are exceptions, of course, especially when entrepreneurs or creative people get together.

Structured Brainstorming Groups

Structured brainstorming groups generate ideas guided by certain rules. Following is one technique:

1. A problem is presented to the group.
2. Each member thinks about the problem and records his or her ideas on a sheet of paper. No comment or discussion is allowed at this time.
3. Each member reads one item from his or her list. Each of these is recorded on a flipchart. No comment or discussion is permitted at this time either, but members may piggyback on the ideas of others.
4. This sequence is repeated until all the ideas are displayed on the chart.
5. Each item is then discussed, amplified, or modified. The originator of each item may be asked to leave the room while his or her idea is discussed. Criticism is now encouraged.
6. Each member ranks the items, and the votes are recorded on the chart.[6]

Note that there are two phases in this approach: the generation phase (steps 1 through 4) and the evaluation phase (steps 5 and 6).

To get the maximum benefit of brainstorming, make certain that participants know beforehand what is going to be discussed and encourage them to come loaded with ideas. Set a good example by bringing a large packet of your own suggestions, including some really wild ones. Lead off with your wildest one.

Think About It

In making any but the simplest of decisions or addressing any but the most elementary of problems, it is always necessary to accept some risk and uncertainty, uncertainty in that you cannot be completely sure that the decision is absolutely the correct one and risk in that there are consequences to making the wrong decision. It is risk and uncertainty that make decision makers uneasy with the process, but if risk and uncertainty were both reduced to zero, there would be no need to decide because the answer would be self-evident.

Questions for Review and Discussion

1. What is the true difference between consultative leadership and participative leadership in decision making?
2. The chapter suggests how autocratic, consultative, and participative managers make decisions. How are bureaucratic managers likely to make decisions?
3. No matter how simple a decision situation seems to be, why can it be said that there are always at least two alternative choices available?
4. Isn't it the responsibility of the boss to make decisions and solve problems? Why push these activities down to employee level?
5. What is the primary drawback likely to be encountered in making a decision when the problem is not your problem?
6. In creative idea-generating situations, why should wild or foolish or even downright stupid-sounding ideas not be rejected as soon as they arise?
7. In diagnosing a problem, it is always necessary to be on guard against mistakenly labeling a problem symptom as the problem itself. What is most likely to happen if what is addressed is a problem symptom and not the causal problem?
8. Why might we say that ignoring or even forgetting a problem can itself be considered a decision?
9. What should be the ultimate determinant of how much time and effort is put into any particular decision situation?
10. What are the essential differences between decision by vote and decision by true consensus?

Case: More Pleasant Dreams

Imagine yourself as night-shift charge nurse on a medical/surgical unit. For several months you have had a problem with a staff nurse whose performance you consider unsatisfactory. She seems to continually take advantage of quiet times during her shift to doze off at the nursing station. You have reprimanded her several times for sleeping on the job, and you have reached the point where you feel you can no longer simply scold her for her conduct.

Her position, however, is that "it's no big deal," that she's always certain to hear any call signals as long as she's at the nursing station. (Your hospital has a clear policy concerning written warnings, but policy is relatively loose concerning oral warnings; these can be unlimited and issued at your discretion, so you can deliver as many as you feel necessary.)

For a written warning to become official and entered into an employee's personnel file, it must be agreed to and countersigned by the unit's nurse manager and the director of nursing. You issued the offending nurse two written warnings; both warnings cleared through the unit manager. However, you feel you can go no further without backing from the office of the director of nursing, and there has been no follow-up from that direction. Meanwhile, the employee continues to be a problem.

Questions:

1. What would your decision be concerning the sleeping employee if it were not necessary to clear such actions through the director of nursing?
2. Assuming you have indeed "hit a wall" as described in the final paragraph of the case, what would you consider doing to try to get some action or support?
3. If you feel stuck with the reality of having your personnel decisions approved—or essentially made—by higher management, what information would you assemble and how would you prepare yourself to try getting a decision favorable to you from your chain of command?
4. What is the director of nursing actually doing by reserving the right to approve or veto your decisions?

Case: The Long-Time Employee

Assume you have been head nurse of the same medical/surgical unit for nearly 20 years. One of your employees, a licensed practical nurse named Hilda, has been part of the unit's day shift for even longer than you have been head nurse. In fact, Hilda is the only original member remaining of the crew that existed when you first took over the unit.

About 6 months ago Hilda returned to work following an extensive illness that left her noticeably changed in a number of ways. Where once she was energetic and seemed to possess considerable stamina, now the hustle and bustle of the day shift and always being on her feet and on the move seem to wear her down rapidly. You have felt a growing concern for Hilda, and for the rest of the team as well, because it has become obvious to you that Hilda is not bearing her share of the load. Other members of your already overworked crew are working extra hard to make up the difference.

Your concern reached a peak this week when three of your staff nurses came to talk to you about Hilda. Although they came with apparent reluctance—Hilda had always been well liked by both staff and patients—they were quite convinced that something had to be done for both Hilda's sake and the sake of the department. It seems that Hilda has barely been able to accomplish half of what she should be expected to do in an 8-hour shift.

Hilda knows only nursing; she has been an LPN for all of her working life. She will not be eligible for retirement for 5 more years.

It is evident that you need to make a decision concerning Hilda and her apparent inability to keep up with the work. Identify at least three alternatives (or more, if you wish) that you believe might be possible solutions.

Questions:

1. Which alternative appears sufficiently workable to be the first one attempted? And what information do you need to assemble in preparing to justify your decision?
2. If your initial decision is found unworkable or unacceptable, which alternative would be your second choice? Why?

REFERENCES

1. Lewin, K. 1951. *Field theory in social science.* New York: Harper & Row.
2. Gantt, H. 1973. *Industrial leadership.* Easton, PA: Hive.
3. Likert, R. 1961. *New patterns of management.* New York: McGraw-Hill.
4. Sullivan, D. 1987. *Work smart, not hard.* New York: Facts on File.
5. DeBono, E. 1970. *Lateral thinking: Creativity step by step.* New York: Harper & Row.
6. Delbecq, A.L., et al. 1975. *Group techniques for program planning.* Glenview, IL: Scott, Foresman.

Chapter 36

Negotiating Skills

Success or failure depends solely on one's attitude.
All things are conquerable. It's simply a matter
of beliefs and accompanying attempts.

—David V.A. Ambrose

An agreement is only as good
as the people involved.

—Jack Nadel

CHAPTER OBJECTIVES

- Introduce the four basic forms of negotiation.
- Provide guidelines to apply in preparing for negotiation.
- Outline the major steps involved in effective negotiation.
- Identify the more common barriers to successful negotiation and suggest how these may be avoided.
- Provide the supervisor with suggestions on how to negotiate with his or her immediate superior.

We all engage in negotiations at work and at home on a daily basis. Many of us start our day negotiating with offspring over what they will wear to school. Supervisors negotiate with vendors; workers negotiate over vacation schedules. When we hold a performance review, a counseling session, or moderate a problem-solving meeting, we often wish that we were better negotiators. A characteristic of effective leaders is that they are persuasive negotiators who obtain commitment rather than obedience from their people.

FOUR BASIC FORMS OF NEGOTIATION

The *power play* or *"gotcha"* approach is authoritarian and is based on marshaling enough power to overwhelm opponents. People who play this game may have prestigious titles, powerful friends, or weighty professional expertise. They consider it naive to believe that cooperation works. These attempts at dominance often meet counter-dominance and become less effective as people learn how to cope with them. The Sherman Tanks we described in Chapter 22 like to play "gotcha." There are several ways to cope with power plays.

- Develop a thick skin. Do not take the nasty things you hear personally.
- Do not be intimidated. Be assertive without being aggressive.
- If someone tries to intimidate you with technical jargon, don't hesitate to speak up (for example, "I need you to put that in one-syllable words").
- Request a third-party mediator.
- Respond to threats with "Why would you want to do that?"

Taking *fixed positions* is a "take-it-or-leave-it" approach. Both sides adopt rigid positions and are reluctant to compromise. They become locked into defending those positions to save face, and negotiations become contests of will rather than problem-solving exercises.

In the *haggling* approach, experienced hagglers ask for more than they expect to get. They offer options that are only favorable to them. They try to create an obligation by giving the other party a little something or make them feel guilty (for example, "I take that remark personally"). They promise more than they know they will deliver. Avoid the high-low dollar game. In that game sellers quote figures that are much higher than they expect to get. Buyers respond with figures much lower than they expect to pay. The expectation is that the agreed-upon amount will be somewhere in the middle. Although this game may be appropriate in some instances, the outcome depends too heavily on the persuasiveness of one party or on how badly the buyer wants the product or service. If you are the buyer and you have done your homework, make one honest offer and stick to it. You have the option of turning around and walking away.

Collaboration or *value adding* is more likely to result in win-win outcomes. You achieve your goals while helping others achieve theirs. Collaboration is based on the premise that you make the pie bigger rather than fighting over the size of each party's slice. The negotiators add value to the package rather than seeking concessions from each other. The more creative they are, the better the results. For example, an employee seeks permission to leave work early each day so she can pick up her child at school. Her supervisor balks. When the employee proposes to make up the time by accepting more weekend assignments, the supervisor readily agrees. They both win.

PREPARING FOR NEGOTIATION

Assembling Your Wish List

Each person has different interests, so being prepared helps you understand these different interests. At least you must know what you want and what you are willing to concede. Sometimes it helps to have not only a specific goal but also several fallback positions or alternative goals. For important negotiations, put these goals in writing.

Before the meeting, try to find out what the other side wants and how badly they want it. What are they likely to propose? What advantages do they have?

Collect Data

The information you take into a negotiation may be copies of laws, policies, protocols, guidelines, or other backup material. Get up-to-date information through your formal and informal communication channels. Organize information so it is concise and understandable. Include handouts, graphs, charts, and other visual displays.

Organize Your Approach

- Sketch out the options you can offer.
- Prepare your opening remarks.
- Ready the arguments you can make to maximize the positive aspects of your interests and to counter the other person's arguments.
- Role-play what you plan to say or offer with a friend or mentor.
- Choose the best time and place for the meeting.

MAJOR STEPS IN NEGOTIATION

1. Clarify interests. Ask people how they view the situation and what is important to them. Paraphrase their message and ask if you have interpreted the view correctly. Then state your position. Do not continue on until these viewpoints and desired outcomes are clear.
2. Focus on points of agreement. Center on what you perceive as areas of agreement. Work from there. Get into the problem areas later.
3. Formulate possible options. Usually the more options you can identify, the better prepared you are. Articulate the benefits of each option to the other person. Do not get stuck believing that your solution is the only good one. Be gracious. If the person has a valid argument, say so. A common mistake that novice negotiators make is to think that something is not negotiable.

This may be based on past experience or what you have been told by others. These assumed constraints are often just that, assumed. You may later regret not exploring such possibilities. Instead of presenting your idea as a proposal, test the waters by stating your case as a question (for example, "I wonder what would happen if we...?"). If it gets a cool reception, you can easily drop the subject with a simple "Yeah, that's right." It you think your idea has great merit and has a good chance of being accepted, the above approach may lead to others taking it over by adding an additional twist. To prevent that, have a written outline of your proposal and introduce it into the discussion.[1]

4. Agree on the best option. If you cannot reach complete agreement, be willing to compromise, but not until you have explored all possible win-win solutions.

5. Be prepared to encounter an impasse. Keep the meeting going even though your initial efforts are unsuccessful. The longer the discussion continues, the more likely the other party is to give in. He or she is reluctant to invest a lot of time in a negotiation without achieving any result. If things continue to stall, call for a break or a postponement. Each of you may need more information or to consult with other individuals.

6. Perfect the deal. Refine the selected deal to ensure that each of you is comfortable with it.

7. Wrap it up. Review what is agreed and document that fact. If it was a long or rigorous negotiation, compliment the other party on being a tough negotiator. This helps you to end on a positive note.

BARRIERS TO SUCCESSFUL NEGOTIATION

Fear

Negotiation may give rise to fear of loss of friendship or future cooperation. Some people cave in quickly because they do not have the stomach for any kind of disagreement. Others are inflexible or demanding because they fear that people will take advantage of them.

When you are negotiating a salary increase and you feel that the organization or your manager is taking advantage of you, there are times when you must threaten to resign. Never do this unless you are willing to follow through. Still better, wait until you have a bona fide offer elsewhere.

Secrecy

Some negotiators mistakenly think that they will win more often if they withhold information.

Ultimatums and Deadlines

Avoid making threats yourself unless they are absolutely necessary. However, sometimes the threat to walk out of a bargaining session will get results. Once you make such a threat, be willing to do it. If you do not, your bluff will be called in future negotiations.

Anger, Induction of Guilt, Ridicule, or Tears

These emotional responses or attempts to manipulate are seldom indicated. Experienced negotiators are not moved by these gimmicks, but some novice negotiators are.

The Team Approach

Although team efforts have some advantages, such as augmented expertise and mutual support, there are potential problems with the team approach. Showing up with a cadre of supporters may suggest that you lack the ability to handle the process by yourself. Sometimes one member of your group makes a remark that hurts your case or reveals disunity among the group's members. The team approach also takes longer and is more likely to end without a consensus being reached.

Reliance on Data

Statistics are useful if valid and not redundant. However, too much reliance on them backfires when the other party finds flaws in your data or comes up with more impressive data of his or her own. You rarely convince people with facts and figures. Search for something in your proposal that appeals to them, and then keep pushing that hot button. Say, for example, that during bargaining the other person frequently mentions paperwork. When negotiation stalls, repeatedly come back to your offer to help with the documentation and reports.

Delaying Tactics

Repeated and unnecessary delays often postpone needed action. They also erode the spirit of cooperation and can be very frustrating to both parties.

NEGOTIATING WITH YOUR BOSS

Unless you are a clone of your manager, the two of you will sometimes experience disagreements. Most of the time, you reach amicable solutions. On rare occasions, your boss will reject something you feel very strongly about (for example, an ethical problem or a raise for you or one of your employees). After the first rebuff, try a second verbal approach at a more convenient time or place and bring more ammunition with you. If that attempt stalls, put your request in writing. Emphasize your strong feelings about the request. If that does not work, you must decide whether the matter is important enough to challenge your boss and possibly to risk your career. If you think it is worth pursuing, tell your manager that you would like the two of you to discuss the problem with his superior. If he declines to accompany you but tells you to go ahead, do so after telling him exactly what you plan to say to his boss. If his response is to threaten you in some way, you must be prepared to react appropriately.

Think About It

Contrary to what some people seem to believe, "compromise" is not a dirty word; it does not connote weakness. Unwillingness to compromise contributes to inflexibility and destroys any chance of achieving a win-win outcome. Be willing to give ground on some issues to get what you want on others. No negotiation is successful unless both parties can feel they have gained something.

Questions for Review and Discussion

1. Concerning the example cited in the discussion of value-added negotiation in which an employee proposes to leave work early each day so she can pick up her child at school by making up the time by accepting more weekend assignments, what critical factor—not mentioned or even inferred in the statement—will have the strongest influence on the extent to which the supervisor can negotiate?

2. What, if anything, is wrong with entering a negotiation with a firm minimum position in mind and announcing that position at the start?

3. What is the principal hazard in negotiating with a single employee a request for a change in the individual's terms and conditions of employment?

4. Reference has been made to negotiations with employees. In what ways, if any, might negotiation enter into a performance appraisal discussion?

5. If you are unable to successfully negotiate a perceived need with your immediate superior, is it ever advisable to go up the chain of command to your superior's boss? When, and why?

Case: An Ultimatum

You are administrative supervisor of the hospital's department of radiology. The department has been having problems with the special procedures area; you have had considerable difficulty recruiting and retaining special procedures technologists. You presently have your allotted staff of three such technologists, but these people are fully utilized, and at least two of them have recently made comments about staffing being inadequate for the workload.

The senior technologist, Carl Smithers, has been especially vocal in his comments about understaffing. Several times, and as recently as Monday of this week, he spoke with you concerning his perception of the need for another technologist. Today, Wednesday the 9th, you received the following note from Smithers:

"As I suggested I would do in our conversation of Monday this week, I am going on record notifying you that additional technologist help must be available by Monday the 21st. If you are unwilling or unable to provide the needed help, I will be unable to continue in my present position beyond Friday the 18th."

You immediately called Smithers and said, "Come to my office right now, Carl. We need to talk." Your intent is to come up with some course of action that will take care of the department's needs and keep your senior technologist in place.

Questions:

1. What has Carl Smithers done to his own negotiating position by delivering an ultimatum?
2. Granted you want to address the problem as soon as possible, but what, if anything, should you have done before sending for Smithers? Why?
3. What are you going to do or suggest doing if available resources continue to forbid adding any new staff?
4. Is there anything positive to immediately come of Smithers' ultimatum? If so, what?

REFERENCES

1. Davidow, W.H., and Uttal, B.K. 1989. *Total customer service: The Ultimate Weapon*. New York: Harper & Row 121.
2. Farnham, A. 1989. The trust gap. *Fortune Magazine* (December 1989): 66.
3. Condodina, J., and Erme, L. 1978. Compensation packages changing shape. *HR Focus* 74(10): S1.
4. Davison, B. 1978. Strategies for managing retention. *HR Focus* 74(10): S3.
5. Zemke, R. 1989. Employee orientation: A process, not a program. *Training* 26: 33–40.
6. Reichheld, F.F. 1993. Loyalty-based management. *Harvard Business Review* 71: 64–73.

RECOMMENDED READING

K. Albrecht and S. Albrecht, *Added Value Negotiating: The Breakthrough Method for Building Balanced Deals* (Homewood, IL: Business One Irwin, 1993).

A.R. Cohen and D.L. Bradford, *Influence Without Authority* (New York: John Wiley & Sons, 1990).

R. Dawson, *Secrets of Power Persuasion* (Englewood Cliffs, NJ: Prentice Hall, 1992).

R. Fisher and W. Ury, *Getting to Yes: Negotiating without Giving In* (New York: HoughtonMifflin, 1988).

H.S. Rindler, *Managing Disagreement Constructively* (Los Altos, CA: Crisp Publishers, 1988).

Chapter 37

Time Management

Regret for time wasted can become a power for
good in the time that remains, if we will only stop
the waste and the idle, useless regretting.

—Arthur Brisbane

By losing present time we lose all time.

—Old Proverb

CHAPTER OBJECTIVES

- Explore the implications of various factors bearing on the use and management of time by the individual supervisor, suggesting the extent to which the supervisor can conceivably take control of his or her work time and surroundings.
- Identify the more commonly encountered time wasters and suggest how the supervisor can counter these when they arise.
- Offer some practical tips for saving time.
- Suggest how the supervisor can effectively address the abuses of time perpetrated by others.

TIME AND THE SUPERVISOR

Most supervisors are well aware of the value of their time. Deadlines, turnaround times, emergencies, and interruptions constantly challenge them. Seldom are there enough hours to complete all their tasks. Most managers put in long hours on the job and often take unfinished work home. Then there are the hours that conscientious supervisors spend at home worrying about problems back at work.

Time management programs, like weight reduction programs, succeed only if one commits to reaching a goal and sticks to that commitment. Experts can tell you how to save time, but you must supply the necessary discipline. To lose weight, people sacrifice things they like to eat. To gain time, people give up some activities they enjoy doing, especially when they do those tasks so well.

Practical time management strategies are twofold: managing your own time and eliminating the time-wasting practices of the people who report to you.

Time Problems of Supervisors

Supervisors who practice management by crisis have major time problems. They react rather than anticipate and plan. They spend large chunks of time running around trying to solve crises instead of preventing them.

Then there are the perfectionists. They are not satisfied with excellence. They strive for perfection. Perfectionists check and double-check everything. They invariably obtain more data and opinions than they need.

Leaders who cannot or will not delegate are always running out of time because they try to do things that others could do for them in addition to the things that only they can do.

Passive individuals have the same kind of time problems as those who fail to delegate. Because they cannot turn down requests that consume their time, they too are constantly struggling to keep up with their own work while serving on numerous committees, doing favors for colleagues, and listening to people problems that should be addressed by others.

Your Office or Workstation

The best place to start a time management program is in your personal work area. There you can see results quickly. To avoid distractions, move your desk so that it does not face the door, or keep your door closed. Arrange filing cabinets and other furnishings to provide ready access to documents.

A messy desk does not necessarily mean a messy mind. If you can quickly find what you are looking for and other folks, such as secretaries, do not need access to items strewn about in your office, keep your organized clutter. Ignore the jibes from your associates. On the other hand, most supervisors spend loads of time looking for things in their offices. Instruct your secretary and others on how you want papers, manuals, office supplies, and other items stored. Revise your filing system. Use a desk drawer file for papers you refer to often. Put other papers in cabinets. Sort and batch your documents, using folders that you label appropriately. Set aside a drawer as a slush file for documents that you are not likely to need but are reluctant to discard right away. Clean out that drawer each month.

Paper Flow

Supervisors often feel overwhelmed by the volume of information they face. It once was thought that the computer would alleviate the paper overload, but it seems to have added to it instead.

Filing begins when you sort your incoming mail. Try to handle each item only once. Practice the 3D idea: Do, Delegate, or Discard. When you hesitate to discard, ask yourself "What is the worst thing that could happen if I do not have this?"

Do not let your hold basket or folder get out of control. Review the items there daily, and act on as many as you can. Jot down a throw-out date on major filed items. Clear off your desk every night to avoid chaos when you arrive the next day.

Additional Ways to Cope with Information Overload

- Be ruthless about what to read and what not to read. Reduce your "to read" pile after screening for relevant information.
- Check the messages you are sending out. Do they improve customer service or provide essential information? If not, rethink their contents.
- Answer memos by writing your responses on the memos rather than preparing additional memos.
- Purge your e-mail of nonessentials.
- Let your computer replace your address/telephone book, Rolodex, "to-do list," calendar, and appointment book.

Maximize the Value of Your Reading Time

- Scan articles, memos, journals, newspapers, or other documents.
- Read the introductions and last paragraphs to decide if you need to read the rest.
- Highlight or underline key passages. Use a scanner to transfer needed information into your computer.
- Prepare and file summaries of important books or lengthy documents.
- Take reading material with you when you have appointments or find it necessary to travel.
- Set aside blocks of time for reading.

Planning and Scheduling

When you fail to plan, you are planning to fail. Establish goals, priorities, schedules, and deadlines for all major undertakings. The more time you spend preparing for meetings, the less time is wasted at those meetings.

Most supervisors have little slack time these days. Make good use of what you have to catch up on correspondence, inventory, files, and low-priority items (busywork). Get your administrative tasks out of the way early or late in the day when there are fewer people around to take up your time. Leave some time for unexpected occurrences. Differentiate between real deadlines, such as for payroll input data, and less urgent ones, such as for the minutes of meetings.

Our physiological clocks are all different. We each have hours of the day when our productivity and ability to concentrate are greater than during the rest of the day. Use those hours to work on major items (for example, presenting ideas to your manager, high-priority discussions, and important correspondence). During periods of low productivity, undertake tasks that are less mentally challenging, such as reading mail, making routine telephone calls, filing, and other routine chores.

Be sure that projects have priorities, due dates, and time estimates. Set realistic time frames. Review long-range goals frequently with superiors.

Use "To-Do" Lists

Group similar tasks together on a "to-do" list. Number the actions in order of importance and urgency. Label each item as must, should, or maybe. Do not expect to accomplish everything on your list every day. Remake or update the list daily. At the end of your workday, the items you did not get to should be low priority ones that you can transfer to the next day's list.

Delegating

The greatest supervisory time saver of all is delegation. Every hour that someone else does something that you previously did is an hour of your time that is saved. See Chapter 31 for a discussion of delegating.

Procrastination

At the very least, procrastination results in spending your time doing tasks that have a lower priority than the one you should be working on. This is compounded when you are immobilized because you have placed the topic on hold.

Practical Suggestions for Minimizing Procrastination

- Use daily prioritized task lists.
- Start the day with the high-priority or unpleasant tasks.
- Avoid the temptation to stall.
- Do not get involved with trivia.

- Block out enough time to complete time-consuming tasks.
- Slice a big task into thin slices that are more easily completed.
- Convince yourself that the task needs doing.
- Challenge your excuses.
- Do not reward procrastination. Do not allow yourself to engage in pleasant activities while you delay action. Sit in a straight chair without coffee or conversation.
- Set a timer for 5 minutes, and force yourself to start when it goes off.

TIME WASTERS AND WHAT TO DO ABOUT THEM

Use a time log to determine how you spend your time. This enables you to ferret out your wasted time and alter your time schedules. It takes 21 days to establish a habit. Select your top five time wasters, and work on them for three weeks. Here are the principal offenders.

- Doing things you do not need to do, including
  tasks that could be delegated,
  trivial things that could be eliminated, and
  excessive socializing.
- Inefficient planning, organizing, and scheduling.
- Unnecessary or poorly run meetings.
- Interruptions, particularly
  drop-in visitors,
  unexpected problems, and
  telephone calls.

Do Not Let People Take Advantage of You

To avoid overcommitment of your time and other resources, say "no" diplomatically but emphatically. With subordinates, this often means not allowing them to delegate their work upward to you. That is not easy if you are readily flattered or manipulated.

Offer alternatives to colleagues. When a superior makes a request that creates a serious time problem for you, nail down priorities (for example, "Should I stop working on the…?" or "Will someone else handle…?").

Visitor Control

Do not refer directly to visitors as annoyances or time wasters, even though many are just that. Most visitors are external or internal customers, and you should treat them as such. Efficient managers save time elsewhere so that they can spend more time with their visitors.

Unfortunately, we all have to deal with people who are excessively verbose or have lots of time to kill. Certain sales representatives and casual acquaintances may be high on your list of pests. The worst of the lot are those who cannot take hints that you are very busy and would like to end the conversation. Here are a few suggestions for handling visitors who abuse your time.

- Train and empower your staff so they have less need to consult with you or to get your permission on routine matters.
- Train your staff to help visitors when you are not immediately available.
- Meet people in their territory. You then control the time of the meeting. Managing by walking around reduces the number of people who walk into your office.
- Shut your door when you really need privacy.
- Intercept visitors outside your office. Once people get into your office, transaction time increases.
- Remain standing and do not invite the visitor to be seated.
- Use verbal and nonverbal language to signal that you wish to end the meeting.
  1. Reduce eye contact.
  2. Glance at the clock or your watch.
  3. Start shuffling papers, tapping a pencil, or drumming your fingers.
  4. Put your hand on your telephone.
  5. Say "Could we continue this later when I'm not so swamped?" or "I won't take any more of your time."
  6. Stand up and extend your hand.
  7. Come out from behind your desk and walk toward the door.

Group Meetings

Try to limit group meetings to 45 minutes. People start becoming restless after that. If you must go on, call a break.

If you are not the chairperson and the meetings always start late, come late or bring busywork with you.

Send members of your staff to represent you. For more on meetings, see Chapter 34.

One-on-One Communication

Apply all of the communication skills discussed in previous chapters. Communication competency prevents misunderstandings, mistakes, and the need for repeats, all of which are major time wasters.

If you tend to be verbose on the telephone, put an egg timer next to the phone. When windy talkers trap you in a corridor, wait until they pause for breath, then summarize what was said and start edging away. If they continue to talk, ask them to excuse you and leave. Say that you have an appointment (you can always have an appointment with your inner soul, can't you?).

TIPS FOR SAVING TIME

Already enumerated as time savers were:

- Avoid procrastination or perfectionism.
- Delegate what others can do or can be trained to do.
- Plan, schedule, and set priorities.
- Improve your communication skills.
- Learn to say "no."
- Reduce wasted time at meetings.
- Use margin replies for informal written correspondence.
- Keep your desk ready for action.
- Select the most appropriate channel for every communication.

Additional time savers:

- Express as much appreciation to people for saving your time as you do to people who help you save money.
- Reduce interruptions by coming to work early or staying late, by finding a good hiding place, or by using a "Thank You for Not Disturbing" sign.
- Monitor your time usage. Keep a log.
- Use waiting times to read or to do short tasks.
- Make phone calls in bunches.
- Refer calls and visitors to others.
- Decrease your socializing time.
- Study and streamline your workflow patterns.
- Use videotapes for repetitive teaching (for example, orientation and training of new hires).
- Use dictation instead of doing the typing yourself.
- Use the telephone for conference calls.
- Ask for help when you need it.

TIME ABUSES BY OTHERS

Time theft may be America's biggest crime. Robert Half, a personnel expert, writes, "The average worker in the United States has an average of 7 to 12 unscheduled absences each year. He wastes 18% of the time he is supposed to be

---

Ten Major Time-Use Blunders

1. Tolerating abuses of your open-door policy
2. Overuse of memos, reports, and electronic messages
3. Unnecessary or poorly run meetings
4. Lack of assigning and delegating
5. Excessive socializing
6. Doing other people's work and solving their problems
7. Accepting too many unimportant assignments
8. Lack of planning
9. Inadequate paper flow and storage
10. Procrastination

---

working. That equals nine 35-hour weeks…a 'vacation' of more than two months per year at work."[1]

Nip bad habits in the bud with better coaching and counseling. Remember, however, that your subordinates number among your customers and should be treated with kindness and consideration. Show compassion for employees who have latchkey children or who have other special situations that sometimes call for a bit of understanding slack.

The first step in eliminating or decreasing this time waste is to be aware of it. Our old strategy of managing by wandering around pays off handsomely. Merely appearing on the scene squelches idle conversations and lets people know that you are aware of their inappropriate absences from the work area.

Changes in workstations can often help. Some employees accomplish more when they work alone; certain others get more done when working in a group.

Major Time Thefts

- Taking unjustified sick days
- Arriving late or leaving early
- Taking long breaks or extended meal periods
- Leaving one's post for personal trips (shopping, banking, etc.)
- Doing personal tasks on the job
- Socializing excessively
- Interrupting others
- Wandering about the facility
- Making excessive personal phone calls
- Allowing personal or family visitors
- Daydreaming

Study workflow patterns and other systems to find out whether you can achieve more efficiency.

Think About It

Always keep in mind that time is the ultimate nonrenewable resource. Most other resources required in operating the organization can be renewed, recovered, or replaced, but a moment of time, once it is gone, is gone forever.

Questions for Review and Discussion
1. Why is delegation clearly identified as the greatest supervisory time saver?
2. What is the strongest force acting to prevent us from improving our use of time? Why is this, and what can be done about it?
3. Why do some individuals spend time focusing on low-priority tasks even when they know there are more important tasks waiting?
4. How might some supervisors feel trapped into overcommitting their time?
5. Why is it often suggested to begin the workday by first tackling the unpleasant tasks?
6. What is the usual fate of material that's set aside to read "when the time is available?" Why does this occur?
7. What particular characteristics might be exhibited by a supervisor who continually seems to become caught up in people problems that should actually be addressed by others?
8. What is wrong with the process of gathering more data and opinions than may be needed? Is this not a sound means of ensuring accuracy?
9. How can you learn to say no when the overload comes via demands of your immediate superior?
10. What is fundamentally wrong with reactive management? Doesn't it ensure that you are working on the most urgent matter of the moment?

Case: Where Does the Time Go?

Kay Thatcher, director of staff education, decided she had to get organized. Recently her work days had been running well beyond quitting time, cutting noticeably into the time required by family responsibilities. And all the while her backlog of work was growing.

Inspired by an article about planning and setting priorities, Kay decided to try planning each day's activities at the end of the previous day. This Monday Kay came to the office with her day planned out to the last minute. During the morning she had to complete a report on a recent learning-needs analysis, write the performance appraisals of two part-time instructors, and assemble the balance of the materials for a 2-hour class she was scheduled to conduct that afternoon. After lunch she had to conduct the class, complete the schedule for the next 3 months' training activities (now 10 days overdue), and prepare no-tices—which should be posted this very day—for two upcoming classes.

Kay got off to a good start; she finished her report before 10:00 and turned her attention to the two performance evaluations. However, at that time the interruptions began. In the next two hours she was interrupted six times—three telephone calls and three visitors. The calls were all appropriate busi-ness calls. Two of the visitors had legitimate problems, one of them taking 30 minutes to resolve. The other visitor was a fellow supervisor simply passing the time of day. Neither performance evaluation was completed, and the training materials were assembled in time only because Kay put them to-gether during lunch while she juggled a sandwich at her desk.

Kay's afternoon class ran 20 minutes overtime because of legitimate ques-tions and discussion. When she returned to her office she discovered she had a visitor, a good-humored, talkative sales representative from whom Kay oc-casionally bought audiovisual materials. The sales rep, who "happened to be in the area" and just dropped in, stayed for an hour and a half.

After the sales rep departed Kay spent several minutes simply wondering what to do next. The performance appraisals, the 3-month class schedules, the class notices—all were overdue. Deciding on the class notices because they were the briefest task before her, she dashed off both notices in long-hand and asked the nursing office secretary to type them, copy them, and post them immediately. Then she tackled the training schedule.

When Kay looked up again from her work it was nearly an hour past quit-ting time. She still had a long way to go on the schedule and had not yet started on the two performance appraisals. As she swept her work aside for the day she sadly reflected that in spite of all her planning she had not ac-complished two thirds of what she intended to do that day. She decided, how-ever, to try again; when she could get a few minutes of quiet time late in the evening, she would plan her next day's activity.

On her way out of the hospital she happened to glance at the main bulletin board. The small satisfaction she felt when she saw the posted class notices vanished instantly when she discovered that both were incorrect—the dates and times of the two classes had been interchanged.

Questions:

1. What apparent mistakes did Kay make in attempting to improve her use of time by planning and establishing priorities?
2. In what respects could Kay possibly have improved her use of time on the Monday described in the case? (State any reasonable as-sumptions you might make in providing possible answers.)

Case: How Time Flies

You are the business office supervisor at Community Hospital. At 9:00 this morning your boss, the controller, called you to his office for "a little chit-chat, 10 minutes or so, on where we stand getting the new procedure manual finished." You scooped up the proper papers and went to his office, bracing yourself because you knew how frustrating these sessions could be.

When you entered and seated yourself, your manager was shuffling through the desktop clutter looking for a particular document. At the same time he found the document he also found a pink telephone message slip apparently left over from the previous day. He said, "Oh-oh, should have done this yesterday. Hang on just a minute."

The "minute" turned into a quarter hour as he transacted some business and engaged in some social conversation. You fidgeted, wondering as you always did at such times whether you should get up and leave and return when he was free.

You were perhaps 5 minutes underway with the true subject of your meeting when the telephone rang. The boss answered it himself, although there was a secretary available who could have taken the call. This time it was 10 minutes before you could return to the subject of the meeting. Before you concluded your business, your manager had taken two more calls and made a brief additional call for something he "just remembered."

When at last you were finished to the boss's satisfaction you rose to leave. He rose also, reaching for his empty coffee mug. On his way out of the office he glanced at his watch and said, "Wow, 10:00 o'clock already. Time sure flies."

You made no comment. You were well aware that the pile of work on your desk had gotten no smaller while you were tied up for a full hour trying to accomplish about 10 minutes worth of true work.

Questions:

1. What assumptions about his time and your time are implicit in your manager's behavior?
2. What can you possibly do—or try to do—to encourage your manager to show more respect for your working time?
3. To pose a question that is considerably broader than time management alone: Of what serious management errors is your manager apparently guilty?

REFERENCES

1. Half, R. 1984. Management roundup. *Management Review* 73: 7.

RECOMMENDED READING

R. Bittel, *Right on Time: the Complete Guide for Time-Pressured Managers*. (New York: McGraw-Hill, 1991).

M.E. Douglass and D.H. Douglass, *Time Management for Teams*. (New York: AMACOM, 1992). D. Scott, *The Telephone and Time Management*. (Los Altos, CA: Crisp Publishers, 1988).

PART VI

Self-Enhancement for Supervisors

Chapter 38

Coping with Stress and Burnout

There are many styles for coping with stress,
ranging from passivity to direct confrontation.
The most important element is the ability
to recognize when individuals are
experiencing stress and its causes.[1]

CHAPTER OBJECTIVES

- Identify the various causes of stress, both internal to the individual and in the environment in which the individual functions.
- Provide the supervisor with guidelines for reducing stress within the department, including the use of departmental stress programs.
- Address the subject of burnout, including recognition of the signs of burnout and its usual stages.
- Suggest what the supervisor can do to minimize personally experienced stress caused and aggravated by conditions and experiences in the workplace.

One of every three workers in the United States who calls in sick is experiencing a stress-related problem. According to a report in *Time*, June 6, 1983, the cost of stress-related illnesses in the United States was $50 to $75 billion a year in the early 1980s. Although current figures are not available, everything that has been experienced in business in general and health care in particular over these recent two decades suggests that the cost of stress-related illness is now considerably greater. In this country, the four most used kinds of drugs—headache remedies, tranquilizers, antihypertensive agents, and ulcer medications—are used primarily for treating stress-related conditions.

EXTERNAL CAUSES OF STRESS

Most working individuals have limited control over factors external to themselves that contribute to stress. External stressors related to work include

- Work environment: parking difficulties, uncomfortable or noisy surroundings, equipment failures, and safety concerns. Infection and safety concerns are especially prevalent in health care institutions.
- The job itself: too much work, time pressures, organizational and procedural changes, and job insecurity.
- Work relationships: harassment, threats, personality incompatibilities, difficult patients or patient families, competition between and among departments and workers.
- Hierarchical factors: lack of goals, mission or objectives, confusing or difficult policies, lack of support from management.
- Poor leadership: flawed communication, favoritism, discrimination, insufficient authority to fulfill responsibilities, nitpicking, unclear responsibilities.
- Outside factors: family, financial, legal, or health concerns.

INTERNAL FACTORS AGGRAVATING STRESS

These causes dwell within ourselves, and they act as multipliers of the external factors that besiege us.

- Lack of confidence or self-esteem due to lack of expertise or experience.
- Health problems resulting in decreased immunity and frequent illnesses.
- Irrational thinking. False perceptions of powerlessness and flawed assumptions may be rampant. Some people set unrealistic goals and aspirations. Employees often stretch virtues into evils (for example, perfectionism, excess emotional involvement in patient care, or making work the most important activity in life).
- Clash of actions with values. Stress occurs when our actions are not congruent with our values. For example, when we spend long hours at work (action) and neglect our family responsibilities (value).
- Emotions. Being buffeted by a negative emotion such as fear, guilt, anger, or resentment is like trying to drive a car with the emergency brake on; movement is limited, and there is a great strain on the parts.
  1. Fears. We are beset with all kinds of fear, with or without real basis: fear of job loss, fear of failure or rejection, and fear of getting AIDS or hepatitis. These fears are compounded by the ever-increasing rate of technological and organizational changes and lack of job security.
  2. Guilt. Guilt is characterized by feelings of inadequacy and inferiority. It makes us indulge in self-criticism and in the criticism of others. People

who feel guilt use "victim language" such as "I should," "I have to," or "It wasn't my fault."

3. Anger. The stress produced by daily contact with difficult people is often associated with anger. When anger is not resolved, frustration sets in. There is usually an underlying hurt or fear, especially the fear that you cannot cope with the situation or that you are regarded as unimportant. Resentment is a subtle, continuous, seething anger that is seldom expressed directly to the person or persons who are resented.

RESPONSIBILITIES OF SUPERVISORS

Because leadership plays an important role in the amount of stress prevalent within a group, supervisors have considerable accountability for stress control. Supervisors' four major stress-related responsibilities are

1. Reducing the stress that they may personally cause;
2. Protecting their employees from stress induced by other people;
3. Empowering their employees and raising their self-esteem; and
4. Recognizing the signs and symptoms of burnout and take remedial steps.

HOW TO REDUCE STRESS IN YOUR DEPARTMENT

Hire Stress-Resistant People

Select employees whose needs and abilities correspond with the demands of the job. See Chapter 7 for the kinds of questions that can help in spotting the susceptible people during employment interviews.

Orient and Train Thoroughly

Well-designed orientation and training programs reduce anxiety, create realistic job expectations, and provide the skills needed to work effectively. Clear and unambivalent policies and procedures, when enforced uniformly and fairly, reduce hierarchical pressures. Active mentoring provides additional stress resistance.

Empower Employees

Individuals who feel that they are in control of their work and their future are better equipped to handle stress. When they are competent and their skills are marketable, they become more burnout resistant. Self-empowerment and empowerment by management are essential to the development of this mindset (see Chapter 31).

Counsel Stressed Workers

Support your employees by word and action, especially when performance drops off. Get them to express their concerns and frustrations. Help them to reinforce the good things about themselves by reviewing their past successes. Encourage them to adopt realistic goals. Refer them to professional counselors if this seems indicated. Eliminate specific stressors when possible without interfering with the workflow or imposing on other workers.

Ensure Time for Breaks

Make certain that your people get their breaks. Encourage them to use the time in a healthy way (for example, socializing, exercising, relaxing, and meditating). If possible, provide health food such as fruit instead of doughnuts and coffee.

Modify Assignments, Team Compositions, Management Style

Rotating assignments or shifts may be appropriate in specific instances. Transfers or changes in work schedules may also be therapeutic.

DEPARTMENTAL STRESS PROGRAMS

Support groups are most effective when they function under their own leadership. Participants can talk openly about their personal responses to the demands of their work. They find common problems and search for remedial measures. At their meetings, they may use guest speakers, audiovisuals, reading materials, and brainstorming.

Coping Methods for Departmental Stress Programs

- Relaxation or meditation techniques
- Exercise
- Diet adjustment
- Review of job designs, policies, and procedures
- Solution of communication, ethical, and workflow problems
- Resolution of conflicts

There is increasing interest in wellness and disease prevention. Exercise, healthy diet, and supplemental vitamins and minerals appear to increase immunity and counter the harmful physiological effects of stress. Health stores feature many herbs and neutraceutical combinations that are alleged to help cope with stress. Also, employees generally appreciate talks from dietitians and health experts.

BURNOUT

Burnout is the condition of emotional and physical collapse caused by the unchecked escalation of stress. Everyone has a breaking point, but most emotionally stable people protect themselves intuitively by focusing on current tasks while shutting out most past or future problems.

The most vulnerable employees are the perfectionists, workaholics, overachievers, insecure job holders, and people with low self-esteem.

Signs and Symptoms of Burnout

Anxiety or depression
Waking up tired
Chronic fatigue
High blood pressure
Insomnia and nightmares
Cardiac irregularities
Headaches, backaches, premenstrual syndrome
Elevated cholesterol
Duodenal ulcers
Loss of appetite
Compulsive eating

What Colleagues and Families Notice

Emotional outbursts
High-pitched, nervous laughter
Increased use of sick leave
Increased resistance to change
Avoidance of decision making
Increased use of alcohol or drugs
Frequent talk about escaping
Increased irritability and complaints
Decline in work performance
Trembling, tics, or stuttering
Lack of enthusiasm and energy

Four Typical Stages of Coping with Burnout

1. Doing nothing, hoping it will go away.
2. Seeking fast relief from alcohol, drugs, and/or pharmaceuticals.
3. Taking it out on others.
4. Seeking professional help.

When an employee is ravaged by full-blown burnout, continued employment is impossible, and the person must receive extended professional counseling. In its early stages remedial measures can reverse the condition.

It is the responsibility of supervisors to be alert for the signs and symptoms of burnout and to persuade those so afflicted to get professional help. Supervisors can also modify or eliminate major stressors and provide psychological support during the employee's therapy.

MANAGING YOUR PERSONAL STRESS

Self-empowerment is the key to immunizing you against stress and preventing burnout. You have more power than you realize. You have some degree of control over each of your major stressors. For example:

- You can reduce or eliminate your job insecurity by making your services more marketable.
- You can fire (for cause) that employee who makes life miserable for you.
- You can exercise your power to make most of the daily decisions you face.
- You can make people smile, laugh, frown, and even cry.
- You do not need permission to do most of the things you do (for example, thank someone, hold a meeting, ask for help, say "no," or pack up and leave).

Augment Your Competencies

- Keep up to date technically and professionally.
- Fine-tune your interpersonal skills.
- Make yourself more marketable.
- Request more educational support.
- Train for alternative jobs or vocations.

Eliminate Perceived Barriers

Separate that which is only a perception from that which is reality. Challenge all of your assumptions.

Improve Your Self-Talk

Shower your subconscious mind with positive affirmations. Affirmations are simple statements that proclaim positive facts about yourself or someone else. Articulate them plainly and emphatically. They are clear, brief, strong, and positive, and they grow more effective with repetition. Some examples are "I will" (instead of "I should" or "I will try"), "I am in control here," "I am a worthy person," "I feel good about that," or "I earned that." Affirmations have a way of becoming reality.

Kick the habit of putting yourself down. Instead of criticizing yourself and telling yourself what you cannot do, congratulate yourself for the things you can do. Do not compare yourself unfavorably with others. When criticized unfairly by a superior, say to yourself "That's only one person's opinion." Neutralize negative information by saying "cancel" when negative thoughts start to flow into your consciousness. Say it aloud instead of just thinking it—the sound provides double reinforcement. Follow the "cancel" with an affirmation.

Surround Yourself with Optimistic, Enthusiastic Doers

The people you associate with affect the way you feel and how you ultimately behave. Examine your friendships and relationships at work and during your leisure hours. If you have been lunching with negative and critical people, find more upbeat folks. Eat with a different group each day. Put some limits on the time you spend with negative friends and relatives.

Join social and community organizations. Most organizations feature optimistic, energetic people. Become a leader in one of these organizations. Almost anyone can be elected to an office in a professional group. All you have to do is attend the business meetings, sit up near the front, and ask an occasional question or make a few comments. On the other hand, do not get bogged down by social or professional activities that are stressful or take too much time away from work or family.

Practice Success Imagery

There are two kinds of success imagery. In results imagery, you visualize a highly successful outcome of a future event. For example, when preparing to give a talk, you picture your audience giving you a standing ovation. In process imagery, you visualize every step of the activity and feel each emotion. For example, in the above scenario, you visualize the moderator introducing you. You feel your heart pounding. You see yourself taking a deep breath and forcing a smile. You hear your introductory remarks.

Laugh More

> *When the going gets tough, the tough lighten up!*

The simple act of laughter increases our body's endorphins, the stress fighters. People who watch a video comedy have higher levels of endorphins and lower levels of adrenaline and cortisol, the stress producers. Snicker when you make a little mistake. Enjoy a hearty laugh, and actively seek humor. When you visit a work site, notice the differences in the amount of joking and smiles. You can sense the deflection of stress.

Also:

- Escape, literally or mentally
- Take a walk on your breaks
- Find a quiet place to relax and daydream
- Learn relaxation or meditation techniques
- Expand your supportive network (see Chapter 41)
- Keep a log of your successes
- Behave assertively (see Chapter 41)

Think About It

Supervisors tend to manage their employees the way they were managed, and their behavior often includes the residual influences of autocratic, authoritarian, stress-inducing management behavior. Today, however, it is necessary to recognize that the supervisor who bosses, pushes, or intimidates creates stresses in the work group that actually hinder effective performance and undermine working relationships. The so-called "hard-driving manager" who knowingly places stressful demands and conditions on the employees is making questionable short-run progress at significantly great expense to future effectiveness.

Questions for Review and Discussion:

1. How can a lack of knowledge of the organization's long-terms goals contribute to stress among rank-and-file employees?
2. How can circumstances in one's private life outside of work contribute to stress on the job?
3. How can ethical considerations affect the level of a supervisor's job-related stress? Provide an example.
4. Describe one way in which a supervisor can at least partially control the level of stress experienced by his or her employees.

5. What should you look for in recruiting for new employees to improve your chances of hiring stress-resistant personnel?
6. Why are appropriately empowered employees less likely than others to experience excessive stress or burnout?
7. How has the recent trend toward reengineering, reorganizing, and the formation of health systems contributed to employee stress? To management stress?
8. What can a supervisor do to protect the department's employees from stress coming from sources outside the department?
9. How can the goals of an individual employee contribute to stress or help to control or avoid stress?
10. What is one present condition or circumstance affecting health care in general that is contributing to increasing stress levels? Why is this so?

Case: Surprise!

On Monday morning when the business office employees arrived at the hospital, they immediately noticed the absence of the office manager. This was not unusual; the manager was frequently absent on Monday. However, he rarely failed to call his department when he would not be there, and on this day he still had not called by noon.

Shortly after lunch the two working supervisors in the business office were summoned to the administrator's office. There they were told that the office manager was no longer employed by the hospital. They, the two supervisors, were told to look after things for the current week and that a new manager, already secured, would be starting the following Monday. All the supervisors were told about the new manager was that it was somebody from outside of the hospital.

The supervisors were not told whether the manager resigned or was discharged, nor were they told whether anyone from within the department had been considered as a replacement.

Questions:

1. What was right or wrong abut the manner in which the change in business office manager was made?
2. What do you suppose would be the attitudes of the business office staff upon hearing of the change?
3. What do you believe would have been the level of stress among the department's staff *before* the change was announced and immediately *after* the change was announced? Why the difference, if any?
4. What can the two working supervisors do to help control the stress level in the group during the week spent waiting for the new manager?

Case: The Forceful Organizer

You are the admitting supervisor for Central Hospital. This morning you were called to attend a meeting about possible union-organizing activity.

On the way to the meeting you observe a man (his back is to you and you do not recognize him) backing one of the building service workers into a corner. The man appears to be trying to get the person to take a card and a pen he is holding.

You cannot hear what is being said, but the worker appears to be close to tears, and she is effectively trapped in the corner. Your first thought is of active solicitation of interest in a union election; you are reasonably certain the man is trying to get the worker to sign a union authorization card.

You move closer in an effort to see the man's face.

Questions:

1. It seems obvious to you that the building service worker is caught in a stressful situation. What can you do to provide the employee with some immediate relief?
2. The individual who is cornered is not one of your employees. What do you believe is your responsibility, if any, to this employee?
3. What will you do if you recognize the man as an employee (of a department other than yours)? Or if you are reasonably certain he is an outsider?
4. What would you recommend as steps to take to reduce the chances of another employee being subjected to the same behavior?

REFERENCES

1. Appelbaum, S.H. 1981. *Stress management for health care professionals.* Rockville, MD: Aspen Systems, 183.

RECOMMENDED RESOURCES

M. English, *How To Feel Great About Yourself and Your Life.* (New York, NY: AMACOM, 1992).

R. Mellott, *Stress Management for Professionals.* (Boulder, CO: CareerTrack Publishers, 1987). Four audiotapes.

B. Sommer, *Psycho-Cybernetics 2000.* (Englewood Cliffs, NJ: Prentice Hall, 1993).

B.E. Statland, "Caught in the Web: Combating Work Stress in the Information Age," *Medical Laboratory* Observer 29, no. 8 (1997): 82–9.

Chapter 39

Career Development
for Supervisors

Luck is where you find it—but you have to find it.
Meanwhile, get as much experience as you can, so
you'll be ready for luck when you run into it.

—Henny Youngman[1]

CHAPTER OBJECTIVES

- Review the generally accepted criteria for success and identify the characteristics of achievers.
- Establish the critical roles of both risk and opportunity in building a productive and satisfying career.
- Suggest how to enhance your career development by increasing your promotability and marketability.
- Present a number of steps to success that have worked for many people and that can enable a person to succeed to the full extent of his or her individual determination and ability.

FIVE CRITERIA FOR SUCCESS

Most people would be content with their lot in life if they were able to meet the following five criteria for success:

1. peace of mind,
2. health and energy,
3. a loving relationship,
4. freedom from financial hardship, and
5. a perception of personal fulfillment.

CHARACTERISTICS OF ACHIEVERS

- Achievers project a winning attitude.
- Achievers are enthusiastic about their work.
- Achievers are flexible, adjusting quickly to change.
- Achievers accept ambiguity and uncertainty.
- Achievers are rapid learners and invest in lifelong education.
- Achievers hold themselves accountable for outcomes.
- Achievers manage their own morale and empowerment.
- Achievers are problem solvers, not complainers.
- Achievers set goals for themselves.
- Achievers use their time wisely.
- Achievers have a reputation for innovativeness.
- Achievers are technically or professionally competent.
- Achievers are assertive and stress resistant.
- Achievers are effective communicators.
- Achievers are customer oriented.

ONLY YOU ARE RESPONSIBLE FOR YOUR CAREER

WORTHWHILE CAREERS INVOLVE TAKING RISKS

By definition, excellence requires deviance from accepted norms. Such deviance involves career risks. You achieve excellence by making unpopular or risky decisions that are avoided by others. This requires courage.

Risk taking is essential if you want to advance. Even standing pat involves risk because any job can become obsolete. Preparing for the future requires making decisions, some of which involve considerable time, expense, and sacrifice. Risk takers exhibit the flexibility that today's employers appreciate. Self-confident, enthusiastic, and optimistic, the risk takers regard mistakes as learning experiences.

We are not recommending that people take foolish risks or neglect to gather sufficient information to make good decisions. Risk taking can be overdone, even becoming foolhardy. Avoid making the same mistake twice. Do not disregard your intuitive warnings and past experience. Reduce risks by adding safety measures. For example, find a new job before putting your present employment on the line.

Eliminate Your Fears

Two of our most powerful fears are fear of failure and fear of the unknown. You must be willing to take career risks and regard failures as learning experiences.

Answer These Questions Before Taking a Major Risk

What is my goal or objective?
What are the best and worst possible outcomes?
What additional information do I need? From what sources?
What are the alternative measures?
What are the relative rewards and risks of each alternative?
What barriers must I overcome?
What support is available?
What contingency plan is available?
How can I eliminate or reduce amount of risk?
How will delay affect the benefit and the risk?

WINDS OF CHANGE BLOW IN OPPORTUNITIES

The contention that opportunity knocks only once is a myth approaching the ridiculous. Opportunity is knocking all the time, if people would only listen. Because opportunities often present themselves without warning, always be prepared to grab the brass ring when it comes around.

Investigate Opportunities in Your Workplace

New services such as patient-focused care present new challenges. Consider projects or new assignments that solve problems for your employer or your leader.

Do not forget all the administrative roles needed to carry out various organizational changes. Reporters comment on the loss of jobs at various institutions. However, perceptive observers note that while employers are eliminating some positions, they are also offering many new ones. The parking lots are still full. Reengineering, alliances, new services, and adjusting to the mandates of state and federal regulations create needs that require new positions.

The best new jobs in your institution are not those you find in the local newspaper or the company newsletter. They may not appear on the bulletin boards outside personnel departments. They reach you via the grapevine or your personal network. Now is a critical time to expand that network and to latch onto mentors who are at the forefront of your organization's initiatives.

Learn all you can about your organization's initiatives. What initiatives are your employer or your manager contemplating? Reflect on how you can benefit from these changes. Still better, suggest some changes of your own. Maybe you can create a new and better job for yourself. Consider possible new services or customers, marketing strategies, satellite operations, or restructuring. Look, sound, and act as someone who is already qualified to assume a new role. You want your boss to feel comfortable when he or she tries to picture you in that slot.

Organizational restructuring creates opportunities for people who are willing and able to move into new careers. Supervisors who dislike controlling others are usually happier when they revert to nonsupervisory roles. Alert professionals are always on the lookout for new positions created by any restructuring in their institutions or elsewhere. Organizations in crises are always in need of capable leaders who can help them survive.

Design a new position for yourself that will make your work more satisfying for you and more valuable to the organization. Before you discuss your proposal, outline a comprehensive plan. What do you want, and what do you need to get there? In these negotiations be assertive, but not demanding, about changing your position description or assignments. Be willing to compromise.

Be Alert for Outside Opportunities

Do your own market research. What are current and future trends in the industry or in other areas where you may have career interests? What skills do you need now and in the future? Consider the advantages and disadvantages of each type of position or employer. For example, professionals who become bored working in the same environment may find more satisfying roles as on-call employees for multiple medical facilities.

Consider a vocational change. Many nurses and other health care supervisors are finding their niches in managed care organizations. See Chapter 25 for a description of some of the positions available in the managed care industry.

Many people use career changes to do things that they never had time for or to develop previously latent talents. Consult with your mentors. Career counselors are just as close as the yellow pages of your phone book.

INCREASE YOUR PROMOTABILITY AND MARKETABILITY

Hard Work Is Not Enough

Hard work alone rarely earns promotions or gets big raises. Employers applaud excellent past performance and usually base rewards and recognition on that basis. Nevertheless, they have an even greater incentive to promote people who have the potential for doing still more for them in the future. The manager who is considering promoting someone is thinking, "How will promoting this person help me?"

Employability requires keeping up with the literature, attending educational and professional meetings, and expanding your personal network. Question mentors and other people in your network about opportunities in your present field or in a new one. Ask them for advice on whom to contact.

The final chapter of this book discusses the importance of workplace politics and networking in securing job advancement and rewards.

What Today's Employers Look For

Employers look for people who can make good and quick decisions, who can come up with solutions to problems, and who exhibit enthusiasm and initiative. They want leaders who can coordinate new teams, integrate new technology across departmental lines, and accept altered supervisory roles created by workforce reductions.

Knowing that frontline supervisors and their staffs can spot opportunities for improvement before executives do, employers want leaders who are observant, proactive, and innovative. They value flexibility and adaptability more than ever.

Review Your Present Status

Take a second look at your career as it now stands by asking yourself the following questions.

- Am I doing what I want to do?
- Do I spend most of the workday doing things I enjoy?
- What aspects of my present situation am I reluctant to change?
- What changes in my present job would decrease the amount of time I spend doing what I dislike doing or increase the time spent on more enjoyable tasks?
- Should I move in the direction of generalist or specialist?
- Would I like to switch from full time to part time or vice versa?
- Are my actions congruent with my personal values? Is my present career hurting my family life?
- To reach my new goals, what must I sacrifice? Am I willing to make that sacrifice?
- How do my family members feel about a change?
- Should I look for a different job within this organization or elsewhere?

Clarify Your Values

Values should weigh heavily in career decisions. A value is what in life is important to you. Without having first established your values, you may lack a clear idea of why you seek a particular goal. With respect to work, do you value challenge, interesting assignments, recognition, involvement, control, or innovation?

Is the absence of stress important? Do you prefer independence to teamwork? With respect to outside values, do you want more time with family, friends, hobbies, or recreational activities? Financial considerations are important. Is a higher income a top priority, or can you postpone monetary rewards while preparing for a new career?

Expand Your Competencies

Each individual must make up his or her own mind about whether to specialize or generalize. Some employers are practically begging for people with a hard-to-find skill, while still more employers want people who can broaden their area of competency when occupational needs change. Having one's ear to the ground helps to know which direction to take. The important action is to continue with education and training.

All health care supervisors must continue to balance their educational efforts between those that are professional or technical and those that are supervisory. In the past health care professionals tended to neglect the latter and concentrate on teachings learned at the meetings of their professional societies or from the professional journals. This is changing as supervisors realize that their performance ratings depend more on their leadership ability than on their professional expertise.

Develop a Reputation for Innovativeness, Flexibility, and Customer Service

Directly or indirectly, customer evaluations of service determines the success of care providers. Hospitals and managed care organizations are soliciting more feedback from patients, physicians, and other external customers. More of them seek the perceptions of internal customers such as departments that service other departments.

When departments fail to live up to expectations, their work may be reassigned to other in-house departments or contracted with outside providers. Heads often roll.

Do your best to build rapport with people outside your department, especially those that you serve—your internal customers. Accept invitations to sit in on their meetings and social functions. Volunteer for special assignments that provide interdepartmental contacts. Socialize with them at organizational training or informational meetings. Invite them to your department.

Promote Your Capabilities

Make yourself more visible, but do it with class. Be assertive but not pushy. Come to meetings prepared, and participate actively. Ask questions and make suggestions. Volunteer to make department presentations or to represent your unit at management meetings. Look like someone who is on the way up; appearances still count.

When you receive compliments, ask the givers if they would put them in writing and send copies to your manager.

Acquire personal calling cards and use them. Keep a file of your accomplishments and bring them up at your performance reviews.

Expand Your Personal Network

Some people complain that "It's not what you know, but who you know." They are right, but you invariably find that the complainers have made little or no effort to get to know people who can help them. When it comes to promotions and finding jobs elsewhere, mentors are among the most important people in your network. We address mentoring and personal networks in the final chapter.

STEPS TO SUCCESS

Most people spend more time planning a vacation than they spend planning their careers. Do not be one of these folks. Try these nine steps to success.

1. Begin with a vision. Martin Luther King Jr. had a vision ("I have a dream"). Do you? You can accomplish what you want, but be sure that you know what that is. Visualize the scene when you have reached your main goals in life. What do you like about that vision? Fame and fortune? Being in charge of a large department? Being highly respected because of your technical expertise? What would you like a speaker to say about you at your retirement ceremony? The answer to that question helps you to elucidate your vision.

2. Select your mission statement and major goals. A mission statement is the "why," the reason for your goals. It is a declaration of direction that has the power to design your activities for the rest of your life. A good mission statement is one that has meaning for you. It may be to improve the medical care in your community by serving as a top official in a health care institution or to spend your retirement in Florida. The final statement may not be as important as the time you take to reflect on your life and what is important to you. Mission statements provide the motivation to accomplish our goals. Hal Lancaster, who writes an excellent column on career managing in *The Wall Street Journal*, invited his readers to submit copies of their mission statements to him.[2] Although he found a great divergence in what the responders regarded as mission statements, he came up with a personal statement that could serve as an example for you with some simple modifications. Hal's mission statement is "My mission is to enlighten

and entertain people through my writing and to help provide a life for my family that is emotionally and financially secure, loving, learning and fun." A goal is the "what." A person without a goal is like a ship without a rudder. Once you've tuned in to your goal, you will find that the workings of your unconscious help you to reach it. You become open to sources of information that you were not aware of and you gravitate toward people who can help you. Besides career goals, consider your family and personal life goals. Because of limitations of time and money, you may have to sacrifice some goals to promote others. We all know of broken homes that result from neglect of family goals. There are many early deaths because a high-powered professional sacrificed his health on the altar of a career. If one of your goals is to get promoted, take a piece of paper and jot down all the advantages and disadvantages of that change. You may decide that at least for the present, this is not a good choice. Before you finalize your goals, discuss them with your family, close friends, mentors, and your manager. You will probably need their help along the way. Document your mission statement and goals. Studies have shown that people who do so are much more likely to succeed. Some people carry their mission statements with them in their wallets. Others review their statements periodically to provide inspiration and motivation.

3. Prepare a list of objectives for each major goal. Objectives are steps to achieving goals. For example, if one of your goals is to be promoted to a higher management position, one of your objectives may be to earn a master's degree in business administration. A good objective should be specific, challenging, realistic, achievable, and measurable.

4. Take an inventory of your strengths and weaknesses. Be honest and forthright about weaknesses. You will not correct them if you refuse to admit that they exist. Review your last performance appraisal and discuss this with your manager. Activities that supervisors frequently feel they do poorly include writing letters and job descriptions, holding disciplinary and employment interviews, delegating, budgeting, and resolving employee conflicts.

5. Prepare a needs analysis. Catalog your development needs using the list of weaknesses you prepared. Break them down into smaller categories if necessary. The acquisition of new education, skills, and experience is imperative. The people with the most intellectual capital and experience find new opportunities with their current employer or with other organizations.

6. Document potential barriers and how you plan to cope with them. Common barriers are time, finances, and resistance from family.

7. Chart your action steps and add target dates. Begin your initiative with a small first step (for example, getting a catalog of educational courses or

signing up for a seminar). See Exhibit 39–1 for examples of goals, objectives, and actions.

8. Implement the process. Transfer your action plans to daily to-do lists.

Monitor, evaluate, and reward. Your motivation is strongest if you enjoy the process as well as reaching your goal. For example, it is much more difficult to continue with a long educational program if you dislike taking the classes. Reward yourself for what you accomplish. Self-evaluation and self-reward decrease your need for approval from other people. The advantage of praising yourself instead of waiting for others to do it is that you can lay it on thick and in the

---

Exhibit 39–1 Example of Goal, Objectives, and Actions

Goal: To be promoted to unit manager

Objectives: To meet professional requirements by [date]; to meet administrative requirements by [date]; to meet supervisory requirements by [date]

Actions:

1. Complete courses needed to get MBA
   - get support of family
   - seek financial support
   - enroll in local university
2. Study administrative functions of unit
   - computer information system
   - quality improvement program
   - budget preparation and use
   - routine and special reports
   - anticipation of next inspection by Joint Commission on Accreditation of Healthcare Organizations
   - procedure manuals and employee handbook
3. Educate self about supervisory functions
   - read at least one book on supervisory skills for new supervisors
   - attend at least one seminar, workshop, or college course on the topics of leadership, planning, counseling, interviewing, writing skills, delegating, negotiating, empowering, and career development
   - volunteer to serve on a cross-functional team or a quality improvement committee
   - find a mentor and expand professional network by at least one new person each month

right places. Do not wait until you have reached your goal or achieved an objective. Do it on a frequent basis.

Watch Out for the Career Killers

People who fail usually blame other people, society, or fate, but most cases represent self-destruction. (See Exhibit 39–2.)

HOW TO NEGOTIATE FOR MORE COMPENSATION

There is a myth of long standing that if you work hard you will be rewarded. Many employees earn big raises, but few actually get them. In a typical health care institution, a person whose performance is rated as outstanding may receive a salary increase that is 2% to 3% above that of the average worker. Big deal! What is even worse is that if you have been getting those kinds of raises for several years, you may find that your salary is lower than that of new people in equivalent roles.[3]

If you never ask, you are not likely to get what you are worth. To receive a substantial salary increase, you must earn it, AND you usually must negotiate for it. If you are as good as they say you are, your superiors should take your requests seriously.

Exhibit 39–2 The Career Killers

- Lack of or inappropriate goals, objectives, or priorities
- Fears and inability to make decisions or to take action
- Poor time management
- Lack of motivation or enthusiasm
- Drifting into obsolescence
- Too many diversions or outside interests
- Lack of self-control, trustworthiness, or integrity
- Lack of flexibility or ability to adjust to change
- Ineffective leadership or followership
- Lack of interpersonal skills
- Problems with alcohol or drugs
- Passivity and negative self-talk
- Inability to be an effective team player

Important Don'ts When Negotiating for More Pay

- Do not tell your manager you deserve a raise because you have been with the organization for umpteen years. Seniority no longer counts for much. It is how valuable you are to the organization and what your potential is that really count.
- Do not try to convince your manager that you should get a raise because you need more money. You may get some sympathy but not much more in your pay envelope.
- Do not rely on your manager giving you more money because you are doing a terrific job and your performance rating is outstanding.
- Do not threaten to resign, at least not early in the process or in haste.

Your manager probably has the power to get you more money despite his or her strong protestations to the contrary. Employees who resign when told that funds were not available often learn that their replacements started at higher salaries than they were being paid.

Preparation for Walking into the Lion's Den

As in all negotiations, preparation, confidence, and sales ability are critical. The first prerequisite is knowing your market value and using that value to decide the figure you will shoot for. Research the pay scale for your kind of work. Know what competitors are paying, and be sure that these comparable jobs are available.

There are several sources for finding your market value. Lancaster claims that few managers know their market value, despite a wealth of salary information.[4] He suggests researching business publications, professional groups, cyberspace, alumni, and your alma mater to see what recruiters are offering. You can also check with your mentors and other members of your personal network and see what you can learn in the library.

If your coworkers all receive about the same compensation, factor in the functions, responsibilities, and special competencies that only you possess. If you are directly instrumental in producing value (for example, finding customers or obtaining grants that can be expressed in terms of dollars), add that information to your presentation.

Do not be passive in your approach. However, it is equally bad to stalk into your manager's office and demand more money. You must use a little finesse. Despite that squeamish feeling about a confrontation over salary, you must be assertive. The meek may inherit the earth, but they seldom get substantial raises. If you are a worthy recipient, your manager will feel just as uncomfortable about your request as you do.

The timing of your pitch is critical. When your employer is in financial difficulty or your manager is experiencing work, health, or family problems, do not expect a favorable response. Never approach a boss who is extremely busy, emotionally upset, or in the middle of an important project or crisis. Sometimes a good opportunity is right after you have received a glowing performance appraisal.

Be prepared to compromise. There are many possible improvements other than salary. Would you be satisfied with a better benefit package? How about funds for continuing education or a research project? Would a work schedule change enable you to earn money elsewhere? In academic centers, professionals value the opportunity to carry on a private practice, do research, write a book, consult, or teach elsewhere.

If you are turned down, ask what you must do or achieve to earn a raise. Use the response to make appropriate modifications to your career development program (or to start looking for another job). Check back periodically with your manager to find out how you are doing.

Think About It

Make up your mind that career development should be a concern throughout your entire working lifetime. And considering the continued acceleration of technological and social change, most working individuals—and especially those supervising and managing in rapidly evolving fields such as health care—may experience two, three, or even four different "careers" in a single working lifetime.

Questions for Review and Discussion

1. What are the apparent advantages and potential disadvantages of focusing your self-development on achieving excellence in a specific technical or professional specialty?
2. Why is it claimed that the acceptance of risk is essential in career development?
3. How do fear of failure and fear of the unknown figure in career development?
4. Explain how personal values can weigh heavily in significant career decisions.
5. In making yourself increasingly visible to higher management, could you experience any risks relative to your home department? Explain.
6. Why can frontline supervisors and their employees spot improvement opportunities before the organization's executives do?
7. What is the difference between an objective and a goal? Provide an example related to career development.
8. Why might one have to look forward to experiencing multiple careers? Why not simply pick one line of work and stick with it?

9. Why is your personal network important in career development, and how does it function to your benefit?
10. How important is it in the development of your career to remain attuned to a specific goal at all times? Why is this so?

Exercise: Success Criteria

Refer to the "Five Criteria for Success" presented in this chapter. Write a proper introduction, and take each of the five criteria in turn and explain how and to what extent they relate to individual motivation, that is, to the search for fulfillment of human needs that drives people to perform. Then select any one of the five criteria and explain how an individual's career development plan might be shaped if this particular criterion is by far the most important one to the person.

Exercise: Your Career Development Plan

In brief, sketch out a career development plan for yourself using the occupation you are now engaged in or are planning to enter. Indicate several major milestones to be encountered in your plan—for example, one might be to secure licensure in a particular professional or technical specialty. Also, indicate what you would imagine your status to be at several points in the future, specifically 5, 10, 15, and 20 years from the present. Then respond to the following questions.

1. How will you adjust your plan if the organization you had planned on remaining with closes its doors and disappears at about the 5-year point in your plan?
2. How will you again adjust your plan if you realize about half way through your career that your chosen occupation is declining toward obsolescence?

REFERENCES

1. Youngman, H. 1997. Lessons in life from Henny Youngman. *Bottom Line-Personal* 18: 13.
2. Lancaster, H. 1997. It's the thoughts that count in putting missions in writing. *The Wall Street Journal,* Tuesday, October 28, 1997, B1.
3. Lancaster, H. 1997. How do you know what you're worth in a job marketplace? *The Wall Street Journal,* Tuesday, September 30, 1997, B1.
4. Lancaster, How do you know what you're worth?

RECOMMENDED RESOURCES

L. Milteer, *Success Self-Programming.* (Boulder, CO: CareerTrack Publishers, 1987). Two audiotapes.
D. Waitley, *Dennis Waitley Live: Powerful Strategies for Reaching Your Potential.* (Boulder, CO: CareerTrack Publishers, 1987). Six audiotapes.

Chapter 40

Succession Planning

If you haven't prepared someone to step into
your shoes, you're not ready to take
a successful step upward.[1]

CHAPTER OBJECTIVES

- Establish the value of succession planning to the individual supervisor.
- Explore the potential risks inherent in selecting and developing a successor.
- Outline the succession planning process from the department supervisor's perspective, including selecting, grooming, and monitoring a potential successor.

In today's uncertain times, the need for succession planning is more vital than ever. Organizations are becoming increasingly unstable. Mergers and acquisitions and other affiliations are causing the movement of supervisors like never before as jobs are changed, upgraded, downgraded, created, and eliminated. Therefore, everyone who is in charge of a work unit should answer these four questions:

1. If my services suddenly become unavailable, how would my responsibilities be discharged?
2. How long would it take to find and train my replacement?
3. Who is on board right now who could take over?
4. What have I done to prepare a successor?

BENEFITS OF SUCCESSION PLANNING

The strength and adaptability of an organization are linked to how fully it has developed the talents of its personnel. This development depends largely on the willingness and capability of supervisors to share their expertise with potential successors.

After you have mastered your job and are looking for advancement within your organization, you need to make yourself dispensable. To fail to do so freezes you into your present job because your superiors will come to regard you as indispensable in that position.

There are other benefits to succession planning. When you have a trained backup, you can do the things you did not have time for previously. This increases your value to the organization and enhances your career. You can be absent from the work scene with the assurance that your unit will function smoothly in your absence. You can skip those frequent calls back to work to check on how things are going while you are not there.

RISKS IN PICKING AND TRAINING A SUCCESSOR

There is always the possibility that you pick a lemon, but remember that the only people who never fall down are those who keep sitting in their chairs. All leaders worthy of the title have made poor decisions and choices, but they regard such mistakes as learning experiences, and they move on. Careful planning and thorough preparation minimize this risk.

A more frequent risk is that your protégé gets promoted out from under you or is enticed away by a competitor. Although this elicits pangs of disappointment proportional to the effort you made in developing the individual, you still get important benefits: a reputation as a career builder, the gratitude of the person you trained, supporters (your former protégés) in other units or organizations, and the ability to repeat the process with greater competency.

Some supervisors fear competition from subordinates, worrying that a protégé may prove to be a more effective leader than the supervisor. They feel they may be putting their jobs in jeopardy. These supervisors usually have already displayed this fear through their reluctance to delegate. However, such concerns are based on false assumptions. It is rare for a supervisor to lose a job because a protégé outperforms the supervisor. On the contrary, because supervisors who develop successors will have more time to expand their own expertise, their security will increase.

SELECTION AND TRAINING PLAN

Finding the appropriate understudy can be simple or complicated. You do not have far to look if you already have an assistant and are satisfied with that person's potential. In that situation, you have probably already trained that person to handle supervisory tasks and to demonstrate leadership ability. You already know his or her strengths and where additional training or experience is needed.

If you do not have an assistant and must choose from several employees who have the same potential, this can be a more delicate matter. Do not take for granted that all these people are interested in your job. This is something you should have learned during performance reviews or during your daily contacts.

Do not waste your time preparing reluctant successors unless they have such impressive leadership talents that it is worth trying to recruit them. Do not be in a hurry to designate a single candidate as the anointed one. The moment such a move becomes apparent, others stop striving for the job. Some may see the handwriting on the wall and leave.

When you have several prospects, treat them as equal contenders. Delegate supervisory and administrative activities to each and document how they handle them. Let them take turns moderating staff meetings or representing you at interdepartmental meetings. When you are going to be absent, appoint different substitutes. Pay close attention to how they handle these situations. Does the work get done? Do they try to do everything themselves, or do they get the cooperation of other team members? How did their fellow workers perceive their performance? The fairness of these delegated responsibilities and the documentation of performance may later save you the embarrassment of being charged with discrimination or favoritism.

Any effective program of supervisory development begins with an appraisal of a person's strengths, weaknesses, and potential. It sets attainable development goals. The program usually includes practical on-the-job coaching, formal educational courses, attendance at management seminars, and selected readings.

GROOMING YOUR SUCCESSOR

How you prepare the chosen one is extremely important. The process consists largely, but not exclusively, of a series of delegations and special assignments. Ensure that the person does each of these tasks often enough to become competent and comfortable. Make certain that he or she has enough time to handle daily responsibilities.

Besides these delegations and assignments, take your protégés to some of your meetings. Let them sit in on interviews you hold and accompany you as you "manage by walking around." Work jointly on things like budgets or plans.

Developing a successor involves much mentoring. Provide opportunities for meeting senior managers and important customers. The latter include internal customers, those units that serve or are served by your department. Provide visibility by letting your successor give reports to the bigwigs and chair meetings.

When your chosen one does something worthy of mention, let your boss know about it. In your performance appraisal reports on your protégé, use phrases such as "shows leadership ability" and "is developing into an excellent facilitator."

Exhibit 40–1 Action Plan for Skill Enhancement

SUBJECT:	(Skill to be enhanced)
PURPOSE:	(Why this is important)
OBJECTIVES:	(How success will be measured)
RESOURCES:	(Funds and other materials needed)
OBSTACLES:	(People, time, other)
	(How they can be removed)
IMPLEMENTATION:	(List in sequence the steps to achieve the desired change. If possible, assign target dates.)

A worthy protégé will do most of the planning and energizing independently. He or she will

- decide what seminars to attend, what courses and workshops to take, what books to study, and what periodicals to read;
- set goals and develop action plans; and
- make the extra effort needed to work on career development while still discharging daily responsibilities.

An outline for a training plan is presented as Exhibit 40–1.

MONITORING YOUR SUCCESSOR

The true test of managerial ability is not only to ensure that the people know how to do things they were taught; it is also how they do the things that they were *not* taught. Meet regularly with the person to discuss progress. Do not wait for the annual formal performance appraisal to review progress.

Think About It

The supervisor who fails to have one or more potential successors undergoing continuing development is committing one of the most common career-limiting errors encountered in management. The supervisor who cannot or does not delegate and develop staff at the firstline management level is unlikely to move to a higher level where those processes assume even greater importance.

Questions for Review and Discussion

1. In addition to fearing competition from subordinates, provide another likely reason why some supervisors fail to develop potential successors.

2. Even if your promotion or departure for a better position is not anticipated to occur for years to come, why is succession planning in the department still essential?
3. Do you believe you should be developing more than one potential successor, or should this activity be limited to a single person? Why?
4. What would you do if it becomes clear to you that the potential successor you were grooming is not going to make the grade as a supervisor?
5. What are likely to be the immediate difficulties experienced if the work unit is left leaderless by the sudden incapacity of the supervisor and no successor is apparent?

Exercise: Justifying Succession Planning

Some supervisors and managers are inclined to resist succession planning for one particular reason that surfaces again and again: they see their well-trained key personnel moving to jobs in other departments and other organizations. They resent training people only to have them leave to go elsewhere.

You are to frame an argument that acknowledges this loss of trained personnel and accepts this phenomenon as a legitimate result of succession planning. In brief, you are to write as strong as possible a justification for practicing succession planning in spite of its apparent drawbacks.

REFERENCES

1. Feinberg, M. 1990. Succession planning. *The Wall Street Journal*, November 12, 1990: A14.

RECOMMENDED READING

C.R. McConnell, "Succeed With Succession Planning," *The Health Care Supervisor* 15, no. 2 (1996): 69–78.

Chapter 41

Networks and Organizational Politics

A wise man knows everything;
a shrewd man knows everybody.

—Old Chinese Proverb

CHAPTER OBJECTIVES

- Define personal networks, review their benefits, and examine their likely composition from the supervisor's perspective.
- Suggest how the supervisor might go about making and maintaining appropriate contacts.
- Briefly examine the increasing utilization of computer networks.
- Review the characteristics of effective networkers.
- Examine the phenomenon of politics in the workplace, and suggest how the supervisor might most effectively cope with job-related politics.
- Provide the supervisor with advice for relating to and coping with his or her immediate organizational superior.

PERSONAL NETWORKS

Developing outside relationships is largely a matter of networking. Luebbert defines a network as "an informal group of contacts that share advice, facts, techniques, job leads, plans and dreams, and who lend each other moral support."[1] We still hear the old (and generally true) cliché, "It's not what you know, but who you know that counts."

Fortunately, there is abundant opportunity to get to know people who can help us if we are willing to make the effort. Networking is largely a matter of knowing how to be helpful to your contacts and how to ask them for help.

BENEFITS OF NETWORKS

Networking is invaluable to teams for improving daily productivity, efficiency, and achievement. It is also a fast track to personal growth for individual members. People who build connections within and outside organizations are much more likely to succeed. The benefits of active networking are

- technical, professional, legal, or fiscal advice;
- advance information about trends, new projects, or organizational changes;
- opinions on proposals, ideas, speeches, or reports;
- moral support;
- mentoring or counseling help;
- learning about job opportunities;
- becoming aware of the availability of job candidates;
- soliciting recommendations or support; and
- sharing experiences, both successes and failures.

POTENTIAL NETWORK PARTICIPANTS

External Customers

Patients, physicians, and other outside customers can provide a constant source of suggestions for improving your service. When you satisfy these clients, you gain enthusiastic supporters.

Internal Customers

These are departments or individuals within your organization that you provide services for or who provide services to you.

Coworkers

These are employees who precede or follow you in work flows, and colleagues who serve with you on committees, task forces, or problem solving groups.

Former Professors and Instructors

These people take pride in responding to your requests to tap into their knowledge bank.

Vendors

Your suppliers are loaded with valuable information and very willing to share it.

Community Associates

Fellow members of civic, service, and social or religious organizations comprise this category.

Gatekeepers

These are people who provide access to important people, services, or knowledge. When a gatekeeper is part of your network, you are operating on the inside track.

Competitors

Keep in touch with "friendly" competitors. You can teach each other how to save costs and avoid problems. If a cross-town competitor warns you about hiring one of his or her former employees, your friendly relationship has proven its worth.

Family Members

Never forget the special people in your life. They serve as your publicists and supporters. Wives and husbands have their own networks. Even when they are not in the same profession, their spheres of influence overlap. Most successful people owe much of their success to their mates, whether they remain at home or have their own professional careers.

HOW TO MAKE AND MAINTAIN CONTACTS

Use your Rolodex or address book, files of correspondence, business cards, membership rosters of organizations you belong to, alumni associations, and Internet rosters. Establish contacts at professional and social meetings, seminars, workshops, committees, churches or synagogues, schools, clubs, hobby groups, and among your neighbors. Your present network can provide contacts with people you would like to include in your network.

The omnipresent lapel name tags on meeting attendees are signs of networking in action. The networking at any given meeting may be more valuable than the program itself.

Raise your visibility by giving talks, holding office, or becoming a spokesperson. Earn a reputation as a recognized expert in some professional or technical aspect of health care. Constantly expand your professional and social network. Do this by getting people obligated to you rather than asking favors.

Gain the respect of your colleagues. Become a resource person and troubleshooter. This goes a long way toward developing a power base. Do not shift blame or point fingers. Never take credit for something others have done. Instead, lead the cheers for their accomplishments. Acknowledge their support, especially to superiors.

With all the current restructuring and realigning, many employees have new contacts with personnel in other departments and institutions. Employees in health care institutions have dealings with people in managed care organizations. There is less stress when people know each other's expectations and strive to collaborate. Ideally these relationships are supportive as well as cordial. However, this is easier said than done; many situations are conducive to antagonistic positions.

Tips for Building Rapport with People Outside Your Work Unit

- Accept invitations to sit in on their meetings or to visit their work areas. Invite them to your meetings and facilities. Ask them to sit with you in the cafeteria.
- Be visible. Introduce yourself to others when you are in the same room.
- Volunteer for assignments that provide interdepartmental contacts.
- Attend organizational social functions.
- Take advantage of training sessions and seminars where you meet people from other departments or agencies.
- Participate in extracurricular activities.

COMPUTER NETWORKS

Computer networking is the sharing of computer resources among various users. These resources may be the computers themselves, databases, printers, or even human expertise. Communication may be one-to-one e-mail between individuals, message sending to a distribution list, and group participation in electronic forums or conferences. Document sharing, central databases, and computer forums now play a vital role in sharing knowledge and expertise. Electronic distribution lists enable managers and professionals to broadcast information or to address concerns to many people. E-mail is rapidly replacing memos and has the advantage over telephone conversations in that the responder can look up information and get back to the sender when it is convenient.

Computer networks enable employees to obtain information directly from sources without having to contact supervisors and middle managers. This computer capability has been a factor in the elimination of some middle manager jobs.

People are learning through their computers how to do things for which they formerly needed the help of staff specialists. For example, supervisors can now develop their own budgets with minimal assistance from the finance department. Greater access to accounts and files enables frontline employees to answer questions and serve their clients better. Personnel on after-hour shifts and those stationed in satellite facilities feel more in touch with each other and with their organization.

CHARACTERISTICS OF GREAT NETWORKERS

- They know how to interact with people. They ask good questions and listen attentively.
- They keep in touch with their contacts.
- They are great joiners.
- They circulate at parties and meetings and introduce themselves rather than wait for someone else to do the honors.
- They are cordial and courteous to all but selective about the people with whom they develop special rapport.
- They use coffee breaks and lunch times to chat with different people.
- They volunteer for committees and other group functions.
- They teach, coach, and mentor.
- They serve as officers in social and professional organizations.
- They go out of their way to establish relationships with newcomers.
- They share clippings, reports, articles, and other information.
- They send out many thank-you notes, and they remember birthdays and other special occasions.
- They express their appreciation for favors in special ways.

WORKPLACE POLITICS

Politics is primarily the pursuit of power. The original meaning of the word was "to act in the service of society." It once meant a high form of public service. Politics has been reinterpreted to mean service to oneself, self-empowerment with a negative connotation. What winners call interpersonal relationships, losers call politics. Career failures can result from political as well as professional incompetence. Unwillingness to address the political components of a job has snuffed out many a promising career. Losers make no effort to find mentors or to build personal networks. They grow resentful toward their employers, their superiors, and their colleagues. Often they become chronic complainers or shrill negativists.

Corporate politics is gamesmanship, using forces other than good performance to improve one's stance in an organization. This includes trying to influence superiors and gain a competitive edge over one's peers. If your political script is a positive one, you play the game fairly and ethically.

At one end of the scale, politics is selfish, unethical, or illegal. At the other end, political behavior supplements professional competency. It is often beneficial not only for the political person but also for his subordinates, superiors, teammates, and employer.

POLITICS AND THE INFORMAL ORGANIZATION

Every organization has an informal structure. Unions are officially sanctioned informal organizations. Cliques represent informal coteries that discriminate against fellow workers. The informal organization selects its own leaders and communicates via the grapevine.

Powerful informal work groups set productivity norms. They may introduce initiation rituals that sometimes include such severe hazing that new hires quit. The culture of the informal organization may allow disloyalty, insubordination, and even sabotage.

Politics overlaps the formal and the informal organizations. Political scripts are flexible because there are few, if any, documented guidelines. The first rule of politics is that nobody will tell you the rules.

NEGATIVE POLITICS

Negative politics may be dysfunctional, unethical, or even illegal. It gets blamed for almost everything: poor communication, inappropriate behavior, unpopular promotions, discrimination, and favoritism.

Block claims that organizational politics is partly based on the time-honored bureaucratic wish to be blameless and safe.[2] Terrell identifies the following factors as the breeding grounds for negative politics.

- Lack of clear organizational goals or lack of communication of the goals
- Autocratic or bureaucratic leadership
- Multiple layers of management (the more layers, the more politics)
- Little upward communication
- Frequent changes
- Controversial management shifts of power
- Poor relationships between workers and managers[3]

Political Games That Subordinates or Colleagues Play

- Taking advantage of being indispensable
- Abusing friendships
- Probing for weaknesses of others and revealing those weaknesses
- Undermining operations or new services
- Starting unfounded rumors or providing misleading information

- Creating crises or discord
- Displaying undue emotional distress to achieve selfish gains
- Discrediting teammates in public or undermining them in private
- Intimidating new employees and provoking sensitive people

Political Games That Managers Play

- Stealing ideas or credit
- Excluding others from meetings or information
- Eliminating or downgrading the jobs of employees whom they dislike or distrust
- Assigning unpleasant tasks
- Delegating work that places delegates at risk or that prevents them from handling their regular work
- Pitting one employee against another
- Giving unfair or false performance appraisals
- Not hiring anyone who could be threatening to them

Manipulation

Manipulators invoke the names of high-level people to get their way. They curry the favor of those who outrank them, sometimes to a degree of obsequiousness. They take advantage of friends and colleagues. Threats or even bribes may be part of their strategy. They usually "forget" their promises. Political savvy to these folks means passing the buck, procrastinating, and saying what they do not mean. They are always cautious about speaking candidly.

You know someone is manipulating you when they lead off with "You don't value my service anymore, do you?" or "You owe me one," or "The boss will back me on this."

POSITIVE POLITICAL SCRIPTS AND TACTICS

Assertiveness

Assertiveness is standing up for one's personal rights and expressing those feelings and beliefs in direct, honest ways that do not violate the rights of others. The theme of the assertive person is "You're OK, I'm OK." Lack of assertiveness chips away at one's self-image and self-respect.

Ask yourself these questions.

* Do you often say yes when you should say no?
* Do you allow people to interrupt you?
* Do you use self-deprecating comments? For example: "I know this sounds stupid, but…"
* At meetings, do you want to speak up but seldom do it?
* Do you always avoid controversial issues?
* Are you doing work that others should do?
* Are you the one who always gives in?
* Do others take advantage of you?
* Do you find it difficult to negotiate?

If you answered yes to several of the foregoing questions, follow the recommendations in the box below.

Increase Your Assertiveness

* Attend a workshop or read a book on assertiveness.
* When others say something negative about you, reply, "Are you trying to make me feel guilty?" Watch them turn red!
* Appreciate the fact that you have more power than you realize.
* Set boundaries or limits. Learn to say "no."
* Rehearse expressing yourself or engage in role-playing with a close friend.

Rapport with People Who Report to You

One thing that employees notice quickly is whether "the score" is being kept equitably. The score refers to how you evaluate performance, how you treat each employee, and how you enforce the rules.

Political power is short circuited when employees feel they are being manipulated or hoodwinked. Negative political statements and unfulfilled promises lead to resentment, anger, and loss of trust. On the other hand, if there are mutual trust and respect and if your people perceive you as their champion, your personal power will skyrocket.

COPING WITH THE PERSON TO WHOM YOU REPORT

It is not likely that your employer will ask you to select a manager, so your manager may or may not be one of whom you would approve. However, if you are job hunting or transferring within your organization, one of your considerations should be the person to whom you will report.

You want someone with whom you can get along. You also want to know as much as you can about the leadership style, morale, and turnover in the new unit. This information is not found in any handout. However, you can learn much with some probing. Question some of the employees who work in the unit.

Get to Know Your Manager's Expectations, Likes, and Dislikes

Managers are often insecure because they do not really know much about what you do on the job. Clarify this by reviewing your goals and priorities with your manager and by asking the manager if he or she agrees with the goals. In this way the manager will also be in a better position to offer more specific support.

We have already mentioned leadership styles. Communication preferences are also important. Learn how the manager wants to receive messages. Some like to read them, as President John Kennedy did. Others prefer to listen to them, as President Harry Truman did. Keep your manager informed. Never hide problems, and when you report them, offer solutions. Do not waste his or her time with trivia or gossip. Learn when to speak up and when to remain silent.

Avoid disagreements in public, and never embarrass the boss in front of others. Pick the right time and place for presenting your ideas. Some managers like input first thing in the morning so they can get a handle on operations. Others do not want to hear or see anyone until they complete their morning chores.

Other considerations are the manager's likes and dislikes, decision-making style, tendency to stereotype, or other hangups. Most importantly, what are his or her expectations and priorities concerning your performance? Ask the manager to review your position description and work standards with you.

Discover the problems that your manager has with his or her superiors and provide whatever support you can. Do everything you can to make your manager look good to upper management.

Accept delegated responsibilities with enthusiasm. Better still, seek out additional responsibilities. For example, volunteer to chair a committee or to lead a focus group. When you pinch-hit for your manager, consider this as a chance to try out the job. Remember that promotions are based not so much on what you have done as on what your superiors think you can do for them in the future.

Direct Your Manager's Behavior: the Carrot and the Stick

This can be done verbally or by means of thank you notes or e-mail. When one of your requests is granted, a thank-you message is appropriate. Do you respond enthusiastically and gratefully when your manager approves your request to attend a professional meeting or to take a long weekend? Depending on how important the favor is, a small gift is not out of order.

Group expressions of appreciation are even more acceptable. Handing out the carrots of praise is much more effective in channeling behavior than using the stick (threats or complaints).

Be Loyal and Show Respect

This means making your boss look good. You can display loyalty by defending your manager when he or she is criticized, arriving on time at meetings, making extra effort, and by expressing enthusiasm.

Most important is a tone of respect in daily communications. Know when and how to dissent. Most managers accept disagreement if it is offered tactfully. Learn how direct you can be, and be diplomatic. Remember that what you think is a bad decision by your manager may be one that had been imposed on him or her. Share credit for your accomplishments with your manager.

When You Have More Than One Immediate Superior

Today, many health care employees report to two or more superiors. This can lead to conflicts of time sharing or priorities or even of conflicting orders. When you get competing assignments, inform the junior member of the pair of the conflict and ask for his or her advice.

Tips for Coping with Your Manager

- Say complimentary things about your manager to other people—your boss will get the message.
- Act as a devil's advocate occasionally, then yield gracefully (bosses like to persuade people).
- Develop a reputation as a problem solver. Be willing to risk your reputation by offering innovative suggestions or introducing new techniques in your unit.
- Have the courage to stand up for what you think is right.
- Deliver on your promises.
- Protect and defend the reputation of your organization and your boss.
- Keep your frustrations and negative thoughts to yourself.
- Know when and how to resign or ask for a transfer.

But, in relations with the boss, do not

- Do anything that would lead your boss to regard you as a threat;
- Say "That's not in my position description" or "I wasn't hired to do that";
- Let pessimism or negativism creep into your attitude;

- Steal credit;
- Criticize your boss, coworkers, or organization in public;
- Distort the truth;
- Develop an amorous relationship with your boss;
- Threaten to resign when you do not get your way; or
- Sacrifice your professional and ethical values.

Never go to your manager's superiors with problems or complaints before discussing them with your boss. These end runs are usually the beginning of the end of a work relationship. The most serious end run is when someone keeps going up the chain of command until he or she finds someone who gives the answer he or she wants. If you are frustrated over not getting satisfaction from your superior and want to talk to a higher authority, disclose your intention to your manager first and suggest that you both make the visit. If the manager refuses, tell him or her exactly what you are going to say to the higher up.

Difficult Bosses

Look at the bright side: inevitably, most of us must deal with an unpleasant or incompetent boss. When you have one of these early in your career, you have a wonderful opportunity to fine-tune your skill in getting along with someone who has power over you. Often you can learn a great deal about management from the negative examples offered by a genuine tyrant.

Before you put all the blame on your manager, examine your own behavior. Are you doing anything that irritates him or her? Is your work area a mess while the boss's office is orderly? Do you show up at meetings late and without excuses? Are you occasionally careless about your appearance while your manager always dresses impeccably? Do you get frequent personal phone calls or visits or have to drop things and run home? Do you routinely get to work after your manager does and consistently leave earlier? Have you been insensitive to things you say or do that you know annoy the boss?

Procrastinators

These are usually agreeable, well-intentioned folks with perfectionist tendencies. They avoid or put off decisions for fear of making mistakes or offending others.

Try to find the reasons for their hesitancy and eliminate them. Praise them when they do make decisions or take action promptly, for example, "Louise, we really appreciate it when you're so proactive. It helps us meet our schedules and get home on time."

Be reassuring of and optimistic toward procrastinators. When you need to get something approved, have all the supporting data ready. Tell them that you have checked out all proposals carefully. Instead of asking permission, send a memo stating what you intend to do unless you hear to the contrary. Make sure that you give them sufficient time to get back to you.

Unfair Bosses

If you are getting more than your share of unpleasant assignments, instead of accusing your manager of sticking it to you, state exactly what it is that is bothering you. You will usually find that the manager is not aware of the situation or that you are upset about it. If the boss is dumping excessive busywork on you or is delegating too much, ask him or her to help you to set your work priorities or provide additional help.

If you think that he or she is discriminating against you, point this out in behavioral terms. If the discrimination gets out of hand, blow the whistle after you are certain that your evidence is firm and specific. Be prepared to provide examples and have corroborative evidence. Check with your mentors and local governmental agencies as necessary.

Bosses Who Bypass You

These managers frequently give orders to your subordinates without your knowledge, usually when you are not right on the spot. You can eliminate most of these intrusions if you discuss the problem with them. Point out how this undermines your authority and confuses your staff. Give specific examples.

Tell your staff that they are to keep you informed about requests from others. Except in emergencies they are not to carry these orders out until they have consulted you. If you feel that your employees can diplomatically tell certain of these order givers that they must get your approval first, try that approach. You may want to authorize your team members to decide when they should honor extrinsic orders. You can provide a discretionary task list.

You must have the courage to protest when a superior repeatedly issues orders to your people in your presence. Try diplomacy first. Tell him or her that results will be better if requests are made to you. If this practice continues, point out that your employees are confused about some of his or her orders and that they are afraid to ask for clarification. If this behavior continues and results in real problems for you and your people, you are justified in going over the superior's head with your complaint.

Laissez-Faire Leaders

These people are not really leaders; they just have the title. They have abdicated their responsibilities. They are never around when you need them. When they are on site, they provide no help.

Know what your authority is, and use it. Revise your position description to include more control over your areas of responsibility. Seek broad approval for your objectives, plans, and schedules, and then go ahead with them. Pin the boss down when vague directives are issued. Gradually assume more responsibility and control.

Think About It

Many an individual new to supervision has vowed to avoid ever becoming embroiled in the politics of the workplace. But these same supervisors soon discover that trying to avoid all workplace politics is like trying to get the job done while avoiding people. Workplace politics is inevitable; the best one can do is participate only when necessary and "play the game" truthfully, ethically, and with respect for others.

Questions for Review and Discussion

1. How can your external customers be of value to you in networking?
2. Why do you suppose networking is frequently a more successful means of finding a new position than other means such as answering employment ads?
3. What kinds of "gatekeepers" in the organization might be especially helpful to you in your position as a department supervisor?
4. How might effective internal networking be of assistance to you during a period of reengineering or reorganizing?
5. Why can we truthfully say that politics is inevitable in organizational life?
6. How would you attempt to relate to a manager who continually projects an attitude that says, "Don't tell me anything I don't want to hear?"
7. What do you believe is the most effective way for you to keep your personal networking channels open and operating?
8. What is the direct and immediate effect of "end running" your boss and why is this particularly harmful?
9. What measures can you take if your boss has never communicated any expectations to you even though you may have asked?
10. How would you propose to deal with the "blindsider," the individual who drops embarrassing or harmful information about you in a meeting of a number of people?

Case: Your Word Against His

You are at a meeting with your manager, another middle manager, and four other supervisors. The subject of the meeting is the manner in which the organization's supervisors are to conduct themselves during the present union organizing campaign.

Your manager makes a statement concerning one way in which supervisors should conduct themselves. You are surprised to hear his statement because earlier that day you read a legal opinion describing this particular action as probably illegal.

You interrupt your manager with, "Pardon me, but I don't believe it can really be done that way. I'm certain it would leave us open to an unfair labor practice charge."

Obviously annoyed at the interruption, your manager says sharply, "This isn't open to discussion. You're wrong."

You open your mouth to speak again but are cut short by an angry glance.

You are absolutely certain that your boss is wrong; he had inadvertently turned around a couple of words and described a "cannot do" as a "can do." Unfortunately, you are in a conference room surrounded by other people, and the document that could prove your point is in your office.

Question:

1. How do you suggest approaching this problem in an effort to a) set the record straight concerning the correct information; b) provide minimal embarrassment for your manager; and c) run the least risk of prejudicing yourself with your manager?

Case: Tough Politics: Coping with the Blindsider

George did not look forward to going to the staff meetings that his middle-manager boss convened once each week. He did not always feel this way about the meetings; in fact, up until 3 months earlier he rather enjoyed what he felt were productive and congenial gatherings. What made the difference was one change in the membership of this group of six supervisors: the addition of Charlie, who replaced a usually silent supervisor of one of the building services sections.

Unlike his predecessor, Charlie was anything but usually silent. In fact, it seemed as though Charlie had made it a point to become conversant with every section of their boss's territory, and he almost always had something critical to say about the other supervisors' weekly reports.

What bothered George most was Charlie's approach to getting his issues or criticisms on the table. Charlie seemed to focus exclusively on problems and weaknesses. As if that in itself wasn't bad enough, what George resented most was Charlie's way of introducing a problem or concern in a way that ensured maximum embarrassment for whoever's area he was commenting on. It was Charlie's practice to openly drop his little bombshells in the staff meeting, where the supervisor whose area was in question first heard of a so-called "problem" or weakness at the same time the others learned of it.

It seemed to George that Charlie's practice of blindsiding the others in the group was coldly calculated to make himself look better by making others look worse. And George found it even more frustrating to note that their boss did not seem to recognize what Charlie was doing.

Questions:

1. What do you recommend that George do about Charlie's staff meeting behavior?
2. Should George take up his concerns directly with Charlie? And if so, should he do it one-on-one or in the context of the staff meeting?
3. Would you recommend that George start addressing this problem by taking it up one-on-one with their mutual middle-manager boss?

REFERENCES

1. Luebbert, P.P. 1987. Networking for survival and success. *Medical Laboratory Observer* 19(6): 39–42.
2. Block, P. 1987. *The empowered manager: Positive skills at work.* San Francisco, CA: Jossey-Bass, 45.
3. Terrell, R.D. 1989. The elusive menace of office politics. *Training* 26(5): 48–54.

RECOMMENDED RESOURCES

S.M. Crow and S.J. Hartman, "Improving the Political Skills of Health Care Supervisors," *The Health Care Supervisor* 14, no. 4 (1995): 35–42.
S. Dellinger, Political Savvy: *The Unwritten Power Skills for Professional Women.* (Boulder, CO: CareerTrack Publishers, 1987). Four audiotapes.

Index